Documentation for Acute Care

D1316927

Jean S. Clark, RHIA
Technical Editor

AHIMA
American Health Information
Management Association®

ISBN 1-58426-112-9
AHIMA Product No. AB100704

AHIMA Staff:

Katherine Kerpan, Senior Editor
Marcia Bottoms, Director of Publications
Jennifer Solheim, Assistant Editor
Michelle Dougherty, RHIA, Content Reviewer

AHIMA strives to recognize the value of people from every racial and ethnic background as well as all genders, age groups, and sexual orientations by building its membership and leadership resources to reflect the rich diversity of the American population. AHIMA encourages the celebration and promotion of human diversity through education, mentoring, recognition, leadership, and other programs.

American Health Information Management Association
233 North Michigan Avenue, Suite 2150
Chicago, Illinois 60601-5800

http://www.ahima.org

Contents

Appendixes Included on Accompanying CD-ROMs

Preface

Clinical documentation and health records play a vital role in every aspect of healthcare delivery and decision making, no matter what the setting. But complete and accurate documentation is especially important for modern acute care facilities, which provide a wide variety of technologically and medically sophisticated diagnostic and therapeutic services. Documentation is also a central focus in current efforts to improve healthcare quality and patient safety as well as the efficiency of the U.S. healthcare system. The development and implementation of electronic health record (EHR) systems promise to revolutionize the collection, use, and management of healthcare data over the next decade.

Ensuring the accessibility, accuracy, and integrity of health records has been the primary mission of health information managers since the profession emerged more than seventy-five years ago. Just as important, health information management professionals continue to champion the protection of patient privacy and the confidentiality of health information. As experts in the documentation requirements of external governmental agencies and accreditation organizations, they also play an invaluable role in managing their facilities' regulatory compliance and accreditation performance.

The goal of this publication is to help health information management students understand the role of health records and clinical documentation in the delivery of direct patient care and the operation of individual healthcare organizations. The book also explains the external environment in which health records function and the documentation requirements of local, state, and federal governments. The process of voluntary accreditation and the development of external practice standards are also explored.

This publication will also be informative for practicing health information management professionals, especially in the area of EHR systems. It provides an integrated overview of all of the external standards relevant to clinical documentation and health records. Included are AHIMA practice guidelines, acute care accreditation standards, Medicare *Conditions of Participation for Hospitals,* national health informatics standards, and state and federal statutory and regulatory requirements.

Specifically, chapter 1 explains the importance of clinical documentation in the context of the U.S. healthcare delivery system. Chapter 2 describes the various uses of health record information in patient care, healthcare operations, healthcare reimbursement, public health, clinical education, and biomedical research. The content of acute care records is explored in detail in chapter 3, which includes dozens of sample health record forms and reports. Chapter 4 explains the organization of acute care health records, including health record formats and identification/storage systems in both paper-based and computer-based systems. The chapter also provides basic information on health record analysis and management, release and disclosure, and retention and destruction as well as the management of master patient indexes and other indexes, registries, and clinical databases. Chapter 5 explains the accreditation, statutory, and regulatory requirements applicable to acute care documentation and the processes of accreditation, licensure, certification, and medical staff credentialing.

This publication also includes nine appendixes in print format and four additional appendixes in electronic format on the two accompanying CD-ROMs. The print appendixes include a complete bibliography, a glossary of the terms used in this book, and a crosswalk between the Medicare *Conditions of Participation for Hospitals* and the 2004 accreditation standards of the Joint Commission on Accreditation of Healthcare Organizations and the American Osteopathic Association's Healthcare Facilities Accreditation Program. Other appendixes cover form and screen design, the AHIMA data quality model, the maintenance of master patient indexes, and principles of health record release and disclosure and retention and destruction. A list of the regulations on documentation for nonacute care settings is also provided.

CD-ROM number one includes a complete acute care record in paper format, a copy of the Health Level Seven EHR functional model, and six AHIMA practice briefs on the subject of EHR implementation. CD-ROM number two provides a functional demonstration of the proprietary EHR software developed by The Shams Group.

AHIMA hopes that the publication of this up-to-the-minute book on documentation for acute care services will help new professionals, as well as those already in practice, to meet the current demands and future challenges of health information management.

Sandra R. Fuller, MA, RHIA
Senior Vice-President and Chief Operating Officer
American Health Information Management Association

Acknowledgments

The publications staff of the AHIMA gratefully acknowledges the contributions of Jean S. Clark, RHIA; Patricia Shaw, MEd, RHIA; Betty N. Mitchell, RHIA; Kamruddin Shams, MA; and Sobia Ahmed. Without the help of these dedicated professionals, this publication would not have been possible.

Jean Clark reviewed the content of the manuscript for its technical accuracy and contributed samples of clinical documentation forms. She also furnished the content for the sample acute care health record in paper format (appendix J). Jean has had more than twenty-five years of experience as a health information management professional. She was the president of the American Health Information Management Association in 1995 and currently serves as the U.S. representative to the International Federation of Health Record Organizations. She was also a member of the health information advisory committee that worked on revising the hospital accreditation manual published by the Joint Commission on Accreditation of Healthcare Organizations in 2004.

Pat Shaw reviewed the manuscript's content, developed chapter review questions, and created the instructor's materials for this textbook. She has been a member of the health information administration and health services administration faculty at Weber State University, Ogden, Utah, for more than thirteen years. Before becoming an educator, Pat managed hospital health information services departments and worked as a nosologist for 3M Corporation's health information systems division.

Betty Mitchell reviewed the manuscript for this book and offered numerous suggestions for improvement. She is currently the director of the health information technology program at Baltimore City Community College in New Freedom, Pennsylvania.

Kam Shams and Sobia Ahmed provided the demonstration model of an acute care electronic health record system as well as sample health record views and screens. Kam is the chairman of The Shams Group, Inc., a health information systems software and consulting company headquartered in Coppell, Texas. Kam is also a visiting professor in health information management and healthcare informatics at the College of St. Scholastica in Duluth, Minnesota, and the University of Tennessee Health Sciences Center in Memphis. Sobia is a communications specialist with The Shams Group.

In addition, we are grateful to Michele Kala, RN, MS, and George Reuther, DO, for providing information on the Healthcare Facilities Accreditation Program offered by the American Osteopathic Association. We also acknowledge the generosity of the Joint Commission on Accreditation of Healthcare Organizations in allowing us to reprint information on its current health information standards for hospitals.

How to Use This Book

This book explains the importance of accurate and timely health record documentation in acute care settings. Many of the principles discussed, however, also apply to other healthcare settings. Information about acute care legal, regulatory, and accreditation requirements is also provided. Sample forms and records are included to demonstrate the application of these principles as well as compliance with applicable external requirements.

The paper-based forms in this book were specifically designed as examples of data capture and management tools and samples of appropriate health record documentation. In some cases, the sample forms have been greatly simplified to fulfill educational purposes. They were also sized and formatted to fit the printed book format. Therefore, direct use for documentation of actual clinical services would not be appropriate. However, educators and students are free to copy and use the forms as part of their classroom activities. Any other usage would require the expressed permission of the American Health Information Management Association.

The sample health record documentation in this book was created exclusively for educational purposes. All of the healthcare organizations, healthcare professionals, and patients represented in this book are fictional. Any similarity to actual organizations or real individuals, living or dead, is entirely coincidental.

Appendix K is an example of a proprietary electronic health record system. The demonstration version of the system is reproduced in this book with the permission of the developer and copyright owner, The Shams Group. Most of the sample electronic documentation in the text is also used with permission from The Shams Group. These samples are meant to be used exclusively for educational purposes. Any other usage would require the expressed permission of The Shams Group.

Appendix L reproduces the Health Level Seven functional model for electronic health records, which was released in a preliminary form in 2004. The model is used with the permission of the copyright owner, Health Level Seven, and may not be reproduced for any other purpose without the expressed permission of Health Level Seven.

Sample lesson plans, answer keys, and other instructional materials that complement this book are provided free of charge to AHIMA members through the AHIMA Assembly on Education. Educators who are not members of the association should contact the publications staff at AHIMA to request a copy of the supplementary materials.

Chapter 1

Clinical Documentation and the Healthcare Delivery System

Learning Objectives

- Outline the basic structure of the U.S. healthcare delivery system

- Explain the significance of recent trends in healthcare delivery

- Describe the distinction between inpatients and outpatients

- Compare the concepts of continuum of care and medical necessity

- Differentiate and explain the different types of healthcare reimbursement systems

- Identify and outline the various private and government-sponsored reimbursement systems for acute care services

- Describe the functions clinical documentation and health records play in the healthcare delivery system

Terminology

Acute care
Ambulatory care
Capitation
Chargemaster
Civilian Health and Medical Program—Veterans Administration (CHAMPVA)
Continuum of care
EHR Collaborative
Fee-for-service reimbursement
Health Level Seven (HL7)
Health maintenance organization (HMO)
Health record
Home health care
Hospice care
Indian Health Service (IHS)
Inpatient
Integrated healthcare network
Longitudinal health record

Long-term care
Managed care
Managed fee-for-service reimbursement
Medical necessity
Medical specialties
Medicare
Medicaid
National Committee on Vital and Health Statistics (NCVHS)
Outpatient
Personal health record (PHR)
Preferred provider organization (PPO)
Primary care
Prospective payment system (PPS)
Prospective reimbursement
Rehabilitation care
Retrospective payment system (RPS)
Secondary care
Skilled nursing facility
State Children's Health Insurance Program (SCHIP)
Subacute care
Surgical specialties
Tertiary care
Third-party payers
TRICARE
Workers' compensation

Introduction

In colonial America, many communities opened public hospitals solely for the purpose of caring for the poor and isolating the sick. Until the twentieth century, most medical care was performed in the homes of patients by physicians with little formal training. In remote areas of the new settlements, there often was little or no help available for the injured and sick, and mortality rates among early settlers were very high.

Reform movements that began during the late nineteenth century improved the overall quality of medical care in the United States. Specific quality improvement efforts were directed at medical school training and hospital care. The new, more scientific approach to medicine set the stage for unprecedented advances in biomedicine that were under way at the turn of the twentieth century.

The number of hospitals and the number of hospital admissions increased dramatically during the first decades of the twentieth century. Organized efforts among healthcare reformers and private foundations led to the standardization of hospital care, and many private hospitals were established. Care in the new, privately funded hospitals, however, was available only to those who could pay for the services. Underfunded public and charity hospitals continued to serve the poor and indigent.

The development of modern surgical techniques and new pharmaceuticals as well as the more widespread use of antibiotics after the Second World War created an even greater demand for hospital care. As a result, the late 1940s and 1950s saw a hospital building boom. Increased hospital utilization was also encouraged by the widespread availability of employer-based, prepaid medical plans.

Until the late 1980s, hospitals continued to provide most of the diagnostic and therapeutic healthcare services in the United States. Long hospital stays were the norm rather than the exception. Patients commonly stayed in the same hospital facility from the time they were admitted for diagnostic testing through their treatment and then until they were well enough to care for themselves at home. Before the development of endoscopic and laser surgery, many routine surgical procedures involved long periods of recovery with weeks or even months of professional nursing and follow-up care. Most of that care was provided in hospitals. And, by custom, hospitals also became places where terminally ill patients went to spend the last days of their lives.

During the decades after the Second World War, most employers added health insurance coverage to the compensation packages they offered to employees and their families. Healthcare services, including hospital care, became more accessible, at least for the families of workers who held permanent jobs. However, as the costs rose, paying for healthcare services became an even greater burden for the aged and the unemployed. As a result, many of the most vulnerable Americans (especially the aged and children from poor families) received inadequate medical care because they could not to pay for it.

In 1965, President Lyndon Johnson signed an amendment to the Social Security Act of 1935. The 1965 legislation established two federal programs designed to provide health insurance coverage to the nation's aged and poor populations: Medicare and Medicaid. **Medicare** is now the primary payer for the healthcare services provided to retired Americans (and their spouses or surviving children) who qualify for federal Social Security benefits. **Medicaid,** a health insurance program provided by individual states with partial support from the federal government, is also a major source of healthcare funding. Medicaid pays for many of the healthcare services provided to indigent or impoverished individuals and their families who qualify for benefits under Medicaid regulations.

The last decades of the twentieth century brought with them another wave of revolutionary advances in the biomedical sciences. The development of new pharmaceutical treatments has made it possible for patients with chronic illnesses to stay healthy longer and to postpone or avoid debilitating complications. Developments in surgical technology and anesthesia have shortened surgical recovery times dramatically. Today, many routine surgeries that once meant lengthy hospitalizations now require patients to spend only a few hours or days in the hospital. Organ transplantations that were cutting edge just a few years ago have become almost commonplace. Many transplant patients now go home in a matter of days rather than weeks or months after surgery.

Americans have come to expect and demand the most advanced medical care available in the world. As a result, the increasing cost and utilization of services during the past twenty years have required fundamental changes in the way healthcare services are provided and paid for. Despite these changes, however, many Americans who do not qualify for health insurance coverage or cannot pay for it continue to receive inadequate medical care. Even healthcare consumers with health insurance coverage are feeling the effects of increasing healthcare costs because they are being asked to pay a larger portion of their expenses through higher premiums, deductibles, and copayments.

According to the Agency for Healthcare Research and Quality (2002), the United States spends more on healthcare than any other large, industrialized nation, and spending continues to increase every year. In 1960, for example, healthcare spending represented approximately 5 percent of the gross domestic product. By 2000, that portion had grown to more than 13 percent. Final numbers for 2001 through 2003 are likely to approach or exceed 15 percent.

Yet, in 2002, according to the U.S. Census Bureau (2003), almost 44 million Americans had no health insurance coverage. (See table 1.1.) In addition, the percentage of Americans who qualified for employer-based health coverage dropped from 62.6 percent in 2001 to 61.3 in 2002. At the same time, the number of people covered by government-sponsored health insurance programs rose to 25.7 percent in 2002. Today, healthcare is more expensive than ever, and economists continue to worry about the potential impact on the nation's economic health in the future.

Since colonial times, physicians and other healthcare providers have documented the patient services they provide. But the increasing cost and complexity of healthcare delivery requires increasingly sophisticated documentation and data collection processes. At this point in the twenty-first century, the documentation of healthcare services and the computerization of health record systems have become critical components in both the quality of healthcare services and the efficiency of the national healthcare delivery system.

Modern Healthcare Delivery

The current healthcare delivery system in the United States is made up of thousands of independent providers and facilities that offer a somewhat bewildering array of health-related services. Reimbursement for healthcare services is accomplished through a complex system of private insurance plans and government-funded programs. The cost of medical–surgical care and pharmaceuticals has grown so much over recent years that many Americans who do not qualify for private or government-sponsored health insurance are unable to find affordable healthcare.

Healthcare Providers and Facilities

Professional healthcare providers include, among others:

- Physicians and physician's assistants
- Nurses and nurse-practitioners

Table 1.1. Health Insurance Coverage in the United States, 1987–2002

Year	Percentage Covered
2002	84.8
2001	85.4
2000	86.0
1999	84.5
1998	83.7
1997	83.9
1996	84.4
1995	84.6
1994	84.8
1993	84.7
1992	85.0
1991	85.9
1990	86.1
1989	86.4
1988	86.6
1987	87.1

Source: U.S. Census Bureau 2003.

- Psychologists and clinical social workers
- Physical, respiratory, speech, and occupational therapists
- Dentists, dental assistants, and dental hygienists
- Medical technologists and cytotechnologists
- Patient care technicians and paramedics
- Podiatrists and chiropractors

Healthcare services are provided in countless public and private facilities, including:

- Public and community hospitals operated by local governments
- Teaching hospitals affiliated with university medical schools
- Specialty hospitals dedicated to providing specialized services (for example, behavioral health and rehabilitation care)
- Private hospitals affiliated with religious organizations
- Private hospitals affiliated with profit-making corporations
- Private hospitals operated by nonprofit organizations
- Integrated healthcare networks (made up of hospitals, postacute care facilities, and ambulatory care facilities operated by the same corporate entity)
- Physicians' offices, group practices, and private medical clinics
- Community-based clinics and public health departments
- Hospital-based and freestanding ambulatory diagnostic and surgical centers
- Hospital-based and freestanding ambulatory rehabilitation centers
- Skilled nursing facilities
- Long-term care and assisted care residential facilities
- Home health care and hospice care agencies

Healthcare Services

Generally, healthcare services are categorized according to the setting in which the services are provided and/or the illness toward which services are directed. For example, **acute care** can be defined as the short-term medical and nursing care provided in an inpatient hospital setting to treat the acute phase of a patient's injury or illness. Other broad categories of healthcare services include:

- **Ambulatory care:** The preventive, diagnostic, and therapeutic medical services provided on a nonresidential basis in healthcare practitioners' offices, group practices, private clinics, community-based clinics, and hospital-based outpatient departments
- **Behavioral health care:** The psychiatric and/or psychological care provided to address mental disorders, developmental disorders, and substance abuse disorders; provided in a variety of settings, including dedicated units in acute care hospitals, psychiatric hospitals, community-based clinics, and physicians' offices

- **Emergency and trauma care:** The medical–surgical care provided to individuals whose injuries or illnesses require urgent care to address conditions that could be life-threatening or disabling if they were not treated immediately; provided through a network of designated hospitals and emergency transportation systems

- **Home health care:** The medical and/or personal care provided to individuals and families in their place of residence with the goal of promoting, maintaining, or restoring health or minimizing the effects of disabilities and illnesses, including terminal illnesses

- **Hospice care:** The medical and/or personal care provided to individuals with life expectancies of six months or less who elect to receive palliative care in place of standard medical treatment for their illnesses; provided in patients' homes and in residential treatment facilities

- **Long-term care:** The medical and/or personal care services provided to chronically ill, aged, disabled, or mentally handicapped individuals who reside in dedicated nursing facilities on a permanent basis

- **Rehabilitation care:** The therapeutic medical services (speech, physical, and occupational therapy) provided to patients who have been disabled by injuries or illnesses; provided in dedicated rehabilitation hospitals, community-based facilities, patients' homes, and hospital-based outpatient departments with the goal of helping patients recover as much function as possible

- **Skilled nursing care:** The professional nursing care and related medical, therapeutic, psychosocial, and personal services provided in a residential setting to individuals recovering from injuries or illnesses or the residual effects of injuries or illnesses after the acute phase of the condition has resolved; sometimes called **subacute care**

Trends in Healthcare Delivery

Today, the medical services provided in the United States are often described as being the best in the world. Still, many critics of the healthcare delivery system consider it to be too costly and inefficient. The current system is a complex amalgam of payers, providers, and facilities that function more or less independently. There are also ongoing concerns related to uneven accessibility, over- and underutilization of services, and cost inflation.

In 2002, more than 15 percent of Americans had no health insurance coverage (U.S. Census Bureau 2003; Center for Studying Health System Change 2003). Today, families who do not receive insurance coverage through their employers and do not qualify for Medicaid assistance are finding it difficult or impossible to find and pay for medical care. Public healthcare facilities are overcrowded and underfunded and are unable to fully address the needs of their communities. Some economists fear that the high cost of pharmaceuticals will threaten the future stability of the Medicare and Medicaid programs. In addition, fraudulent and erroneous medical claims cost private and government insurers billions of dollars each year (almost $12 billion for the Medicare program alone in 2002) (Centers for Medicare and Medicaid Services 2003).

Since the 1960s, the cost of healthcare services has grown at a rate much faster than overall inflation. For example, in 2000, the cost of inpatient hospital services increased by about 6 percent, while the overall consumer price index increased by less than 4 percent. In 2002, the cost of inpatient hospital services increased almost 9 percent over the previous year, and the overall cost of medical care rose almost 5 percent. In contrast, overall cost inflation for that period was less than 2 percent (Agency for Healthcare Research and Quality 2002).

Concerns over the growing cost of healthcare services have brought significant changes in the healthcare system over the past two decades. The most significant has been the movement of most diagnostic services and noncritical therapeutic services away from the acute care hospital setting.

In response to competition from ambulatory care facilities, many hospitals have enhanced their service offerings in the areas of ambulatory diagnostic and surgical services and subacute nursing care. In addition, many hospitals have merged with other general and specialty hospitals and subacute and ambulatory care providers to form integrated healthcare networks. An **integrated healthcare network** is a group of healthcare organizations that collectively provides a full range of coordinated health-related services. These services range from simple preventive care to complex surgical care.

Hospital-Based Services

Today, the inpatient services provided in acute care hospitals are reserved for the sickest patients and the most invasive medical procedures. Noninvasive diagnostic procedures, same-day surgery, chemotherapy, and radiation therapy are now routinely performed in separate ambulatory care facilities or in the outpatient departments of acute care hospitals. Most convalescent care is provided in dedicated skilled nursing facilities or through home health agencies. But some hospitals have opened dedicated nursing units to care for patients who no longer require acute care services but are too ill to return home. Similarly, most rehabilitation care is now provided in dedicated rehabilitation hospitals, skilled nursing facilities, freestanding community-based facilities, or hospital-based outpatient departments.

Patients who receive healthcare services in a hospital are categorized as either inpatients or outpatients. An **inpatient** is an individual who receives healthcare services as well as room, board, and continuous nursing care in a hospital unit dedicated to providing around-the-clock patient care.

An **outpatient** is an individual who receives healthcare services in a hospital-based clinic or department but who is not admitted to a dedicated acute care unit. For example, a patient who is treated exclusively in the emergency department of a hospital is considered an outpatient rather than an inpatient. But if that same patient were admitted to an acute care unit of the hospital after receiving emergency services, the patient would then be considered an inpatient for the rest of his or her hospital stay.

Continuum of Care

Hospital-based services make up only one component in the broad spectrum of healthcare services available to Americans today. The current healthcare delivery system is extremely complex. And until recently, little effort was made to coordinate the services offered by the hundreds or thousands of independent healthcare practitioners and providers working in any one community. Since the early 1990s, however, healthcare organizations, accreditation and standards organizations, healthcare-related trade and professional associations, and federal agencies have been attempting to integrate the components of the delivery system. The goal is to improve the quality of medical care provided to Americans and at the same time make healthcare services more affordable and accessible.

The concept of a continuum of care was initially developed during the mid-1990s in response to increasing healthcare costs. According to the 1995 hospital accreditation manual from the Joint Commission on Accreditation of Healthcare Organizations (JCAHO), an integrated continuum of healthcare services would match "an individual's ongoing needs with the appropriate level and type of medical, psychological, or social care. . . ." Ideally, every patient would receive the appropriate service at the appropriate time from the appropriate practitioner or facility.

The **continuum of care** can be defined as the sum of all the healthcare services provided in all settings, from the least intensive and specialized (and the least expensive) to the most intensive and specialized (the most expensive). The services that make up the continuum then can be further categorized into three levels of care: primary, secondary, and tertiary. The levels of care reflect the cost of the services as well as the intensity of the services provided. For example, the basic services provided in physicians' offices are generally the least expensive, and the intensive medical services provided in acute care hospitals are generally the most expensive.

Primary Care

The most appropriate setting for routine healthcare services falls at the **primary care** level. Primary care services are generally provided by physicians working in private offices, group practices, private clinics, or community-based clinics. Primary care physicians usually receive their training in the more general fields of medicine: family practice, pediatrics, and general internal medicine. In addition, many women of reproductive age receive primary care services from physicians specializing in gynecology. Nurse-practitioners (nurses who hold advanced clinical degrees) and physician's assistants also provide primary care services under the supervision of physicians.

Primary care services include the following:

- Preventive care (such as immunizations)

- Early detection of neoplastic diseases and other serious illnesses through routine screening and laboratory tests (such as mammograms and blood tests)

- Periodic physical examinations (such as well-baby checkups, well-child checkups, and annual checkups for adults)

- Diagnosis and treatment of minor infectious illnesses (such as influenza and other viral infections and common bacterial and fungal infections such as strep throat and athlete's foot), which may be diagnosed with a combination of examination and laboratory testing and treated with prescription drugs

- Diagnosis and management services for chronic illnesses (such as asthma, hypertension, and diabetes), which are monitored through periodic examinations and laboratory testing and treated with prescription drugs

- Diagnosis and treatment of minor injuries (such as lacerations, sprains, and uncomplicated orthopedic injuries)

Primary care physicians also coordinate their patients' hospital care and diagnostic services, specialty care consultations, and psychosocial services.

Secondary Care

Secondary care encompasses the diagnostic and therapeutic services provided by medical specialists working in private offices, specialty group practices, private clinics, community-based clinics, and general and community hospitals. Patients may arrange to consult specialists directly. However, it is more common for primary care physicians to refer patients to specialists for the diagnosis and treatment of complex conditions that require more intensive services than the primary care physician can provide.

Specialty care can be divided into two groups of services: medical and surgical. The **medical specialties** include the following:

- Internal medicine
- Pediatrics
- Cardiology
- Endocrinology
- Psychiatry
- Oncology
- Nephrology
- Neurology
- Pulmonology
- Gastroenterology
- Dermatology
- Radiology and nuclear medicine

The **surgical specialties** include:

- Obstetrics/gynecology
- Opthalmology
- Orthopedics
- Cardiovascular surgery
- Otorhinolaryngology
- Trauma surgery
- Neurosurgery
- Thoracic surgery
- Urology
- Plastic and reconstructive surgery
- Anesthesiology
- Pathology

Most medical and surgical specialists provide both office-based and hospital-based care. However, because of the nature of their specialties, some specialists work predominantly in hospitals and ambulatory surgery settings: pathologists, radiologists, and anesthesiologists.

Tertiary Care

Tertiary care is centered on the provision of highly specialized and technologically advanced diagnostic and therapeutic services in inpatient and outpatient hospital settings. Most tertiary care is provided by medical specialists working in large, urban hospitals and specialty clinics affiliated with nearby medical schools and universities.

Tertiary care services include medical–surgical services such as trauma care, burn care, organ transplantation, and medical–surgical intensive care for neonatal, pediatric, and adult patients. In addition, most tertiary care hospitals perform medical research and conduct resident training programs for physicians and other healthcare practitioners.

Medical Necessity

Defining exactly which healthcare services can be considered appropriate for an individual patient at any point in his or her lifetime has proven to be extremely difficult. Today, the concept of the continuum of care has merged with the requirement that every healthcare service provided can be shown to have been reasonable and necessary. **Medical necessity** is based on whether the services provided to a specific patient will have a reasonably beneficial effect on his or her physical needs and quality of life at a specific point in his or her illness or life.

For example: Suppose that a screening test for colon cancer performed on an otherwise healthy fifty-year-old man were positive and that further tests showed that the cancer had not advanced beyond its original site. Surgical removal of the neoplasm along with chemotherapy and radiation treatment would meet medical necessary standards for the patient because he would have a very reasonable chance of surviving the cancer and living a full life for many years to come. But a similar finding on a ninety-year-old man who was already being treated for end-stage emphysema might result in a different medical necessity decision. In his case, the patient and his family and physicians might decide that he should receive only radiotherapy to ease the symptoms of his cancer because he is too ill to endure major surgery. In addition, his severe respiratory disease would make it unlikely that he would survive for more than a few months no matter what treatment he received. Aggressive cancer treatment would likely have little beneficial effect for the patient, and complications from the surgery or chemotherapy might even shorten his life. In this case, physicians would probably conclude that surgery and chemotherapy would not meet medical necessity standards in the second man's case.

Modern Reimbursement Systems

Medical necessity is an important consideration in modern reimbursement systems. That is one of the reasons why complete and accurate clinical documentation is so important. Today's managed care systems attempt to control costs by controlling access to healthcare services. That is, managed care plans work by ensuring that only those services that will truly benefit individual patients are performed. Medical necessity is also a prime consideration in Medicare and Medicaid reimbursement decisions and in virtually all other reimbursement arrangements.

Currently, most healthcare expenses are reimbursed in one of six ways:

- Through commercial health insurance plans partially or fully paid for by employers and provided to employees as part of their employment agreement

- Through Blue Cross and Blue Shield plans and other health plans structured as nonprofit entities and partially or fully paid for by employers and provided to employees as part of their employment agreement

- Through employer-based self-insurance plans funded directly by employers and provided to employees as part of their employment agreement

- Through government-sponsored health insurance programs

- Through commercial or nonprofit health insurance plans purchased by private individuals

- Through payments made directly to providers by healthcare consumers

Enrollees in health plans associated with their employment usually pay part of the premiums while their employers pay the larger part. Medicare beneficiaries also pay part of the cost of their medical coverage through premiums. Individuals who purchase insurance directly usually pay the highest premiums for coverage. Unfortunately, many older individuals (those between ages fifty and sixty-five who are too young to qualify for Medicare coverage) and individuals of any age who have a history of chronic or serious illness may not qualify for personal coverage at any price.

Most prepaid health insurance plans are based on a contractual cost-sharing arrangement between the plan and the beneficiary. As healthcare costs have risen, the cost of health insurance premiums has also risen dramatically. In addition, enrollees in prepaid plans now pay a significantly larger share of their healthcare expenses as deductibles and copayments than they did just a few years ago.

Retrospective Reimbursement

Retrospective payment systems are based on the payment of fees charged according to the actual medical services provided. The fees are billed to the patient or the patient's insurance provider after the services are complete, or retrospectively.

Traditional Fee for Service

Until the 1970s, most healthcare services were paid for after the service was provided. Reimbursement was based on a fee schedule developed by the provider. For example, the physician first performed the service for the patient. After the service was provided, the physician's office staff sent a bill for that service to the patient for payment. The cost of the service was determined according to the physician's established fee schedule, and the patient was expected to pay the bill in full.

When the patient was enrolled in a health insurance plan, he or she then submitted a claim to the insurer. Proof of the expenditures was submitted along with the claim. Subsequently, the insurer reimbursed the patient for all or part of the charges he or she had paid to the physician. (Most insurance plans were based on a cost-sharing arrangement whereby the patient was responsible for paying a percentage of the cost [commonly 20 percent], while the plan paid the rest.) Claims for hospital charges were processed in a similar way, with the insurance plan paying its portion of the fixed hospital charges first. The hospital then billed the patient for the unpaid portion of the charges.

Managed Fee for Service

Today, only uninsured healthcare consumers pay full charges based on traditional **fee-for-service reimbursement** arrangements for most types of healthcare services. Virtually all of the commercial, nonprofit, and employer-based health plans now negotiate discounted fee schedules with providers. This arrangement is called **managed fee-for-service reimbursement.**

Managed fee-for-service arrangements, however, are not considered to be true examples of **managed care** reimbursement. True managed care systems combine payment and delivery under a single entity. (Managed care is discussed in more detail later in this chapter.)

Prospective Reimbursement

Prospective reimbursement plans appeared early in the history of health insurance plans. Beneficiaries or their employers paid a set fee for membership in a prepaid health plan. The plan then provided all of the services the beneficiaries needed for the period of time covered by their agreement. For example, in the early 1930s, Baylor University Hospital offered a prepaid hospital plan to Dallas schoolteachers. Each teacher paid $0.50 per month, and the dues went into a fund that was used to pay for any hospital services needed by the teachers for the duration of the agreement. In other words, services were paid for prospectively, before the services were provided. Prospective plans were gradually replaced by retrospective plans during the Second World War and did not appear again until the advent of cost-cutting measures in the 1980s.

Private Managed Care Plans

Since Medicare and Medicaid were implemented in 1966, the cost and utilization of healthcare services in the United States have increased exponentially. Recent biomedical research has resulted in the development of safer anesthetics and less invasive surgical techniques as well as thousands of new pharmaceutical treatments for acute and chronic illnesses. But these unprecedented improvements have come with an unexpectedly high price tag.

By the late 1960s, public policy makers, commercial and nonprofit insurance providers, and employers began looking for less costly ways to provide healthcare benefits to Americans. A number of provider and payer organizations responded to the need to cut the cost of healthcare services by developing managed care plans.

Until the advent of managed care, delivering healthcare services and paying for healthcare services had been accomplished through separate, independent systems. In other words, healthcare providers and facilities were responsible for providing patient services. Separate entities were then responsible for paying the providers on behalf of the patients. These reimbursement entities are often referred to as **third-party payers** (the first party is the patient and the second party is the healthcare provider).

Managed care is a generic term used to describe several types of prepaid health plans that combine the delivery and financing components of healthcare. Modern managed care plans first appeared in the early 1970s. Since that time, traditional health plans have incorporated elements of managed care into their services as a way to cut costs. Most commercial and nonprofit health plans now offer managed care options to their beneficiaries. And virtually all third-party payers negotiate discounted fee schedules with hospitals, physicians, and other healthcare providers.

Today, health maintenance organizations and preferred provider organizations are the two most common types of managed care plans available.

Health Maintenance Organizations

A **health maintenance organization** (HMO) is a prepaid voluntary health plan that provides healthcare services to its enrollees. Enrollees and/or their employers pay monthly premiums in exchange for all of the medical–surgical services and drug benefits the enrollees will need over the life of the HMO contract. Some HMOs (staff model HMOs) provide healthcare services in their own facilities and directly employ the healthcare professionals who provide the services. Other types of HMOs negotiate contracts with independent healthcare providers and facilities, who agree to provide services to enrollees in exchange for a set fee over the duration of the contract.

HMO premiums are based on statistical calculations that estimate what it will cost a plan to provide necessary healthcare services to its enrollees for the period of time covered by the contract. Managed care plans attempt to control healthcare spending by preventing unnecessary utilization of the most costly services. Because hospital care is so resource intensive, it is among the most expensive healthcare services available. That is why managed care plans concentrate on finding alternatives to hospital care. Managed care plans also limit access to clinical specialists and expensive diagnostic procedures. They also control the availability of especially costly pharmaceuticals.

HMO premiums are usually shared by enrollees and their employers. In general, employers and enrollees pay less for HMO coverage than for other types of health plans, and enrollees have lower out-of-pocket healthcare expenses. In return for these cost savings, however, enrollees agree to give up some of their medical decision-making power. HMOs require that their enrollees use physicians and other providers from a preapproved list. When HMO enrollees wish to use the services of providers who are not on the preapproved list, enrollees must pay for those services themselves. In addition, it is not uncommon for HMOs to deny enrollees access to healthcare services that the HMO considers medically unnecessary.

Preferred Provider Organizations

Preferred provider organizations (PPOs) are more like traditional health insurance organizations than HMOs. Beneficiaries and their employers pay premiums, but enrollees are free to select their own physicians and other healthcare providers from a large network of preapproved providers. Providers also sign contracts with the PPOs whereby they agree to accept discounted fees for the services they provide to the PPOs' beneficiaries. Beneficiaries are also free to receive services from providers outside the network, but they are required to pay a larger portion of the cost for those services.

PPOs cut healthcare spending primarily by cutting the cost of services rather than by limiting access to services. PPOs are different from HMOs in that they do not restrict the services their enrollees may receive and generally do not directly employ healthcare providers. However, PPO beneficiaries pay significantly more for healthcare services through higher deductibles and copayments than do HMO enrollees. In fact, many HMOs pay 100 percent of the cost of covered healthcare services as long as there is proof of the services' medical necessity.

PPO agreements with providers are also different from managed fee-for-service arrangements. Under managed fee-for-service arrangements, providers agree to accept discounted fees from the third-party payer just as PPO network providers do. But managed fee-for-service providers are then free to bill patients for the unpaid portion of the charges. Under PPO contracts, providers agree to accept the discounted payment as payment in full and are not allowed to seek further compensation directly from patients.

Government-Sponsored Prospective Payment Systems

In another effort to control healthcare spending, the federal government began implementing prospective payment systems for the Medicare program in 1983. The Medicare **prospective payment systems** base reimbursement on patient classification groups. For reimbursement purposes only, each individual patient is assigned to a diagnostic group primarily on the basis of his or her clinical diagnosis. The assumption is that patients who have the same diagnosis and undergo the same treatment will consume similar amounts of medical resources.

For example: Suppose that a patient was readmitted to an acute care hospital after a broken leg treated during a previous admission led to a pulmonary embolism. Treatment for the pulmonary embolism would be assigned to diagnosis-related group number 078. This group includes several specific conditions:

415.1, Embolism and infarction, pulmonary
958.0, Complications, early, trauma, embolism, air
958.1, Complications, early, trauma, embolism, fat
999.1, Complications, not elsewhere classified, embolism, air

The ICD-9-CM diagnostic code that represents the patient's principal diagnosis (958.1) during the second admission determines the diagnosis-related group assignment (078). A set reimbursement amount is assigned to each diagnostic group, but a number of additional factors affect the actual payment made to the provider. These factors include the following:

- Principal and secondary diagnoses

- Principal and secondary surgical procedures

- Age and gender of the patient

- Discharge status of the patient

- Presence of complicating or comorbid conditions

The Medicare program has implemented several prospective payment systems and patient classification schemes for various services and delivery settings since 1983:

- Inpatient acute care: diagnosis-related groups (DRGs)

- Physicians' services: resource-based relative value scale (RBRVS)

- Skilled nursing facilities: resource utilization groups (RUGs)

- Outpatient care: ambulatory payment classification groups (APCs)

- Home care: home health resource groups (HHRGs)

- Inpatient rehabilitation: case-mix groups (CMGs)

A prospective payment system for inpatient psychiatric care was also in development at the time this book was published. Medicare programs are discussed in more detail in the next section of this chapter.

Reimbursement for Acute Care Services

As explained in the preceding section, the acute care services provided to hospital inpatients are paid for through a number of private plans and public programs. In some cases, they are paid for directly by healthcare consumers. The various healthcare reimbursement entities all have different qualification requirements. Each payer also requires slightly different types of information to support reimbursement claims and verify the medical necessity of the services that were provided.

The source of this information is the clinical documentation collected and stored in each patient's **health record.** A traditional axiom among health information managers—*if it wasn't documented, it didn't happen*—reflects the importance of complete, timely, and accurate clinical documentation in every healthcare setting. But the quality of the information in acute care health records is especially critical because of the complexity of hospital care and the potentially serious consequences incorrect or incomplete information can have for hospital patients and caregivers. Less obviously, poor quality documentation can also adversely affect the hospital's ability to claim appropriate reimbursement from third-party payers. This, in turn, can damage the short-term and long-term financial health of hospitals and their continued ability to provide high-quality patient care.

Chargemasters

Regardless of the source of reimbursement, acute care hospitals must be able to calculate the actual cost of providing services. With realistic cost information, they can compare the expense of providing a service with the payment they are likely to receive. In this way, they will be able to determine whether the reimbursement they are receiving is adequate to meet the cost of providing a service.

Hospitals collect information on the services they provide in the accounts of individual patients. The charges for the services and the underlying costs associated with those services are maintained in a database called the **chargemaster.** Billing for patient services is performed through an automated process linked to the hospital's chargemaster. (Many facilities refer to this financial tool by other names, for example, the charge data master or the charge description master.)

The chargemaster database is used to organize information on all of the goods and services the hospital provides to patients. Patient charges are captured in the chargemaster as the services are provided and the expenses are incurred. To ensure accuracy, the chargemaster must be updated frequently as new services are offered, costs increase, and procedure or service descriptions change (Rhodes 1999).

The information maintained in the chargemaster is determined by the types of services the hospital provides, and so each hospital's chargemaster is unique. (See figure 1.1 for an example.) Most chargemasters, however, include at least the following components (Rhodes 1999):

- Charge dollar amount: The specific amount charged for a procedure or service

- Charge code: A unique number used internally by the facility to identify the individual services and procedures in the chargemaster

- Item description: A short title that represents the procedure or service

- General ledger key: The accounting code that ties patient charges to the facility's accounting system

- Revenue code: A three-digit number (required for Medicare billing) that represents a specific accommodation, ancillary service, or billing calculation

- Activity date: The date the procedure or service was performed

Many hospital chargemasters also include one or more of the following additional data elements (Davis 2002):

- The CPT or HCPCS codes that correspond to the facility's services and procedures

- The charge codes used by major insurance plans to represent the procedures and services

- The department code numbers that identify the ancillary departments that provide the procedures and services

The function of chargemaster information in claims processing and billing is obvious. Perhaps less obvious is its usefulness in negotiating future contracts with third-party payers. Hospital administrators use chargemaster information to determine:

- The types of illnesses and injuries the beneficiaries of a particular health plan are likely to experience in the future

- The number and types of services the beneficiaries of a particular health plan are likely to use in the future

- The adequacy of current or proposed charges compared to the actual cost of providing those services

Figure 1.1.   Section from a Typical Chargemaster

| Charge Code | Item Description | CPT/HCPCS Code | | | Revenue Code | G/L Key | Activity Date |
		Insurance Code A	Insurance Code B	Insurance Code C			
2110410000	ECHO ENCEPHALOGRAM	76506	76506	Y7030	320	15	12/2/1999
2110410090	F/U ECHO ENCEPHALOGRAM	76506	76506	Y7040	320	15	12/2/1999
2110413000	PORT US ECHO ENCEPHALOGRAM	76506	76506	Y7050	320	15	12/2/1999
2120411000	ULTRASOUND SPINAL CONTENTS	76800	76800	Y7060	320	15	12/2/1999
2130401000	THYROID SONOGRAM	76536	76536	Y7070	320	15	1/1/2001
2151111000	TM JOINTS BILATERAL	70330	70330	Y7080	320	15	8/12/2000
2161111000	NECK LAT ONLY	70360	70360	Y7090	320	15	10/1/1999
2162111000	LARYNX AP & LATERAL	70360	70360	Y7100	320	15	10/1/1999
2201111000	LONG BONE CHLD AP	76061	76061	Y7110	320	15	8/12/2000
2201401000	NON-VASCULAR EXTREM SONO	76880	76880	Y7120	320	15	10/1/1999
2210111000	SKULL 1 VIEW	70250	70250	Y7130	320	15	1/1/2001
2210112000	SKULL 2 VIEWS	70250	70250	Y7140	320	15	8/12/2000
2210114000	SKULL 4 VIEWS	70260	70260	Y7150	320	15	8/12/2000
2211111000	MASTOIDS	70130	70130	Y7160	320	15	1/1/2001
2212111000	MANDIBLE	70110	70110	Y7170	320	15	12/2/1999
2213111000	FACIAL BONES	70140	70140	Y7180	320	15	12/2/1999
2213114000	FACIAL BONES MIN 4	70150	70150	Y7190	320	15	12/2/1999
2214111000	NASAL BONES	70160	70160	Y7200	320	15	1/1/2001
2215111000	ORBITS	70200	70200	Y7210	320	15	1/1/2001
2217111000	PARANASAL SINUSES	70220	70220	Y7220	320	15	1/1/2001

Commercial and Employer-Based Health Insurance Plans and Nonprofit Health Insurance Plans

As noted earlier in the chapter, most health insurance plans and nonprofit insurance plans such as Blue Cross/Blue Shield negotiate discounted payment schedules with healthcare providers, including acute care hospitals. The contract between a payer and a hospital stipulates how much the hospital will be paid for the services it will provide to the beneficiaries of the plan throughout the period during which the contract is in force. The negotiated fees represent a specific discount off the hospital's standard charges (that is, the charges listed in the hospital's chargemaster).

Managed Care Plans

Some large HMOs directly own and operate the healthcare facilities that provide services to their enrollees. The Kaiser Permanente Health Plan is an example of one such HMO. Founded in 1945 and headquartered in Oakland, California, Kaiser Permanente is the largest nonprofit health plan in the United States, with more than 8 million members (Kaiser Permanente 2004). The HMO provides inpatient and outpatient services through the Kaiser Permanente Foundation Hospitals and a network of outpatient clinics and hospitals along the West Coast and in Hawaii. The HMO also operates a network of physicians' practices known as the Permanente Medical Groups.

Many smaller health maintenance organizations enter into contracts with local hospitals to provide acute care services to their enrollees. Under some arrangements, the hospital agrees to provide all of the acute care services needed by a specific population of enrollees over the duration of the contract. In return, the HMO agrees to pay the hospital a negotiated fee as payment in full for the services the hospital is to provide to the enrollees. If the enrollees actually use fewer services than anticipated, the hospital may make a profit. If the enrollees use more services than anticipated, the hospital may lose money. This arrangement is known as **capitation.** Other healthcare providers, including physicians, also provide services under capitated agreements with managed care organizations.

Not all managed care organizations contract for acute care services through capitated agreements, however. Many HMOs and most PPOs negotiate acute care services contracts on the basis of discounted fee schedules. In such cases, the HMOs control acute care expenditures by limiting their enrollees' utilization of hospital services. The HMOs control utilization by requiring enrollees to seek preauthorization before undergoing surgery or using emergency care and other hospital-based diagnostic and therapeutic services.

Government-Sponsored Health Programs

The federal government sponsors several healthcare programs that finance acute care and other healthcare services for specific groups of individuals. Most of the federal programs are reimbursement mechanisms, but a few programs operate hospitals and clinics for specific populations (for example, the Indian Health Service hospitals and clinics, the Department of Defense military hospitals, and the Veterans Administration network of hospitals).

The following list includes the largest federal healthcare reimbursement programs:

- *Medicare:* A program that pays for the healthcare services provided to Social Security beneficiaries sixty-five years old and older; also covers some other groups, including permanently disabled individuals and individuals with end-stage renal disease of any age

- *Medicaid:* A program that works with individual state governments to provide health-care coverage to low-income individuals and families

- *TRICARE:* A program that provides healthcare coverage to members of the military forces and their families

- *Civilian Health and Medical Program—Veterans Administration (CHAMPVA):* A program that provides healthcare coverage to the dependents and survivors of permanently and totally disabled veterans, survivors of veterans who died as a result of service-related injuries, and survivors of military personnel who died in the line of duty

- *Workers' Compensation:* A program that covers the healthcare costs and lost income of federal employees who suffer work-related injuries or illnesses

Medicare

The Medicare program was implemented in 1966 for retired workers over sixty-five who qualify for Social Security benefits. In 1973, federal legislation expanded Medicare benefits to include individuals of any age with permanent disabilities or end-stage renal disease.

Social Security beneficiaries receive hospitalization insurance (Medicare Part A) at no charge. Beneficiaries also have the option of purchasing supplemental medical insurance (Medicare Part B) to cover physicians' services and other healthcare expenses not covered by Part A. Many beneficiaries also purchase private insurance (commonly referred to as medigap insurance) to supplement their Medicare benefits. Medicare Part C (or Medicare+Choice) was implemented in 1997 to expand the options for participation in private healthcare plans. In addition, a new Medicare prescription drug program was enacted by the Medicare Modernization Act of 2003. The new program will be implemented in 2006.

The Centers for Medicare and Medicaid Services (CMS) is a federal agency within the Department of Health and Human Services. The CMS is responsible for administering the Medicare program and the federal portion of the Medicaid program. The CMS estimates that approximately 19 million Americans were enrolled in the Medicare program in 1966. By 2001, according to the CMS, approximately 40 million people were enrolled in Parts A and/or B, but less than 6 million enrollees participated in a Medicare+Choice plan (Centers for Medicare and Medicaid Services 2003).

Medicare is the largest single payer for healthcare services in the United States. The implementation of the Medicare acute care prospective payment system in 1983 and the outpatient prospective payment system in 2001 have had a tremendous impact on the financial operations of most acute care hospitals in the country.

Because most Medicare participants are past retirement age, they suffer from a number of chronic and degenerative diseases linked to the process of aging (for example, heart disease and many types of cancer). Medicare beneficiaries are sick more often, suffer more complications, and take longer to recover from surgery and acute illnesses. Therefore, Medicare beneficiaries consume more acute care services than any other age-group. That is why any changes in the Medicare program have an immediate financial impact on acute care providers.

Medicare Part A
Medicare Part A covers acute care services as well as the following:

- Long-term care services
- Skilled nursing facility services

- Home health services
- Hospice care service

Medicare Part A covers inpatient hospital care, but medical necessity must be demonstrated in order to qualify for reimbursement. Under Medicare Part A, inpatient hospital care is usually limited to ninety days during each benefit period. There is no limit on the number of benefit periods covered by Medicare hospital insurance during a beneficiary's lifetime, but copayment requirements apply to stays of more than sixty days. Once a beneficiary has used all ninety days of inpatient coverage during a benefit period, a nonrenewable lifetime reserve of sixty additional days of inpatient care will be paid for by Medicare. Copayments are required for such additional days.

Several types of hospitals are still exempt from the Medicare acute care prospective payment system: psychiatric and rehabilitation hospitals and dedicated psychiatric and rehabilitation units within larger facilities, long-term care hospitals, children's hospitals, and cancer hospitals. These specialty hospitals are paid on the basis of reasonable costs per discharge. A prospective payment system for psychiatric hospitals, however, is under development. A three-year gradual implementation is planned, beginning in 2004.

The CMS updates the list of diagnosis-related groups at the beginning of each fiscal year. The acute care payment schedules for Medicare Part A are also adjusted every year.

Medicare Part B

Medicare Part B is an optional supplemental medical insurance plan that covers the medical–surgical services provided by physicians and other approved clinical professionals (physician's assistants and clinical psychologists, among others). Part B also covers some of the services not covered under the Medicare hospitalization plan and a number of ambulatory services, including:

- Emergency department services
- Ambulatory surgery
- Psychiatric care
- Durable medical equipment
- Occupational, physical, and speech therapy
- Outpatient diagnostic and therapeutic services such as radiation therapy and renal dialysis

As with Medicare Part A, the medical necessity of services must be documented under Part B. Deductibles and copayments also apply to Part B services. In addition, special payment rules apply to certain medical services, such as blood transfusions, outpatient physical and occupational therapy, and outpatient psychiatric care.

Medicare Part C

Several healthcare services and supplies are covered by neither Medicare Part A or B, including:

- Long-term nursing care
- Dental care
- Eyeglasses and hearing aids
- Self-administered prescription drugs

Medicare Part C is also called Medicare+Choice. Most individuals who qualify for Medicare Parts A and B may choose Part C coverage as an alternative. Part C products include HMOs, private plans that choose to participate in the program, and medical savings accounts.

Medicare Prescription Drug Program

A new Medicare prescription drug program is set for implementation in 2006. The plan was enacted as part of the Medicare Modernization Act of 2003. The plan will be open to all Medicare beneficiaries. Benefits will be made available through Medicare-approved drug discount plans. Minimum monthly premiums will be $35 for most beneficiaries. The plans will also include significant deductibles and copayments for most beneficiaries. People with low incomes and limited assets may be able to qualify for lower premiums and deductibles (Centers for Medicare and Medicaid Services 2004).

Medicaid

Medicaid was enacted in 1965 under Title XIX of the Social Security Act. The Medicaid program contributes federal funds to the medical assistance programs operated by individual states. These programs must meet national qualification guidelines in order to receive federal funds.

Medicaid benefits are designed to help individuals and families who have low incomes and limited financial resources to obtain needed medical services. Individual states establish the Medicaid eligibility standards for their residents and determine which services will be covered. They also calculate the rate of reimbursement for covered services and administer local programs.

Medicaid Eligibility

Medicaid eligibility and services vary considerably among states, although all of the states must follow basic federal guidelines. States use the income levels and other financial resources of applicants to determine eligibility. To qualify for federal funds, however, states must provide Medicaid coverage to recipients of federally assisted income maintenance payments as well as related groups of individuals who do not receive cash payments. These eligibility groups include:

- Individuals who qualify for Temporary Assistance for Needy Families

- Children below age six whose family income is at or below 133 percent of the federal poverty level

- Pregnant women whose family income is below 133 percent of the federal poverty level (services, however, may be limited to those related to pregnancy, labor, and delivery)

- Supplemental Security Income recipients in most states

- Recipients of adoption or foster care assistance under Title IV of the Social Security Act

- Special protected groups (for example, individuals who lose their cash assistance but are temporarily allowed to keep their Medicaid coverage)

- All children born after September 30, 1983, who are under age nineteen and live in families with incomes at or below the federal poverty level

- Some Medicare beneficiaries

States also have the option of providing Medicaid coverage to other similar groups.

In 1996, Congress passed the Personal Responsibility and Work Opportunity Reconciliation Act (also known as the welfare reform act). The act instituted changes in the eligibility requirements for Supplemental Security Income and Medicaid. The changes also affected Medicaid eligibility for some resident aliens. However, states are still required to provide resident aliens with Medicaid coverage for emergency medical services.

Medicaid Services

To be eligible for federal matching funds, every state Medicaid program must cover the following basic services:

- Inpatient hospital services

- Outpatient hospital services

- Prenatal care

- Vaccinations for children

- Physicians' services

- Skilled nursing services for individuals over age twenty-one

- Family planning services and supplies

- Rural health clinic services

- Home health services for individuals eligible for skilled nursing services

- Laboratory and X-ray services

- Pediatric and family nurse practitioner services

- Nurse–midwife services

- Ambulatory health services at federally qualified health centers

- Early and periodic screening and diagnostic and therapeutic services for children under age twenty-one

State Children's Health Insurance Program

The **State Children's Health Insurance Program** (SCHIP) was enacted by the Balanced Budget Act of 1997. This program provides additional federal funding to encourage states to expand Medicaid eligibility to include more poor and uninsured children.

TRICARE

TRICARE is a federal program that finances healthcare services for active-duty armed forces personnel and their families. The Department of Defense also operates acute care facilities designed to meet the needs of military personnel. Walter Reed Hospital in Washington, DC, is probably the most well known military hospital in the United States.

Military retirees and their families as well as survivors of deceased members of the armed services also qualify for TRICARE services. The Department of Veterans Affairs operates a nationwide network of hospitals dedicated to providing healthcare services to retired military personnel.

Civilian Health and Medical Program—Veterans Administration

The **Civilian Health and Medical Program—Veterans Administration** (CHAMPVA) provides healthcare coverage for dependents and survivors of permanently disabled veterans, survivors of veterans who died from service-related conditions, and survivors of military personnel who died in the line of duty.

Indian Health Service

The **Indian Health Service** (IHS) provides federally funded healthcare services to American Indians and Alaska natives. The IHS is a part of the Department of Health and Human Services. The IHS operates a network of acute care and ambulatory care facilities on Indian reservations and in native communities around the United States. In some areas, the services are provided through local and state hospitals and health agencies under contract with the IHS.

Workers' Compensation Programs

Most Americans are covered by some type of **workers' compensation** insurance. These programs cover the healthcare costs and lost wages of employees who are injured in connection with their employment. The programs also cover the healthcare costs and lost wages of employees who suffer work-related illnesses.

The program for civilian employees of the federal government was enacted as part of the Federal Employees' Compensation Act of 1916. The program is administered by the Office of Workers' Compensation Programs in the Department of Health and Human Services.

Every state except Texas provides some type of workers' compensation insurance. The plans are supported by premiums paid by employers operating in the states.

Private disability insurance is also widely available. This type of insurance is designed to cover any type of disabling injury or illness and not just work-related disabilities. Disability insurance generally covers lost income but not health-related expenditures.

Other Sources of Funding for Acute Care Services

Many city and county governments operate public hospitals to serve the healthcare needs of their residents, especially those who are uninsured and cannot pay for healthcare services. The services provided by public hospitals are supported by property taxes and other sources of local funding as well as by payments from private insurers, the Medicare program, and the state Medicaid programs for patients who qualify for medical assistance. Cook County Hospital in Chicago, Charity Hospital in New Orleans, and Bellevue Hospital in New York City are well-known public hospitals.

Many state governments also operate public hospitals. State-run inpatient psychiatric facilities are the most common. Services for residents with developmental disabilities and chronic mental illnesses are often provided in state psychiatric hospitals and financed in part by state Medicaid funds.

Many charitable foundations, religious orders, churches, and labor unions operate not-for-profit hospitals. The acute care services provided by such hospitals are financed in part by individual contributions as well as through reimbursement from Medicare, Medicaid, private insurance plans, and other third-party payers. These not-for-profit hospitals provide free acute care services to many patients who might otherwise be left underserved. St. Jude's Children's Research Hospital (in Memphis, Tennessee) is one well-known charitable institution that provides free acute care services to any child who needs them.

Clinical Documentation and the Health Record

Every healthcare provider is required to document the clinical services it performs on behalf of individual patients. Providers include healthcare organizations such as hospitals as well as independent practitioners such as physicians working from private offices or clinics. Nurses, psychologists, allied health professionals, licensed dependent practitioners (for example, physician's assistants), and clinical social workers are all considered healthcare providers.

A separate record must be created for each individual patient, and records must be created and maintained by providers in every healthcare setting. Clinical documentation may be stored in a paper-based format, in a mixed-media format, or in a computer-based electronic format. But it must include certain specific data elements no matter what format it is stored in. (Chapter 3 of this book discusses the content of health records in more detail.)

Accreditation standards, licensing requirements, and federal and state regulations all dictate the specific kinds of health-related information that must be collected for each patient. Standards and regulations also specify when the information must be collected and by whom. (Acute care documentation standards and regulations are discussed later, in chapter 5 of this book.) The content and style of clinical documentation also depend somewhat on a combination of other factors, including:

- The profession and specialty training of the healthcare provider (physician, surgeon, registered nurse, or respiratory therapist, for example)

- The healthcare setting (physician's office, ambulatory surgery center, or acute care hospital, for example)

- The type of healthcare service (routine screening, cataract surgery, or pulmonary intensive care, for example)

As subsequent chapters will explain, the **health record** is the tool that healthcare providers use to collect and store the clinical documentation they create for individual patients. In the context of the overall healthcare delivery system, health records serve several other important purposes, including:

- Ensuring the continuity of patient care among providers and along the continuum of care

- Providing a means for evaluating the outcomes, quality, and medical necessity of care

- Providing documentation to substantiate reimbursement claims

- Protecting the legal interests of patients, caregivers, and healthcare organizations

- Providing clinical data for biomedical research

- Supporting professional education for physicians, nurses, and allied health professionals

- Supporting the operational management of healthcare organizations

- Providing health services data for public health planning and governmental policy making

(The functions of clinical documentation and the health record are discussed in more detail in chapter 2 of this book.)

Owners of the Health Record

Legally, health records are considered the property of the healthcare providers that created them. Ethically, however, the personal information in each record still belongs to the patient. Recent federal regulations have been enacted to protect the patients' right to control access to their personal health information.

Until 2002, few federal regulations protected the confidentiality of health record information. Federal laws did protect a few special-circumstances records, such as the records of addiction treatment and HIV status. And in many states, laws were in place to govern the use and disclosure of health information. But, in general, the protection of patient privacy and health record security was the responsibility of individual healthcare providers. In hospitals, the privacy of confidential health information and the security of health records were managed primarily by health information management professionals.

The implementation of the Health Insurance Portability and Accountability Act (HIPAA) in 2002 established a consistent set of privacy and security rules for the first time. These rules apply to virtually every provider in the United States, including healthcare insurance companies. The rules were designed to protect the privacy of patients, but they were also created to simplify the sharing of health information for legitimate purposes.

For example: Before the implementation of the privacy rule, a provider who needed access to a health record maintained by another provider usually could not request the information directly. The previous provider needed the patient's written permission in order to release the information to the current provider. In many cases, it was up to the patient or the patient's legal representative to ask the previous provider to duplicate the record and send the copy to the current provider. Under the new federal privacy regulations, the healthcare provider would be able to request the information directly and would not need to obtain the patient's formal consent.

As long as the information is to be used for the purposes of treatment, payment, or healthcare operations, providers are allowed to access, use, or disclose patient information without a formal authorization signed by the patient. However, the regulations stipulate that only the information needed to satisfy the specified purpose can be used or disclosed. The release of information for purposes unrelated to treatment, payment, or healthcare operations still requires the patient's formal authorization. (Current privacy and security standards and regulations are discussed in detail in chapter 5.)

The new health information regulations under HIPAA have also established the rights of patients to access and amend their own health records. Before the Internet and widespread applications of information technology, most patients had little interest in the contents of their health records. In fact, state regulations and provider policies allowed patients very limited access to their records. Today, however, patients are more aware of the huge amounts of personal information stored in their health records, and they are more concerned about the information's accuracy and the record's security. (The rights of patients to access their own health records are explained in detail in chapter 5.)

Users of the Health Record

The number of organizations and individuals who have a legitimate need for access to confidential patient information has grown along with the complexity of the healthcare delivery system. Physicians, nurses, allied health professionals, and patient care technicians provide clinical services directly to patients, but clinicians are supported by many other people working in support and administrative roles. During a short hospital stay, dozens of clinicians, ancillary staff, administrative staff, and support staff will access the information in the patient's health record. (Chapter 2 provides more detailed information on the functions and uses of the health record documentation in acute care settings.)

Definition of the Health Record for Legal Purposes

Until the widespread use of computer technology in the last part of the twentieth century, the definition of what constituted a legal health record seemed relatively straightforward. The contents of the paper-based health records became the provider's legal business record of the services it provided to specific patients.

Because of the complexity of modern medical care and healthcare delivery systems, using a simple definition of the "legal record" is no longer possible. To help healthcare organizations define the content of their health records for legal purposes, the American Health Information Management Association (AHIMA) has broken down the information maintained in a typical health record system into four components (Amatayakul 2001):

- The legal health record
- Patient-identified source data
- Administrative data
- Derived data

Legal Health Record

The legal health record can be defined as the official business record created by or for the healthcare organization. The legal record is the portion of the health record that would be released upon request to parties outside the organization.

The legal health record includes documentation of the healthcare services provided to an individual patient in any aspect of healthcare delivery by a healthcare provider organization. This documentation includes all patient-identifiable information collected and directly used by caregivers, for example:

- Advance directives
- Anesthesia records
- Care plans
- Consents for treatment
- Consultation reports
- Discharge summaries
- Medication orders
- Minimum data sets
- Multidisciplinary progress notes
- Nursing assessments
- Operative and procedure reports
- Orders for diagnostic tests
- Pathology reports
- Records of history and physical examination
- Records of telephone orders and consultations

Generally, the legal health record should not include copies of health record information created by another provider and furnished directly by the patient. Similarly, personal health records created or controlled by the patient should not be included in the legal health record. However, if any of these materials (for example, patients' glucose/insulin-tracking records) are actually used by the current provider organization to deliver care, they may be included in the legal health record.

Patient-Identifiable Source Data

Patient-identifiable source data include data that are maintained in a separate database or location but are summarized in the legal health record in the form of clinical interpretations, notes, or other derivative reports. Such source information is usually retrievable, and it is kept in a secure environment. Source data are not considered part of the legal record as long as the source information is included in the legal record as a summary or report. Examples of patient-identifiable source data include:

- Patient photographs used for identification purposes

- Original audio recordings of transcribed dictation

- Diagnostic films and images

- Electrocardiographs

- Videos of procedures and telemedical consultations

Administrative Data

Administrative data include patient-identifiable information used for regulatory, operational, and reimbursement purposes. Administrative data should not be considered part of the legal health record. Examples include:

- Authorizations for release of information

- Birth and death certificates

- Patient identifiers such as health record numbers and biometrics

- Protocols, clinical pathways, practice guidelines, and other decision-support materials that do not include patient data

Derived Data

Derived data include information collected or summarized from health records in a form that does not include patient identifiers. Derived data are sometimes called aggregate data or de-identified data. Examples of derived data include the following:

- Accreditation reports

- Public health records

- Statistical reports

- Anonymous patient data used for research purposes

Documentation Guidelines for Acute Care

Health records may be called by different names in different healthcare settings, for example:

- Resident records in long-term care facilities

- Client records in psychiatric clinics

- Patient records in physicians' offices

- Medical records in acute care hospitals

And, as mentioned earlier in this chapter, the style and content of health records depend, in part, on the setting in which the healthcare services are provided. The regulatory and accreditation requirements for the various healthcare settings are quite different, as are the reimbursement requirements, patient demographics, and services mix. (See table 1.2 for a comparison of acute care to long-term care.)

Because of these differences, the documentation requirements for acute care facilities are unique to the setting. There are also different types of acute care hospitals, some of which have their own special documentation requirements. For example, psychiatric hospitals also treat patients who are in an acute phase of their illness, but the documentation of the diagnostic and therapeutic services for developmental disabilities and psychiatric conditions is somewhat different than the documentation for acute care medical–surgical services. However, other specialty hospitals, such as children's hospitals and women's hospitals, provide services similar to general acute care facilities and follow the same general guidelines. The same is true of critical access hospitals, very small and geographically isolated hospitals that provide a limited range of services.

It should be kept in mind that some hospitals are not considered acute care facilities. Long-term hospitals treat patients who require intensive medical and life support services (for example, ventilator-dependent patients) but are no longer in the acute phase of their illness. Rehabilitation hospitals provide nursing, medical, and rehabilitative services to patients who require physical, speech, and/or occupational therapy in addition to medical and nursing services (for example, stroke patients) but are no longer in the acute phase of their illness.

Virtually all acute care hospitals must comply with the federal documentation guidelines established by the Centers for Medicare and Medicaid Services for Medicare participants. In addition, most acute care hospitals choose to participate in voluntary accreditation programs, which also publish health record documentation standards. (Appendix C of this book outlines and compares the Medicare *Conditions of Participation for Hospitals* and the documentation standards of the two most common acute care accreditation programs. Chapter 5 discusses the accreditation and regulatory requirements for acute care documentation in detail.)

Table 1.2. Comparison of Acute Care with Long-Term Care

Setting	Licensure/ Certification	Primary Accreditation Organizations	Primary Payers	Patients	Diagnoses	Services
Acute care	State agencies, federal programs	JCAHO, AOA	All payers	All age-groups	Acute conditions	Intensive medical–surgical
Long-term care	State agencies, federal programs	JCAHO	Medicare/Medicaid, Veterans Administration, private health plans	Mostly elderly adults	Chronic conditions	Skilled nursing, custodial

The AHIMA (Smith 2001) also offers the following general guidelines for inpatient documentation:

- Hospital health record policies should be based on all applicable standards, including accreditation standards, state and local licensure requirements, federal and state regulations, reimbursement requirements, and professional practice standards.

- Hospital health records should be uniform in content and format, and health record entries should be legible and complete.

- Hospital health records should be organized systematically in a way that facilitates data retrieval and compilation.

- Only authorized clinicians should be permitted to author health record documentation. This requirement should be included in the hospital's medical staff rules and regulations and/or in the facility's administrative guidelines.

- Hospital policy and/or medical staff rules and regulations should specify the parties responsible for receiving and transcribing the verbal (telephone) orders of physicians.

- Health record entries should be completed at the time the documented services were performed, and entries should be dated.

- The authorship of health record entries should be clearly identified in the documentation.

- Only approved abbreviations and symbols should be used in health record documentation. This requirement should be included in the hospital's medical staff rules and regulations. (Alternately, some hospitals issue lists of prohibited abbreviations and symbols rather than lists of approved abbreviations and symbols.)

- All documentation in health records should be permanent.

- Documentation errors should never be obliterated or changed. Instead, documentation errors should be corrected according to the procedure established in the hospital's documentation policy and/or medical staff rules.

- Patients should never be allowed to change the original documentation in their health records. Instead, patients' comments should be entered into their health records as amendments to the originals.

- The qualitative and quantitative analysis of health record documentation should be conducted according to procedures developed and implemented by the hospital's health information management department.

Future of Clinical Documentation for Acute Care

Healthcare has lagged far behind other segments of the economy in the application of digital technology to operations and communications. But the development and implementation of computer-based systems, including electronic health record systems, is inevitable for all types of healthcare organizations.

The evolution of computer-based systems in acute care facilities began with the development of automated systems for administrative operations (admissions, billing, and claims processing). In the 1980s and 1990s, automated systems for laboratory and pharmacy services were implemented in most hospitals. Today, hospitals use a wide variety of computer-based technologies to provide clinical services and to support administrative functions. Yet, the application of advanced computer technology to health record systems has been slow to evolve.

In 1991, the Institute of Medicine (a division of the National Academy of Science) published the results of an eighteen-month study on the quality of patient records (Detmer and others 1991). The report advocated the development of computer-based systems for health records, and it mapped out the features computer-based records should contain. In a follow-up publication in 1997, the institute reported that progress toward implementing computer-based records (CPRs) had been much slower than anticipated (Dick and others 1997, p. 9):

> Most healthcare institutions are standing at the fork, trying to decide whether or not to begin implementing a CPR system. Those who have made the decision to invest in a CPR system are grappling with the complicated issue of how to do so. Many organizations implement the CPR system in some, but not all areas. Others implement a partial system and depend on a combination of paper and electronic documentation. All adopters of CPR systems must address how to integrate the components of the CPR and how to integrate the CPR with other institutional information systems. The challenge of implementing such an expansive, robust system is daunting, but the option of continuing to manage the clinical and administrative data of an IDS [integrated delivery system] on paper is increasingly becoming a nonviable alternative.

(The term *electronic health record* [EHR] is now preferred over *computer-based record* [CPR], a term that was in use during the 1990s.)

Several additional factors are driving the movement toward the universal adoption of EHR systems. First, the 2002 implementation of the privacy and security provisions of the Health Insurance Portability and Accountability Act (HIPAA) has established broad-based federal regulations on health record operations for the first time. Initially enacted in response to the widespread use of electronic communications systems in healthcare operational transactions, HIPAA regulations may actually be stimulating the development of additional healthcare applications of computer technology.

Second, in 2003, the **National Committee on Vital and Health Statistics** (a public policy advisory board made up of representatives from numerous healthcare trade and professional organizations) recommended the adoption of a new diagnostic and procedural coding system. Based on the international version of ICD-10, the new system is to replace the outdated ICD-9-CM in the near future. ICD-10-CM and ICD-10-PCS require meticulous clinical documentation to substantiate code assignment, because ICD-10-CM contains more codes and allows greater specificity in diagnostic code assignments. But in offering this enhanced feature, the classification system has become very complex, and computer-enhanced coding systems will probably be needed to make implementation practical. Adopting a computer-based health record system in conjunction with ICD-10-CM and ICD-10-PCS software would make sense for large healthcare providers, especially acute care hospitals.

Finally, **Health Level Seven** (HL7), an organization that develops standards related to healthcare delivery, released the draft version of a new EHR functional model in late 2003. The **EHR Collaborative,** a group of organizations representing the key stakeholders in healthcare, worked with HL7 to publicize and refine the draft model. The model was revised several times before industry representatives voted to adopt the model in April 2004. The model will be used by healthcare organizations over a two-year trial period in preparation for final changes and implementation sometime after 2006. The adoption of these universal EHR guidelines is likely to stimulate the development of new and refined health record products by software technology vendors. In turn, the availability of more authoritative, and perhaps less costly, electronic record systems is likely to make implementation more practical for healthcare organizations.

The implementation of EHR systems may also support the development of longitudinal health records. A **longitudinal health record** is a health record that includes all of the health-related information generated for an individual during his or her lifetime. A longitudinal health record would have obvious benefits for individual patients. However, the maintenance of such records for every American will be impossible until EHR systems have been implemented by every healthcare provider in the country.

Under the current system of mixed-media records, every provider keeps a separate health record for every patient it treats. As a result, an individual's medical history is documented in hundreds of separate records created over the span of a lifetime. By the time a person reaches retirement age, most of those records have been lost or destroyed.

It is possible for individual patients and families to create and maintain their own longitudinal records. Health records maintained by patients and their families are called **personal health records,** or PHRs. Several tools for creating and maintaining PHRs are available over the Internet, including one from the AHIMA. Personal health records, however, are not considered legal documents, and so they cannot be included in the official records of healthcare providers at this time.

Summary

Healthcare services in the United States are distributed via a complex delivery system made up of innumerable clinical professionals, allied health professionals, healthcare administrators, and healthcare provider organizations. Many more organizations and governmental agencies manage healthcare reimbursement processes, institute healthcare standards and policies, and conduct healthcare-related research. Although the U.S. healthcare system is considered to be one of the best in the world, the cost of providing services and the challenge of meeting the needs of every American remain a concern in the twenty-first century.

The quality of the clinical documentation in patients' health records is vital to virtually every aspect of healthcare, including delivery, reimbursement, education, and research. Health information management professionals play a pivotal role by ensuring the availability, completeness, and accuracy of health record documentation at the same time they protect the patients' right to confidentiality and privacy. To be effective, health information management professionals working in acute care settings must understand every aspect of the healthcare environment, including state and federal laws and regulations, accreditation standards and processes, quality improvement practices, and information system technology.

References

Agency for Healthcare Research and Quality. 2002. *Health Care Costs.* Rockville, MD: U.S. Department of Health and Human Services.

Amatayakul, Margret, and others. 2001. Practice Brief: Definition of the health record for legal purposes. *Journal of the American Health Information Management Association* 72(10). Available at www.ahima.org.

Cassidy, Bonnie. 2002. Healthcare delivery systems. In *Health Information Management: Concepts, Principles, and Practice,* edited by Kathleen LaTour and Shirley Eichenwald. Chicago: American Health Information Management Association.

Center for Studying Health System Change. 2003. Tracking health care costs. *Data Bulletin* 25:1–2.

Centers for Medicare and Medicaid Services. 2003. Medicare+Choice program in 2001 and 2002. Available at www.cms.hhs.gov.

Centers for Medicare and Medicaid Services. 2004. The facts about upcoming new benefits in Medicare. Available at www.cms.hhs.gov.

Davis, Nadinia. 2002. Financial management. In *Health Information Management: Concepts, Principles, and Practice,* edited by Kathleen LaTour and Shirley Eichenwald. Chicago: American Health Information Management Association.

Detmer, Don, and others, editors. 1991. *The Computer-Based Patient Record: An Essential Technology for Health Care.* Washington, D.C.: National Academy Press.

Dick, Richard, and others, editors. 1997. *The Computer-Based Patient Record: An Essential Technology for Health Care,* revised edition. Washington, D.C.: National Academy Press.

Fletcher, Donna. 1999. Practice Brief: Best practices in medical record documentation and completion. *Journal of the American Health Information Management Association* 70(10). Available at www.ahima.org.

Glondys, Barbara. 2003. Practice Brief: Ensuring legibility of patient records. *Journal of the American Health Information Management Association* 74(5). Available at www.ahima.org.

Green, Michelle. 2002. Reimbursement systems. In *Health Information Management: Concepts, Principles, and Practice,* edited by Kathleen LaTour and Shirley Eichenwald. Chicago: American Health Information Management Association.

Joint Commission on Accreditation of Healthcare Organizations. 1995. *Accreditation Manual for Hospitals.* Oakbrook Terrace, Il.: JCAHO.

Kaiser Permanente. 2004. About Kaiser Permanente. Available at www.newsmedia.kaiserpermanente.org.

Rhodes, Harry. 1999. Practice Brief: The care and maintenance of charge masters. *Journal of the American Health Information Management Association* 70(7). Available at www.ahima.org.

Smith, Cheryl. 2001. Practice Brief: Documentation requirements for the acute care inpatient record. *Journal of the American Health Information Management Association* 72(3). Available at www.ahima.org.

U.S. Census Bureau. 2003. *Health Insurance Coverage in the United States: 2002.* Washington, D.C.: U.S. Census Bureau.

Review Quiz

Directions: Choose the best answer for each of the following items.

1. ___ What is the primary reason why many Americans cannot find affordable health insurance?
   A. The complexity of private insurance plans and government-funded programs
   B. The cost of medical–surgical care and pharmaceuticals
   C. The difficulty and complexity of healthcare delivery under the HMO system
   D. The inefficiency of the national healthcare delivery system

2. ___ What is acute care?
   A. Short-term treatment in an inpatient setting to address the acute phase of a patient's illness or injury
   B. Medical–surgical care provided to patients who require urgent care for an illness or injury
   C. Preventive, diagnostic, and therapeutic medical services provided on a nonresidential basis
   D. Therapeutic medical services provided to patients who have been disabled by illness or injury

3. ___ Which of the following terms can be defined as the sum of all the healthcare services provided in all settings, from the least to the most intensive, specialized, and expensive?
   A. Primary care
   B. Fee-for-service care
   C. Continuum of care
   D. Subacute care

4. ___ What is the main difference between primary, secondary, and tertiary care?
- A. The degree of specialization
- B. The quality of care
- C. The care setting
- D. The duration of care

5. ___ Health maintenance organizations and preferred provider organizations are two types of what?
- A. Prospective payment systems
- B. Prospective reimbursement systems
- C. Integrated healthcare networks
- D. Managed care plans

6. ___ What is the term for health records maintained by patients and/or their families?
- A. Electronic health records
- B. Mixed-media records
- C. Personal health records
- D. Longitudinal health records

7. ___ Due to the widespread use of the Internet to distribute health-related information, Americans have become more aware of what?
- A. The insurance options available to them
- B. The differences between care settings
- C. The large quantity of personal information stored in their health records
- D. The health information management profession

8. ___ What is the term used for the patient-identifiable information collected and used directly by caregivers?
- A. Minimum data record
- B. Legal health record
- C. Mixed-media health record
- D. Electronic health record

9. ___ Health records are often called by different names. What factor determines the name that is used?
- A. The healthcare setting
- B. The patient's preference
- C. The physician's preference
- D. The age of the patient

10. ___ What condition will make it possible to adopt longitudinal health records on a widespread basis?
- A. Patients keep tabs on all of the facilities where their health records are housed
- B. Healthcare facilities adopt a universal health record format
- C. EHR systems are implemented by every healthcare provider
- D. Mixed-media health records are maintained instead of an EHR system

11. ___ How has the overall percentage of Americans with health insurance coverage changed since the late 1980s?
- A. It has decreased
- B. It has stayed the same
- C. It has increased
- D. It has fluctuated by 5 to 10 percent each year

12. ___ Under what circumstances would an outpatient become an inpatient?
    A. The patient was admitted for an overnight stay after receiving emergency room services
    B. The patient was released after receiving emergency room services during the course of which the date changed
    C. The patient received medical treatment at the same facility on two consecutive days
    D. The patient was treated for the same health condition over the course of several months

13. ___ The concept of the continuum of care has been increasingly emphasized in response to what trend in the healthcare environment?
    A. The growing lack of communication between healthcare providers and HIM departments
    B. The increasing use of the Internet in healthcare
    C. Patients' growing awareness of the information contained in their health records
    D. The increasing cost of healthcare

14. ___ What factor is medical necessity based on?
    A. The beneficial effects of a service on the patient's physical needs and quality of life
    B. The cost of a service compared with the beneficial effects on the patient's health
    C. The availability of a service at the facility
    D. The reimbursement available for a given service

15. ___ Which healthcare consumers are subject to fee-for-service reimbursement systems today?
    A. Medicare and Medicaid patients
    B. The underinsured
    C. The uninsured
    D. Patients over the age of 65 years

16. ___ Which of the following is a major difference between health maintenance organizations (HMOs) and preferred provider organizations (PPOs)?
    A. PPOs pay at least part of the cost for medically necessary services provided to beneficiaries by any qualified physician
    B. HMOs pay at least part of the cost for medically necessary services provided to beneficiaries by any qualified physician
    C. HMOs are more expensive than PPOs for the patient
    D. HMOs, but not PPOs, are considered managed care organizations

17. ___ According to the Centers for Medicare and Medicaid Services, how did the number of Americans enrolled in Medicare change from 1966 to 2001?
    A. It has remained the same
    B. It has tripled
    C. It has decreased by one-half
    D. It has more than doubled

18. ___ Which of the following statements applies to Medicaid eligibility?
    A. Eligibility is based entirely on federal regulations
    B. Eligibility varies from state to state
    C. Eligibility is determined on the basis of the patient's age
    D. Eligibility is based entirely on the patient's need

19. ___ _____, health records are the property of the healthcare providers who created them; _____, the personal information contained in each record belongs to the patient.
    A. Legally; ethically
    B. Morally; logically
    C. Ethically; legally
    D. In theory; in reality

20. ___ How do healthcare providers use the administrative data they collect?
    A. For regulatory, operational, and reimbursement purposes
    B. For statistical data purposes
    C. For electronic health record tracking purposes
    D. For continuity of patient care purposes

21. ___ The current healthcare delivery system in the United States can be characterized by which of the following phrases?
    A. Simple and affordable
    B. Simple and expensive
    C. Complex and expensive
    D. Complex and affordable

22. ___ How have recent biomedical advances affected healthcare?
    A. Recent advances have simplified healthcare services
    B. Recent advances have streamlined healthcare services
    C. Recent advances have revolutionized healthcare services
    D. Recent advances have professionalized healthcare services

23. ___ Where do acute care facilities store confidential clinical documentation?
    A. On employees' personal computers
    B. In health records
    C. At the Centers for Medicare and Medicaid Services
    D. In integrated healthcare networks

24. ___ What level of care is provided by medical specialists working in private offices, specialty group practices, private clinics, community-based clinics, and general and community hospitals?
    A. Primary
    B. Secondary
    C. Tertiary
    D. Managed

25. ___ What is the term used for a database that stores the facility's fee schedules for services and information on the underlying costs associated with those services?
    A. Master patient index
    B. Prospective payment system
    C. Cost–benefit database
    D. Chargemaster

Chapter 2

Functions of the Acute Care Health Record

Learning Objectives

- Define and explain the term health record

- Explain the difference between information and data

- Identify and explain the principal and ancillary functions of the health record in the acute care setting

- List the main users of acute care health records

- List the most common secondary indexes, registries, and databases maintained by hospitals and explain the content and purpose of each

- Explain the basic differences between paper-based and computer-based health record systems

Terminology

Accreditation
Accreditation organizations
Advanced decision support
Aggregate data
Allied health professionals
Biomedical research
Case management
Case mix
Centers for Medicare and Medicaid Services (CMS)
Certification
Claims processing
Clinical practice guidelines
Coding specialist
Confidentiality
Continuous quality improvement (CQI)
Core measures
Credentialing
Data

Diagnostic codes
Disease index
Electronic data interchange (EDI)
Electronic health record (EHR)
Health Level Seven (HL7)
Health record
Healthcare Integrity and Protection Data Bank (HIPDB)
Information
Informed consent
Licensure
Master patient index (MPI)
Medical necessity
Medicare Provider Analysis and Review File (MEDPAR)
National Practitioner Data Bank (NPDB)
Notifiable diseases
Operation index
Performance improvement
Physician index
Population-based statistics
Privacy
Procedural codes
Quality improvement organization (QIO)
Registry
Reimbursement
Risk management (RM)
Systematized Nomenclature of Medicine Clinical Term® (SNOMED CT®)
Third-party payers
Transcriptionist
Utilization management (UM)
Utilization review (UR)

Introduction

The **health records** created and maintained by acute care hospitals contain large amounts of clinical documentation stored as data and information. That information must be readily accessible for legitimate healthcare functions and yet protected from unauthorized intrusion, damage, and loss.

The terms *data* and *information* are often used interchangeably, but there are distinct differences in meaning between the two terms when they are used in reference to health records. **Data** represent objective descriptions of processes, procedures, people, and other observable things and activities. Data are collected in the form of dates, numbers, symbols, images, illustrations, texts, lists, charts, and equations. The analysis of data for a specific purpose results in **information.** Data represent facts; information conveys meaning. In other words, data themselves have no meaning until they are considered in the context of a specific purpose or function.

For example, a chart showing a series of columns with times, dates, initials, numbers, and symbols would have little meaning unless it were put in the context of patient care. Then, the numbers and symbols would represent observations of the vital signs of a specific patient. And the times, dates, and initials would constitute authentication for the health record documentation of those observations. Taken further, the information on the patient's temperature, pulse rate, respirations, and blood pressure would have even more specific meaning if it were considered in the context of the patient's age and medical condition.

Before the widespread use of computer technology in healthcare, all of the information in acute care health records was collected and stored in paper format. Each record was a compilation of handwritten progress notes, paper forms, photographs, graphic tracings, and typewritten reports. Many of the typewritten reports of medical findings and operative procedures were originally dictated by physicians and surgeons and subsequently converted into written format by medical **transcriptionists** (specially trained typists who understand medical terminology). The paper record was organized in a paper folder (called a chart). When an episode of care was complete, the paper record was moved from the patient care unit and stored in a large file room. After a predetermined amount of time, the record might be moved to a more remote storage facility or converted to a film image (called microfiche) that consumed much less space in storage. Eventually, the paper records were destroyed.

Many healthcare organizations, including hospitals, continue to use paper-based health record systems. Most combine handwritten documentation with computer printouts and documents generated in other media, such as digital images, e-mail communications, and video images.

Hospitals and other large healthcare organizations have been slow to adopt new information technologies. The high cost of developing and implementing computer-based health record systems and the reluctance of clinical professionals to learn new documentation processes account for some of the resistance. Another factor has been the lack of national standards on electronic record content, which has hampered the commercial development of health record systems. In addition, the federal government, the largest healthcare payer in the United States, had been silent on the issue until the president's state of the union address in January 2004.

The movement toward **electronic health record** (EHR) systems has gained momentum since the implementation of the Health Insurance Portability and Accountability Act (HIPAA) in 2002. Similarly, the future adoption of the new diagnostic and procedural coding system (ICD-10-CM and ICD-10-PCS) and the standardized definitions from the **Systematized Nomenclature of Medicine Clinical Terms**® (SNOMED CT®) is also likely to spur the inevitable change from paper and mixed-media to electronic health record systems (AHIMA 2003). (The HIPAA regulations as well as other regulations that pertain to health records are explained in chapter 5. Chapter 5 also discusses SNOMED CT in more detail.)

Health Level Seven (HL7) began working on a functional model for EHRs in 2003. (HL7 is a standards development organization that addresses issues at the applications [or seventh] level of healthcare system interconnections.) HL7 and industry stakeholders are set to begin a two-year trial of the EHR model in preparation for the release of final EHR standards some time after 2006. (The transition to electronic health record systems is discussed in more detail in chapter 4 and appendixes L and M.)

Principal Functions of the Acute Care Record

The main function of the health record is the same, no matter what format it is stored in: The health record serves as the principal repository for the clinical documentation relevant to the care and treatment of one specific patient. Health records also have many additional functions. The principal functions are related to specific healthcare encounters between providers and patients. The ancillary functions are related to the environment in which healthcare services are provided.

According to the Institute of Medicine (Dick and others 1997), the principal functions of the acute care health record can be organized into four categories:

- Patient care delivery
- Patient care management
- Patient care support
- Billing and reimbursement

Patient Care Delivery

The acute care record combines information about the patient's illness with documentation of the services provided during the patient's hospital stay. Clinical observations of the patient, results of physical examinations and diagnostic tests, details of medical–surgical procedures, and descriptions of therapeutic outcomes are all compiled in one record. This record is accessible to all of the clinical professionals and **allied health professionals** who provide services to the patient. Therefore, first and foremost, the health record is a data and information collection and storage tool. However, it has a number of additional and equally important functions:

- The health record is a service documentation tool. The information in the patient's record constitutes a permanent account of the services the patient received.

- The health record is a communications tool for the patient's caregivers. Effective communication among caregivers ensures the continuity of patient services.

- The health record is a diagnostic tool. The information in the patient's health record helps physicians make informed decisions about the patient's current condition and treatment requirements.

- The health record is a tool for patient assessment and care planning. Nursing assessments document the level of nursing assistance and personal care needed by the patient.

- The health record is a risk assessment tool. The information in the patient's record forms the basis for evaluations of potential threats to the welfare of individual patients.

- The health record is a discharge planning tool. The purpose of discharge planning is to ensure that the patient is able to leave the hospital safely and that the patient will receive appropriate follow-up care after leaving the hospital.

Electronic records are based on sophisticated information processing technology. Therefore, EHRs perform several additional clinical functions that traditional records are not equipped to do. For example:

- The electronic health record is an **advanced decision support** tool. Advanced decision support makes the latest clinical guidelines and research findings available to physicians at a click.

- The electronic health record is a medical error prevention tool. Drug interaction and dosage warnings are issued automatically when conflicting medication orders are entered into the record. Other reminders for clinicians can also be issued automatically.

- The electronic health record is an enhanced discharge planning tool. EHR systems can be linked to clinic schedules so that follow-up appointments can be made for patients before they leave the hospital. EHRs may also supply patient aftercare instructions automatically.

Patient Care Management and Support

The patient care support function includes activities related to:

- The allocation of the healthcare organization's resources (for example, staff scheduling)

- The analysis of trends in the usage of patient services (for example, new service planning)

- The forecasting of future demand for services (for example, new equipment acquisitions)

- The communication of information among different clinical departments (for example, laboratory services planning)

The patient care management function of health records encompasses the activities related to the management of the acute care services provided directly to patients. For example:

- Health record information is analyzed to determine the hospital's case mix. **Case-mix analysis** is a method of grouping patients according to a predefined set of characteristics. Case-mix information is used in determining Medicare reimbursement.

- Health record information provides the basis for case management. **Case management** is the ongoing review of clinical care conducted during the patient's hospital stay. The purpose of case management is to ensure the necessity and quality of the services being provided to the patient.

- Health record information is used to develop clinical pathways and other types of **clinical practice guidelines.** Clinical practice guidelines help clinicians make knowledge- and experience-based decisions on medical treatment. The guidelines also make it easier to coordinate multidisciplinary services.

Quality Management and Performance Improvement

Accreditation organizations and licensing bodies expect hospitals and other healthcare organizations to strive for the highest possible quality in patient care. **Third-party payers** also review the quality of care their members receive.

Quality Management

The Joint Commission on Accreditation of Healthcare Organizations (JCAHO) uses the concept of **core measures** to assess the quality management efforts of healthcare organizations. Hospitals submit information on core patient care areas (for example, heart failure and myocardial infarction), and the JCAHO compares the hospital's results with those of similar facilities.

The Medicare program first established a system of quality review in the 1980s. Today, local **quality improvement organizations** (QIOs) work under contract with the **Centers for Medicare and Medicaid Services** (CMS), the federal agency that administers the Medicare and Medicaid programs. Hospitals submit patient information collected from health records to the QIOs, which then review the appropriateness of the admissions and discharges. The Seventh

Scope of Work for QIOs, which was developed in 2002 and 2003, includes four national projects aimed at improving the care of Medicare beneficiaries in acute care hospitals (Centers for Medicare and Medicaid Services 2003b):

- The acute myocardial infarction project focuses on improving patient outcomes by increasing the implementation of evidence-based treatment processes.

- The heart failure project focuses on the evaluation of left ventricular systolic function and the use of angiotensin-converting enzyme inhibitors in heart failure patients.

- The pneumonia project focuses on improving pneumonia treatment processes and increasing rates of vaccination against influenza and pneuomococcal disease.

- The surgical infection prevention project focuses on improving the selection and administration of prophylactic antibiotics.

Similarly, managed care organizations and other third-party payers review information on the hospital services provided to their beneficiaries. Their focus is on the appropriateness of care as well as the quality of care.

The process of medical staff credentialing is also considered an element of quality management in hospitals. **Credentialing** is the process of reviewing and validating the qualifications of physicians who have applied for permission to treat patients in the facility. The JCAHO has established credentialing standards to guide hospitals and other healthcare organizations. (The credentialing process is discussed in more detail in chapter 5.)

Performance Improvement

Healthcare organizations systematically look at their processes and outcomes to ensure the quality of the services they provide. Most large hospitals employ quality management professionals. Quality managers work directly with clinical and ancillary staff to identify patient care issues and then develop process improvements. In the past, quality assurance efforts concentrated on the identification of mistakes and substandard individual performance. In contrast, contemporary **performance improvement** (PI) efforts emphasize the importance of identifying the shortcomings of processes and systems rather than individuals.

Hospitals use a number of different PI models, and the models tend to go in and out of fashion rather quickly. No matter what model is chosen, however, PI processes must be driven by patient care information to be effective. Currently, most healthcare organizations employ some form of **continuous quality improvement** (CQI). The CQI philosophy emphasizes the critical importance of three factors:

- Knowing and meeting customer expectations
- Reducing variation within processes
- Relying on data to build knowledge for process improvement

CQI entails a continuous cycle of planning, measuring, and monitoring performance and making periodic knowledge-based improvements. Quality managers use a number of tools to monitor performance and identify areas for improvement. Many hospitals use a model originally developed by the Hospital Corporation of America (LeBlanc and White 2002). The model is known as FOCUS-PDCA® and is based on five steps:

1. Find a clinical process to improve.

2. Organize a team made up of people who understand the process.

3. **C**larify the team's current knowledge of the process.

4. **U**nderstand the causes of the undesired variation.

5. **S**elect the improvement to be made in the process.

Like other CQI models, FOCUS-PDCA then calls for applying the plan–do–check–act process, which is basically a cycle of trial, measurement, and learning. During the planning phase, the PI team analyzes the process to be improved. The team identifies what the process is, how it currently works, who is involved, and other performance factors. Then, the team develops a proposed change to address the problem identified. Team members also develop a system for measuring the outcomes of the proposed change to determine whether the change will actually represent an improvement. In the doing phase, the proposed improvement is implemented for a trial period, and data are collected. The checking phase involves analyzing the data that were collected. If the proposed change actually did result in a measurable improvement in the process, the cycle moves on to the action step. The change is adjusted on the basis of the knowledge gained and/or implemented. If the proposed change had no observable effect, the team goes back to develop another solution. They go through the entire PDCA cycle again and again until they identify a solution that works.

Utilization Management

The process of **utilization management** (UM) focuses on how healthcare organizations use their resources. Hospital utilization management programs ensure that patients receive appropriate levels of services and that the services are performed in an efficient and cost-effective way. State and federal government regulations require hospitals to conduct utilization reviews. Most commercial health insurance plans also conduct their own utilization reviews for both inpatient and outpatient services. Health record information is used as the basis of utilization review and management activities.

Utilization review (UR) is a formal process conducted to determine the medical necessity of the services provided to, or planned for, an individual patient. Determinations of **medical necessity** are based on whether the services can be expected to have a reasonably beneficial effect on the patient's physical needs and quality of life.

The Medicare *Conditions of Participation for Hospitals* specifically require acute care facilities to perform utilization review for Medicare and Medicaid patients to determine the medical necessity of hospital admissions, lengths of stay, and professional services (including drugs and biological substances). The process uses preestablished, objective screening criteria. The criteria are based on the severity of the patient's illness and the intensity of the services needed to effectively treat the patient's illness. Hospitals may conduct utilization review at several points before, during, and after the patient's stay to determine whether the patient's condition and need for services necessitate inpatient treatment. In most cases, the Medicare regulations permit hospitals to conduct utilization for a sample of patients rather than for every Medicare or Medicaid patient.

Risk Management

Health record information is also used in risk management activities. The main purpose of **risk management** (RM) is to prevent situations that might put hospital patients, caregivers, or visitors in danger. Risk management also includes investigating reported incidents, reviewing liability claims, and working with the hospital's lawyers. Most hospitals employ professional risk managers, who may also manage the hospital's safety programs and disaster planning.

Legal Proceedings

The contents of health records constitute the healthcare organization's legal business record. In most states, the records created and maintained during the regular course of business may be used in court proceedings. In order for a health record to be admissible as evidence, four conditions must be met (Dougherty 2002):

- The record must have been created as part of the provider's regular business activities.

- The record must have been maintained as part of the provider's regular business activities.

- The record must have been created at or near the time that the events occurred.

- The record must have been created by a person who had first-hand knowledge of the acts, events, conditions, and observations described in the record.

These conditions apply to both paper-based health records and electronic health records as long as the records are shown to be accurate and trustworthy. To be considered trustworthy, records must be secured in a manner that protects them from tampering. (See figure 2.1 for additional guidelines.) (Health record security is discussed in more detail in chapter 5.)

Personal injury lawsuits and other legal proceedings are often conducted long after the original events took place. Because witnesses often cannot remember the circumstances that led to the injury, the patient's health record is usually the only reliable evidence available to substantiate the care and treatment that the patient received. Incomplete or illegible documentation can lead to judgments against the facility and caregivers.

Billing and Reimbursement

The clinical documentation collected in health records supports the hospital's billing and claims management processes. In modern healthcare reimbursement systems, two main factors determine the amount of payment to which the hospital is entitled: (1) the illnesses for which the patient received care and (2) the services and procedures the patient received. Third-party payers often require hospitals and other healthcare providers to furnish copies of patient records to verify the legitimacy of reimbursement claims. In addition, the federal government conducts regular studies to identify inaccurate and fraudulent Medicare claims. The penalties for filing inaccurate claims may cost provider organizations millions of dollars. Providers that systematically defraud the government by claiming more reimbursement than they are entitled to may be disqualified from future participation in federal healthcare programs.

Diagnostic and Procedural Coding

Reimbursement claims communicate information about the patient's illnesses through the use of **diagnostic codes.** Information about the services and procedures provided to the patient are communicated in the form of **procedural codes.** The codes applied to acute care services are based on a clinical modification of the *International Classification of Diseases, Ninth Revision* (ICD-9-CM), which was designed exclusively for use in the United States. ICD-9-CM diagnostic codes are applied in all healthcare settings, but ICD-9-CM procedural codes apply only to acute care services. Hospital-based outpatient services are coded under a different system: *Common Procedural Terminology, Version 4* (CPT).

Figure 2.1. AHIMA General Documentation Guidelines for Legal Purposes

- The organization's health record policies must stipulate the persons who are authorized to make entries in the health record.
- Every page or screen in the health record must be identified with the patient's name and health record number.
- Health record entries must be made as soon as possible after the observation or event occurred.
- Health record entries must indicate the actual time and date (month, day, and year) when each entry was made. (Predating and postdating are both unethical and illegal.)
- The language used in health record entries must be specific, factual, and objective. (Opinions and speculations must not be included.)
- Health record entries must include all of the pertinent facts and information related to the observation or event being described.
- Health record policy must include a list of the abbreviations that may be used in the health record. The list must include definitions for the abbreviations, and only acceptable abbreviations must be allowed in documentation.
- Health record entries must be legible and permanent whether they are handwritten, computer-generated, or electronic. Policies must be in place to protect health records from alteration, tampering, and loss.
- In paper-based health records, entries must be continuous (no gaps or extra spacing between entries). Blank lines in forms must be crossed out.
- All of the data fields on assessments, flowsheets, and checklists must be completed even when one or more of the fields does not apply to the patient. (Dashes or the abbreviation NA, for not applicable, can be entered in blanks to prevent tampering.)
- Entries must be consistent with previous entries. Any contradictions must be explained.
- Every change in the patient's condition and all significant treatment issues must be noted until the patient's condition becomes stable or the treatment issue is resolved. Documentation must provide evidence of follow-through.
- The patient's informed consent for procedures and treatment must be documented in the health record.
- The patient's initial admission note and discharge summary must fully and accurately describe the patient's condition at that time.
- All communications and attempts at communication with the patient's family and personal physician must be documented.
- The charge nurse or nurse manager must ensure the consistency and completeness of all health record entries made by patient care technicians and other clinical staff with delegated responsibilities.
- The facts behind any adverse incidents must be documented in the progress notes. However, no mention of an incident report should be made in the health record.
- The authors of health record documentation must create and sign their own entries in both paper-based and electronic health record systems. Authors must never create or sign entries on behalf of another author.
- Health record entries must contain nothing other than documentation that pertains to the direct care of the patient (no personal statements or complaints).
- When it is necessary to refer to another patient in describing an event, the other patient's health record number must be used in place of his or her name.
- Every health record entry must be authenticated. The healthcare organization's health record authentication policy must stipulate the manner in which handwritten signatures, electronic signatures, fax signatures, or rubber-stamp signatures are to be used.
- When countersignatures are required by state regulations, only qualified persons must countersign health record entries.
- The healthcare organization's health record policies must stipulate the process that is to be followed to correct errors in health record entries.
- Late entries must include the time and date the late entry was entered into the health record, not the date when the entry should have been made.
- Health records must never be removed from the healthcare facility except in response to a legitimate court order or subpoena.

Source: Dougherty 2002.

A clinical modification of the tenth revision of the diagnostic system (ICD-10-CM) is currently available and will likely be implemented within the next few years. ICD-10-CM codes are significantly more detailed than ICD-9-CM codes. Therefore, in the near future, accurate coding—and precise documentation—will become even more important than they are now.

ICD-9-CM and CPT codes are based directly on the documentation in patient health records. Inaccurate or incomplete documentation can result in underpayment or overpayment. Underpayments may affect the financial viability of the hospital, but overpayments can lead to serious charges of fraud and abuse. Delays in completing health record documentation may also result in delays in reimbursement.

Hospitals also use coded information based on health records for purposes other than reimbursement (Prophet 2002, p. 107). Comparing health record information in the form of alphanumerical codes makes it possible:

- To improve the quality and effectiveness of patient care

- To expand the body of medical knowledge

- To make appropriate decisions related to healthcare policies, delivery systems, funding, expansion, and education

- To monitor resource utilization

- To permit identification and resolution of medical errors

- To improve clinical decision making

- To identify potential fraud-and-abuse problems

- To permit valid clinical research, epidemiological studies, outcomes and statistical analyses, and provider profiling

- To provide comparative cost and outcome information to consumers

Documentation of Medical Necessity

Third-party payers deny reimbursement for services that they do not consider to have been reasonable and necessary. For example, Medicare carriers and fiscal intermediaries (organizations that manage payments under Medicare Part A and Part B) have identified the diagnostic codes that support the medical necessity of specific diagnostic tests. When claims for such tests are made but not supported by the ICD-9-CM diagnostic codes reported, payment is denied.

Health record documentation should include a physician's order for every service rendered during the patient's stay. Documentation should also clearly indicate that the only appropriate setting for the patient to receive necessary services was an acute care hospital. The record should include evidence that discharge planning took place early in the stay. It should also demonstrate that the patient was released from the hospital as soon as treatment was complete and the patient's safety could be assured.

Specifically, every acute care record should include dated and authenticated documentation to support the level and types of services provided (Prophet 2002). (See figure 2.2 for a list of general documentation guidelines for reimbursement purposes.) Following are a few additional suggestions that may also be helpful (Glondys 1999, pp. 293–94):

- Clinicians should indicate the location where each service was performed in the patient's health record.

Figure 2.2. AHIMA Minimum Documentation Requirements for Reimbursement Purposes

- The reason for hospitalization
- The level of care needed as evidenced by the initial orders for patient care
- The patient's medical history and the results of the physical examination
- The types and numbers of services provided
- The reasons why services, procedures, and supplies were needed
- The initial assessments of the patient's condition
- The patient's reaction to treatment and the patient's progress and outcomes
- The treatment plan, including treatments and medications (with frequency and dosages), orders for referrals and consultations, requirements for patient and family education, discharge plan, and follow-up instructions
- Changes to the treatment plan with a rationale for the changes
- The medical rationale for the intensity of services provided
- The evidence that the standards for medical necessity were met
- The physician's analysis of abnormal test results
- Any relevant health risk factors
- The complexity of medical decision making

Source: Prophet 2002, pp. 15–16.

- Physicians should enter final diagnostic information in the same place on every health record, for example, on the discharge summary or in the final progress note.

- Physicians should report the results of any preadmission tests or evaluations that led to the inpatient hospitalization.

- Physicians should document the patient's specific diagnosis rather than the patient's symptoms when a definitive diagnosis is known.

- Physicians should document their actions in response to consultations with other physicians or departments.

- Clinicians should use the same medical terminology throughout the health record.

- Clinicians should document any circumstances that resulted in treatment delays or slowed progress.

- Clinicians should indicate the method of administration for medications and treatments (oral, intravenous, etc.).

Claims Processing

Reimbursement claims for the clinical services provided to patients constitute the hospital's primary source of operating revenue. **Claims processing** involves calculating charges, preparing and submitting reimbursement forms, and following up to make sure that appropriate payments were made (Davis 2002). Claims processing for inpatient and outpatient services is handled by the hospital's patient accounts department.

Third-party payers generally will not issue payment for claims that do not include appropriate diagnostic and procedural codes. For this reason, claims processing can be thought of as a responsibility shared by several hospital departments. Incomplete or inaccurate clinical documentation results in incomplete or inaccurate coding. In turn, the reporting of incomplete or inaccurate codes results in reimbursement problems.

For example: Suppose that a hospital submitted a claim for a surgical procedure performed to treat a Medicare patient's colon cancer. The Medicare fiscal intermediary would look for specific diagnostic codes that documented the necessity of the surgery. If the claim included only a nonspecific diagnostic code, the intermediary would issue a notice to the hospital that requested supporting documentation. The claims manager would then go back to the coder for more specific information. The coder would look through the patient's health record to find the information needed to support the assignment of a more specific code. If the final pathology report on the specimens collected during surgery were missing, the coder would then need to query the pathologist for a copy of the final report. If the pathologist remembered dictating the report but could not find a copy, the health information manager would need to locate the missing report before the reimbursement claim could be resubmitted.

Most reimbursement claims are submitted to third-party payers electronically. **Electronic data interchange** (EDI) is the computer-based transmission of information in a standard format between individuals and institutions engaged in a business relationship. EDI makes it possible for healthcare providers and third-party payers to exchange billing information quickly and inexpensively (Green 2002). The information transmitted via EDI is subject to HIPAA regulations. (HIPAA is discussed in chapter 5.)

Ancillary Functions of the Acute Care Record

The ancillary functions of the health record are not associated with specific patients and specific healthcare encounters. They are related to the environment in which patient care is provided. Accreditation, certification, and licensure processes are linked to how hospitals operate, and these processes require health record information. State and federal regulations also dictate a number of specific operational and information-reporting requirements. Providing information for biomedical research and clinical education is also considered an ancillary function of the health record.

Health record data are the basis of morbidity and mortality (vital statistics) reports and healthcare-related indexes, registries, and databases. (*Morbidity* refers to illness, and *mortality* refers to death.) Much of the statistical data collected in hospital reports, indexes, registries, and databases is submitted to state, national, and international agencies. These agencies are responsible for policy making on healthcare delivery, services, research, and education. For example, the World Health Organization, a component of the United Nations, uses record-based statistics to track the incidence of disease worldwide and to plan public health initiatives accordingly.

Accreditation, Licensure, and Certification

Hospitals and other healthcare organizations are subject to a number of practice standards. The purpose of the standards is to ensure the safety of patients and the quality of medical care. The accreditation, licensure, and certification processes that hospitals undergo are based on these standards.

Because hospitals are large, complex organizations, the processes of accreditation, licensure, and certification are also complex (Shaw and others 2003, pp. 243–50). **Accreditation** is the process of granting formal approval to a healthcare organization. The approval is based on whether the organization meets a set of voluntary standards developed by the accrediting organization. The Joint Commission on Accreditation of Healthcare Organizations (JCAHO) publishes operational standards for several types of healthcare organizations, including acute care hospitals. The purpose of accreditation is to confirm the quality of the services being provided in participating healthcare organizations. After an organization has been accredited by the JCAHO, accreditation surveys are conducted periodically to determine whether the facility continues to meet the JCAHO's standards. Accreditation has a number of benefits for hospitals and other healthcare organizations. For example, when a hospital is accredited by the JCAHO, Medicare automatically allows the hospital to participate in the program. (Accreditation is discussed in more detail in chapter 5.)

Licensure is the process of granting an organization the right to provide healthcare services. Licensure requirements are established by state governments. Unlike accreditation, which is a voluntary process, licensure is mandatory. Some individual healthcare practitioners are also subject to state licensure requirements. For example, physicians, dentists, and nurses must be licensed in order to practice in every state. Specific licensure requirements are determined by state regulations and vary somewhat from state to state. However, it is illegal to operate healthcare facilities and practice medicine without a license in all fifty states.

Certification is the process of granting an organization the right to provide healthcare services to a specific group of individuals. For example, healthcare organizations must meet certain federal regulations in order to receive funding through the Medicare program. These regulations are published in the Medicare Conditions of Participation.

Many individual healthcare practitioners undergo a voluntary certification process. Clinical and ancillary professional certifications are based on requirements established by specialized professional organizations. The requirements usually specify the level of education that must have been achieved, and most involve passing certification examinations. In addition, most certified professionals are required to meet continuing education requirements to maintain their credentials. For example, a physician specializing in dermatology would seek certification from the American Academy of Dermatologists. Health information management technicians and administrators are certified through the American Health Information Management Association.

Biomedical Research

Biomedical research is the process of systematically investigating subjects related to the functioning of the human body. Biomedical research often leads to a greater understanding of disease processes and the development of new or improved treatments and medical technologies. For example, research conducted over the past thirty years has led to the development of new drugs that control several debilitating mental illnesses, such as clinical depression and schizophrenia. Similarly, the development of endoscopic technology has revolutionized the way many surgical procedures are performed.

The goal of scientific research of any kind is to prove or disprove theoretical explanations of observable phenomena. To be valid, the results of research must be based on findings that can be reproduced in subsequent studies conducted by different research teams. The general purpose of biomedical research studies is to develop or improve treatment interventions for the benefit of humans. Such developments are the cumulative result of many studies conducted over many years.

Biomedical research is usually conducted at large, urban hospitals affiliated with universities and medical schools. Funding for biomedical research comes from a number of different sources, including the federal government, pharmaceutical and medical equipment manufacturers, and charitable foundations. Many acute care facilities are not involved in long-term research projects, although they often participate in clinical trials.

Biomedical research studies explore the safety and effectiveness of drugs, diagnostic procedures, therapeutic procedures, and disease prevention approaches. A large portion of biomedical research is conducted on the microscopic level or with nonhuman subjects. However, many biomedical research studies involve human subjects directly, or they study clinical cases gleaned from health records.

Studies that involve human subjects must meet federal and international ethical guidelines. The guidelines are intended to protect the welfare of human subjects. In the United States, the *Belmont Report: Ethical Principles and Guidelines for the Protection of Human Subjects of Biomedical and Behavioral Research,* first released in 1979, is still applicable. Internationally, the Declaration of Helsinki represents the ethical principles to be followed in biomedical studies that involve biological specimens or medical information that comes from an identifiable human source (Osborn 2002b).

Federal regulations require that researchers provide human subjects with specific information before biomedical studies are initiated. The information is meant to make it possible for the subjects to give their **informed consent** to participation. (See figure 2.3.) This information must include at least the following:

- A statement that describes the purpose of the research, the expected duration of the subject's participation, the procedures to be followed, and the nature of any experimental procedures involved

- A description of possible risks or discomforts

- A description of the possible benefits to the subject or others

- A disclosure of any alternative procedures or courses of treatment that might benefit the subject

- A statement that describes the level of **confidentiality** that will be applied to any records that identify the subject

- An explanation of the compensation or medical treatment available to address possible injuries during the study if the study involves more than minimal risk for the subject

- An explanation of where information would be made available if the subject were injured during the study and a contact who would answer questions

- A statement that explains that participation is voluntary and that refusal to participate would involve no penalties and that the subject may discontinue participation at any time

The JCAHO has also established specific standards related to research and clinical trials conducted in hospitals. The JCAHO's standards are similar to the federal regulations on human research. To meet the accreditation standards, the consent form must also include the name of the person who provided the information, the date the form was signed, and an acknowledgment of the patient's right to **privacy,** confidentiality, and safety. Any information given to the patient along with the informed consent form must be documented in the patient's health record or research file (JCAHO 2003).

Education

Health records are used as educational tools by medical schools, dental schools, nursing schools, and allied health training programs. The case studies derived from health record information provide real-world experience for students. Case studies are also useful for in-service training for all of the health professions, including health information management.

Figure 2.3.   Template for Informed Consent for Research Involving Human Subjects

---

Consent to Investigational Treatment or Procedure

I, _____ , hereby authorize or direct _____
or associates of his/her choosing to perform the following treatment or procedure (describe in
general terms), upon _____ (myself).

The experimental (research) portion of the treatment or procedure is:

This is part of an investigation entitled:

1. Purpose of the procedure or treatment:

2. Possible appropriate alternative procedure or treatment (not to participate in the study is always
   an option):

3. Discomforts and risks reasonably to be expected:

4. Possible benefits for subjects/society:

5. Anticipated duration of subject's participation (including number of visits):

I hereby acknowledge that _____ has provided information about the
procedure described above, about my rights as a subject, and he/she answered all questions to my
satisfaction. I understand that I may contact him/her at phone no. _____
should I have additional questions. He/she has explained the risks described above, and I
understand them; he/she has also offered to explain all possible risks or complications.

I understand that, where appropriate, the U.S. Food and Drug Administration may inspect records
pertaining to this study. I understand further that records obtained during my participation in this
study that may contain my name or other personal identifiers may be made available to the sponsor
of this study. Beyond this, I understand that my participation will remain confidential.

I understand that I am free to withdraw my consent and participation in this project at any time after
notifying the project director without prejudicing future care. No guarantee has been given to me
concerning this treatment or procedure.

I understand that in signing this form that, beyond giving consent, I am not waiving any legal rights
that I might have, and I am not releasing the investigator, the sponsor, the institution, or its agents
from any legal liability for damages that they might otherwise have.

In the event of injury resulting from participation in this study, I also understand that immediate
medical treatment is available at _____ and that the costs of such
treatment will be at my expense; financial compensation beyond that required by law is not
available. Questions about this should be directed to the Office of Research Risks at
_____.

I have read and fully understand the consent form. I sign it freely and voluntarily. A copy has been
given to me.

_____   _____
Signature   Date

Source: Osborn 2002b, p. 431.

Morbidity and Mortality Reporting

In the United States, official vital statistics are maintained under the **National Vital Statistics System** (NVSS). The NVSS is a federal agency that operates within the **Centers for Disease Control and Prevention** (CDC). (The CDC is a group of federal agencies that oversee health promotion and disease control and prevention activities in the United States.) Vital statistics include information on the number of births and the number of deaths that occur during a calendar year. Hospitals and other healthcare providers report the births and deaths in their facilities to designated state authorities. (Most states have their own reporting requirements for vital statistics.) The state authorities then report the statistics to the NVSS. State and federal agencies also collect and report other types of morbidity and mortality data submitted by healthcare providers. The source of all this information is the health record (Osborn 2002a).

To ensure consistency in data collection, standard forms and procedures are provided by the NVSS. The forms are revised regularly, about every ten years. Standard forms include the U.S. Standard Certificate of Live Birth (figure 2.4), the U.S. Standard Certificate of Death (figure 2.5), and the U.S. Standard Report of Induced Termination of Pregnancy (figure 2.6). The U.S. standard report for fetal deaths is very similar to the certificate of live birth (CDC 1997).

The individual states also maintain public health databases to manage information on the incidence of communicable diseases. The CDC maintains a database that contains similar information. The World Health Organization's (WHO) international health regulations also require incidence reporting from participating nations so that the organization can track potential worldwide epidemics. (The WHO is the United Nations' agency that oversees global health initiatives.) The SARS epidemic that spread from China to Europe, Canada, and the United States in 2003 is an example of how quickly communicable diseases can be carried from continent to continent via international transportation systems.

A number of communicable illnesses must be reported to the CDC, as shown in figure 2.7. National data on these diseases (classified as **notifiable diseases**) are reported weekly. Case-specific information is included in the CDC's reports. The CDC also investigates cases where the cause of an illness or the source of an epidemic cannot be determined at the local level.

Hospitals also calculate population-based health statistics at the local level. **Population-based statistics** represent estimates of the incidence of a disease as a percentage of the total population that could have been affected. For example, the crude birth rate for a community can be calculated by dividing the number of live births in a community during a specific period of time by the estimated population of the same community for the same time period.

Morbidity statistics are calculated as incidence rates (the number of people who contracted the disease during a specific time period compared to the number of people who could have contracted the disease). Incidence rates usually include information on race, gender, and age so that the relative incidence rates among different populations can be compared. Examples of commonly computed mortality statistics include the following:

- Crude death rate

- Neonatal mortality rate

- Postneonatal mortality rate

- Infant mortality rate

- Crude mortality rate

- Cause-specific mortality rate

- Maternal mortality rate

Figure 2.4.   U.S. Standard Certificate of Live Birth

U.S. STANDARD CERTIFICATE OF LIVE BIRTH

LOCAL FILE NO.   BIRTH NUMBER:

CHILD

1. CHILD'S NAME (First, Middle, Last, Suffix)
2. TIME OF BIRTH (24hr)
3. SEX
4. DATE OF BIRTH (Mo/Day/Yr)

5. FACILITY NAME (If not institution, give street and number)
6. CITY, TOWN, OR LOCATION OF BIRTH
7. COUNTY OF BIRTH

MOTHER

8a. MOTHER'S CURRENT LEGAL NAME (First, Middle, Last, Suffix)
8b. DATE OF BIRTH (Mo/Day/Yr)

8c. MOTHER'S NAME PRIOR TO FIRST MARRIAGE (First, Middle, Last, Suffix)
8d. BIRTHPLACE (State, Territory, or Foreign Country)

9a. RESIDENCE OF MOTHER-STATE
9b. COUNTY
9c. CITY, TOWN, OR LOCATION

9d. STREET AND NUMBER
9e. APT. NO.
9f. ZIP CODE
9g. INSIDE CITY LIMITS? • •Yes • •No

FATHER

10a. FATHER'S CURRENT LEGAL NAME (First, Middle, Last, Suffix)
10b. DATE OF BIRTH (Mo/Day/Yr)
10c. BIRTHPLACE (State, Territory, or Foreign Country)

CERTIFIER

11. CERTIFIER'S NAME: _____
TITLE: • •MD • • DO • •HOSPITAL ADMIN. • •CNM/CM • • OTHER MIDWIFE
• • OTHER (Specify)_____
12. DATE CERTIFIED __MM__/__DD__/__YYYY__
13. DATE FILED BY REGISTRAR __MM__/__DD__/__YYYY__

INFORMATION FOR ADMINISTRATIVE USE

MOTHER

14. MOTHER'S MAILING ADDRESS: • •Same as residence, or: State: City, Town, or Location:

Street & Number: Apartment No.:   Zip Code:

15. MOTHER MARRIED? (At birth, conception, or any time between) • •Yes • •No
IF NO, HAS PATERNITY ACKNOWLEDGMENT BEEN SIGNED IN THE HOSPITAL? • •Yes • •No
16. SOCIAL SECURITY NUMBER REQUESTED FOR CHILD? • •Yes • •No
17. FACILITY ID. (NPI)

18. MOTHER'S SOCIAL SECURITY NUMBER:
19. FATHER'S SOCIAL SECURITY NUMBER:

INFORMATION FOR MEDICAL AND HEALTH PURPOSES ONLY

MOTHER

20. MOTHER'S EDUCATION (Check the box that best describes the highest degree or level of school completed at the time of delivery)
• • 8th grade or less
• • 9th - 12th grade, no diploma
• • High school graduate or GED completed
• • Some college credit but no degree
• • Associate degree (e.g., AA, AS)
• • Bachelor's degree (e.g., BA, AB, BS)
• •Master's degree (e.g., MA, MS, MEng, MEd, MSW, MBA)
• • Doctorate (e.g., PhD, EdD) or Professional degree (e.g., MD, DDS, DVM, LLB, JD)

21. MOTHER OF HISPANIC ORIGIN? (Check the box that best describes whether the mother is Spanish/Hispanic/Latina. Check the "No" box if mother is not Spanish/Hispanic/Latina)
• • No, not Spanish/Hispanic/Latina
• • Yes, Mexican, Mexican American, Chicana
• • Yes, Puerto Rican
• • Yes, Cuban
• • Yes, other Spanish/Hispanic/Latina (Specify)_____

22. MOTHER'S RACE (Check one or more races to indicate what the mother considers herself to be)
• • White
• • Black or African American
• • American Indian or Alaska Native (Name of the enrolled or principal tribe)_____
• • Asian Indian
• •Chinese
• •Filipino
• •Japanese
• •Korean
• •Vietnamese
• • Other Asian (Specify)_____
• • Native Hawaiian
• • Guamanian or Chamorro
• • Samoan
• • Other Pacific Islander (Specify)_____
• • Other (Specify)_____

FATHER

23. FATHER'S EDUCATION (Check the box that best describes the highest degree or level of school completed at the time of delivery)
• • 8th grade or less
• • 9th - 12th grade, no diploma
• • High school graduate or GED completed
• • Some college credit but no degree
• • Associate degree (e.g., AA, AS)
• • Bachelor's degree (e.g., BA, AB, BS)
• •Master's degree (e.g., MA, MS, MEng, MEd, MSW, MBA)
• • Doctorate (e.g., PhD, EdD) or Professional degree (e.g., MD, DDS, DVM, LLB, JD)

24. FATHER OF HISPANIC ORIGIN? (Check the box that best describes whether the father is Spanish/Hispanic/Latino. Check the "No" box if father is not Spanish/Hispanic/Latino)
• • No, not Spanish/Hispanic/Latino
• • Yes, Mexican, Mexican American, Chicano
• • Yes, Puerto Rican
• • Yes, Cuban
• • Yes, other Spanish/Hispanic/Latino (Specify)_____

25. FATHER'S RACE (Check one or more races to indicate what the father considers himself to be)
• • White
• • Black or African American
• • American Indian or Alaska Native (Name of the enrolled or principal tribe)_____
• • Asian Indian
• •Chinese
• •Filipino
• •Japanese
• •Korean
• • Vietnamese
• • Other Asian (Specify)_____
• • Native Hawaiian
• • Guamanian or Chamorro
• • Samoan
• • Other Pacific Islander (Specify)_____
• • Other (Specify)_____

Mother's Name____   Mother's Medical Record No.____

26. PLACE WHERE BIRTH OCCURRED (Check one)
• •Hospital
• •Freestanding birthing center
• •Home Birth: Planned to deliver at home? • •Yes • •No
• •Clinic/Doctor's office
• •Other (Specify)_____

27. ATTENDANT'S NAME, TITLE, AND NPI
NAME: _____ NPI:____
TITLE: • •MD • •DO • •CNM/CM • •OTHER MIDWIFE
• •OTHER (Specify)_____

28. MOTHER TRANSFERRED FOR MATERNAL MEDICAL OR FETAL INDICATIONS FOR DELIVERY? • •Yes • •No
IF YES, ENTER NAME OF FACILITY MOTHER TRANSFERRED FROM:
_____

REV. 11/2003

(Continued on next page)

51

Figure 2.4.   (Continued)

MOTHER	29a. DATE OF FIRST PRENATAL CARE VISIT _____ /_____ /_____ • •No Prenatal Care M M D D YYYY	29b. DATE OF LAST PRENATAL CARE VISIT _____ /_____ /_____ M M D D YYYY	30. TOTAL NUMBER OF PRENATAL VISITS FOR THIS PREGNANCY _____ (If none, enter "0".)

31. MOTHER'S HEIGHT _____ (feet/inches)	32. MOTHER'S PREPREGNANCY WEIGHT _____ (pounds)	33. MOTHER'S WEIGHT AT DELIVERY _____ (pounds)	34. DID MOTHER GET WIC FOOD FOR HERSELF DURING THIS PREGNANCY? • •Yes • •No

35. NUMBER OF PREVIOUS LIVE BIRTHS (Do not include this child)	36. NUMBER OF OTHER PREGNANCY OUTCOMES (spontaneous or induced losses or ectopic pregnancies)	37. CIGARETTE SMOKING BEFORE AND DURING PREGNANCY For each time period, enter either the number of cigarettes or the number of packs of cigarettes smoked. IF NONE, ENTER "0". Average number of cigarettes or packs of cigarettes smoked per day.	38. PRINCIPAL SOURCE OF PAYMENT FOR THIS DELIVERY • •Private Insurance • •Medicaid • •Self-pay • •Other (Specify) _____
35a.Now Living Number _____ • •None	35b. Now Dead Number ____ • •None	36a. Other Outcomes Number _____ • •None		

Three Months Before Pregnancy   # of cigarettes OR # of packs
First Three Months of Pregnancy _____ OR _____
Second Three Months of Pregnancy _____ OR _____
Third Trimester of Pregnancy _____ OR _____

35c. DATE OF LAST LIVE BIRTH _____ /_____ MM YYYY	36b. DATE OF LAST OTHER PREGNANCY OUTCOME _____ /_____ MM YYYY	39. DATE LAST NORMAL MENSES BEGAN _____ /_____ /_____ M M D D YYYY	40. MOTHER'S MEDICAL RECORD NUMBER

MEDICAL AND HEALTH INFORMATION	41. RISK FACTORS IN THIS PREGNANCY
	(Check all that apply)
	Diabetes
	• • Prepregnancy (Diagnosis prior to this pregnancy)
	• • Gestational (Diagnosis in this pregnancy)
	Hypertension
	• • Prepregnancy (Chronic)
	• • Gestational (PIH, preeclampsia)
	• • Eclampsia
	• • Previous preterm birth
	• • Other previous poor pregnancy outcome (Includes perinatal death, small-for-gestational age/intrauterine growth restricted birth)
	• • Pregnancy resulted from infertility treatment-If yes, check all that apply:
	  • • Fertility-enhancing drugs, Artificial insemination or Intrauterine insemination
	  • • Assisted reproductive technology (e.g., in vitro fertilization (IVF), gamete intrafallopian transfer (GIFT))
	• • Mother had a previous cesarean delivery If yes, how many _____
	• • None of the above
		43. OBSTETRIC PROCEDURES (Check all that apply)
		• • Cervical cerclage
		• • Tocolysis
		External cephalic version:
		  • •Successful
		  • •Failed
		  • •None of the above
			46. METHOD OF DELIVERY
			A. Was delivery with forceps attempted but unsuccessful?
			  • •Yes • • No
			B. Was delivery with vacuum extraction attempted but unsuccessful?
			  • •Yes • • No
			C. Fetal presentation at birth
			  • • Cephalic
			  • • Breech
			  • • Other
			D. Final route and method of delivery (Check one)
			  • Vaginal/Spontaneous
			  • Vaginal/Forceps
			  • Vaginal/Vacuum
			  • Cesarean
			  If cesarean, was a trial of labor attempted?
			  • •Yes
			  • •No

44. ONSET OF LABOR (Check all that apply)
• • Premature Rupture of the Membranes (prolonged, ≥12 hrs.)
• • Precipitous Labor (<3 hrs.)
• • Prolonged Labor (≥20 hrs.)
• • None of the above

45. CHARACTERISTICS OF LABOR AND DELIVERY (Check all that apply)
• • Induction of labor
• • Augmentation of labor
• • Non-vertex presentation
• • Steroids (glucocorticoids) for fetal lung maturation received by the mother prior to delivery
• • Antibiotics received by the mother during labor
• • Clinical chorioamnionitis diagnosed during labor or maternal temperature ≥38°C (100.4°F)
• • Moderate/heavy meconium staining of the amniotic fluid
• • Fetal intolerance of labor such that one or more of the following actions was taken: in-utero resuscitative measures, further fetal assessment, or operative delivery
• • Epidural or spinal anesthesia during labor
• • None of the above

42. INFECTIONS PRESENT AND/OR TREATED DURING THIS PREGNANCY (Check all that apply)
• • Gonorrhea
• • Syphilis
• • Chlamydia
• • Hepatitis B
• • Hepatitis C
• • None of the above

47. MATERNAL MORBIDITY (Check all that apply) (Complications associated with labor and delivery)
• • Maternal transfusion
• • Third or fourth degree perineal laceration
• • Ruptured uterus
• • Unplanned hysterectomy
• • Admission to intensive care unit
• • Unplanned operating room procedure following delivery
• • None of the above

NEWBORN INFORMATION

NEWBORN	48. NEWBORN MEDICAL RECORD NUMBER: 49. BIRTHWEIGHT (grams preferred, specify unit) _____ • grams • lb/oz	54. ABNORMAL CONDITIONS OF THE NEWBORN (Check all that apply) • • Assisted ventilation required immediately following delivery • • Assisted ventilation required for more than six hours • • NICU admission	55. CONGENITAL ANOMALIES OF THE NEWBORN (Check all that apply) • • Anencephaly • • Meningomyelocele/Spina bifida • • Cyanotic congenital heart disease • • Congenital diaphragmatic hernia • • Omphalocele • • Gastroschisis

50. OBSTETRIC ESTIMATE OF GESTATION:
_____ (completed weeks)

51. APGAR SCORE:
Score at 5 minutes:_____
If 5 minute score is less than 6,
Score at 10 minutes: _____

52. PLURALITY - Single, Twin, Triplet, etc.
(Specify)_____

53. IF NOT SINGLE BIRTH - Born First, Second, Third, etc. (Specify)_____

• • Newborn given surfactant replacement therapy
• • Antibiotics received by the newborn for suspected neonatal sepsis
• • Seizure or serious neurologic dysfunction
• • Significant birth injury (skeletal fracture(s), peripheral nerve injury, and/or soft tissue/solid organ hemorrhage which requires intervention)
• • None of the above

• • Limb reduction defect (excluding congenital amputation and dwarfing syndromes)
• • Cleft Lip with or without Cleft Palate
• • Cleft Palate alone
• • Down Syndrome
  • • Karyotype confirmed
  • • Karyotype pending
• • Suspected chromosomal disorder
  • • Karyotype confirmed
  • • Karyotype pending
• • Hypospadias
• • None of the anomalies listed above

Mother's Name _____
Mother's Medical Record No. _____

56. WAS INFANT TRANSFERRED WITHIN 24 HOURS OF DELIVERY? • • Yes • • No IF YES, NAME OF FACILITY INFANT TRANSFERRED TO:_____	57. IS INFANT LIVING AT TIME OF REPORT? • •Yes • •No • •Infant transferred, status unknown	58. IS THE INFANT BEING BREASTFED AT DISCHARGE? • • Yes • • No

REV. 11/2003

Source: Centers for Disease Control and Prevention 2003.

Figure 2.5. U.S. Standard Certificate of Death

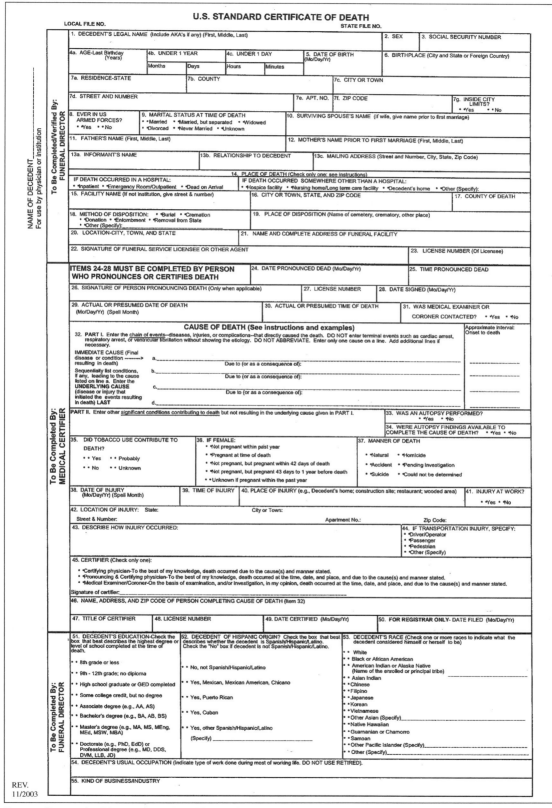

Source: Centers for Disease Control and Prevention 2003.

Figure 2.6.   U.S. Standard Report of Termination of Pregnancy

U.S. DEPARTMENT OF HEALTH AND HUMAN SERVICES—CENTERS FOR DISEASE CONTROL AND PREVENTION—NATIONAL CENTER FOR HEALTH STATISTICS—1997 REVISION

U.S. STANDARD
REPORT OF INDUCED TERMINATION OF PREGNANCY

STATE FILE NUMBER

1. FACILITY NAME *(If not clinic or hospital, give address)*	2. CITY, TOWN, OR LOCATION OF PREGNANCY TERMINATION	3. COUNTY OF PREGNANCY TERMINATION

4. PATIENT'S IDENTIFICATION	5. AGE LAST BIRTHDAY	6. MARRIED? ☐ YES ☐ NO	7. DATE OF PREGNANCY TERMINATION *(Month, Day, Year)*

8a. RESIDENCE—STATE	8b. COUNTY	8c. CITY, TOWN, LOCATION	8d. INSIDE CITY LIMITS? ☐ YES ☐ NO	8e. ZIP CODE

9. OF HISPANIC ORIGIN? (If yes, specify Cuban, Mexican, Puerto Rican, etc.) ☐ YES ☐ NO Specify: _____	10. RACE ☐ American Indian ☐ Black ☐ White ☐ Other *(Specify)* _____	11. EDUCATION *(Specify only highest grade completed)*
		Elementary/Secondary (0–12) / College (1–4, 5+)

12. DATE LAST NORMAL MENSES BEGAN *(Month, Day, Year)*

13. CLINICAL ESTIMATE OF GESTATION *(Weeks)*

14. PREVIOUS PREGNANCIES *(Complete each section)*

	LIVE BIRTHS		OTHER TERMINATIONS	
	14a. Now living	14b. Now dead	14c. Spontaneous	14d. Induced *(Do not include this termination)*
	Number: _____	Number: _____	Number: _____	Number: _____
	☐ None	☐ None	☐ None	☐ None

15. TYPE OF TERMINATION PROCEDURE *(Check only one)*

☐ Suction Curettage

☐ Medical (Nonsurgical), Specify Medication(s) _____

☐ Dilation and Evacuation (D&E)

☐ Intrauterine Instillation (Saline or Prostaglandin)

☐ Sharp Curettage (D&C)

☐ Hysterotomy/Hysterectomy

☐ Other *(Specify)* _____

16. NAME OF ATTENDING PHYSICIAN *(Type/Print)*	17. NAME OF PERSON COMPLETING REPORT *(Type/Print)*

PHS-T008
REV.12/97

Source: Centers for Disease Control and Prevention 1997.

Figure 2.7. Infectious Diseases That Require Notification to the Centers for Disease Control and Prevention

Acquired immunodeficiency syndrome (AIDS)	Meningococcal disease
Anthrax	Mumps
Botulism	Pertussis
Brucellosis	Plague
Chancroid	Poliomyelitis, paralysis
Chlamydia trachomatis genital infections	Psittacosis
Cholera	Q fever
Coccidioidomycosis	Rabies, human and animal
Cryptosporidiosis	Rocky Mountain spotted fever
Cyclosporiasis	Rubella
Diphtheria	Rubella congenital syndrome
Ehrlichiosis, human, other, or unspecified agent	Salmonellosis
Encephalitis/meningitis, Arboviral, California serogroup viral, eastern equine, Powassan, St. Louis, western equine, West Nile	Severe acute respiratory syndrome-associated Coronavirus (SARS-CoV) disease
Enterohemorrhagic Escherichia coli	Shigellosis
Enterohemorrhagic *Escherichia coli, shiga* toxin positive (serotyped and nonserotyped)	Smallpox
	Streptococcal disease, invasive, group A
	Streptococcal toxic-shock syndrome
Giardiasis	*Streptococcus pneumoniae,* drug-resistant, invasive disease
Gonorrhea	
Haemophilus influenzae, invasive disease	Syphilis
Hansen disease (leprosy)	Syphilitic stillbirth
Hantavirus pulmonary syndrome	Tetanus
Hemolytic uremic syndrome, postdiarrheal	Toxic-shock syndrome
Hepatitis A, acute and chronic	Trichinosis
Hepatitis B, acute and chronic	Tuberculosis
Hepatitis C (past and present)	Tularemia
HIV infection	Typhoid fever
Legionellosis	Vancomycin-intermediate *Staphylococcus aureus* (VISA)
Listeriosis	
Lyme disease	Vancomycin-resistant *Staphylococcus aureus* (VRSA)
Malaria	Varicella (morbidity and mortality)
Measles	Yellow fever

Source: Centers for Disease Control and Prevention 2004.

Management of the Healthcare Delivery System

The Centers for Medicare and Medicaid Services (CMS) collects information from reimbursement claims in a national database. The database is used as the basis for decision making related to the effectiveness of healthcare delivery systems and reimbursement systems. Federal and state governments also use the data reported by hospitals and other healthcare organizations to develop public health policies.

Professional organizations and trade organizations use information reported from health records to develop professional practice standards. They also base their support for public actions on healthcare policy issues on clinical information derived from health records. Professional health organizations include the American Medical Association and the American College of Surgeons. The largest trade organization in the healthcare industry is the American Hospital Association.

Primary versus Secondary Data

The principal source of health services-related information is the health record. Primary health record data can be categorized as patient identifiable; that is, the data relate specifically to one individual's diagnoses and treatment. Primary data compiled from multiple patient records can be categorized as secondary data. With the exception of several facility-specific indexes and registries, most secondary data are used in the form of **aggregate data,** or data that are no longer identifiable as belonging to specific patients (Bowman 2002).

Hospitals and other healthcare organizations create and maintain facility-specific secondary data for several reasons. The main reason is that secondary data provide information in formats that can be analyzed and compared more easily than the information in health records. By analyzing secondary data sources, medical and administrative staff are able to identify trends and patterns among patients with similar personal or clinical characteristics. Such information is valuable in long-range business planning and budgeting. Secondary aggregate data can also be released to researchers, policy makers, and other external users without affecting the confidentiality of the original patient records.

Facility-Specific Indexes

Facility-specific indexes are compilations of patient- and provider-identified data. The indexes are maintained by hospitals and other healthcare organizations to facilitate operational functions. Before the implementation of computer-based information systems, healthcare organizations maintained indexes on paper index cards stored in specially designed files. Today, most healthcare organizations maintain indexes in database format.

Most acute care organizations use four indexes:

- The master patient index
- The master physician index
- The index of diseases
- The index of operations

Master Patient Index

The **master patient index** (MPI) is made up of separate entries for every patient the facility has ever treated. Each entry includes the patient's name, address, and date of birth; the dates of past hospitalizations and outpatient encounters; the name of the patient's primary physician; and the patient's health record number. Most hospitals that still use paper-based health record systems file records according to health record number rather than patient's name. For these hospitals, the MPI is an important tool for quickly determining whether a patient already has a health record on file and retrieving the record from storage. The master patient index is sometimes called the master population index or the master person index. (Figure 2.8 shows a section of a typical MPI.) (Guidelines for managing MPIs are provided in appendix F.)

Physician Index

The **physician index** is a list of all the cases that have been treated in the hospital. The cases are identified by health record number and arranged according to the physician who admitted the patient to the facility. Some hospitals use the names of physicians, and others use the physicians' identification numbers. Additional information such as admission and discharge dates

Figure 2.8. Subset of a Master Patient Index

MRN	SSN	Last Name	First Name	Middle Name	DOB	Payment Type	Zip Code
096543	123-23-2345	Jones	Georgia	Louise	11/21/1957	Self	29425
065432	789-99-3456	Lexington	Milton	Robert	08/12/2000	Private	29425
467345	022-45-5378	Lovingood	Jill	Karen	10/14/1992	Medicaid	29401
678543	222-56-7777	Martin	Chloe	Mary	05/30/1978	Private	29465
234719	654-33-2222	Martin	John	Adams	06/22/1961	Private	29401
786543	435-89-0034	Nance	Natalie	JoAnn	11/27/1902	Medicare	29464

may also be included. The physician index makes it possible to review the practice patterns of individual physicians. Such information is especially helpful when a physician has applied for renewal of his or her medical privileges at the facility.

Disease and Operation Indexes

The **disease index** is a list of all the patients who have been treated in the hospital over a specified period of time. The entries are arranged numerically by ICD-9-CM diagnostic code, and each entry includes the patient's health record number. Additional information may include admission and discharge dates and the name of the patient's physician.

Similarly, the **operation index** is arranged numerically by procedural code (either ICD-9-CM or CPT, depending on hospital policy). The operation index contains the same information as the disease index except that the surgeon's name may be used in addition to, or instead of, the physician's name.

Registries

A **registry** is a collection of information related to a specific disease, condition, or procedure. Registries contain more information than indexes, but like indexes, registries usually include patient identifiers such as health record numbers. The main purpose of registries is to make health record information available for analysis and comparison of cases. Some registries include mechanisms for tracking periodic follow-up on patient outcomes. Information from registries is also used in biomedical research.

Disease Registries

The most common type of disease registry is the cancer registry. The first cancer registry was developed in the 1920s, and since then, most hospitals that provide cancer-related treatment maintain a cancer registry. The Cancer Registries Amendment Act of 1992 instituted a national program of cancer registries. The act called for the funding of population-based registries in all fifty states.

State cancer registries include the following types of information about each patient reported to have a diagnosis of neoplastic disease (Bowman 2002, p. 233):

- Demographic information

- Occupational information

- Administrative information including the date of the diagnosis and the source of the information on the case

- Specific information about the neoplasm, including its site, stage, incidence, and treatment

Figure 2.9 shows an example of a data entry screen and figure 2.10 an example of a cancer registry report.

Most acute care facilities also compile disease registries to collect information on the incidence of severe traumatic injuries, birth defects, HIV infections, and diabetes.

Procedure Registries

Common procedure registries include implant registries, transplant registries, and immunization registries. The information in procedure registries is especially helpful for tracking the safety of implants such as cardiac pacemakers and breast implants. Immunization registries provide important information on the healthcare services provided to children.

Healthcare Databases

Healthcare databases have been developed by the federal government as a method of tracking the quality of healthcare services in the United States. The three national administrative databases are used to conduct research, identify unqualified healthcare practitioners, and organize information on instances of fraud and abuse related to healthcare reimbursement.

- The **Medicare Provider Analysis and Review File** (MEDPAR): MEDPAR is a collection of data collected from reimbursement claims submitted to the Medicare

Figure 2.9. Data Collection Screen for a Cancer Registry

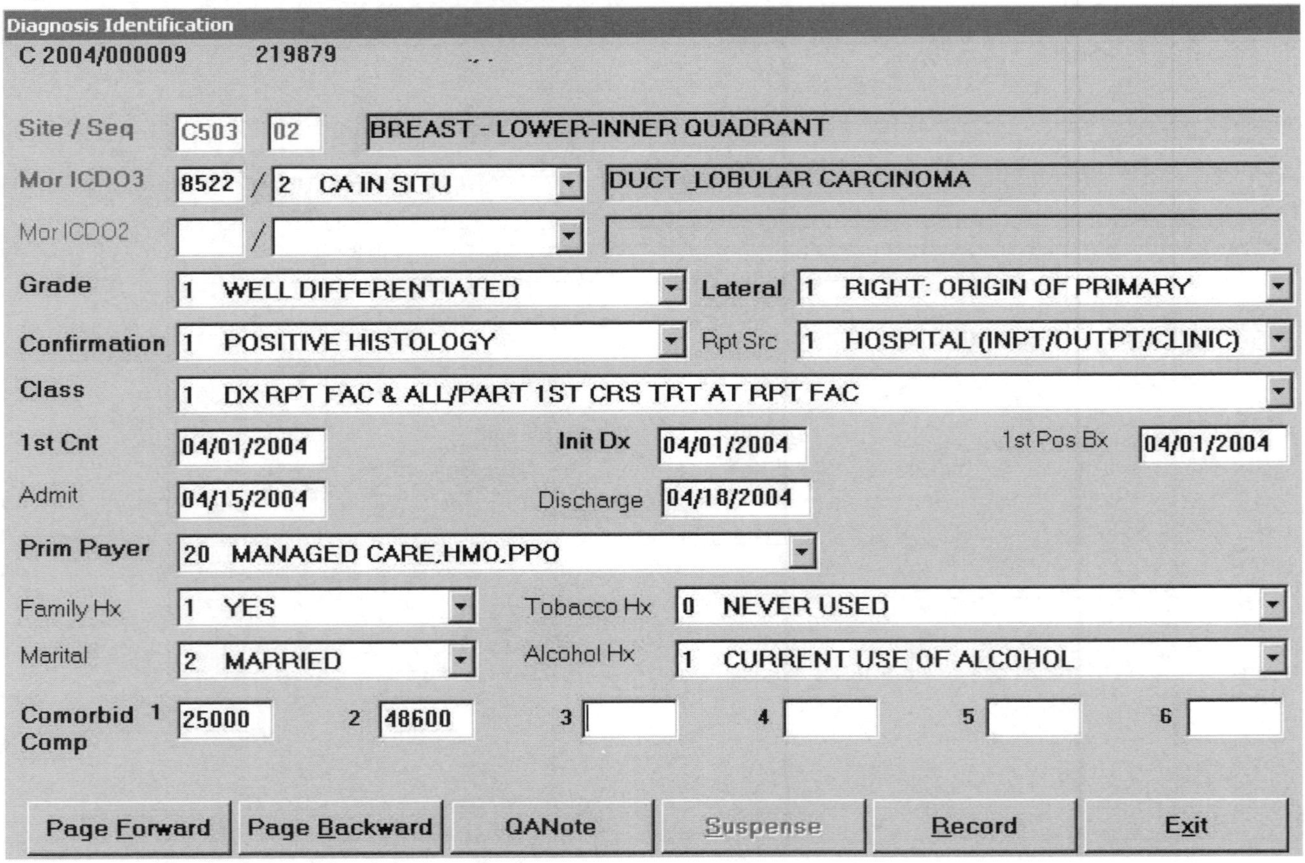

Source: IMPAC MRS™ Cancer Registry Software. Used with permission from IMPAC Medical Systems. All rights reserved.

Figure 2.10. Cancer Registry Report

RPT 30 FREQUENCY REPORT - BODY SYSTEM FORMAT PAGE 1
National Composite SUMMARY BY LOCATION/SEX/CLASS/STATUS/AJCC
RUN-DATE 05/08/2002
CIRF: CASES ACCESSIONED IN 2000

PRIMARY SITE	TOTAL	PERC	SEX M	SEX F	CLASS OF CASE ANALY	CLASS OF CASE N-ANALY	ALIVE	EXP	AJCC STAGE/ANALYTIC ONLY 00	01	02	03	04	99	88	B/B
LIP	245	.2	174	71	245	0	227	18	12	165	20	2	14	30	2	0
TONGUE	909	.6	619	290	909	0	720	189	24	181	113	159	372	53	7	0
SALIVARY GLANDS	409	.3	226	183	409	0	352	57	0	203	34	24	111	22	15	0
FLOOR OF MOUTH	240	.2	163	77	240	0	185	55	15	59	44	23	84	14	1	0
GUM & OTHER MOUTH	517	.3	263	254	517	0	413	104	26	119	106	58	154	37	17	0
NASOPHARYNX	203	.1	144	59	203	0	168	35	0	14	41	36	82	23	7	0
TONSIL	505	.3	398	107	505	0	426	79	8	37	57	123	254	23	3	0
OROPHARYNX	172	.1	124	48	172	0	131	41	1	21	15	35	81	16	3	0
HYPOPHARYNX	311	.2	248	63	311	0	208	103	4	11	37	66	170	21	2	0
OTHER BUCCAL CAV & PHAR	83	.1	58	25	83	0	49	34	0	6	15	13	32	14	3	0
BUCCAL CAV & PHARYNX	3594	2.4	2417	1177	3594	0	2879	715	90	816	482	539	1354	253	60	0
ESOPHAGUS	1725	1.2	1342	383	1725	0	811	914	45	168	340	280	452	405	35	0
STOMACH	2257	1.5	1443	814	2257	0	1116	1141	33	342	218	383	725	387	169	0
SMALL INTESTINE	0	.0	0	0	0	0	0	0	0	0	0	0	0	0	0	0
CECUM	2854	1.9	1266	1588	2854	0	2166	688	170	598	723	698	479	146	40	0
APPENDIX	172	.1	86	86	172	0	142	30	2	17	33	15	38	5	62	1
ASCENDING COLON	2266	1.5	1064	1202	2266	0	1758	508	147	432	682	535	321	133	16	0
HEPATIC FLEXURE	664	.4	338	326	664	0	525	139	44	140	211	130	84	49	6	0
TRANSVERSE COLON	1123	.8	537	586	1123	0	861	262	65	234	348	239	173	52	12	0

(Continued on next page)

Figure 2.10. (Continued)

RPT 30 FREQUENCY REPORT - BODY SYSTEM FORMAT   PAGE 2   RUN-DATE 05/08/2002
National Composite   SUMMARY BY LOCATION/SEX/CLASS/STATUS/AJCC   CIRF: CASES ACCESSIONED IN 2000

PRIMARY SITE	TOTAL	PERC	SEX M	SEX F	CLASS OF CASE ANALY	CLASS OF CASE N-ANALY	ALIVE	EXP	00	01	02	03	04	99	88	B/B
												AJCC STAGE/ANALYTIC ONLY				
SPLENIC FLEXURE	461	.3	256	205	461	0	335	126	20	73	142	110	80	32	4	0
DESCENDING COLON	732	.5	426	306	732	0	599	133	69	155	207	149	101	47	4	0
SIGMOID COLON	3925	2.6	2155	1770	3925	0	3314	611	458	972	905	759	532	275	24	0
LARGE INTESTINE, NOS	817	.5	446	371	817	0	559	258	81	133	121	125	213	125	19	0
COLON, EXCL RECTUM	13014	8.7	6574	6440	13014	0	10259	2755	1056	2754	3372	2760	2021	864	187	1
RECTOSIGMOID JUNCTION	1620	1.1	907	713	1620	0	1330	290	106	373	362	401	247	118	13	
RECTUM	3854	2.6	2240	1614	3854	0	3293	561	342	1069	693	720	391	476	163	0
RECTUM & RECTOSIGMOID	5474	3.7	3147	2327	5474	0	4623	851	448	1442	1055	1121	638	594	176	0
ANUS, ANAL CANAL, ANORECT	535	.4	212	323	535	0	463	72	66	100	178	78	19	80	14	0
LIVER	1106	.7	825	281	1106	0	432	674	1	43	85	233	426	261	57	0
INTRAHEPATIC BILE DUCT	229	.2	118	111	229	0	78	151	1	8	13	34	64	94	15	0
LIVER & INTRAHEPATIC BI	1335	.9	943	392	1135	0	510	825	2	51	98	267	490	355	72	0
GALLBLADDER	0	.0	0	0	0	0	0	0	0	0	0	0	0	0	0	0
OTHER BILIARY	0	.0	0	0	0	0	0	0	0	0	0	0	0	0	0	0
PANCREAS	3156	2.1	1645	1511	3156	0	904	2252	16	241	243	329	1699	499	129	2
RETROPERITONEUM	0	.0	0	0	0	0	0	0	0	0	0	0	0	0	0	0
PERITONEUM, OMENTUM, MESE	0	.0	0	0	0	0	0	0	0	0	0	0	0	0	0	0
OTHER DIGESTIVE ORGANS	0	.0	0	0	0	0	0	0	0	0	0	0	0	0	0	0
DIGESTIVE SYSTEM	27496	18.4	15306	12190	27496	0	18686	8810	1666	5098	5504	5218	6044	3184	782	3

program by acute care hospitals and skilled nursing facilities. MEDPAR information is used to evaluate the quality and effectiveness of the care being provided to Medicare beneficiaries.

- The **National Practitioner Data Bank** (NPDB): The National Practitioner Data Bank is a collection of information on medical malpractice payments, sanctions issued against physicians by medical examiners and licensing boards, and other actions taken against physicians and healthcare practitioners who provide substandard care. The data bank was established in 1986 as a means for making information on dangerous practitioners available nationally. Hospitals are now required to report disciplinary actions taken against physicians to the data bank. Hospitals are also required to query the data bank before granting physicians medical staff privileges.

- The **Healthcare Integrity and Protection Data Bank** (HIPDB): The Healthcare Integrity and Protection Data Bank is a collection of information related to fraudulent and abusive healthcare practices. The data bank includes information on federal and state convictions, civil judgments, and other legal actions and decisions. Only federal and state governmental agencies and health programs are required to report information to the national data bank.

Users of the Acute Care Record

The Institute of Medicine broadly defines the users of health records as "those individuals who enter, verify, correct, analyze, or obtain information from the record, either directly or indirectly through an intermediary" (Dick and others 1997, p. 75). All of the users of health records influence patient care in some way, but they use the information for various reasons and in different ways. Some users (nurses, physicians, allied health professionals, and **coding specialists**) refer to the health records of specific patients as an integral part of their daily work responsibilities. In contrast, many other users never have direct access to the records of individual patients. Instead, they use aggregate (summarized and deidentified) clinical and demographic information derived from health record documentation.

The main users of health records are the clinicians who are responsible for direct patient care. They are authorized to record and access clinical documentation for the patients to whom they provide services. It should be noted, however, that most clinicians are only authorized to access the records for their own patients. Accessing or disclosing health record information without a valid reason would be considered a violation of the ethical principles of every healthcare profession. It would also violate institutional policies protecting the confidentiality of patient information. (Privacy and security are discussed in detail in chapter 5.)

Nurse managers who supervise nursing services and physicians on the faculty of university-based medical schools supervise the work of less experienced clinicians and unlicensed students, and so they need access to patient-identifiable health information. Risk managers and utilization managers also need access to patient-identifiable information. Coding and billing staff consult patient-identifiable information as the basis for clinical coding and reimbursement. (Figure 2.11 provides a list of representative users of health record information.)

Patients, patients' next of kin, and patients' legal representatives all have access to the health records of individual patients but under very restricted circumstances. (The patient's right to access and amend his or her own health record is explained in chapter 5.)

Figure 2.11. Representative Users of the Health Record: Individuals

Patient Care Delivery (Providers)
- Chaplains
- Dental hygienists
- Dentists
- Dietitians
- Laboratory technologists
- Nurses
- Occupational therapists
- Optometrists
- Pharmacists
- Physical therapists
- Physicians
- Physician assistants
- Podiatrists
- Psychologists
- Radiology technologists
- Respiratory therapists
- Social workers

Patient Care Delivery (Consumers)
- Patients
- Families

Patient Care Management and Support
- Administrators
- Financial managers and accountants
- Quality managers
- Records professionals
- Risk managers
- Unit clerks
- Utilization review managers

Patient Care Reimbursement
- Benefit managers
- Insurers (federal, state, and private)

Other
- Accreditors
- Government policy makers and legislators
- Lawyers
- Healthcare researchers and clinical investigators
- Health sciences journalists and editors

Source: Dick and others 1997, p. 76.

As explained earlier in this chapter, a number of healthcare-related organizations use information derived from health records. Healthcare providers such as HMOs and physicians' practices use patient-identifiable information, as do third-party payers. Quality improvement organizations and other entities working under contracts with hospitals or with third-party payers such as Medicare often review copies of health record documentation. Many other organizations use aggregate health information in activities related to accreditation, research, and policy making. (See figure 2.12 for a more comprehensive list of the institutions that rely on information from health records.)

Summary

The primary functions of the acute care health record can be grouped into four categories: patient care delivery, patient care management, patient care support, and billing and reimbursement. In examining these functions, this chapter focused on the concept that data represent facts but information conveys meaning. Primary users of the acute care health record include nurses, physicians, allied health professionals, and administrative personnel as well as patients and their family members or legal representatives.

The ancillary functions of the acute care health record are related to the care environment. Ancillary functions include accreditation, licensure, and certification; biomedical research; clinical education; and morbidity and mortality reporting.

The principal functions of the health record use primary, patient-identifiable information. Most ancillary functions use secondary, deidentified health record information, usually in an aggregate form that protects the confidentiality of patient records.

Figure 2.12. Representative Users of the Health Record: Institutions

Healthcare Delivery (Inpatient and Outpatient)
- Alliances, associations, networks, and systems of providers
- Ambulatory surgery centers
- Donor banks (blood, tissue, organs)
- Health maintenance organizations
- Home care agencies
- Hospices
- Hospitals (general and specialty)
- Nursing homes
- Preferred provider organizations
- Physician offices (large and small group practices, individual practitioners)
- Psychiatric facilities
- Public health departments
- Substance abuse programs

Management and Review of Care
- Medicare peer review organizations
- Quality management companies
- Risk management companies
- Utilization review and utilization management companies

Reimbursement of Care
- Business healthcare coalitions
- Employers
- Insurers (federal, state, and private)

Research
- Disease registries
- Health data organizations
- Healthcare technology developers and manufacturers (equipment and device firms, pharmaceutical firms, and computer hardware and software vendors for patient record systems)
- Research centers

Education
- Allied health professional schools and programs
- Schools of medicine
- Schools of nursing
- Schools of public health

Accreditation
- Accreditation organizations
- Institutional licensure agencies
- Professional licensure agencies

Policy Making
- Federal government agencies
- Local government agencies
- State government agencies

Source: Dick and others 1997, p. 77.

References

American Health Information Management Association. 2003. Press Release: AHIMA urges Secretary Thompson to adopt ICD-10. July 25, 2003. Available at www.ahima.org.

Bowman, Elizabeth. 2002. Secondary records and healthcare databases. In *Health Information Management: Concepts, Principles, and Practice,* edited by Kathleen LaTour and Shirley Eichenwald. Chicago: American Health Information Management Association.

Centers for Disease Control and Prevention, National Center for Health Statistics. 1997. *State Definitions and Reporting Requirements for Live Births, Fetal Deaths, and Induced Terminations of Pregnancy,* revised edition. Washington, D.C.: U.S. Department of Health and Human Services. Available at www.cdc.gov.

Centers for Medicare and Medicaid Services. 2003a. Medicare+Choice program in 2001 and 2002. Available at www.cms.hhs.gov.

Centers for Medicare and Medicaid Services. 2003b. Seventh Scope of Work for Quality Improvement Organizations. Available at www.cms.hhs.gov.

Davis, Nadinia. 2002. Financial management. In *Health Information Management: Concepts, Principles, and Practice,* edited by Kathleen LaTour and Shirley Eichenwald. Chicago: American Health Information Management Association.

Dick, Richard, and others, editors. 1997. *The Computer-Based Patient Record: An Essential Technology for Health Care,* revised edition. Washington, D.C.: National Academy Press.

Dougherty, Michelle. 2002. Practice Brief: Maintaining a legally sound health record. *Journal of the American Health Information Management Association* 73(9). Available at www.ahima.org.

Glondys, Barbara. 1999. The patient record: content and reimbursement. In *Documentation Requirements for the Acute Care Patient Record,* 1999 edition. Chicago: American Health Information Management Association. [Out of print.]

Glondys, Barbara. 2003. Practice Brief: Ensuring legibility of patient records. *Journal of the American Health Information Management Association* 74(5). Available at www.ahima.org.

Green, Michelle. 2002. Reimbursement systems. In *Health Information Management: Concepts, Principles, and Practice,* edited by Kathleen LaTour and Shirley Eichenwald. Chicago: American Health Information Management Association.

Homan, Cheryl. 2002. Functions of the health record. In *Health Information Management Technology: An Applied Approach,* edited by Merida Johns. Chicago: American Health Information Management Association.

Joint Commission on Accreditation of Healthcare Organizations. 2003. *2004 Accreditation Manual for Hospitals.* Oakbrook Terrace, Il.: JCAHO.

LeBlanc, Madonna, and White, Andrea Weatherby. 2002. Work design and performance improvement. In *Health Information Management: Concepts, Principles, and Practice,* edited by Kathleen LaTour and Shirley Eichenwald. Chicago: American Health Information Management Association.

McCain, Mary Cole. 2002. Paper-based health records. In *Health Information Management: Concepts, Principles, and Practice,* edited by Kathleen LaTour and Shirley Eichenwald. Chicago: American Health Information Management Association.

Osborn, Carol. 2002a. Healthcare statistics. *Health Information Management: Concepts, Principles, and Practice,* edited by Kathleen LaTour and Shirley Eichenwald. Chicago: American Health Information Management Association.

Osborn, Carol. 2002b. Biomedical and research support. *Health Information Management: Concepts, Principles, and Practice,* edited by Kathleen LaTour and Shirley Eichenwald. Chicago: American Health Information Management Association.

Prophet, Sue. 2002. *Health Information Management Compliance: A Model Program for Healthcare Organizations,* 2002 edition. Chicago: American Health Information Management Association.

Schanz, S. J. 1999. *Developing and Implementing Clinical Practice Guidelines.* Chicago: American Medical Association.

Shaw, Patricia, and others. 2003. *Quality and Performance Improvement in Healthcare: A Tool for Programmed Learning,* second edition. Chicago: American Health Information Management Association.

Smith, Cheryl. 2001. Practice Brief: Documentation requirements for the acute care inpatient record. *Journal of the American Health Information Management Association* 72(3). Available at www.ahima.org.

Zeman, Vicki. 2002. Clinical quality management. *Health Information Management: Concepts, Principles, and Practice,* edited by Kathleen LaTour and Shirley Eichenwald. Chicago: American Health Information Management Association.

Review Quiz

Directions for items 1 through 18: Select the best answer for the following items.

1. ___ What is the most important factor in determining the best storage method for acute care health records?
   A. Ensuring that the records are readily accessible and secure
   B. Ensuring that the records are factual and informational
   C. Ensuring that the records are both electronic and paper based
   D. Ensuring that the records are personal and private

2. ___ What term is used in reference to objective descriptions of processes, procedures, people, and other observable objects and activities?
   A. Information
   B. Data
   C. Knowledge
   D. Notices

3. ___ What is the most important component of the health record?
   A. Demographic information
   B. Format
   C. Quality
   D. Clinical documentation

4. ___ What is the term usually used in reference to the process of calculating charges, preparing and submitting reimbursement claims, and following up to make sure that appropriate payments have been made?
   A. Case-mix management
   B. Risk management
   C. Claims processing
   D. Certification processing

5. ___ Which of the following processes is an ancillary function of the health record?
   A. Medical error prevention
   B. Data and information storage
   C. Patient assessment and care planning
   D. Resource allocation

6. ___ What term is used in reference to electronically accessed information that provides physicians with pertinent health information beyond the health record itself?
   A. Core measures
   B. Advanced decision support
   C. Clinical practice guidelines
   D. Enhanced discharge planning

7. ___ Which of the following is a method of grouping patients according to a predefined set of characteristics?
   A. Case-mix analysis
   B. Case management
   C. Clinical practice guidelines
   D. Core measures

8. ___ What process is being carried out when a hospital reviews the quantity and type of resources being used in the provision of chemotherapy treatments?
   A. FOCUS-PDCA review
   B. Accreditation review
   C. Continuous quality improvement review
   D. Utilization management review

9. ___ Which of the following processes would investigate a medical error that resulted in the death of a patient?
   A. Security management
   B. Risk management
   C. Diagnostic review
   D. Accreditation

10. ___ Which of the following processes is an element of claims processing?
    A. UR
    B. CQI
    C. EDI
    D. FOCUS-PCDA

11. ___ Which of the following would be used to communicate information about a patient's injuries on a reimbursement claim?
    A. Payment codes
    B. Procedural codes
    C. Diagnostic codes
    D. Utilization codes

12. ___ Before a physician will be permitted to provide patient services in a specific facility, he or she must first go through which of the following processes?
    A. Credentialing
    B. Accreditation
    C. Examination
    D. Investigation

13. ___ What is the outcome of analyzing data for a specific purpose?
    A. Facts
    B. Numbers
    C. Charts
    D. Information

14. ___ Which of the following terms refers to the computer-based transmission of standardized information among the parties in a business relationship?
    A. Electronic data interchange
    B. Electronic health data
    C. Computer transmission formats
    D. Computer language processing

15. ____ Before an acute care hospital is permitted to provide medical services in a particular state, the organization must first go through which of the following processes?
    A. Accreditation
    B. Licensure
    C. Qualification
    D. Certification

16. ____ What is the principal function of health records?
    A. To provide information for performance improvement activities
    B. To support billing and reimbursement processes
    C. To serve as the repository of clinical documentation relevant to the care of individual patients
    D. To determine appropriate resource allocation

17. ____ To which of the following authorities do hospitals report vital statistics?
    A. The World Health Organization
    B. The National Vital Statistics System
    C. The Centers for Disease Control
    D. The designated state authority

18. ____ Which of the following types of data is derived from documentation related to a specific patient's medical treatment?
    A. Primary
    B. Secondary
    C. Aggregate
    D. Facility-specific

Directions for items 19 through 25: Match each of the following indexes/databases with the appropriate definition.

19. ____ Healthcare Integrity and Protection Data Bank

20. ____ Medicare Provider Analysis and Review File

21. ____ National Practitioner Data Bank

22. ____ Master Patient Index

23. ____ Disease Index

24. ____ Physician Index

25. ____ Operation Index

    A. A list arranged according to admitting physician and health record number that includes all of the patients admitted to the facility
    B. A list arranged by diagnostic code that includes all of the patients who have been treated in the hospital during a specified period
    C. A collection of information on healthcare professionals who have been sanctioned by medical examiners or licensing boards or who have been subject to medical malpractice judgments that involved damage awards
    D. A list of data entries for every patient who was ever treated in the hospital
    E. A collection of data gathered from reimbursement claims that is used to evaluate the quality and effectiveness of the care provided to the beneficiaries of a federal healthcare program
    F. A collection of information related to fraudulent and abusive healthcare practices
    G. A list arranged by procedural code that includes entries for all of the patients who were treated in a hospital during a specified period

Chapter 3

Content of the Acute Care Health Record

Learning Objectives

- List the types of demographic information collected in health records and explain the purpose of each data element

- List the types of administrative information collected in health records and explain the purpose of each data element

- List the types of clinical information collected in health records and explain the purpose of each data element

- List the data elements collected in the report of history and physical examination and explain their relevance to patient treatment

- Describe the types of services covered in physicians' orders

- List the various types of documentation authored by physicians and explain their content and functions

- Explain the conditions under which medical consultations should be ordered

- List the various types of documentation authored by nurses and explain their content and functions

- Explain the functions of general and special consents

- List the data elements that must be included in laboratory reports

- List the data elements that must be included in imaging reports

- Explain the purpose and content of anesthesia assessments and reports

- List the data elements that must be included in operative reports

- List the data elements that must be included in pathology reports

- List the data elements that should be collected in implant and transplantation records

- Explain the function and content of discharge summaries

- Explain the function and content of patient instructions

- List the various types of specialty documentation maintained in acute care records

- List the data elements that must be collected in emergency and trauma records

- List the data elements that must be collected in ambulatory surgery records

- List the data elements that must be collected in outpatient records of diagnostic and therapeutic services

- List the standard clinical data sets that are collected for hospital patients and describe their content

Terminology

Activities of daily living (ADL)
Administrative information
Advance directive
Ancillary services
Autopsy report
Care plan
Case management
Charting by exception
Clinical information
Clinical pathways
Clinical practice guidelines
Clinical protocols
Comorbidity
Complication
Consent to treatment
Consultation reports
Data Elements for Emergency Department Systems (DEEDS)
Demographic information
Discharge summary
Do-not-resuscitate (DNR) order
Dumping
Essential Medical Data Set (EMEDS)
Expressed consent
Financial data
Flow charts
History
Hospitalist
Implied consent
Interval note
Intraoperative anesthesia record
Labor and delivery record
Master patient index (MPI)
Medication record

Notice of privacy practices
Nursing assessment
Nutritional assessment
Operative report
Orders for restraint or seclusion
Pathology report
Patient assessment instrument (PAI)
Patient's rights
Physician's orders
Postoperative anesthesia record
Preoperative anesthesia evaluation
Principal diagnosis
Principal procedure
Progress notes
Recovery room record
Transfusion record
Uniform Ambulatory Care Data Set (UACDS)
Uniform Hospital Discharge Data Set (UHDDS)
Unique identifier

Introduction

A separate health record is maintained for every patient who receives services in an acute care facility. The content of the record reflects the patient's illness and the types of services that are planned and provided to the patient during his or her hospital stay.

The inpatient services provided by acute care hospitals are separated into two broad categories: medical and surgical. The category for each admission is determined by the specialty of the admitting physician in addition to the nature of the patient's illness. For example, a patient with a diagnosis of myocardial infarction could be admitted as a medical patient either to the internal medicine service or to the cardiology service, depending on the specialty of the admitting physician. Another patient with a history of cardiac ischemia who requires cardiac bypass surgery would be admitted as a surgical patient to the cardiovascular surgery service. In this case, the admitting physician would be a cardiovascular surgeon.

The documentation in acute care records includes both administrative and clinical information. **Administrative information** includes personal information about the patient, such as name, address, birth date, and age. It includes consents for treatment and use of healthcare information. Administrative information also describes the nature of the patient's admission and the patient's health insurance coverage. Administrative information is usually collected before or during the admissions process.

The **clinical information** in acute care records documents the patient's condition and course of treatment. The following types of information are documented in the inpatient record:

- The patient's physical condition upon initial examination and the reason why the patient's condition required acute care treatment

- The patient's medical history

- The diagnostic and therapeutic orders given by the patient's physician(s)

- The observations made by clinicians over the course of the patient's hospital stay

- The outcomes of diagnostic and therapeutic services, including surgical interventions

- The patient's final diagnosis and condition at discharge

The same administrative and clinical information is collected in both paper-based and electronic health record systems. Only the data collection, storage, authentication, and security technologies differ. This chapter provides examples of both paper and electronic data collection tools. (Electronic health records are discussed in more detail in chapter 4. A complete sample record in paper format is included in appendix J, and a demonstration of an electronic health record system is provided in appendix K.)

In addition to fulfilling operational and clinical information requirements, the content of acute care health records must comply with state and federal regulations, accreditation standards, and professional practice guidelines. (Standards and regulations are discussed in detail in chapter 5.)

The data in hospital records must also conform to one of two uniform healthcare data sets: the **Uniform Hospital Discharge Data Set** (UHDDS) for inpatient services and the **Uniform Ambulatory Care Data Set** (UACDS) for outpatient services. A third data set has been developed for emergency and trauma departments in hospitals, but the use of **Data Elements for Emergency Department Systems** (DEEDS) is voluntary.

Uniform data sets have two purposes: (1) They ensure that the same types of data are collected for every patient, and (2) they provide standardized definitions of the data to be collected. Thus, the data sets collected by different hospitals can be compared, and the data can be combined for national analysis and healthcare delivery planning.

Administrative and Demographic Information

For elective hospital admissions, administrative and demographic information is often submitted by the patient or the admitting physician's office staff via telephone before the patient comes to the hospital. Alternatively, the patient may provide the information to registration staff on the day of admission. Administrative information for unplanned admissions is often provided by the patient or the patient's representative in the hospital's emergency department.

Admitting and Registration Information

Registration staff collect personal information about the patient as well as information about the patient's health insurance coverage at the time of admission. Virtually all acute care organizations currently use a computer-based registration system tied to a database called the **master patient index.** When the patient has been treated in the facility in the past, registration personnel check the patient's current information against the information in the database to ensure that it is current and correct. The patient's administrative information is then recorded on an identification sheet (often called a face sheet). In paper-based record systems, a printout of the identification sheet is used as the front page in the patient's record. (See figures 3.1 through 3.3, pp. 73–76, for examples.)

Figure 3.1. Admission Record in Paper Format

University of Anystate Hospitals

ADMISSION RECORD

PATIENT LABEL

	Health Record #	Admission Date/Time	Discharge Date/Time	Service	Station	Room #	Patient Type	Financial Class.	BL/Account #

Patient

Location(s)		Language	Sex	Race	Marital Status	Date of Birth	Age

Patient Name and Address	SSN	Patient Employer	Telephone #
	Primary Telephone #		

Guarantor

Guarantor Name and Address	SSN	Guarantor Employer	Telephone #
	Relationship		

Employers

Insurance

Insurance 1

Insurance 2

Miscellaneous

Emergency Contact

Spouse

Home: Work:

Home: Work:

Admission Dx/Presenting Complaint		Arrival Mode	Admission Type/Source

Admitting Physician	Attending Physician	Referring Physician	Primary Care Physician

Alerts	Previous Admission Date

For Emergency Department Use Only

Allergies   LMP   T   R   P   BP   Time   Signature

Diagnoses/Procedures	DRG/Code(s)
Principal Diagnosis:	
Other Diagnoses:	
Principal Operation/Procedure:	
Other Operation(s)/Procedure(s):	

Physician Signature: _____   Date: _____

ADMISSION RECORD
000001 (11/2002)

Figure 3.2.   Admission Record in Electronic Format

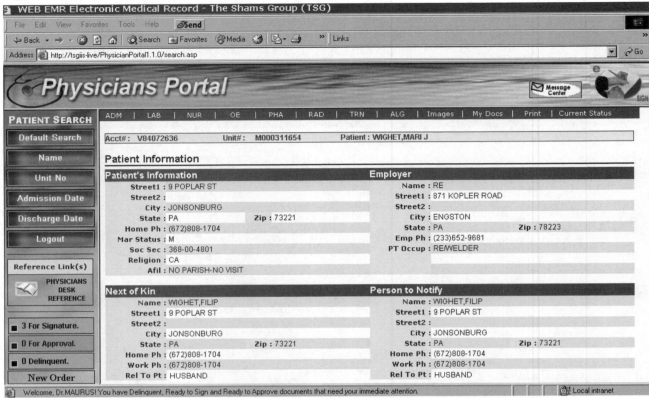

Demographic Data

The term *demographics* refers to the study of statistical information about human populations. In the context of healthcare, **demographic information** includes basic factual information about the individual patient, including:

- Patient's full name

- Patient's address

- Patient's telephone number

- Patient's gender

- Patient's date and place of birth

- Patient's race or ethnic origin

- Patient's marital status

- Name and address of the patient's next of kin

- Patient's Social Security number

The main purpose of collecting demographic information is to confirm the identity of the patient. Hospitals and other healthcare-related organizations also use the demographic information collected from patients as the basis of statistical records, research, and resource planning.

Figure 3.3. Obstetric Admitting Record in Paper Format

Anytown Community Hospital

OBSTETRIC ADMITTING RECORD
PAGE 1 OF 2

PATIENT LABEL

Admission Date ____ / ____ / ____ Time_____
- ☐ Ambulatory   ☐ Stretcher   ☐ Oriented to Unit
- ☐ Wheelchair   ☐ Transfer from _____ ☐ Safety/Security

G	T	Pt	A	L	LMP / /	EDD / /	Weeks

EDD by Fetal Assessment ___ / ___

Race/Ethnicity _____ Age _____
Advance Directives ☐ None ☐ Living Will
                    ☐ Medical Power of Attorney
Organ Donor ☐ Yes ☐ No
Pain ☐ No ☐ Yes (site: _____)
   Intensity   0 _____ 10
              None   Highest
Last Oral Intake
   Fluids ____ / ____ / ____ Time _____
   Solids ____ / ____ / ____ Time _____

Allergy/Sensitivity ☐ None ☐ Latex
☐ Other: _____

Reasons for Admission
- ☐ Onset of Labor
- ☐ Induction of Labor
- ☐ Spontaneous Abortion
- ☐ Cesarean Section
   - ☐ Primary ☐ Repeat
   - (Reason for primary: _____)
- ☐ Tubal Ligation
- ☐ Vaginal Bleeding
- ☐ ROM ☐ Premature ☐ Prolonged
- ☐ Preterm Labor
- Reasons for Admission: _____

Observation Evaluation
- ☐ Fetal Status
- ☐ Ultrasound
- ☐ Amniocentesis
- ☐ NST ☐ CST
- ☐ Medical Complications
   _____
- ☐ Obstetric Complications
   _____

Medications ☐ None

Type/Dose	Last Taken	With Patient No / Yes	Disposition
_____	_____	☐ ☐	_____
_____	_____	☐ ☐	_____
_____	_____	☐ ☐	_____

Personal Effects		Disposition		
Item	With Patient	With Support Person	Other (Describe)	

MD/CDM   Phone # | Support Person/Relationship Phone #:

Patient Triage Data
Contractions ☐ None ☐ Palpation ☐ Tocotransducer
Frequency _____ Duration _____ Intensity _____
Began on ____ / ____ / ____ Time _____
Pain intensity 0 _____ 10
               None   Highest
Membranes ☐ Intact ☐ Bulging
           ☐ Ruptured (date ____ / ____ / ____ Time _____)
           ☐ Nitrazine test ☐ pos ☐ neg ☐ Sterile speculum exam
           ☐ Fern test ☐ pos ☐ neg (findings: _____)

Fluid ☐ Clear ☐ Bloody ☐ Meconium stained
       ☐ Foul odor ☐ No foul odor ☐ None observed
Vaginal Bleeding ☐ None ☐ Normal show
                  ☐ Bleeding (describe:_____)
Cervical Exam   By: _____
   Station _____ Effacement _____ Dilatation _____ cm
   Presentation ☐ Vertex   ☐ Transverse lie
                 ☐ Face/brow   ☐ Compound
                 ☐ Breech   ☐ Unknown
                 (type: _____)

Physical Assessment

Height	Weight Pregrav/Grav	T	P	R	BP

Detail Abnormal Findings

System	Normal	Abnormal		Normal	Abnormal
HEENT	☐	☐	Respiratory	☐	☐
Neurologic	☐	☐	Abdomen	☐	☐
Skin	☐	☐	Gastrointestinal	☐	☐
Breasts	☐	☐	Urinary	☐	☐
Extremities	☐	☐	Genitalia	☐	☐
Cardiovascular	☐	☐			

Initial Problems Identified ☐ None   Plan
1. _____   _____
2. _____   _____
3. _____   _____

Fetal Evaluation Data   Multiple Gestation ☐ No ☐ Yes
Fundal Height _____ cm
Fetal Weight (est.) _____   Presentation   Position
FHR _____   1. _____   _____
☐ Fetoscope ☐ Fetal Monitor   2. _____   _____
☐ Doppler ☐ Other: _____   3. _____   _____

Specimens Obtained (Check all that apply)

Urine Test	Time	Results	Blood Test	Time	Results
☐ Urinalysis			☐ Hgb		
☐ C+S			☐ Hct		
☐ Glucose			☐ VDRL/RPR		
☐ Albumin			☐ Type/Screen		
☐ Ketones			☐		
☐ pH			Cervical Culture		
☐ Blood			☐ GBS		
☐ Toxicology			☐		
Admitting Signature	Date/Time		Examiner Signature	Date/Time	

Figure 3.3. (Continued)

Anytown Community Hospital

OBSTETRIC ADMITTING RECORD
PAGE 2 OF 2

PATIENT LABEL

Significant Prenatal Data

Prenatal Records Available on Admission

☐ No ☐ Yes Source _____

First Visit by 13 Weeks ☐ Yes ☐ No

Regular Care ☐ Yes ☐ No

Prenatal Classes ☐ Yes ☐ No

Pediatric Provider _____

General Health ☐ Healthy

☐ Functional Deficit (Type_____)

☐ Recent Exposure to Communicable Disease

　Type/Date _____ ___ / ___ / ___

　☐ Illness (≤14 days prior to admission)

　Type/Treatment _____

☐ Chronic Condition _____

Nutritional Status ☐ Well-nourished ☐ Malnourished ☐ Obese

☐ Special Diet _____

Eating Disorder ☐ None ☐ Identify _____

Nutritional Problems ☐ None ☐ Identify _____

Lab Findings

☐ None

Blood Type & Rh ____

Rubella Titer ____

Serology ____

HBsAg ____

HIV ____

GBS ____

____

Fetal Assessment Tests

☐ None

Date	Test	Result
/		
/		
/		
/		

Hospitalizations ☐ None

1. ___/___/___ Reason _____

2. ___/___/___ Reason _____

Plans for Birth and Hospital Stay ☐ Birth Plan Attached

Support Person Present in L&D ☐ No ☐ Yes _____

Other Family Members in L&D ☐ No ☐ Yes _____

Anesthesia ☐ None ☐ Local ☐ Epidural ☐ Spinal ☐ General

Delivery Site/Position _____

Personal Requests _____

Adoption ☐ No ☐ Yes Contact with Infant ☐ No ☐ Yes

　Adoption Contact _____

Feeding Preference ☐ Breast ☐ Bottle

☐ Tubal Ligation Authorization Signed ☐ Yes ☐ No

☐ Circumcision Authorization Signed ☐ Yes ☐ No

Problems Identified ☐ None

	Active	Resolved
1. _____	☐	☐
2. _____	☐	☐
3. _____	☐	☐
4. _____	☐	☐

Psychosocial Data ☐ See Prenatal Records

Emotional Status ☐ Happy ☐ Ambivalent ☐ Concerned

☐ Depressed ☐ Angry ☐ Other _____

Communication Barriers ☐ None

☐ Language ☐ Interpreter _____

☐ Vision ☐ Reading ☐ Writing ☐ Hearing

☐ Speech ☐ Other _____

Support System

Marital Status S M Sep D W Father involved ☐ Yes ☐ No

Other Support ☐ None ☐ _____

Occupation _____

Religion ☐ N/A ☐ _____

Personal/Cultural/Religious Customs Affecting Care and/or Learning

☐ None ☐ Identify _____

_____

Basic Needs Met Yes No If No, Explain

Food ☐ ☐

Clothing ☐ ☐

Housing ☐ ☐

Transportation ☐ ☐

Finances ☐ ☐

Life Stress	No	Yes	If Yes, Explain
Physical Abuse	☐	☐	
Emotional Abuse	☐	☐	
Major Change	☐	☐	
Self-Care Needs	☐	☐	
Serious Illness	☐	☐	
Other _____	☐	☐	

Substance Abuse	No	Yes	If Yes, Amount/Day, Last Use
Tobacco	☐	☐	_____
Alcohol	☐	☐	_____
Prescribed Drugs	☐	☐	_____
Illicit Drugs	☐	☐	_____

Educational Needs	Mother	Support Person	Comments
Stages/Phases of Labor	☐	☐	
Coping Techniques	☐	☐	
Infant Feeding	☐	☐	
Infant Care	☐	☐	
Other _____	☐		

Preferred Learning Methods	Yes	No
One-on-One Instruction	☐	☐
Group Instruction	☐	☐
Written Information	☐	☐
Audio/Visual Information	☐	☐
Demonstration/Practice	☐	☐

Discharge Planning Data Planned Length of Stay _____ Days

Home Setting

	Yes	No
Heat, running water, refrigeration	☐	☐
Infant Care Supplies/Car Seat	☐	☐
Phone in home	☐	☐
Transportation available	☐	☐
Adult assistance available	☐	☐

Referrals

☐ RN Case Manager ☐ Utilization Review ☐ Other _____

☐ Home Care RN ☐ Social Service

☐ Nutritionist/Dietitian ☐ Pediatric Provider

MD/CNM

Notified by _____ Date/Time _____

Admitting

Signature _____ Date/Time _____

OBSTETRIC ADMITTING RECORD
200305 (06/2003)

Social Security numbers are often used to help identify patients because they are one type of **unique identifier,** that is, a number that represents one and only one individual. Hospitals assign unique identifiers to individual health records to ensure that the information in the records is not misplaced or lost.

Financial Data

Information about the patient's occupation, employer, and insurance coverage is also collected at the time of admission. This information is used to complete the claims forms that will be submitted by the hospital to third-party payers. **Financial data** include the following:

- Patient's name
- Name of the insured party and his or her relationship to the patient if the patient is a dependent of the insured party
- Insured party's member identification number
- Name of the insurance company and the group policy number
- Employer's name and address

Clinical Data

Basic clinical data are also recorded during the admissions process. The reason for the patient's admission and the patient's preliminary diagnosis should be provided or confirmed by the admitting physician. The accuracy of this information is important because it becomes the basis of care plans and determinations of medical necessity.

Consents, Authorizations, and Acknowledgments

Hospitals and other healthcare organizations are required to obtain written consents and authorizations before they provide treatment or release confidential patient information. Acknowledgments usually apply to the patient's confirmation that he or she has received specific information. All consents, authorizations, and acknowledgments that have been signed by patients or their legal representatives in connection with services to be provided in a hospital should be stored in the patients' health records.

Consents Related to Clinical Care

The need to obtain the patient's consent before performing medical and surgical procedures is based on the legal concept of battery. Battery is the unlawful touching of a person without his or her implied or expressed consent.

Implied consent is assumed when a patient voluntarily submits to medical treatment. The rationale behind this conclusion is that it is reasonable to assume that patients must understand the nature of the medical care or they would not submit to it. **Expressed consent** is permission that is either spoken or written. Although the courts recognize both spoken and written forms of consent, spoken consent is more difficult to prove in a legal proceeding.

Most hospitals ask patients or their legal representatives to sign a general **consent to treatment.** By signing a general consent to treatment, the patient agrees to submit to routine clinical procedures and medical and nursing care while he or she is a hospital outpatient or inpatient. Except in emergency situations, patients are usually asked to sign a general consent form during the admissions process. (See figure 3.4, p. 78.) More specific consents are required for procedures that involve significant risk, such as invasive diagnostic tests, transfusions, and surgery. Specific consents are discussed later in the chapter.

Figure 3.4. **Combined Consent to Treatment and Consent to the Use and Disclosure of Protected Health Information**

University of Anystate Hospitals

CONSENT FOR TREATMENT AND DISCLOSURE
OF PROTECTED HEALTH INFORMATION
PAGE 1 OF 2

PATIENT LABEL

To the Patient (or his/her parent, guardian, or legal representative):

Before University of Anystate Hospitals and Clinics or any of its departments can provide inpatient or outpatient services to you, you will need to understand the services you are to receive, give the hospital your consent to perform those services, and agree to pay for them. You will also need to understand the ways the hospital uses the information in your health record and agree to allow the hospital to use that information.

Part I of this form covers your consent to treatment and explains other important matters related to your healthcare. Part II explains the use of your personal health information. You may ask a member of the admissions staff to read this form to you, and we encourage you to ask any questions you may have about it. When you fully understand the form's content, please sign it in the place indicated on the back of the form. Thank you very much for helping us to fulfill the hospital's responsibility to you and the rest of the community we serve.

Part I: Treatment-Related Information

Consent to the Treatment

You authorize your physician and/or other qualified medical providers to perform medical treatments and services on your behalf. You also consent to all of the hospital medical and/or diagnostic services ordered for you during your outpatient visit or inpatient stay in the hospital. This consent includes testing for infections such as hepatitis B and HIV and providing blood or body fluids for such tests in order to protect you and/or those who care for you.

Payment for Services and Insurance

You are directly responsible for paying for the services provided during your hospital visit or stay. The hospital will work directly with the third parties who provide coverage of your medical expenses, including health insurance companies, Medicare, Medicaid, Workers' Compensation, and various types of liability, accident, and disability insurance providers. By signing this form, you attest that your insurance coverage is current, valid, and effective and that you will promptly pay any required copayment amounts and unpaid deductibles. If your stay qualifies for Medicare coverage, the benefits you will receive include coverage for the physician services that were performed as part of your hospital care.

You guarantee payment to the hospital for all noncovered services and any unpaid, billed amounts not covered by insurance benefits when your insurance plan allows the hospital to bill you for any unpaid balances. You understand and accept that your physician's orders may include services not paid by insurance plans but will be provided to you by the hospital. Also, you accept that insurance plans may deny payment for what you believed were covered services, resulting in your responsibility for paying for these services. You may be billed for the professional component of any hospital services, such as the professional component for clinical laboratory tests.

Valuables

You accept full responsibility for your valuables, especially money or jewelry. The hospital does not accept any liability for your valuables. The hospital expects you will entrust any valuables to family or friends for safekeeping. Alternatively, you may deposit them in the safe that the hospital provides for that purpose. This is especially important when you are an inpatient, but this responsibility also extends to when you are an outpatient and must change into a hospital gown, remove jewelry, or undergo sedation during a medical procedure.

Special Note for Medicare or CHAMPUS Beneficiaries

You acknowledge and certify by your signature that all of the information you have provided to the hospital for Medicare or CHAMPUS benefits is correct. You also agree to allow the hospital or others who have information on your Medicare or CHAMPUS benefits claim to provide this information to Medicare or CHAMPUS or their agents in order for them to determine your eligibility for benefits. To carry out this activity, the hospital may use a copy rather than the original of this consent form. You also acknowledge that you have received a copy of the *Important Message from Medicare* or the *Important Message from CHAMPUS* form. This acknowledgement does not waive your rights for a review or make you liable for payment.

Figure 3.4.   (Continued)

University of Anystate Hospitals

**CONSENT FOR TREATMENT AND DISCLOSURE
OF PROTECTED HEALTH INFORMATION**
PAGE 2 OF 2

PATIENT LABEL

Part II: Health Record-Related Information

Consent to the Use and Disclosure of Protected Health Information

You agree to honestly, completely, and correctly provide all requested information. You also agree to permit the hospital to share your health record as applicable under the law with your physician, your insurers, Medicare, Medicaid, or their designated agents. They may review your record and copy it in full or in part in order to obtain billing and payment information. Insurers (private or government) may also use your health record to determine whether they cover your services. You agree to allow the hospital to use the record created during this visit to meet any reporting requirements related to your care and to collect payment for the services you received. You agree to allow your physicians to send copies of your health records to other physicians, hospitals, and healthcare facilities as they deem necessary for continuity of care. You also agree to have your name posted on scheduling boards and outside your hospital room.

Specific Uses of Your Protected Information

The hospital originates and maintains health records describing your health history, symptoms, examination and test results, diagnoses, treatment, and any plans for future care or treatment. This information serves as:

- The basis of care planning and treatment

- A means of communication among the many healthcare professionals who contribute to your care

- A source of information for applying diagnosis and surgical information to your bill

- A means by which a third-party payer (usually your insurance company or a government healthcare program) can verify that the services billed were actually provided

- A tool for routine healthcare operations, such as assessing quality and reviewing the competence of healthcare professionals

Your signature acknowledges that you received the *Notice of Information Practices,* which provides a description of information uses and disclosure practices. You accept and understand that:

- You have the right to review the notice prior to signing this consent.

- The hospital reserves the right to change the notice and its information practices, for past, current, or future information. The new notice will contain the effective date on its first page and be made available on our Web site.

- You have the right to object to the use of your health information for the hospital's patient directory.

- You have the right to request restrictions on the use or disclosure of your health information to carry out treatment, payment, or healthcare operations and to correct error(s) in your record. The hospital, however, is not required to agree to the restrictions requested.

- You may revoke in writing the consent that you provide to the hospital. The revocation does not apply to any uses of your information made by the hospital in reliance upon this consent form and on the belief that your consent was still effective.

I certify that I have read (or had read to me) both parts of this form and fully understand and agree to the content.

Patient/Agent: _____   Date: _____

If you are signing as the patient's agent, please state your relationship to the patient (parent, guardian, or legal representative): _____

Witness (when form is accepted verbally,
by telephone, or by electronic means): _____   Date: _____

CONSENT FOR TREATMENT AND DISCLOSURE
000002 (11/2002)

Consents Related to Confidential Health Information

Since the implementation of the Health Insurance Portability and Accountability Act, hospitals and other healthcare organizations have been required to provide information to patients about the facilities' use of confidential health information. The explanation must be provided in the form of a **notice of privacy practices.** The notice must describe how the patient's health information will be used, and it must provide examples of those uses in hospital treatment and operations as well as reimbursement. (See figure 3.5, p. 81. The release and disclosure of health information is discussed in more detail in chapter 5 and appendix G.)

Acknowledgments

Several types of administrative information are provided or collected by admissions staff. Patients are asked to sign forms to verify that they have received the required information. The acknowledgments then become part of the patient's health record.

Advance Directives

Admissions staff are required by law to ask patients whether they have established advance directives and to inform patients that they have the right to accept or refuse medical treatment. An **advance directive** is a written document that describes the patient's healthcare preferences in the event that he or she is unable to communicate directly at some point in the future. Examples of advance directives include living wills and durable powers of attorney for healthcare purposes.

Hospitals are also required to provide written information to patients that explains hospital policies regarding advance directives. The information must describe the treatment decisions that patients may make and any related hospital policies.

When the patient has executed such a document, federal law also requires that fact to be noted in the patient's health record. A copy of the document may be included in the record, but it is not required. Evidence that the patient's physician has discussed the patient's wishes with the patient or the patient's next of kin constitutes sufficient health record documentation.

Patient's Rights Information

The Medicare *Conditions of Participation* also require hospitals to provide patients with a **patient's rights** statement at the time of admission. The patient's healthcare rights include the following:

- The right to know who is providing their treatment
- The right to confidentiality
- The right to receive information about their treatment
- The right to refuse treatment
- The right to participate in care planning
- The right to be safe from abusive treatment

Some hospitals ask patients to sign an acknowledgment that they have received patient's rights information. The signed acknowledgment then becomes a permanent part of the patient's record. State regulations often require similar explanations and stipulate additional patient's rights, such as the right to privacy in treatment.

Other Administrative Information

Some hospitals ask patients to sign a release that absolves the facility from any responsibility for the loss or damage of personal property. This form is signed during the admissions process and then becomes part of the patient's health record.

Figure 3.5. Acknowledgment of Notice of Privacy Practices

Anytown Community Hospital

**ACKNOWLEDGMENT OF NOTICE
OF PRIVACY PRACTICES**

PATIENT LABEL

I understand that as part of my healthcare, this organization originates and maintains health records describing my health history, symptoms, examination and test results, diagnoses, treatment, and any plans for future care or treatment. I understand that this information serves as:

- A basis for planning my care and treatment
- A means of communication among the many health professionals who contribute to my care
- A source of information for applying my diagnosis and surgical information to my bill
- A means by which a third-party payer can verify that services billed were actually provided
- And a tool for routine healthcare operations such as assessing quality and reviewing the competence of healthcare professionals

I understand and have been provided with a *Notice of Information Practices* that provides a more complete description of information uses and disclosures. I understand that I have the right to review the notice prior to signing this consent. I understand that the organization reserves the right to change their notice and practices and prior to implementation will mail a copy of any revised notice to the address I've provided. I understand that I have the right to object to the use of my health information for directory purposes. I understand that I have the right to request restrictions as to how my health information may be used or disclosed to carry out treatment, payment, or healthcare operations and that the organization is not required to agree to the restrictions requested. I understand that I may revoke this consent in writing, except to the extent that the organization has already take action in reliance thereon.

☐ I request the following restrictions to the use or disclosure of my health information:

_____

_____

_____   _____
Signature of Patient or Legal Representative   Date

_____   _____
Witness   Date

_____
Notice Effective Date or Version

☐ Accepted   ☐ Denied

_____   _____ _____
Signature   Title   Date

ACKNOWLEDGMENT OF PRIVACY NOTICE
100093 (1/2002)

Birth and death certificates are not considered part of the legal health record, although copies may be stored in patients' records. Hospital personnel often prepare this administrative documentation and submit it to state and local departments of health. (The content of birth and death certificate was discussed in chapter 2.)

Clinical Information

As noted in chapters 1 and 2, the most important function of the acute care health record is the collection of information on the patient's medical condition and progress throughout his or her stay in the hospital. Physicians, surgeons, and nurses are the main authors of clinical documentation.

Allied health professionals who provide direct patient care also document their services and author health record entries. Allied health professionals who provide patient care include respiratory, physical, occupational, and speech therapists.

Depending on hospital policy, social workers, psychologists, and dietitians may also document their services directly in the health record. Dietitians write nutritional assessments and nutrition plans. Psychologists report the results of developmental assessments and behavioral tests. Social workers report assessments related to psychosocial functioning, living arrangements, and postacute care requirements.

Many other healthcare specialists provide information that becomes part of the patient's record, for example:

- Pharmacists provide information on the formulation of intravenous medications and nutritional substances for parenteral administration.

- Medical technologists and bacteriologists provide documentation of the results of blood tests and other laboratory analyses.

- Audiologists provide documentation of the results of hearing tests.

- Other technicians provide copies of tracings from electrocardiographs (EKGs) and electroencephalographs (EEGs).

Physicians working in ancillary service departments report on the results of many diagnostic procedures. Pathologists issue reports on their examinations of specimens collected during diagnostic and surgical procedures. Radiologists document the results of X-ray examinations, computed tomography (CT) examinations, and magnetic resonance imaging (MRI) procedures. Radiologists who specialize in nuclear medicine document radiation therapy services.

Medical History

The **history** is a summary of the patient's illness from his or her point of view. The purpose of documenting the patient's medical history is to gather background information about the patient's condition before he or she was admitted to the hospital. In most hospitals, the history is documented in the patient's record by the admitting physician. In teaching hospitals, the history may be collected and documented by a physician employed by the hospital. (See figures 3.6 and 3.7, pp. 83–84.)

When a patient is unable to communicate and the history is provided by a second party, that fact should be recorded in the health record. Similarly, documentation should note that no history could be taken in cases where the patient is alone and unable to communicate.

Figure 3.6.   History Report in Paper Format

University of Anystate Hospitals and Clinics

HISTORY

| PATIENT LABEL |

Order of Recording:

1. Chief complaint

2. History of present illness

3. History of past illness

4. Family history

5. General history

6. System review:

    Skin
    HEENT
    Neck and thyroid
    Lymphatics
    Respiratory
    Cardiovascular
    Gastrointestinal
    Genitourinary
    Neuropsychological
    Musculoskeletal
    Endocrine

7. Allergies (medications and drugs)

For Children and Adolescents:

8. Evaluation of developmental age

9. Immunization status

Physician Signature: _____   Date:_____

HISTORY
000005 (11/2002)

Figure 3.7. History Report in Electronic Format

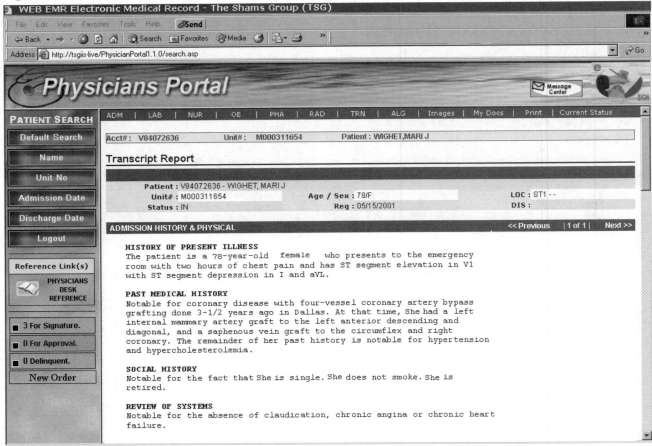

The physician bases his or her approach to assessing and treating the patient on the information provided by the patient or the patient's representative. The physician gathers this information by asking a series of questions about the patient's current and past health-related problems and circumstances, for example:

- What brought you to the hospital today?
- How long have you had these symptoms?
- What were you doing when you first experienced the problem?
- Have you ever had this problem before?
- What medications are you taking?
- Are you experiencing any other symptoms?

The physician attempts to record the patient's responses in the patient's own words to create a subjective account of the illness. Health record documentation of the patient's medical history usually includes the following elements:

- Chief complaint: a subjective description of the reason why the patient sought medical treatment

- Present illness: a subjective description of the development of the patient's illness

- Past medical history: a subjective account of current and past illnesses, injuries, surgeries, and hospitalizations, including information on current medications and allergies

- Social and personal history: a subjective description of the patient's occupation, marital status, personal habits, and living conditions

- Family medical history: a subjective description of illnesses that occurred among close family members

- Review of systems: a subjective description of other symptoms or illnesses organized by body system

Table 3.1 (p. 86) provides examples of the information collected in a complete medical history.

Report of Physical Examination

After taking the patient's medical history, the physician usually performs a physical examination of the patient. The physical examination provides objective information on the patient's condition. Most hospital policies require that admitting physicians perform an initial physical examination within twenty-four hours of admission. Accreditation standards require that the documentation of the physical examination must be available in the patient's record before any surgical procedures may be performed (McCain 2002, p. 144).

For planned admissions, the physical examination may also be performed before admission. However, the *Medicare Conditions of Participation for Hospitals* require that the examination must be performed no more than seven days before admission. In addition, a legible copy of the results of the preadmission physical examination must be included in the patient's acute care record.

The initial physical examination includes an assessment of the main body systems. The physician gathers this information by observing the patient's physical condition and behavior, palpating (touching) the patient's body, tapping the patient's chest and abdomen, listening to the patient's breath and heart sounds, and taking the patient's vital signs. Table 3.2 (p. 87) shows the types of information usually documented for a physical examination. (See also figures 3.8 and 3.9, pp. 88–89.)

Patients are sometimes readmitted to the same hospital for treatment of the same condition. When the readmission occurs within thirty days after the previous discharge, the admitting physician may add an interval note to the patient's record in place of a complete history and physical. An **interval note** includes information about the patient's current complaint, any relevant changes in his or her condition, and the physical findings since the last admission. However, when the patient is admitted for treatment of a different condition, a complete history and physical must be performed and documented.

Diagnostic and Therapeutic Orders

Hospital-based diagnostic and therapeutic services are provided under the direction of the patient's physician or physicians. **Physician's orders** are the instructions that the physician gives to the other healthcare professionals who perform diagnostic and therapeutic procedures, provide nursing care, formulate and administer medications, and provide nutritional services to the patient. (See figures 3.10 and 3.11, pp. 90–91.) Orders are changed and updated often as the patient's condition progresses.

Table 3.1. Information Usually Included in a Complete Medical History

Components of the History	Complaints and Symptoms
Chief complaint	Nature and duration of the symptoms that caused the patient to seek medical attention as stated in his or her own words
Present illness	Detailed chronological description of the development of the patient's illness, from the appearance of the first symptom to the present situation
Past medical history	Summary of childhood and adult illnesses and conditions, such as infectious diseases, pregnancies, allergies and drug sensitivities, accidents, operations, hospitalizations, and current medications
Social and personal history	Marital status; dietary, sleep, and exercise patterns; use of coffee, tobacco, alcohol, and other drugs; occupation; home environment; daily routine; and so on
Family medical history	Diseases among relatives in which heredity or contact might play a role, such as allergies, cancer, and infectious, psychiatric, metabolic, endocrine, cardiovascular, and renal diseases; health status or cause and age at death for immediate relatives
Review of systems	Systemic inventory designed to uncover current or past subjective symptoms that includes the following types of data: • *General:* Usual weight, recent weight changes, fever, weakness, fatigue • *Skin:* Rashes, eruptions, dryness, cyanosis, jaundice; changes in skin, hair, or nails • *Head:* Headache (duration, severity, character, location) • *Eyes:* Glasses or contact lenses, last eye examination, glaucoma, cataracts, eyestrain, pain, diplopia, redness, lacrimation, inflammation, blurring • *Ears:* Hearing, discharge, tinnitus, dizziness, pain • *Nose:* Head colds, epistaxis, discharges, obstruction, postnasal drip, sinus pain • *Mouth and throat:* Condition of teeth and gums, last dental examination, soreness, redness, hoarseness, difficulty in swallowing • *Respiratory system:* Chest pain, wheezing, cough, dyspnea, sputum (color and quantity), hemoptysis, asthma, bronchitis, emphysema, pneumonia, tuberculosis, pleurisy, last chest X ray • *Neurological system:* Fainting, blackouts, seizures, paralysis, tingling, tremors, memory loss • *Musculoskeletal system:* Joint pain or stiffness, arthritis, gout, backache, muscle pain, cramps, swelling, redness, limitation in motor activity • *Cardiovascular system:* Chest pain, rheumatic fever, tachycardia, palpitation, high blood pressure, edema, vertigo, faintness, varicose veins, thrombophlebitis • *Gastrointestinal system:* Appetite, thirst, nausea, vomiting, hematemesis, rectal bleeding, change in bowel habits, diarrhea, constipation, indigestion, food intolerance, flatus, hemorrhoids, jaundice • *Urinary system:* Frequent or painful urination, nocturia, pyuria, hematuria, incontinence, urinary infections • *Genitoreproductive system:* Male—venereal disease, sores, discharge from penis, hernias, testicular pain, or masses; female—age at menarche, frequency and duration of menstruation, dysmenorrhea, menorrhagia, symptoms of menopause, contraception, pregnancies, deliveries, abortions, last Pap smear • *Endocrine system:* Thyroid disease; heat or cold intolerance; excessive sweating, thirst, hunger, or urination • *Hematologic system:* Anemia, easy bruising or bleeding, past transfusions • *Psychiatric disorders:* Insomnia, headache, nightmares, personality disorders, anxiety disorders, mood disorders

Table 3.2. Information Usually Documented in the Report of a Physical Examination

Report Components	Content
General condition	Apparent state of health, signs of distress, posture, weight, height, skin color, dress and personal hygiene, facial expression, manner, mood, state of awareness, speech
Vital signs	Pulse, respiration, blood pressure, temperature
Skin	Color, vascularity, lesions, edema, moisture, temperature, texture, thickness, mobility and turgor, nails
Head	Hair, scalp, skull, face
Eyes	Visual acuity and fields; position and alignment of the eyes, eyebrows, eyelids; lacrimal apparatus; conjunctivae; sclerae; corneas; irises; size, shape, equality, reaction to light, and accommodation of pupils; extraocular movements; ophthalmoscopic exam
Ears	Auricles, canals, tympanic membranes, hearing, discharge
Nose and sinuses	Airways, mucosa, septum, sinus tenderness, discharge, bleeding, smell
Mouth	Breath, lips, teeth, gums, tongue, salivary ducts
Throat	Tonsils, pharynx, palate, uvula, postnasal drip
Neck	Stiffness, thyroid, trachea, vessels, lymph nodes, salivary glands
Thorax, anterior and posterior	Shape, symmetry, respiration
Breasts	Masses, tenderness, discharge from nipples
Lungs	Fremitus, breath sounds, adventitious sounds, friction, spoken voice, whispered voice
Heart	Location and quality of apical impulse, trill, pulsation, rhythm, sounds, murmurs, friction rub, jugular venous pressure and pulse, carotid artery pulse
Abdomen	Contour, peristalsis, scars, rigidity, tenderness, spasm, masses, fluid, hernia, bowel sounds and bruits, palpable organs
Male genitourinary organs	Scars, lesions, discharge, penis, scrotum, epididymis, varicocele, hydrocele
Female reproductive organs	External genitalia, Skene's glands and Bartholin's glands, vagina, cervix, uterus, adnexa
Rectum	Fissure, fistula, hemorrhoids, sphincter tone, masses, prostate, seminal vesicles, feces
Musculoskeletal system	Spine and extremities, deformities, swelling, redness, tenderness, range of motion
Lymphatics	Palpable cervical, axillary, inguinal nodes; location; size; consistency; mobility and tenderness
Blood vessels	Pulses, color, temperature, vessel walls, veins
Neurological system	Cranial nerves, coordination, reflexes, biceps, triceps, patellar, Achilles, abdominal, cremasteric, Babinski, Romberg, gait, sensory, vibratory
Diagnosis(es)	

Figure 3.8. Physical Examination Report in Paper Format

University of Anystate Hospitals and Clinics

PATIENT LABEL

PHYSICAL EXAMINATION

Date: _____ Age: _____ Sex: _____ Height: _____ Weight: _____

T: _____ P: _____ R: _____ BP: _____

Order of Recording:

1. General appearance
2. Skin
3. HEENT
4. Lymph glands
5. Neck
6. Breasts
7. Chest
8. Heart
9. Abdomen
10. Genitalia
11. Musculoskeletal
12. Neurological
13. Rectal
14. Vaginal

Impression: _____

_____

Course of Action Planned: _____

Physician Signature: _____ Date: _____

PHYSICAL EXAMINATION
000006 (11/2002)

Figure 3.9. Physical Examination Report in Electronic Format

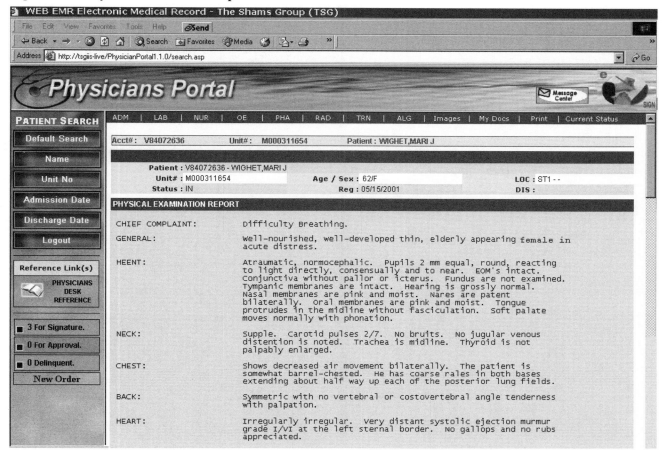

In most states, only licensed physicians are allowed to issue orders for the medications, diagnostic tests, therapeutic services, ancillary medical services, and medical devices to be provided to patients. They may also order the use of seclusion or restraints when required. In some states, however, psychologists, physician's assistants, and certified nurse-practitioners are also allowed to write orders under limited conditions. In all cases, health record documentation must support the medical necessity of the services and materials ordered.

State regulations and hospital medical staff policies also stipulate which healthcare professionals may receive and execute physicians' orders. For example, only licensed nurses and pharmacists are allowed to receive and fulfill medication orders in most states. However, most allied health professionals are allowed to accept physicians' orders for services within their area of practice. Examples include nurse-anesthetists, physical therapists, and respiratory therapists.

In paper-based health record systems, it is vital that physicians submit orders that are legible and complete. The orders must include the physician's signature and the date the orders were entered into the patient's record. Many hospitals also permit physicians to communicate verbal orders via telephone. In such cases, state regulations and the hospital's medical staff rules stipulate which healthcare practitioners are allowed to accept and carry out verbal orders and how such orders are to be authenticated.

Many hospitals use electronic order-entry systems. The systems include safeguards that ensure the authenticity, accuracy, and completeness of physicians' orders. Such computer-based order-entry systems are an integral part of electronic health record systems.

Figure 3.10.   Physician's Order Sheet in Paper Format

University of Anystate Hospital

PHYSICIAN ORDERS

PATIENT LABEL

Drug Allergies

Date and Time	RN Signature	

PHYSICIAN ORDERS
000122 (02/2003)

Figure 3.11. Physician's Order in Electronic Format

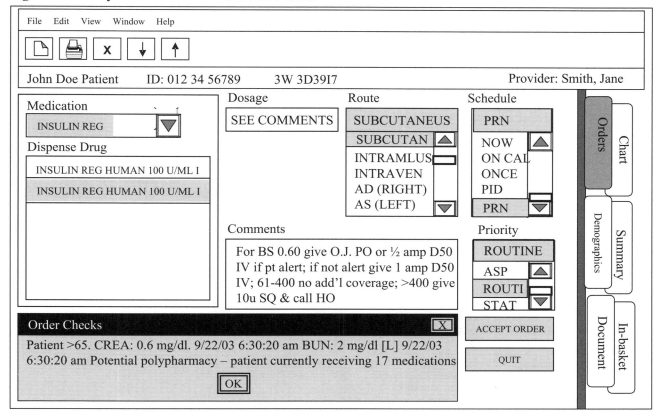

Standing orders are routine physicians' orders that have been established by individual physicians or by the hospital's medical staff. (See figure 3.12, p. 92.) Each standing order applies to a specific diagnosis or procedure. For example, a standing order might be established for the postoperative care to be provided to all patients who have undergone an appendectomy. Some facilities allow nurses to implement standing orders that have been previously approved by the medical staff. Others require physicians to specifically order the implementation of standing orders for their patients (McCain 2002, p. 146).

Authentication Requirements

State and federal regulations require that physicians sign and date their orders for diagnostic and therapeutic services. The authentication requirements for physicians' orders are the same in paper-based and electronic health record systems. Only the mechanism for authentication is different. (See the discussion of authentication processes in chapter 4.)

Special Orders

Two types of special orders are relatively common in acute care hospitals: do-not-resuscitate orders and orders for restraint and seclusion. **Do-not-resuscitate** (DNR) **orders** are issued when it has been decided that the patient is near death and that no resuscitation attempts should be made when the patient stops breathing. In addition to the order, health record documentation must indicate that the decision to withhold resuscitation efforts was discussed with the patient or the patient's legal representative, when the decision was made, and who took part in making the decision.

Figure 3.12.   Physician's Standing Order in Paper Format

Midwest Medical Center

HEPARIN ORDER: REGULAR UNFRACTIONATED HEPARIN FOR ADULTS

PATIENT LABEL

Diagnosis: _____

Allergies: _____

Total Body Weight: _____lb = _____kg

Warning: Due to an increased risk of serious bleeding, patients should not receive both regular heparin and low-molecular-weight heparin.

Patients should also be evaluated for continuance of other medications such as aspirin, clopidogrel, and NSAID therapy.

1. Check baseline PTT, PT/INR, heme panel

2. Check the appropriate bolus regimen according to diagnosis/disease
   a. ☐ No initial bolus
   b. ☐ Acute coronary syndrome—heparin bolus 75 units/kg = _____ units IV
      (round to the nearest 1000 units—maximum bolus = 10,000 units)
   c. ☐ In combination with thrombolytic therapy for acute MI (TNKase, Retavase, TPA)
      ☐ 5000 units bolus if 65 kg or greater
      ☐ 4000 units bolus if less than 65 kg
   d. ☐ Treatment of DVT/PE—heparin bolus 80 units/kg = _____ units IV
      (round to the nearest 1000 units—maximum bolus = 10,000 units)

3. Following bolus, begin IV heparin infusion (check the appropriate regimen):
   • Premixed IV bag contains heparin 25,000 units in 250 ml of D5W (100 units/ml)
   • Maximum initial infusion rate not to exceed 2000 units/h
   ☐ All cardiology regimens: 16 units/kg/h = _____ ml/h
   ☐ Treatment of DVT or PE: 18 units/kg/h = _____ ml/h

4. Check PTT 6 hours after initiation of heparin infusion

5. Adjust heparin based on guidelines below
   (document all changes on MAR and physician's orders sheet):

PTT (seconds)	Bolus Dose	Rate Changes	Repeat PTT after Each Dosage Change
PTT <35	Bolus 4000 units	Increase rate 200 units/h	6 h
PTT 35–45	Bolus 3000 units	Increase rate 200 units/h	6 h
PTT 46–70	No bolus	No rate change	Next a.m.
PTT 71–90	No bolus	Decrease rate 100 units/h	6 h
PTT 91–100	No bolus	Hold infusion 1 h, then decrease rate by 200 units/h	6 h
PTT >100	No bolus	Hold infusion 1 h, then decrease rate by 300 units/h	6 h

6. Check PTT and heme panel every morning (while patient is on heparin protocol).

7. Check stools daily for occult blood and notify physician if positive.

8. Notify physician for bleeding, hematoma, or heart rate above 120 bpm.

Physician Signature: _____ Date/Time:_____

RN Signature: _____ Date/Time:_____

HEPARIN ORDER
000013 (11/2002)

Orders for physical or pharmaceutical restraint or seclusion must comply with Medicare regulations, state laws, and accreditation standards. In general, **orders for restraint or seclusion** should be issued only when the procedures are necessary to protect the patient or others from harm. Regulations and standards require specific time limits and continuous observation to prevent injuries to the patient, such as suffocation. Accreditation standards for psychiatric facilities provide more specific guidelines. (See figure 3.13, p. 94.)

Discharge Orders

Only the patient's physician can decide when the patient is ready to be discharged from the hospital. Discharge orders must be made in writing. When a patient leaves the hospital against medical advice, a note describing the situation should be included in the patient's health record. Similarly, when patients die, a note should be added to their health records in lieu of a discharge order. (See figure 3.14, p. 95.)

Clinical Observations

In acute care hospitals, the records of clinical observations are usually referred to as **progress notes.** The purpose of this type of documentation is to create a chronological record of the patient's condition and response to treatment during his or her entire hospital stay. The progress notes also allow clinicians to communicate their observations to other members of the healthcare team.

The collection of information on the patient's progress is also required for reimbursement purposes. This information serves to justify continued acute care treatment and support the medical necessity of the services provided to the patient. Specifically, the progress notes should indicate why the intervention of medical professionals was required and why that intervention needed to be performed in an acute care setting. In addition, the notes should support the logic behind the patient's care and demonstrate how the services were planned and coordinated.

The rules of the hospital's medical staff specify which healthcare professionals are allowed to enter clinical documentation into the health record. Typically, the patient's principal physician, consulting physicians, house medical staff, nurses, dietitians, social workers, and clinical therapists are authorized to create and access health record documentation. Like physicians, nurses and allied health professionals sign and date all of their record entries and include their credentials after their names. (See table 3.3, p. 96.) Depending on the record format used by the hospital, each discipline may maintain a separate section of the health record. Alternatively, all of the observations may be combined in the same chronological report. (Health record formats are discussed in more detail in chapter 4.)

Progress notes include the following types of information:

- Patient's health status on admission and discharge

- Findings of physical examinations

- Observations of vital signs, including pain assessments

- Chronological record of the patient's course, including his or her response to treatment

- Results of laboratory and imaging procedures along with interpretations and plans for follow-up

- Requests for consultations and reasons for the requests

- Records of patient and family education

Figure 3.13. Special Order for Use of Restraints in Paper Format

Anytown Community Hospital

RESTRAINT ORDER

PATIENT LABEL

Patient Behavior/Criteria Present:
- ☐ Climbing out of bed
- ☐ Pulling at dressings, lines, or tubes
- ☐ Attempting to remove dressings, lines, or tubes
- ☐ Unable to follow directions with results that may injure self or others
- ☐ Standing up from chair
- ☐ Other: _____

Patient Behavior Related To:
- ☐ Confusion
- ☐ Delirium
- ☐ Marked agitation
- ☐ Sedation/analgesia
- ☐ Impaired attention and/or concentration
- ☐ Impaired learning ability
- ☐ Other: _____

Type and Number of Restraints:
- ☐ ×1 ☐ ×2 Soft wrist restraint
- ☐ ×1 ☐ ×2 Soft ankle restraint
- ☐ ×1 ☐ ×2 Soft mitten restraint
- ☐ ×4 Leather restraint
- ☐ Vest restraint
- ☐ Chair restraint
- ☐ Other: _____

Time Limitation:
- ☐ Continuous usage
- ☐ At night only
- ☐ When up in chair
- ☐ When family/visitors not at bedside
- ☐ Other: _____

Renewal Order Only
- ☐ Patient examined by physician.
- ☐ Alternatives to use of restraints reviewed by physician/staff.
- ☐ Patient continues to demonstrate behavior leading to use of restraints, as indicated above.

_____
Physician Signature   Date/Time

Telephone/Verbal Order:

Dr. _____ /

_____ ,RN _____
                                    Date/Time

RESTRAINT ORDER
000011 (11/2002)

Figure 3.14. **Discharge Order in Paper Format**

University of Anystate Hospitals

PHYSICIAN ORDERS

PATIENT, PETUNIA P.
000000001
DOB: 08/14/1949

Drug Allergies: *Codeine*

Date/Time	RN Signature	Physician Order/Physician Signature
10/11/04 **6:00 a.m.**	**Claire Barton, RN**	*(1) Admit via surgery (2) NPO* *(3) CBC, urinalysis (4) BCP 8* *(5) Prothrombin time, PTT (6) Type and screen* *(7) PA chest X-ray* *(8) EKG* *(9) Prep abdomen* *(10) Start IV fluids: 1000 cc D5LR at 125 cc/h via 18g Jelco* *(11) Mefoxin 2 g IV at 7:45 a.m.* Myron P Gynesurg MD 10/11/04
10/11/04 **10:00 a.m.**	**Claire Barton, RN**	*(12) Morphine sulfate 2 mg PCA IV RR q.1.0-1.5.h.* *(13) Mefoxin 2 g IV in 8 h then discontinue* *(14) D5LR 1000 cc at 125 cc/h (15) Liquid diet* *(16) Bed rest* *(17) Vital signs every 4 h* Myron P Gynesurg MD 10/11/04
10/11/04 *2:00 p.m.*	*Nancy Nurse, RN*	*Telephone order from Dr. Gynesurg:* *(18) Morphine sulfate 2 mg IV push* Myron P Gynesurg MD 10/12/04
10/11/04 *3:00 p.m.*	*Nancy Nurse, RN*	*Telephone order from Dr. Gynesurg:* *(19) Temporarily discontinue PCA pump until vital signs return to normal* *(20) Vital signs every hour* Myron P Gynesurg MD 10/12/04
10/12/04 *12:05 p.m.*	*Nancy Nurse, RN*	*(21) Remove Foley* *(22) Begin to ambulate* *(23) Soft diet* *(24) Vital signs every 4 h* Myron P Gynesurg MD 10/12/04
10/13/04 *12:15 p.m.*	*Nancy Nurse, RN*	*(25) Discontinue morphine* *(26) Darvacet-N 100 mg, one or two tablets q.4h. as needed for pain* *(27) Solid diet* Myron P Gynesurg MD 10/13/04
10/14/04 *8:00 a.m.*	*Nancy Nurse, RN*	*(28) Discontinue IVs* *(29) Discharge to home—see discharge instruction sheet* Myron P Gynesurg MD 10/14/04

PHYSICIAN ORDERS
000010 (11/2002)

Table 3.3.   Clinical Credentials of Healthcare Professionals Who Author Health Record Documentation

Credential	Abbreviation	Health Record Documentation
Registered nurse	RN	Nursing assessments, progress notes, medication records, vital signs, care plans, transfer records, flow charts
Licensed practical nurse or licensed vocational nurse	LPN or LVN	Nursing assessments, progress notes, medication records, vital signs, transfer records, flow charts
Nurse-anesthetist	CRNA	Anesthesia records
Nurse-midwife	CRNM	Obstetrical records
Nurse-practitioner	NP	Records associated with specialized nursing practice (pediatric, geriatric, obstetric, and others)
Clinical social worker	LSW	Psychosocial assessments, progress notes
Respiratory therapist	CRT	Records of respiratory therapy, progress notes
Occupational therapist	OT	Records of occupational therapy, progress notes
Speech therapist or speech–language pathologist	SLP	Records of speech therapy, progress notes
Physical therapist	PT	Records of physical therapy, progress notes
Dietitian	RD	Nutritional assessments and plans
Physician assistant	PA	Records of assessments and patient education
Surgeon assistant	SA	Records of assessments and patient education
Pharmacist	RPh	Records of pharmaceuticals and intravenous solutions formulated and dispensed
Clinical psychologist	PhD	Reports of psychological assessments, progress notes
Medical physician	MD	Records of history and physical, orders, progress notes, discharge summaries
Surgeon	MD	Reports of history and physical, orders, progress notes, discharge summaries, and preoperative, intraoperative, and postoperative reports
Radiologist	MD	Records of radiotherapy (nuclear medicine) and imaging results
Pathologist	MD	Records of pathology results and laboratory results and blood bank records
Osteopathic physician	DO	Reports of history and physical, orders, progress notes, and discharge summaries
Oral surgeon	MD/DDS	Records of oral surgery (preoperative, intraoperative, and postoperative), orders, progress notes, and discharge summaries

Documentation of Physicians' Services

In teaching hospitals affiliated with university medical schools, resident physicians and house staff provide medical services to patients as part of their postgraduate medical training. They work under the supervision of attending physicians who are fully qualified in their medical specialties and are members of the faculty for the medical school affiliated with the hospital.

In the past, resident physicians worked long hours and were responsible for providing much of the patient care in teaching hospitals. Starting in the 1980s, however, several highly publicized cases of patients dying while under the care of overworked and underqualified residents created significant concern about the way teaching hospitals operate. Recent changes in federal regulations now limit the number of hours residents may work and require teaching hospitals to employ fully qualified physicians to coordinate patient care. These changes have resulted in the development of a new category of physician known as a **hospitalist.** When patients enter the hospital under the care of emergency physicians or medical faculty, hospitalists play the role that admitting physicians fulfill in hospitals that are not affiliated with resident training programs.

Physicians' Progress Notes

As explained earlier in this section, the physician who is primarily responsible for the patient's care performs an initial assessment of the patient's condition early in the hospitalization. The physician's report of the patient's history and physical examination describes the patient's condition on admission and constitutes the first progress note in the patient's record. Subsequently, the physician's clinical decision making is documented in additional progress notes. Physicians' orders for diagnostic tests, medications, and other therapeutic services are usually documented on a separate order sheet in paper-based records or in a separate section in computer-based records.

The patient's daily progress and reactions to therapeutic interventions are documented by the patient's principal physician. The physician also notes the results of diagnostic tests and documents his or her interpretation of the results and plans for follow-up care.

Physicians' progress notes report conversations with the patient and the patient's family. Progress notes are also used to document discharge planning and instructions for posthospital care. The physician's final progress note usually describes the patient's status upon discharge.

Consultation Reports

Physicians often seek the advice of other physicians before making final diagnostic and therapeutic decisions. The patient's principal physician documents the request for a consultation in the patient's record. The consulting physician then documents his or her examination of the patient as a progress note. The consultant may discuss the case with the patient's physician to arrive at a mutual diagnostic decision or treatment plan. The consultant's findings and recommendations may also be documented as a progress note in the patient's record or supplied to the physician who requested the consultation in the form of a written report. The consultant's report then becomes part of the patient's record.

Consultation reports usually contain the following types of information (see figure 3.15, p. 98, for an example):

- Name of the physician who requested the consultation and the reason for the consultation

- Date and time the consultant examined the patient

- Pertinent findings of the examination

- Consultant's opinion, diagnosis, or impression

- Recommendations for diagnostic tests and/or treatment

- Signature, credentials, and specialty of the consultant

Figure 3.15. Consultation Report

Anytown Community Hospital	PATIENT, BLUTO P. 070095111 DOB: 04/01/1930

CONSULTATION REPORT
PAGE 1 OF 2

I was asked by Dr. Doctor to evaluate Mr. Patient for consideration of left VATS talc pleurodesis.

CHIEF COMPLAINT: Shortness of breath

HISTORY OF PRESENT ILLNESS: Mr. Patient is a 73-year-old male who has a history of metastatic pancreatic cancer. He was found to have left pleural effusion and underwent thoracentesis. He returned with a recurrent effusion. He was admitted on 05/12/2003 and underwent left chest tube thoracostomy and an attempt at talc pleurodesis through the chest tube. He has had residual pneumothorax and continues to drain from the left chest tube. He was referred for the purpose of left VATS talc pleurodesis.

PAST SURGICAL HISTORY: His past surgical history is remarkable for Whipple procedure.

PAST MEDICAL HISTORY: His past medical history is remarkable for prostate cancer and pancreatic cancer.

MEDICATIONS: Avalide and pancrease

ALLERGIES: He has no known drug allergies.

FAMILY/SOCIAL HISTORY: Remarkable for being married. He drinks socially.

REVIEW OF SYSTEMS: Remarkable for no history of seizure or stroke, no history of previous pneumonia, no history of previous myocardial infarction, no history of previous liver failure, renal failure. He has had no swelling in his legs.

PHYSICAL EXAMINATION: He is 5 feet 6 inches tall. He weighs 158 pounds. His blood pressure is 126/70. His pulse is 62. His respiratory rate is 20. His temperature is 97.1. His neurological exam is remarkable for a normal affect. He is oriented × 3. His gross motor examination is 5/5 in all four extremities. His head and neck exam is remarkable for no icteric sclerae. He has no oral lesions. His neck demonstrates no cervical or supraclavicular adenopathy. He has no carotid bruits. His chest exam is remarkable for no use of accessory muscles, no dullness to percussion. He has a left chest tube in place with no air leak. He has serous-appearing drainage from his left chest tube. His breath sounds are remarkable for a slight decrease in breath sounds in the left lateral lung. His cardiovascular exam is remarkable for no lift, heave, or thrill. He has a normal S1, S2 without murmurs. Abdomen is remarkable for well-healed Whipple incision. His abdomen is nontender, nondistended without evidence of masses or organomegaly. His extremities are without clubbing, cyanosis, or edema.

His chest CT shows a loculated left pneumothorax with small residual effusion. He has chest tube in place. This is a small caliber tube. His chest X ray shows loculated left pneumothorax.

Figure 3.15.   (Continued)

Anytown Community Hospital

CONSULTATION REPORT
PAGE 2 OF 2

PATIENT, BLUTO P.
070095111
DOB: 04/01/1930

His laboratory studies are further remarkable for urinalysis that is normal, an EKG that is normal sinus rhythm, sodium of 133, potassium 3.8, chloride 95, BUN 19, creatinine 1.1, PPTT of 11.8, INR of 0.9, PTT of 29.

My impression is that Mr. Patient is a 73-year-old male with metastatic pancreatic cancer status post Whipple. He has a recurrent left pleural effusion. He has undergone previous tube thoracostomy and pleurodesis and now has a residual left pneumothorax and residual chest tube drainage from his malignant effusion.

I have recommended to Mr. Patient that we proceed with left VATS talc pleurodesis today. He understands that his risks include, but are not limited to, death (1–2%), bleeding requiring blood transfusion, infection, prolonged air leak from the cut surface of his lung, and a 30% chance of recurrent effusion. Understanding these risks as well as the alternative of continued drainage, he wishes to proceed today with left VATS talc pleurodesis.

Thank you very much for allowing me to participate in his care.

Signature:

James W. Medman, MD   5/17/03

James W. Medman, MD   Date

d: 05/17/2003
t: 05/20/2003
JWM, MD/mc

The Medicare *Conditions of Participation* require the hospital's medical staff to set rules regarding consultations. Some hospitals have very specific requirements that define the circumstances under which a consultation is or is not required. For example, consultations may be required on every patient who is critically ill. Physicians responsible for the following types of cases usually choose to request consultations:

- Patients who are not good risks for surgery

- Patients whose diagnoses are unclear

- Patients whose physicians are not sure which treatment regime would have the most favorable results

- Patients whose illnesses or injuries may be the result of criminal activities

Medical staff rules may also categorize the types of consultations. For example, consultations that allow the consultant to write orders may be considered materially different than consultations that do not allow the consultant to write orders. Medical staff rules also determine whether partners in multispecialty group practices may provide patient care to each other's patients without going through a formal consultation process (Glondys 1999, pp. 59–61).

Physicians who are routinely involved in providing inpatient care are not considered consultants. Examples include radiologists who interpret imaging results, cardiologists who interpret electrocardiograms, neurologists who interpret electroencephalograms, and pathologists who examine tissue specimens.

Documentation of Nursing Services

Registered nurses (RNs) and licensed practical (or vocational) nurses (LPNs or LVNs) maintain chronological records of the patient's vital signs (blood pressure, heart rate, respiration rate, and temperature) and level of discomfort throughout the patient's hospital stay. They also maintain medication records, write progress notes, and document patient assessments. In hospitals that employ patient care technicians and nursing assistants, registered nurses verify any information provided by unlicensed patient care staff before it becomes part of the permanent health record.

Nursing Assessments

An initial **nursing assessment** is usually performed to obtain clinical and personal information about the patient shortly after he or she has been admitted to the nursing unit. Hospital policy dictates the timing requirements. At a minimum, the initial nursing assessment summarizes the date, time, and method of admission as well as the patient's current condition, symptoms (including level of pain), and vital signs. Most hospitals develop and use a nursing assessment instrument to collect additional information about the patient's physical condition and psychosocial status at admission. The instruments are designed to solicit the following types of information (see figure 3.16, p. 101):

- Patient's reason for being in the hospital

- Patient's current and past illnesses

- Patient's current medical condition, including the condition of his or her skin and the level of pain

Figure 3.16. Initial Nursing Assessment in Paper Format

Midwest Medical Center

INITIAL NURSING ASSESSMENT

PATIENT LABEL

Baseline Information

Date:	Time:	Age:		Arrived: AMB WC Stretcher EMS Carried Other:	Primary MD:

Initial/Chief Complaint/History of Present Illness:

T: PO R TM	P:	R:	BP: R L	⊕ O$_2$ Sats %	Sex: M F	Height:	Weight: Actual: Stated:

⊕ Tetanus/Immunizations:	Pneumococcal Vaccine ☐ No ☐ Yes Most Recent Date:
⊕ Pregnant ☐ No ☐ Yes LNMP:	Influenza Vaccine ☐ No ☐ Yes Most Recent Date:

Allergies: ☐ None   ☐ Medications   ☐ Latex   ☐ Food   ☐ Anesthesia   ☐ Other

List Names and Reactions:

TB Assessment (Initiate airborne isolation if 4 or more criteria are checked yes)

Persistent Cough > 2 weeks ☐ No ☐ Yes	Abnormal Chest X-Ray	☐ No ☐ Yes	Respiratory Isolation
Fever > 100.4 (night sweats) ☐ No ☐ Yes	Physician Order for AFB (smear/culture)	☐ No ☐ Yes	Ordered ☐ No ☐ Yes
Unexplained Weight Loss ☐ No ☐ Yes	Recent Exposure to Person with Suspected TB or +PPD	☐ No ☐ Yes	

RN/LPN Signature: _____

☐ See Home Medication Orders   Medication/Over the Counter/Herbal History   ☐ Investigation Drugs/Devices

Medication	Dose	Freq	Last Dose	Medication	Dose	Freq	Last Dose

Hospitalizations/Surgeries:

Medical History

Neurological	☐ No	☐ Yes		Sensory Impairment	☐ No	☐ Yes	
Cardiovascular	☐ No	☐ Yes		Endocrine	☐ No	☐ Yes	
Hypertension	☐ No	☐ Yes		Blood Disorder	☐ No	☐ Yes	
Respiratory	☐ No	☐ Yes		Cancer	☐ No	☐ Yes	
Gastrointestinal	☐ No	☐ Yes		Psychological	☐ No	☐ Yes	
Renal/Urological	☐ No	☐ Yes		Tobacco Use	☐ No	☐ Yes	
Gynecological	☐ No	☐ Yes		Alcohol/Drug Use	☐ No	☐ Yes	
Musculoskeletal	☐ No	☐ Yes		Infectious Disease	☐ No	☐ Yes	
Integumentary	☐ No	☐ Yes		Cough/Cold Past 2 Weeks	☐ No	☐ Yes	
EENT	☐ No	☐ Yes		Anesthesia	☐ No	☐ Yes	

Source of Information   ☐ Patient   ☐ Family   ☐ Unable to Obtain   ☐ Other   ☐ Medications Sent Home with Patient: _____

Arrival Date:	Arrival Time:	T: PO R TM	P:	R:	BP: R L	O$_2$ Sats %: (If applicable)

RN Initial: _____   **RN Signature:** _____   Date: _____ Time: _____   Unit: _____

RN Initial: _____   **RN Signature:** _____   Date: _____ Time: _____   Unit: _____

INITIAL NURSING ASSESSMENT
000039 (10/2002)

- Patient's current cognitive status, including his or her ability to communicate and to understand and follow instructions

- Patient's current functional status, including his or her level of physical activity and ability to walk, move, and perform personal care)

- Patient's current psychosocial status, including his or her marital status, living arrangements, personal habits (such as smoking, alcohol consumption, and use of illegal drugs), and occupation)

- Patient's family history, including information about his or her parents, children, and siblings and their current health status or cause of death

- Patient's current nutritional status, including his or her ability to feed himself or herself and any special dietary requirements or food allergies

- Patient's known drug allergies, including any sensitivity to latex products

- Patient's current medications

- Patient's need for special discharge planning

Care Plans

Current accreditation standards and the Medicare *Conditions of Participation* require hospitals to develop patient-specific care plans. A **care plan** is a multidisciplinary tool for organizing the diagnostic and therapeutic services to be provided to a patient. The purpose of the care plan is to ensure the efficacy and efficiency of patient services and the quality of patient outcomes. Care plans usually include the following elements (see figure 3.17, p. 103):

- Initial assessment (medical and nursing) of the patient's immediate and long-term needs

- Statement of treatment goals based on the patient's needs and diagnosis

- Description of the activities planned to meet the treatment goals

- Patient education goals

- Discharge planning goals

- Timing of periodic assessments to determine progress toward meeting the treatment goals

- Indicators of the need for reassessing the plan to address the patient's response to treatment and/or the development of complications

Clinical Practice Guidelines and Protocols

Several types of clinical tools are available to support clinical decision making, ensure clinical quality, and facilitate interdisciplinary care planning. Clinical tools include the following (Barnes 2002):

- **Clinical practice guidelines:** Systematically developed statements designed to support clinical decision making for specific medical conditions. Practice guidelines are based on scientific evidence and research and are issued by authoritative organizations such as medical societies, professional associations, and government agencies. See figure 3.18, p.105, for an example.

Figure 3.17. Patient Care Plan in Paper Format

University of Anystate Hospital

PATIENT CARE PLAN
PAGE 1 OF 2

PATIENT LABEL

Admitting Physician:

Admission Date: | Diagnosis: | Isolation:

Operative/Special Procedures: | Date: | Allergies:

Vital Signs	**Activity**	**Bladder/Bowel**	**Treatments**

Vital Signs
- ☐ TPR _____
- ☐ BP _____
- ☐ Neuro checks _____
- ☐ Circ. checks _____
- ☐ Weight _____
- ☐ Telemetry _____
- ☐ Transport S Tele _____

Diet and Fluids

Diet:
- ☐ NPO _____
- ☐ Regular _____
- ☐ Other _____
- ☐ Snack _____
- ☐ Tube Feedings _____
- ☐ Supplemental _____
- ☐ Restrict _____
- ☐ Force _____
- ☐ Ice Chips _____

Fluids:
- ☐ Intake _____
- ☐ Output _____
- ☐ Others _____

Activity
- ☐ Bedrest _____
- ☐ BRP _____
- ☐ Up in Chair _____
- ☐ Ambulate _____
- ☐ Up Ad Lib _____
- ☐ Head of Bed _____
- ☐ Foot of Bed _____
- ☐ TCDB _____
- ☐ Leg Exercises _____
- ☐ Others _____

Hygiene
- ☐ Self
- ☐ Assist
- ☐ Complete
- ☐ Tub/Shower
- ☐ Mouth/Denture Care
- ☐ Shampoo _____
- ☐ Skin Care _____
- ☐ Others _____

Bladder:
- ☐ Strain Urine
- ☐ Check Voiding _____
- ☐ Cath PRN _____
- ☐ Foley Cath
  - ☐ Date Inserted_____
- ☐ S.P. Cath
- ☐ Condom Cath
- ☐ Irrigate Cath q. ____ h. with: _____
- ☐ Bladder Irrigation _____
- ☐ IDEO Conduit_____
- ☐ Incontinent _____

Bowel:
- ☐ Check BMs _____
- ☐ Suppository _____
- ☐ Enema _____
- ☐ Ostomy _____
- ☐ Incontinent _____
- ☐ Others _____

Treatments
- ☐ S&A _____
  - ☐ Self _____
- ☐ NG _____
- ☐ Gomco _____
  - ☐ Clamp _____
  - ☐ Irrigate _____
- ☐ Chest Tube _____
- ☐ Wound _____
- ☐ Others: _____

Respiratory
- ☐ Ventilator _____
- ☐ O_2 _____
  - ☐ Mask
  - ☐ Nasal Cannula
  - ☐ AMT
- ☐ Suction
- ☐ Triflow
- ☐ IPPB/HHN _____
- ☐ Others _____

Tube Feeding

Type of Tube	Type and Strength of Feeding	Rate	Count	Irrigation	Bag ▲

Safety Measures
- ☐ Siderails
  - ☐ Upper _____
  - ☐ Lower _____
- ☐ Restraints
- ☐ Seizure Precautions
- ☐ High Risk for Falls
- ☐ Self-Injury Precautions

IV Therapies

#	Solution	Additives	Rate	Count				

Site Care/Tubing Change

Start/Date				
Type/Size				

Blood Transfusions

Figure 3.17. **(Continued)**

University of Anystate Hospital

PATIENT CARE PLAN
PAGE 2 OF 2

PATIENT LABEL

Date	Daily Lab Work	Date	Lab Work	Date	X-Ray/Special Procedures

Date	Preps for Procedures

Special Equipment	Miscellaneous
☐ Traction _____	
☐ Trapeze _____	
☐ _____ Bed	
☐ _____ Mattress	
☐ Sheepskin	
☐ Crutches	
☐ Walker	
☐ Teds	
☐ Others _____	
_____	
Therapies	
☐ Physical _____	
_____	
☐ Speech _____	
_____	
☐ OT _____	
_____	
Transportation	
☐ Wheelchair	
☐ Stretcher	
☐ Ambulatory	
☐ Bed	
Consultations	
_____	
_____	
_____	

PATIENT CARE PLAN
000072 (10/2002)

Figure 3.18. Example of a Clinical Practice Guideline

TITLE:	Recognition and initial assessment of Alzheimer's disease and related dementias
SOURCE(S):	Rockville (MD): U.S. Department of Health and Human Services, Public Health Service, AHCPR; 1996 Nov. 128 (Clinical practice guidelines number 19)
ADAPTATION:	Not applicable: Guideline was not adapted from another source
DATE:	November 1996

MAJOR RECOMMENDATIONS:	Triggers for Recognition and Initial Assessment for the Presence of Dementia
	Initiation of an Assessment for Alzheimer's Disease and Related Dementias
	    An initial clinical assessment should be performed . . . (strength of evidence = B)
	    A focused history is critical . . . (strength of evidence = C)
	    The history should be obtained from the patient and a reliable informant
	        (strength of evidence = C)
	    The Functional Activities Questionnaire . . . (strength of evidence = A)
	    . . . Mental status test is clearly superior . . . (strength of evidence = A)
	    . . . Visual impairment, sensory impairment, and physical disability . . .
	        (strength of evidence = B)
	Assessment for Delirium and Depression
	Interpretation of Findings and Recommended Actions
	    . . . Normal . . . reassessment in 6–12 months . . . referral for second opinion
	        (strength of evidence = C)
	    Further clinical evaluation . . . if abnormal . . . mental . . . functional status
	        (strength of evidence = C)
	    . . . Neuropsychological, neurological, or psychiatric . . . if mixed results
	        (strength of evidence = C)
	    Confounding factors . . . should be . . . considered in the interpretation
	        (strength of evidence = B)
	Neuropsychological Testing

CLINICAL ALGORITHMS(S):	Algorithms are provided for the clinical assessment of dementia
DEVELOPER(S):	Agency for Healthcare Research and Quality (AHRQ)
COMMITTEE:	Alzheimer's Disease and Related Dementias Guideline Panel
GROUP COMPOSITION:	AHCPR solicited nominations for an expert panel . . . AHCPR appointed 18 panel members, including 5 psychologists, 3 psychiatrists, 2 neurologists, 2 nurses, 1 internist, 2 geriatricians, 1 social worker, and 2 consumer representatives . . .
ENDORSEMENT(S):	Not stated
GUIDELINE STATUS:	This is the current release of the guideline. An update is not in progress at this time.
GUIDELINE AVAILABILITY:	Electronic copies: Available from the National Library of Medicine's HSTAT database Print copies: Information regarding the availability of these publications can be found in the Agency for Healthcare Research and Quality's publications catalog
COMPANION DOCUMENTS:	The following documents are available . . .
PATIENT RESOURCES:	
NGC STATUS:	
COPYRIGHT STATUS:	The contents of these clinical practice guidelines are in the public domain within the United States only and may be used and reproduced without special permission in America, except for those copyrighted materials noted for which further reproduction, in any form, is prohibited without the specific permission of copyright holders. Citation as to source is requested.

- **Clinical pathways:** Tools designed to coordinate multidisciplinary care planning for specific diagnoses and treatments. Clinical pathways are sometimes called critical paths, critical pathways, or care maps. Some of these tools incorporate patient-specific information, and so the tools are included in the health record in place of, or in addition to, the patient's care plan documentation. Clinical pathways are usually developed by specific clinical areas of healthcare organizations, such as the obstetrics department or outpatient surgery department of an acute care hospital. See figure 3.19, pp. 107–9, for an example.

- **Clinical protocols:** Specific instructions for performing clinical procedures established by authoritative bodies, such as medical staff committees, and intended to be applied literally and universally. A hospital's established procedure for preparing intravenous solutions is an example of a clinical protocol.

The Institute of Medicine and other public and private organizations concerned with the quality of healthcare actively support the development of evidence-based clinical tools. For example, the National Guideline Clearinghouse (NGC) is an initiative of the Agency for Healthcare Research and Quality (U.S. Department of Health and Human Services). The NGC is a comprehensive database of evidence-based clinical practice guidelines and related documents. The purpose of the NGC is to provide physicians, nurses, and other healthcare professionals; healthcare facilities and networks; health insurance plans; and healthcare consumers an accessible source for objective, authoritative, and detailed information on effective clinical practices. The NGC's mission also includes facilitating the dissemination, implementation, and use of clinical guidelines in the United States (National Guideline Clearinghouse 2004).

Case Management Reports

In many hospitals, registered nurses called case managers prepare patient assessments and care plans. Most clinical case managers are highly experienced nurses, many of whom hold advanced degrees. In some hospitals, clinical social workers are responsible for case management functions. **Case management** involves a process of ongoing and concurrent review performed to ensure the necessity and effectiveness of the clinical services being provided to the patient. Specifically (Shaw and others 2003, p. 93):

> Case managers review the condition of patients to identify each patient's care needs and to integrate patient data with the patient's course of treatment. . . . [In many organizations] the case manager [compares] the patient's course [to] a predetermined optimal course (known as a care map, critical path, or practice guideline) for the patient's condition. [The case manager] identifies the actions to be taken when the patient's care is not proceeding optimally.

Case management follows a five-step process that is documented in the patient's acute care record (Shaw and others 2003, pp. 93–96):

1. *Perform preadmission care planning.* The case manager reviews the patient's needs with the admitting physician or emergency department physician. The case manager may also contact the patient or the patient's insurance carrier to confirm that the patient is covered for the planned hospital services.

2. *Perform care planning at the time of admission.* The case manager reviews the patient's health record shortly after admission to confirm that the patient requires acute care services. The case manager then consults the treatment guidelines for the patient's diagnosis and verifies that all of the necessary services have been ordered.

Figure 3.19.   Example of a Clinical Pathway

University of Anystate Hospitals

CLINICAL PATHWAY:
CESAREAN SECTION DELIVERY
PAGE 1 OF 3

PATIENT LABEL

This document should be considered a *guideline*. Outcomes will vary depending on the patient's severity of illness and other factors/conditions that affect or alter expected outcomes.

Key: Fill in appropriate location for nursing unit. Initial completed intermediate and discharge outcomes. Circle any variances and document on variance log. Once variance is resolved, date and inital clinical pathway.

Expected Discharge Outcomes	Preop Date _____ Time _____	Operative/Recovery Date _____ Time _____
	Nursing Unit _____	Nursing Unit _____

Cardiovascular
• Hemodynamically stable
• Chest clear to auscultation bilaterally
	Stable BP (< 140/90 or no increases
	   > 30 mm systolic or
	   > 15 mm diastolic) _____
	Chest clear _____
		Stable BP (< 140/90 or no increases
		   > 30 mm systolic or
		   > 15 mm diastolic) _____

Gastrointestinal • Bowel sounds present • Tolerates regular diet • Passing flatus	NPO	
Genitourinary • Normal bladder function		Foley patent, draining clear yellow urine _____ UOP ≥ 30 cc/h _____

Reproductive
• Delivery of well newborn
• Involution progressing
• Minimal physical discomfort
• Breast: Skin and nipples intact
	Adequate prenatal care _____
	Reassuring father _____
	No signs/symptoms of
	   uterine/vaginal bleeding _____
		Fundus firm, lochia small
		   to moderate _____
		Pain control initiated _____
		EBL ≤ 1000 cc _____
		Delivery of well newborn _____

Integumentary • Incision intact with evidence of healing • No signs/symptoms of infection		Abdominal dressing dry and intact _____
Psychosocial • Patient/family demonstrates adjustment to parental role		

Education
• Patient/family able to identify problems
   that require immediate medical attention
• Patient/family able to verbalize under-
   standing of care needs (wound, etc.)
	States/understands
	plan of care _____	

Discharge Planning
• Patient/family able to verbalize support
   system(s) and/or support system for
   home care established
• Patient/family able to manage
   continuing care needs
• Patient discharged
	Patient/family identifies
	support system
	for home care _____	

Date	Initials	Signature	Date	Initials	Signature	Date	Initials	Signature

Figure 3.19.　(Continued)

University of Anystate Hospitals

CLINICAL PATHWAY:
CESAREAN SECTION DELIVERY
PAGE 2 OF 3

PATIENT LABEL

This document should be considered a *guideline*. Outcomes will vary depending on the patient's severity of illness and other factors/conditions that affect or alter expected outcomes.

Key: Fill in appropriate location for nursing unit. Initial completed intermediate and discharge outcomes. Circle any variances and document on variance log. Once variance is resolved, date and inital clinical pathway.

Expected Discharge Outcomes	Postoperative Day Date _____ Time _____	Postop Day #1 Date _____ Time _____
	Nursing Unit _____	Nursing Unit _____
Cardiovascular • Hemodynamically stable	Able to turn, cough, and 　deep-breathe every 2 h _____ Chest clear _____	Ambulates with assistance _____ Chest clear _____
Gastrointestinal • Bowel sounds present • Tolerates regular diet • Passing flatus	Tolerates clear liquids, no nausea or vomiting _____	Bowel sounds present _____ Tolerates regular diet _____
Genitourinary • Normal bladder function	Foley patent, draining clear 　yellow urine _____ UOP > 240 cc/8 h _____	Normal bladder function _____ UOP < 240 cc/8 h _____
Reproductive • Delivery of well newborn • Involution progressing • Minimal physical discomfort • Breast: Skin and nipples intact	Fundus firm, lochia small 　to moderate _____ Pain controlled _____	Fundus firm, lochia small 　to moderate _____ Pain controlled _____
Integumentary • Incision intact with evidence of healing • No signs/symptoms of infection	Abdominal dressing dry 　and intact _____ Afebrile (<100.4ºF) _____	Wound edges approximated, 　no signs/symptoms 　of infection _____ Afebrile (<100.4ºF)
Psychosocial • Patient/family demonstrate adjustment 　to parental role	Demonstrates appropriate 　parent/infant interaction _____	Demonstrates appropriate 　parental/infant interaction_____
Education • Patient/family able to identify problems 　that require immediate medical attention • Patient/family able to verbalize under- 　standing of care needs (wound, etc.)	States/understands postop 　plan of care _____ Initiates breast-feeding _____	Establishes infant feeding _____
Discharge Planning • Patient/family able to verbalize support 　system(s) and/or support system for 　home care established • Patient/family able to manage continu- 　ing care needs • Patient discharged		Discusses plan for discharge_____
Date	Initials	Signature	Date	Initials	Signature	Date	Initials	Signature

Figure 3.19.   (Continued)

University of Anystate Hospitals

CLINICAL PATHWAY:
CESAREAN SECTION DELIVERY
PAGE 3 OF 3

PATIENT LABEL

This document should be considered a *guideline*. Outcomes will vary depending on the patient's severity of illness and other factors/conditions that affect or alter expected outcomes.

Key: Fill in appropriate location for nursing unit. Initial completed intermediate and discharge outcomes. Circle any variances and document on variance log. Once variance is resolved, date and inital clinical pathway.

Expected Discharge Outcomes	Postop Day #2 Date _____ Time _____	Postop Day # 3/Discharge Outcomes Date _____ Time _____
	Nursing Unit _____	Nursing Unit _____

Cardiovascular
• Hemodynamically stable
	Participates in self-care _____
	Ambulates in hall _____
	Chest clear _____
	Stable BP (<140/90 or no
	  increases > 30 mm systolic
	  or > 15 mm diastolic _____
		Responsible for self-care _____
		Vital signs within normal _____
		Chest clear _____

Gastrointestinal • Bowel sounds present • Tolerates regular diet • Passing flatus	Active bowel sounds _____ Passing flatus _____ Tolerates regular diet _____	Active bowel sounds _____ Passing flatus _____ Tolerates regular diet _____
Genitourinary • Normal bladder function	Bladder function normal _____ UOP >240 cc/8 h	Normal bladder function _____
Reproductive • Delivery of well newborn • Involution progressing • Minimal physical discomfort • Breast: Skin and nipples intact	Fundus firm, lochia small to moderate _____ Pain controlled _____	Delivery of well newborn _____ Involution progressing _____ Minimal physical discomfort _____ Breasts and nipples intact _____

Integumentary
• Incision intact with evidence of healing
• No signs/symptoms of infection
	Wound edges approximated,
	  no signs/symptoms
	  of infection _____
	Remains afebrile (<100.4ºF) _____
		Incision intact with evidence
		  of healing _____
		No signs/symptoms
		  of infection _____

Psychosocial
• Patient/family demonstrates adjustment to parental role
	Parental adjustment
	  progressing _____
	Demonstrates appropriate
	  parental–infant interaction _____
	Patient/family verbalizes thoughts/
	  feelings about childbirth _____
		Patient/family demonstrates
		  adjustment to parental role _____

Education
• Patient/family able to identify problems that require immediate medical attention
• Patient/family able to verbalize understanding of care needs (wound, etc.)
	Verbalizes/demonstrates
	  self-care knowledge
	  and skills _____
	Demonstrates infant
	  feeding _____
		Patient/family able to identify
		  problems that require immediate
		  medical attention _____
		Patient/family able to verbalize
		  understanding of care needs
		  (wound, infant feeding) _____

Discharge Planning
• Patient/family able to verbalize support system(s) and/or support system for home care established
• Patient/family able to manage continuing care needs
• Patient discharged
	Support system for home
	care established _____
		Patient/family able to verbalize support
		  system(s) and/or support system
		  for home care established _____
		Verbalizes understanding
		  of follow-up care _____
		Discharged home _____

Date	Initials	Signature	Date	Initials	Signature	Date	Initials	Signature

CLINICAL PATHWAY: C-SECTION
300111 (5/2004)

3. *Review the progress of care.* The case manager reviews the patient's progress throughout the period of hospitalization. When progress is slower than expected, the case manager coordinates interventions among clinicians.

4. *Conduct discharge planning.* Once the patient's progress ensures his or her recovery, the case manager finalizes the discharge plan. The patient and the patient's family as well as his or her primary care physician are included in the process. Postdischarge medications and medical equipment and supplies are ordered, and follow-up appointments are scheduled. Arrangements for transporting the patient to a subacute facility are made, if necessary, as are arrangements for home care or hospice services.

5. *Conclude postdischarge planning.* After the patient has been discharged, the case manager provides information about the patient's hospital course to the clinicians who will continue the patient's care in nonacute care settings.

Nurses' Progress Notes

The nursing staff begins writing progress notes in the patient's health record when the patient is first admitted to the nursing unit. Because nurses have frequent contact with patients, the progress notes written by nurses provide a complete record of the patient's care and response to treatment. Nurses also ensure the continuity of patient care by confirming that all physicians' orders have been carried out and appropriately documented.

Nurses usually record the patient's vital signs at least every two hours. (See figure 3.20, p. 111.) Intensive care nurses provide continuous patient monitoring. A complete assessment of the patient's condition is performed every time the nursing shifts change (McCain 2002). When problems are noted, a member of the nursing staff contacts the patient's physician and recommends appropriate action.

Nursing notes are written in a narrative style. (See figures 3.21 and 3.22, pp. 112–114, for examples.) The notes are recorded in a handwritten format in paper-based health records. Many hospitals that have implemented electronic health records provide bedside computer terminals to make the process of documentation more efficient and timely. Some intensive care monitoring systems record vital signs automatically.

Some hospitals follow a system called **charting by exception** or focus charting. Under this system, only abnormal or unusual findings are documented. Progress notes focus on abnormal events and describe any interventions that were ordered and the patient's response. The purpose of charting by exception is to reduce the amount of routine record keeping required.

Medication Records

Nurses keep a separate log for each patient's medications. The **medication record** includes all of the medications administered to the patient while the patient is in the nursing unit. (See figures 3.23 and 3.24, pp. 115–116, for examples.) The surgery department and ancillary departments that perform diagnostic and therapeutic procedures also maintain records of the medications administered to patients under their care.

The medication record indicates the date and time each drug was administered, the name of the medication, the form of administration, and the medication's dosage and strength. The entry for each medication is signed or initialed and dated by the person who administered the drug.

Surgical patients and others who experience severe levels of pain are sometimes treated with patient-controlled analgesics such as morphine. The medications are administered through a pump that delivers continuous doses controlled manually by the patient. Monitoring equipment automatically records the patient's respiration rate, level of sedation, and pain level as well as pump volume, dose received, and cumulative dosage since the beginning of the monitoring period. (See figure 3.25, p. 117.)

Figure 3.20. Vital Signs Documentation in Graphic Format

University of Anystate Hospitals

GRAPHIC VITAL SIGNS

PATIENT LABEL

Date																																
Hospital Day/Postop																																
Hour			a.m.			p.m.			a.m.			p.m.			a.m.			p.m.			a.m.			p.m.			a.m.			p.m.		
	°C	°F	12 (2400)	4 (0400)	8 (0800)	12 (1200)	4 (1600)	8 (2000)	12 (2400)	4 (0400)	8 (0800)	12 (1200)	4 (1600)	8 (2000)	12 (2400)	4 (0400)	8 (0800)	12 (1200)	4 (1600)	8 (2000)	12 (2400)	4 (0400)	8 (0800)	12 (1200)	4 (1600)	8 (2000)	12 (2400)	4 (0400)	8 (0800)	12 (1200)	4 (1600)	8 (2000)
Temperature	40.0	104																														
	39.5	103																														
	38.9	102																														
	38.4	101																														
	37.8	100																														
	37.2	99																														
	36.7	98																														
	36.1	97																														
	35.6	96																														
P																																
R																																
BP																																

S&As a.m.					
(time/results) p.m.					
Height: _____ Weight: _____	_______ Bed/Chair/Stand	_______ Bed/Chair/Stand	_______ Bed/Chair/Stand	_______ Bed/Chair/Stand	_______ Bed/Chair/Stand

Stool					24-H				24-H				24-H				24-H				24-H
	Shift	7-3	3-11	11-7	Total	7-3	3-11	11-7	Total	7-3	3-11	11-7	Total	7-3	3-11	11-7	Total	7-3	3-11	11-7	Total
Intake	Tube Feedings																				
	Oral																				
	Intravenous																				
	Piggyback																				
	Blood																				
	Shift Total																				
Output	Voided																				
	Catheter																				
	Gastric																				
	Emesis																				
	Shift Total																				

GRAPHIC VITAL SIGNS
000029 (11/2002)

Figure 3.21. Interdisciplinary Progress Notes in Paper Format

University of Anystate Hospitals

PROGRESS NOTES
PAGE 1 OF 2

PATIENT LABEL

Barriers to Patient Education

☐ No Barriers ☐ Language
☐ Physical ☐ Reading Difficulties
☐ Cognitive ☐ Lacks Readiness
☐ Emotional ☐ Lacks Motivation
☐ Other _____

Patient/Family Instructions	Outcome	Initials	Discipline
☐ Nutrition **P/F**			
☐ Medications **P/F**			
☐ Activity/Rehabilitation **P/F**			
☐ Safety **P/F**			
☐ Signs/Symptoms **P/F**			
☐ Wound/Skin Care **P/F**			
☐ Pre/Postop Care **P/F**			
☐ Equipment **P/F**			
☐ Procedures **P/F**			
☐ Treatments **P/F**			
☐ Pain Management **P/F**			
☐ PEARLS **P/F**			
☐ Other **P/F**			

Outcome Key:
1. Able to state understanding and/or return demonstration.
2. Unable to state understanding and/or return demonstration. Continue to reinforce. (See progress notes.)

Date	Time	Discipline	PROGRESS NOTES

Figure 3.21.   (Continued)

University of Anystate Hospitals

PROGRESS NOTES
PAGE 2 OF 2

PATIENT LABEL

Date	Time	Discipline	PROGRESS NOTES

Key

CM = Case Manager	NSG = Nursing	RD = Registered Dietitian
CR = Cardiac Rehabilitation	NSPY = Neuropsychology	RT = Respiratory Therapy
DTC = Diabetes Treatment Center	OT = Occupational Therapy	SLP = Speech/Language Pathologist
ETN = Enterostomal Nurse	PC = Pastoral Care	SW = Social Worker
FSR = Financial Services Representative	PHM = Pharmacy	TR = Therapeutic Recreation
HCC = Home Care Coordinator	PT = Physical Therapy	

Figure 3.22. Interdisciplinary Progress Notes in Electronic Format

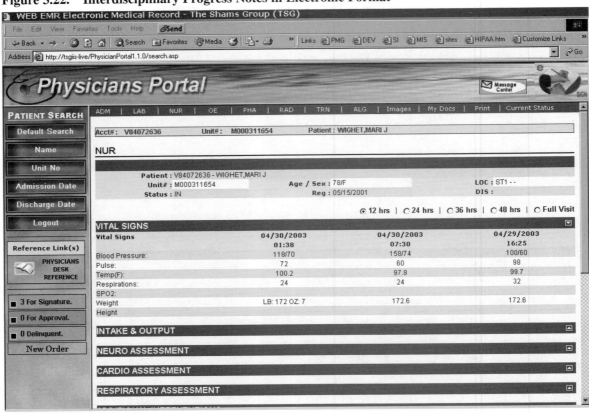

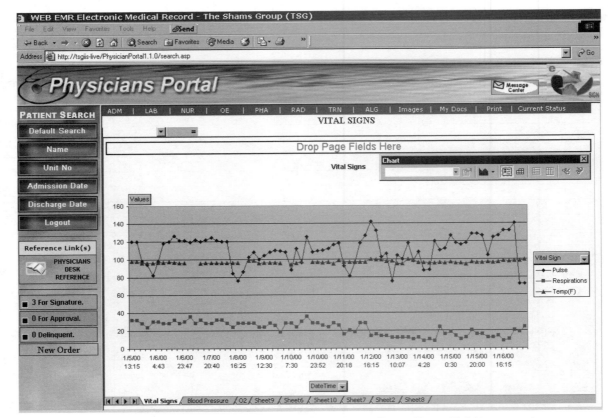

Figure 3.23. Medication Administration Record in Paper Format

University of Anystate Hospitals and Clinics

MEDICATION ADMINISTRATION RECORD

PATIENT LABEL

Site Codes: A = L upper arm
B = R upper arm
C = L hip
D = R hip
E = L thigh
F = R thigh
G = Abdomen
H = Chest

IV Site Codes: 1 = L extremity
2 = R extremity
3 = Central line
4 = Other

Reasons Doses Not Given: Ⓝ = NPO   Ⓡ = Refused   Ⓢ = Sleeping
Ⓟ = On pass   Ⓞ = Other
Ⓣ = Testing   ⒹⒸ = Discontinued

Drug/Dose/Route	Order #	Scheduled	Start	Stop	7–3	3–11	11–7

Stat/One-Time Medications	Date	Time	Site	Initials

Initials	Signature	Initials	Signature	Initials	Signature

MEDICATION ADMINISTRATION RECORD
000028 (11/2002)

Figure 3.24. Medication Administration Record in Electronic Format

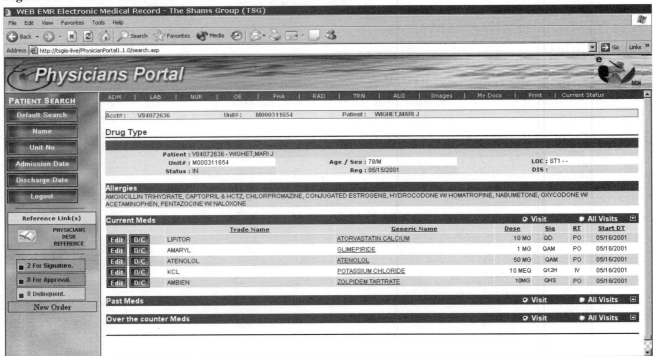

Medication errors are not uncommon in acute care hospitals, and such mistakes can have serious consequences. Every medication error must be described fully in the patient's health record. The time the incorrect medication was administered and the names of the correct and incorrect medications involved must be included in the documentation. The patient's response to the incorrect medication must also be documented, as well as any treatment interventions performed to address the effects of the medication and the patient's response to the interventions.

Adverse reactions to drugs administered correctly or incorrectly must be documented in a progress note and reported to the patient's principal physician. Most hospitals have policies that dictate when adverse reactions and medication errors should also be reported to the risk management and performance improvement departments.

Flow Charts

Flow charts are graphic illustrations of data and observations. Flow charts make it easy to visualize patterns and identify abnormal results. Flow charts are often used in addition to narrative progress notes for recording the patient's fluid consumption (input) and elimination (output) patterns. Blood glucose records for diabetic patients are also maintained as flow charts. Pain assessments can be charted as well. (See figure 3.26, p. 118, for an example of a flow chart.)

Transfer Records

Nurses maintain records of patient transfers from one hospital department to another, for example, from their rooms to the surgery department. They also document any instances when the patient left the facility for a physician's appointment or a procedure to be performed outside the hospital. (See figure 3.27, p.119.)

Figure 3.25. Patient-Controlled Analgesia Record in Paper Format

Midwest Medical Center

**PATIENT-CONTROLLED ANALGESIA
FLOW CHART**

PATIENT LABEL

Physician Order:

_____ Morphine   1 mg/ml = 50 mg/50 ml
_____ Mependine   10 mg/ml = 500 mg/50 ml
_____ Hydromorphone   1 mg/ml = 50 mg/50 ml

Customized

_____ _____ mg/ml = ____ /50 ml
   List Medication   List Concentration

Order Date	Dose		Delay	Basal	1-H Limit	Load	Bolus		Physician
_____		mg	mg	mg	mg	mg	mg	q. ____ h.	
_____		mg	mg	mg	mg	mg	mg	q. ____ h.	
_____		mg	mg	mg	mg	mg	mg	q. ____ h.	
_____		mg	mg	mg	mg	mg	mg	q. ____ h.	
_____		mg	mg	mg	mg	mg	mg	q. ____ h.	

Start Date: _____   Signature (MD/RN): _____
Time:_____a.m./p.m.   Cosignature: (RN): _____

☐ Check if syringe change only.   **Initial Baseline Vital Signs:**   BP: ____ P: ____ R: ____   15 min. after administration: BP: ____ P: ____ R: ____

Date	Time	R	Sedation Level	Pain Level (greater than or equal to 5 × 2 requires documented intervention)	O₂ Sat. (peds required; adults only if ordered)	Total Given	Syringe Volume Infused	Syringe Infused (syringe volume Infused × concentration)	Loading or Bolus Dose	Initials
_____	a.m. p.m.					mg	cc	mg	mg	
_____	a.m. p.m.					mg	cc	mg	mg	
_____	a.m. p.m.					mg	cc	mg	mg	
_____	a.m. p.m.					mg	cc	mg	mg	

Vital Signs: Date: _____ Time: _____ BP: _____ P: _____ R: _____   *Document additional boluses on BP graphic sheet.*
15 Min. after Rebolus: Date: _____ Time: _____ BP: _____ P: _____ R: _____

Initials	Signature	Initials	Signature	Initials	Signature	Initials	Signature	Initials	Signature

---

Pain Scale: For the Conscious Patient

0	5	10
no pain	bad pain	worse pain

For Adult Patients: Stop infusion and call physician for respiratory rate of 10/minute or less.
For Pediatric Patients: Stop infusion and call physician for oxygen saturation less than 94% and/or respiratory rate of 14/minute or less.

Pain Scale: For the Pediatric Patient
Wong-Baker FACES Pain Rating Scale

0 NO HURT	2 HURTS LITTLE BIT	4 HURTS LITTLE MORE	6 HURTS EVEN MORE	8 HURTS WHOLE LOT	10 HURTS WORST

Pain Scale: For the Cognitively Limited

Observe	Criteria	Points	Observe	Criteria	Points
Emotion	Smiling	0	Facial Cues	Relaxed, calm expression	0
	Anxious/irritable	1		Drawn around mouth and eyes	1
	Almost in tears	2		Facial frowning, wincing	2
Movement	None	0	Positioning/Guarding	Relaxed body	0
	Restless/slow or decreased movement	1		Guarding/tense	1
	Immobile, afraid to move	2		Fetal position/jumps if touched	2
Verbal Cues	States no pain	0			
	Whining/whimpering/moaning	1			
	Screaming, crying out	2			

Sedation Level: Modified Ramsay Scale
1. Patient anxious, agitated, or restless
2. Patient cooperative, oriented, and tranquil
3. Patient responds to commands only
4. Patient responds to gentle shaking
5. Patient responds to noxious stimulus
6. Patient has no response to firm nail bed pressure or other noxious stimuli

PATIENT-CONTROLLED ANALGESIA FLOW CHART
000031 (10/2002)

Figure 3.26.   Example of a Flow Chart

Midwest Medical Center

VASCULAR FLOW CHART

PATIENT LABEL

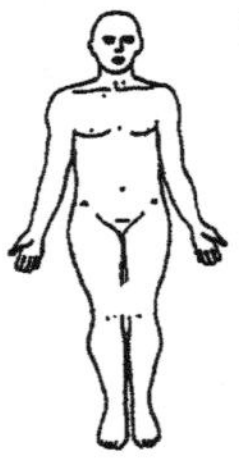

Use diagram to identify graft site

Key	RL/LL = Right Leg/Left Leg	**Date**												
	RA/LA = Right Arm/Left Arm	**Time**												
	Graft Site = A, B, C	**Extremities**												
Pain	Pain Level (0–10)													
	Homan's Sign (+ or −)													
Sensation	N = Normal NB = Numbness T = Tingling A = Absent													
P	0 = No Pulse 1+ = Diminished 2+ = Normal 3+ = Bounding DM = Doppler Monophasic DB = Doppler Biphasic													
Color	R = Red PK = Pink PL = Pallor MOT = Mottled CY = Cyanotic													
T	H = Hot W = Warm C = Cool CD = Cold													
Capillary Refill	N = Normal (1–3 sec) S = Sluggish (>3 sec) B = Brisk (<1 sec)													
Edema	A = Absent 1+, 2+, 3+, 4+													
Two-Pt. Discrim.	1–10 mm (normal = 3–5 mm)													
Vital Signs	T													
	P													
	R													
	BP													
	Initials													

Initial	Signature	Comments

Signature: _____   Date/Time: _____

VASCULAR FLOW CHART
000032 (10/2002)

Figure 3.27.   Interdepartmental Transfer Record in Paper Format

Anycity General Hospital

INTERDEPARTMENTAL TRANSFER RECORD

PATIENT LABEL

Admit/Transfer to Room #: _____   From: _____   Via   ☐ Stretcher   ☐ Wheelchair   Time Report Given: _____

Date: _____   Diagnosis: _____   ☐ Falls prevention protocol
                                                                                                          must be initiated on unit.

Vital Signs (within 30 min):   T: _____   P: _____   R: _____   BP: _____   Pain Scale: _____

Valuables: ☐ N/A   ☐ Given to Patient   ☐ Given to Family   ☐ Other: _____

Assessment

Cardiovascular	Respiratory	Neurological
Rhythm:_____	☐ Lungs Clear	Responds: ☐ Alert/Oriented × 3 2 1
Edema: ☐ Yes ☐ No	☐ Lung Sounds Abnormal	☐ Verbal
Where: _____	Explain: _____	☐ Pain
Amt.:_____	_____	☐ Unresponsive
Pulses × 4 3 2 1	Oxygen Sat. _____ % on room air	Pupils: ☐ ERLA ☐ Other: _____
☐ Other: _____	Oxygen at _____ liters/min via:	Weakness: ☐ Yes ☐ No
_____	☐ N/C ☐ Mask ☐ Other: _____	Where: Right _____
	☐ Other: _____	Left: _____
		☐ Other: _____
Gastrointestinal	**Renal**	**Musculoskeletal**
Abd: ☐ Soft, nontender	☐ Incontinent	☐ Fracture: _____
☐ Distended	☐ Foley Size: _____	☐ Dislocation: _____
☐ Tender	☐ Dialysis	Immobilization:
Bowel Sounds:	Type: _____	☐ Cast ☐ Splint
☐ All quadrants	Intake: _____	☐ Traction
☐ Absent	Output: _____	Neurovascular Status:
☐ Other: _____	☐ Other: _____	☐ Intact
☐ Other: _____		☐ _____
		☐ Other: _____

Integumentary
☐ Intact   ☐ Ecchymosis/Redness: _____   ☐ Decubitus/Breakdown: _____   ☐ Wounds: _____

Interventions

IV Access ☐ N/A	Drip Infusions ☐ N/A	Medications ☐ N/A
☐ INT ☐ IV ☐ Implanted Port	_____ Rate: _____	_____ @_____
Size: _____ Site: _____	_____ Rate: _____	_____ @_____
Fluid: _____ Amount: _____ Rate: ____	_____ Rate: _____	_____ @_____
Other: _____	_____ Rate: _____	_____ @_____
Labs ☐ N/A	**Procedures** ☐ N/A	**Miscellaneous** ☐ N/A
☐ CBC ☐ Heme Panel	☐ EKG	_____
☐ B/CMP ☐ Fingerstick Glucose	☐ X Rays ☐ CXR ☐ KUB	_____
☐ CIP ☐ PT/PTT	☐ Other:_____	
☐ UA ☐ Urine Dip ☐ HCG	☐ Tube Insertion	
☐ Hemoccult ☐ Amylase ☐ Lipase	Type:_____ Size: _____ Location: ___	
Other: _____	Type:_____ Size: _____ Location: ___	**Infection Control** ☐ N/A
Abnormals: _____	Other: _____	☐ Contact ☐ Droplet ☐ Airborne
Equipment Needed in Room ☐ N/A	**Nurse Preparing Report**	**Nurse Receiving Patient**
☐ Oxygen ☐ IV Pump ☐ Suction		☐ Agree with Above Assessment
☐ Monitor ☐ Other:_____	**Unit Phone #:**_____	☐ See Nurses' Notes

INTERDEPARTMENTAL TRANSFER RECORD
000102 (10/2002)

Nutritional Services

Nutritional care plans are based on an initial **nutritional assessment** performed by a registered dietitian. The assessment includes the patient's diet history, weight and height, appetite and food preferences, and information on food sensitivities and allergies. Nutritional care plans usually include the following information:

- Confirmation that a diet order for the patient was issued within twenty-four hours of admission

- Summary of the patient's diet history and/or the nutritional assessment performed upon admission

- Documentation of nutritional therapy and/or dietetic consultation

- Timely and periodic assessments of the patient's nutrient intake and tolerance of the prescribed diet

- Nutritional discharge plan and patient instructions

- Documentation that a copy of the plan was forwarded to the facility to which the patient was transferred after discharge from the hospital, if applicable

- Dietitian's signature, credentials, and date

Diagnostic and Therapeutic Reports

Acute care patients usually undergo a variety of diagnostic and therapeutic procedures, depending on the nature of their illnesses. Some procedures are performed as a part of general patient management, for example, basic blood and urine analyses. Other procedures are performed to determine the extent and nature of the patient's illness, for example, brain scans. Surgical interventions are performed to determine the extent and nature of the patient's disease as well as to provide definitive treatment, for example, breast cancer surgery.

The most common diagnostic and management procedures performed by hospitals include routine laboratory analyses of blood and other bodily fluids, X-ray examinations, and other imaging procedures. Surgical procedures such as biopsies, endoscopic examinations, and surgical explorations, excisions, and resections are performed for both inpatients and outpatients. The circumstances and findings of these procedures require precise documentation in the form of reports to be placed in the patient's health record.

Special Consents

Special consents are required for procedures that involve a significant risk for the patient, such as invasive diagnostic tests, transfusions, and surgical procedures. Medical staff rules and/or hospital policies usually list which types of services always require written documentation of the patient's expressed consent. In general, the following types of procedures usually require special consent:

- Procedures that involve the use of anesthetics

- Treatments that involve the use of experimental drugs

- Surgical procedures that involve the manipulation of organs and tissues

- Procedures that involve a significant risk for complications

In addition, some states require documentation of the patient's written consent for specific types of diagnostic procedures, for example, HIV testing.

It is primarily the responsibility of the patient's physician or surgeon to explain the nature of the specific procedure to be performed. The physician should make sure that the patient or the patient's legal representative understands the procedure's potential risks, complications, and benefits. Patients or their representatives should also be made aware of the comparative risks and benefits of any alternative treatments that are available. Only then should the patient or the patient's representative be asked to sign and date the consent form.

Special consents become a permanent part of the patient's health record. The content of the consent form varies according to the type of procedure to be performed, but most include at least the following information:

- Patient identification, including name and record number

- Name of the procedure to be performed

- Name of the person who is to perform the procedure, if applicable

- Description of the procedure to be performed

- Date the procedure is to be performed

- Patient's or representative's signature (with a note on the representative's relationship to the patient)

- Date the consent was signed

Ancillary Services

The results of every diagnostic procedure performed on the patient's behalf must be permanently documented in the patient's health record. In acute care hospitals, laboratory and imaging procedures are performed in separate departments and are known collectively as **ancillary services.**

Laboratory Reports

Clinical laboratories routinely examine samples of blood, urine, spinal fluid, and other fluids and substances collected from patients. Laboratory tests require a physician's order. The samples for testing are usually collected from patients by nurses or phlebotomists (technicians specially trained to draw blood samples) and then delivered to the laboratory.

When the samples are received in the laboratory, a medical technologist or another laboratory specialist performs the standardized testing procedures ordered. Medical technologists receive training in four-year college programs, where they learn a combination of manual and automated biochemical analysis techniques. Large clinical laboratories may also employ bacteriologists, biologists, and other scientists to conduct more complex analyses, such as genetic testing.

In hospitals, the results of most routine laboratory procedures are generated automatically by electronic testing equipment. Laboratory computer systems generate reports on the test results, which are returned to the physician who ordered the tests. Paper or electronic copies of the results are also placed in the patient's health record. (See figures 3.28 and 3.29, pp. 122–23.) Reports of laboratory results include the following information:

- Patient identification, including name and record number

- Name of the test performed

Figure 3.28.   Example of a Laboratory Report in Paper Format

Midwest Medical Center

LABORATORY SERVICES REPORT:
COAGULATION

PATIENT, WYLIE C.
090241237
DOB: 10/10/1918

ADMISSION DATE: 05/14/03

ADMITTING PHYSICIAN: M. D. Doctor

SPECIMEN DATE: 05/20/03

COLLECTED TIME: 4:55 p.m.

WEEKDAY: Tuesday

——ROUTINE COAGULATION——		UNITS	REFERENCE	
PT	**17.6 H**	SEC	11.2–13.8	
INR	1.9			(1)
PTT	32.0	SEC	22.1–32.5	(2)

H = High

Footnotes

(1) The INR therapeutic range (1.5–4.0) for patients on warfarin therapy will depend on the clinical disorder being treated.

(2) Effective August 19, 2002, the suggested therapeutic range may vary from 40.9–68.3 sec for inpatients on heparin therapy.

Figure 3.29.   Example of a Laboratory Report in Electronic Format

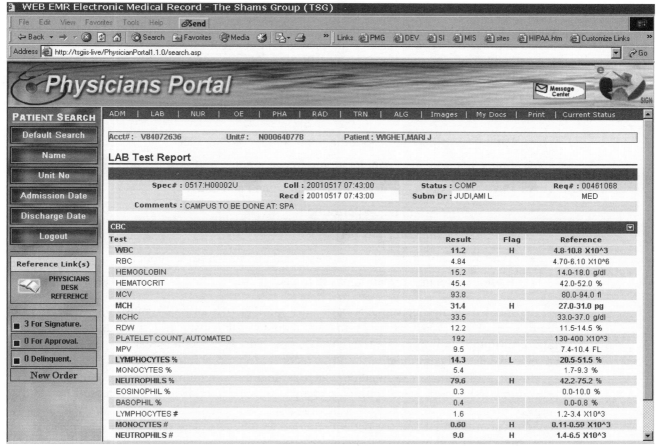

- Date the test was performed and time in/time out of the laboratory

- Signature of the laboratory technologist or scientist who performed the test

- Name of the laboratory where the test was performed

- Results of the test

In hospitals with clinical computer systems, laboratory test results are available to physicians and nurses as soon as the results are generated by the laboratory reporting system. A laboratory summary is available electronically throughout the patient's hospital stay, and a final summary of laboratory results is available soon after the patient's discharge. Copies of the summaries are placed into paper-based records.

Imaging Reports

Scans and X-ray images of various parts of the body and organs are frequently performed by inpatient and outpatient imaging departments. Most hospital imaging departments are equipped to perform X-ray examinations and computed tomography (CT) scans. Many large, urban hospitals also provide more advanced imaging services including magnetic resonance imaging (MRI) and positron-emission tomography (PET). Some imaging procedures require the administration of radiopharmaceuticals, radioactive contrast media administered to the patient before or during the procedure to make it possible to visualize physiological processes and tissues more clearly.

Imaging procedures require a physician's order. Most imaging procedures are performed by specially trained radiology technicians. However, the interpretation of scans and images must be performed by physicians specially trained in radiology. The radiologist's written report, signed and dated, becomes part of the patient's permanent record. (See figure 3.30, p. 125.) The original scans and images are generally stored in the radiology department rather than in patient records. However, most electronic health record systems are capable of storing copies of diagnostic scans and images for easy reference.

Imaging reports generally include the following information:

- Patient identification, including name and record number
- Image identification data including image number and hospital number
- Physician's order for the examination, signed and dated
- Name of the examination performed
- Date the examination was performed
- Type and amount of radiopharmaceutical administered, if applicable
- Radiologist's interpretation of the images, authenticated by date and signature

Hospital imaging departments perform a number of routine diagnostic tests that do not require sedation in most cases. Examples of routine diagnostic tests include mammograms, fetal ultrasounds, and preoperative chest X-rays. These procedures carry a very low risk of adverse events and complications, and so recordkeeping requirements are minimal.

Invasive diagnostic examinations such as angiocardiography and image-guided surgical procedures require recordkeeping and special consents similar to those required for regular surgical procedures. Procedures that involve conscious sedation require documentation of the sedatives administered and the patient's period of recovery. The physicians who perform the procedures must author short discharge progress notes in addition to full reports of the procedures and any findings. For procedures performed under general anesthesia, documentation is required for the entire perioperative period. The facility should establish a list of the imaging procedures that require special consents and documentation.

Specialty Diagnostic Services

Several diagnostic tests are performed by clinical specialists rather than as ancillary services. The most common are tests related to cardiac and neurological functioning.

Cardiology Reports

Cardiologists perform and/or report on a number of different cardiac diagnostic tests performed in the hospital on both inpatients and outpatients. Many patients being treated primarily for noncardiac diagnoses may also have preexisting cardiac conditions that need monitoring through routine electrocardiography. (See figures 3.31 through 3.33, pp. 126–29.) Other specialized tests performed and/or interpreted by cardiologists include:

- Exercise and pharmacological stress tests
- Tilt-table tests
- Holter monitoring
- Pacemaker checks
- Electrocardiography

Figure 3.30.   Example of an Imaging Services Report in Paper Format

Midwest Medical Center

IMAGING SERVICES REPORT

OUTPATIENT, OLIVE O.
121212000
DOB: 02/27/1942

EXAM DATE: 5/12/03

REFERRING PHYSICIAN: B. Interary

Check-in #: 62

Order #: 1201

Exam #: 36080

FXR: Chest Single View

DIAGNOSIS: V72.84

PA AND LATERAL CHEST: 5/12/03

COMPARISON: 6/8/98

FINDINGS: The lungs are clear. The heart and mediastinum are normal in size and configuration. There are minor degenerative changes of the lower thoracic spine.

CONCLUSION: Minor degenerative change of the lower thoracic spine; otherwise negative chest.

Signature: _N~DR~ll_____   _5/12/03_____

Norman D. Radiol, MD   Date

d: 05/12/2003
t: 05/14/2003
NDR, MD/na

Figure 3.31.   Example of a Cardiac Catheterization Report in Paper Format

Midwest Medical Center

CARDIAC CATHETERIZATION REPORT
PAGE 1 OF 2

PATIENT, SYLVESTER Q.
00999067
DOB: 01/03/1960

DATE: 05/17/2003

REFERRING PHYSICIAN(S): M. D. Doctor

PROCEDURES PERFORMED:

1. Left heart catheterization
2. Selective coronary artery study
3. Left ventriculography
4. Insertion of an intra-aortic balloon pump

DESCRIPTION OF PROCEDURE: The patient was brought over from Anyplace General Hospital, where he had been admitted last week with acute respiratory failure. It was felt that it was on the basis of an acute myocardial event. The above procedures were performed. He was taken to the cardiac diagnostic unit at Midwest Medical Center, where the right groin was prepped and draped in the usual sterile manner. One percent Xylocaine was instilled in the region surrounding the right femoral artery. An 18-gauge needle was advanced into the right femoral artery area. Using exchange guide wire technique, a #5 French sheath was placed. This was later exchanged for a #8 French sheath when the intra-aortic balloon pump was placed.

Hemodynamic Data: (1) ascending aortic pressure was 188/62; (2) left ventricle was 188/23-35.

With the patient in the right anterior oblique position, 12 cc of Isovue was injected into the left ventricular chamber. The ejection fraction is approximately 50–55%.

Selective coronary arteriography was performed of both the right and left coronary arteries in multiple oblique projections.

Left Main Coronary Artery: The left main coronary artery was markedly narrowed. The ostium was very significantly obstructed. As the catheter tip barely entered the main coronary artery, the pressure dipped to near 0%. This was confirmed on two further very careful positionings of the catheter. Direct injection into the left main coronary artery was not possible.

Left Anterior Descending Artery: The very proximal portion of the left anterior descending artery shows very high-grade near-total occlusion. The distal vessel is irregular, however, free of high-grade occlusions. There is a large intermediate branch.

Left Posterior Circumflex Coronary Artery: The left posterior circumflex coronary artery was nearly totally occluded at its origin. Minor disease is noted throughout the system.

Right Coronary Artery: The right coronary artery was irregular; however, there was no evidence of significant obstructive disease.

Figure 3.31.   (Continued)

Midwest Medical Center

CARDIAC CATHETERIZATION REPORT
PAGE 2 OF 2

PATIENT, SYLVESTER Q.
00999067
DOB: 01/03/1960

At the conclusion of the procedure, Dr. Surgeon was contacted regarding the possibility of urgent surgery. With Dr. Doctor and Dr. Surgeon consulting by phone, it was elected to place an intra-aortic balloon pump.

The intra-aortic balloon pump was placed without difficulty. Its position was confirmed by fluoroscopy. It appeared to be functioning normally.

During the procedure when the intra-aortic balloon pump was put in, the patient was given 5000 units intravenous heparin and will be on an intravenous heparin drip.

IMPRESSIONS:

1. Relative preservation of left ventricular systolic function at rest with ejection fraction of approximately 50%.
2. Coronary artery disease—three vessels involved
    a. Near-total occlusion of left main coronary artery
    b. High-grade near-total occlusion of the left anterior descending artery proximally
    c. High-grade near-total occlusion of the left posterior circumflex coronary artery proximally
    d. Mild diffuse disease, right coronary artery, as described above
3. Placement of intra-aortic balloon pump in patient with left main coronary artery disease and history of flash pulmonary edema.

Signature:

M. Denn Heartmann

M. Dennis Heartmann, MD

5/17/03

Date

d: 05/17/2003
t: 05/18/2003
MDH, MD/dq

Figure 3.32.   Example of an Echocardiography Report in Paper Format

Anytown Community Hospital

ECHOCARDIOGRAPHIC REPORT

TEST, PATIENT
009999999
DOB: 04/01/1930

DATE: 06/02/2003

REFERRING PHYSICIAN: Dr. Doctor

INDICATION FOR STUDY: Murmur

TAPE: House 528

Outpatient Study

Two-dimensional and M-mode echocardiograms were performed

The left atrium is at the upper limits of normal size at 3.7 cm compared to an aortic root diameter of 2.9 cm. The left ventricle is at the upper limits of normal size with a normal internal dimension of 5.6 cm in diastole and 3.3 cm in systole. There is normal wall thickness. There is hyperdynamic left ventricular systolic performance. The ejection fraction is estimated at greater than 70%. No specific regional wall motion abnormalities were identified. The cardiac valves appear structurally normal. No intracardiac masses were identified and a pericardial effusion was not visualized.

Conventional as well as color-flow Doppler imaging was performed. There are findings of mitral regurgitation which is estimated to be at least moderate to severe, if not severe. There is tricuspid regurgitation with peak right ventricular systolic pressure of 31 mmHg. No other significant valvular stenoses or regurgitation were identified.

IMPRESSION:

1. The left atrium and left ventricle at the upper limits of normal size with a hyperdynamic left ventricular systolic performance.

2. There is evidence of mitral regurgitation which is at least moderate to severe. Would consider transesophageal echocardiography to further assess the severity of the mitral regurgitation as well as potentially its etiology.

Signature: _____   _____

Philip Default, MD   Date

d: 06/02/2003
t: 06/02/2003

Figure 3.33.   Example of an Electrocardiography Report in Paper Format

University of Anystate Hospitals

GRAPHIC EKG REPORT

PATIENT, PETUNIA P.
000000001
DOB: 08/14/1949

NAME: Patient, Petunia

TECHNICIAN: SKH

PROCEDURE DATE/TIME: 10/11/04 9:59:02

CARDIOLOGIST: Julius W. Cardiolini, MD

SEX/RACE: Female, White

REPORT DATE: 10/08/04

REQUESTED BY: M. Gynesurg, MD

RESULTS: Normal EKG
PR   200   Normal sinus rhythm rate: 59
QRST   73
QT   407
QTc   403
Axes
P   28
QRS   36
T   35

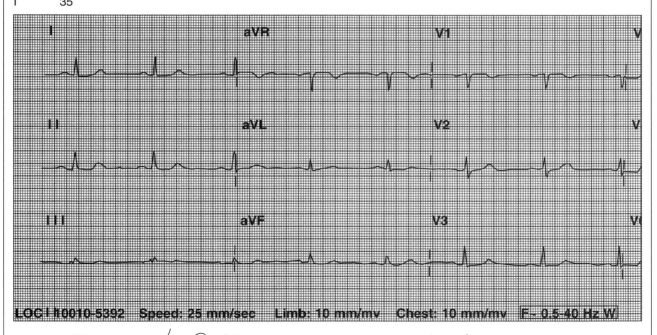

LOC I h0010-5392   Speed: 25 mm/sec   Limb: 10 mm/mv   Chest: 10 mm/mv   F - 0.5-40 Hz W

Julius W. Cardiolini, MD   Date
Cardiologist

10/8/04

- Echocardiography

- Cardioradionucleide imaging

- Myocardial imaging

- Cardiac catheterization

Cardiac catheterizations may also include treatment interventions such as the insertion of stents and balloons.

Neurology Reports

Neurologists are often called upon to evaluate the neurological status of patients being treated for other types of illnesses. For example, neurological dysfunction is common among patients suffering from systemic disorders such as alcoholism, cancer, cerebrovascular and cardiovascular disease, and autoimmune disease. It can be difficult to distinguish neurological impairment from psychiatric illness, and so psychiatrists sometimes ask for neurological evaluations of patients with ambiguous symptoms. In addition, because critically ill patients can be maintained indefinitely on cardiopulmonary support after their other systems have shut down, neurologists may be called upon to perform an examination to confirm brain death. (See figure 3.34, p. 131.)

Common diagnostic tests that must be performed or interpreted by neurologists include the following:

- Mental status examinations

- Electroencephalography

- Echoencephalography

- Cerebral angiography

- Myelography

- Lumbar puncture

Surgical Services

Hospital-based surgery departments provide services to both inpatients and outpatients, although many hospitals maintain separate preoperative and recovery areas for outpatients. The documentation requirements for outpatient surgery (also called ambulatory surgery and same-day surgery) are exactly the same as the requirements for inpatient surgical procedures.

Consents for Surgery

Except in emergency situations, surgeons or their representatives must receive written documentation of the patient's consent to surgery before the operation can begin. After the surgery is complete, surgical consent forms become part of the surgical section of the patient's permanent health record.

In day-surgery clinics, patients are usually asked to sign consent forms during the admissions process. The assumption is that the patient's surgeon explained the benefits and risks of the procedure before the surgery was scheduled. Similarly, in inpatient settings, patients about to undergo planned, elective surgery should already understand the nature of the surgery. It would have been discussed during preadmission office visits with the surgeon. However, the surgeon or the patient's principal physician must explain the nature of unplanned inpatient surgical procedures before asking patients or their legal representatives to sign the consent forms. (See figure 3.35, p. 132, for an example of a surgical consent form.)

Figure 3.34. Example of a Neurological Assessment in Paper Format

University of Anystate Hospitals

NEUROLOGICAL ASSESSMENT AND REASSESSMENT

PATIENT LABEL

			Date and Time														
Glasgow Coma Scale																	
Eye Opening	Spontaneous	= 4															**C** = Eyes Closed by Swelling
	To Voice	= 3															
	To Pain	= 2															
	None	= 1															
Verbal Response	Oriented	= 5															**T** = Endotracheal Tube or Tracheostomy
	Confused	= 4															
	Inappropriate Words	= 3															
	Incomprehensible Words	= 2															
	None	= 1															**A** = Aphasia
Motor Response	Obeys Command	= 6															
	Localizes Pain	= 5															
	Withdraws	= 4															Record Best Arm Response
	Flexion	= 3															
	Extension	= 2															
	None	= 1															
Total Score		3–7 = Severe 8–13 = Moderate 13+ = Mild															

Limb Movement
Grade limb movement either spontaneous or to command. Do not rate reflex movement. Use scale below.

	RA															
	RL															
	LA															
	LL															

Limb Movement Scale: 0 = No Response   1 = Flicker or Trace of Movement   2 = Active Movement without Gravity
3 = Active Movement against Gravity   4 = Active Movement against Gravity with Limited Resistance   5 = Normal Power

Pupils	**Reaction**	Size	R														
Size	C = Closed by swelling		L														
1 mm 2 mm 3 mm 4 mm 5 mm 6 mm 7 mm 8 mm	B = Brisk S = Sluggish F = Fixed	Reaction	R														
	Shape		L														
	R = Round O = Oval K = Keyhole I = Irregular	Shape	R														
			L														

Ventriculostomy Data	ICP															
	CSF Output															
Key: CL = Clear R = Red	Color															
Y = Yellow PK = Pink CLO = Cloudy	Character															

Vital Signs	Temperature															
	Pulse															
	Respirations															
	Blood Pressure															

Other: _____

Other _____

Comments: _____

Signature: _____ Date/Time: _____

NEUROLOGICAL ASSESSMENT
000080 (10/2002)

Figure 3.35. Example of an Informed Consent for Operation with Blood Products

University of Anystate Hospitals

**INFORMED CONSENT FOR OPERATION/
PROCEDURE/ANESTHESIA INCLUDING
BLOOD AND BLOOD PRODUCTS**

PATIENT LABEL

1. I give permission to Dr.(s) _____ to perform
   the following procedure(s): _____
   _____
   _____ on _____ (patient's name).

2. I understand that during the procedure(s), new findings or conditions may appear and require an additional procedure(s) for proper care.

3. My physician has explained the following items:
   - the nature of my condition
   - the nature and purpose of the procedure(s) that I am now authorizing
   - the possible complications and side effects that may result, problems that may be experienced during recuperation, and the likelihood of success
   - the benefits to be reasonably expected from the procedure(s)
   - the likely result of no treatment
   - the available alternatives, including the risks and benefits
   - the other possible risks that accompany any surgical and diagnostic procedure (in addition to those already discussed). I acknowledge that neither my physician nor anyone else involved in my care has made any guarantees or assurances to me as to the result of the procedure(s) that I am now authorizing.

4. I know that other clinical staff may help my physician during the procedure(s).

5. I understand that the procedure(s) may require that I undergo some form of anesthesia, which may have its own risks.

6. Any tissue or specimens taken from my body as a result of the procedure(s) may be examined and disposed of, retained, preserved, or used for medical, scientific, or teaching purposes by the hospital.

7. I understand that my procedure(s) may be photographed or videotaped and that observers may be present in the room for the purpose of advancing medical care and education.

8. I understand that during or after the procedure(s) my physician may find it necessary to give me a transfusion of blood or blood products. My physician has explained the alternatives to, and possible risks of, transfusion.

9. I understand what my physician has explained to me and have had all my questions fully answered.

10. Additional comments: _____
    _____

After talking with my physician and reading this form, I give my consent to the procedure(s) described above.

Signature of Patient or
Legal Representative: _____ Date: _____ Time: _____

If Legal Representative, Relationship to Patient:_____

Witness: _____

Verbal or Telephone Consent

Name of Legal Representative:_____ Date: _____ Time: _____

Relationship to Patient: _____

Witness:_____ Witness: _____

I have explained the risks, benefits, potential complications, and alternatives of the treatment to the patient and have answered all questions to the patient's satisfaction, and he/she has granted consent to proceed.

Physician Signature: _____ Date: _____ Time: _____

INFORMED CONSENT FOR OPERATION
000015 (11/2002)

Preoperative History and Physical Reports

Except in emergency situations, every surgical patient's chart must include a report of a complete history and physical conducted no more than seven days before the surgery is to be performed. This requirement is the same for inpatient and outpatient procedures. The report of the history and physical must be present in the patient's chart before surgery can begin. Ideally, advance directives and organ donation forms should also be placed in the chart before surgery. (These documents are discussed later in the chapter.)

Anesthesia Evaluations and Records

The anesthesia and/or sedation administered to patients during surgical procedures represents a significant risk independent of the risks involved in the surgery itself. Regulations and accreditation standards require anesthesiologists (who are physicians) and certified nurse-anesthetists (advanced practice nurses who work under the direction of anesthesiologists) to perform and document their own **preoperative anesthesia evaluations.** The evaluation collects information on the patient's medical history and current physical and emotional condition. The evaluation becomes the basis for an anesthesia plan that stipulates the type of anesthesia to be used; addresses the patient's risk factors, allergies, and drug usage; and considers the patient's general medical condition. (See figures 3.36 and 3.37, pp. 134–36.)

The professional who is to administer anesthesia to the patient must also perform a reevaluation of the patient's condition immediately before the procedure. The purpose of the reevaluation is to confirm that it is safe to begin the operation. The timing and dosage of any preanesthesia medications should also be documented at this point.

The professional administering anesthesia during the procedure must also maintain an **intraoperative anesthesia record.** The intraoperative record is created while the procedure is being performed. (See figures 3.38 and 3.39, pp. 137–39.) The record describes the entire surgical process and includes the following information:

- Patient identification, including name and record number

- Name of the anesthesiologist or nurse-anesthetist

- Type and amount of anesthesia administered

- Induction mechanisms

- Medication log, including medical gases and fluid administration

- Usage of blood products

- Placement of lines and monitoring devices

- Patient's reaction to anesthesia

- Results of continuous patient monitoring, including vital signs and oxygen saturation levels

The **postoperative anesthesia record** contains information on any unusual events or complications that occurred during surgery. The postoperative anesthesia record also documents the patient's condition at the conclusion of surgery and after recovery from anesthesia. (See figures 3.40 and 3.41, pp. 140–43.)

Figure 3.36. Preprocedure Record in Paper Format

University of Anystate Hospitals

PREPROCEDURE RECORD
PAGE 1 OF 2

PATIENT LABEL

Preprocedure Care (Day of Procedure)

Date: _____ Time: _____

☐ NPO Since: _____ Voided? ☐ Yes ☐ No

Valuables (check if present, put O if removed)?
☐ Clothing ☐ Dentures ☐ Glasses ☐ Contact
☐ Hearing aid ☐ Hair piece/wig ☐ Jewelry Lenses
☐ Other: _____
☐ Patient was informed hospital is not responsible for lost
  valuables
Signature of Person Responsible for Valuables

Disposition if no one is present: _____
☐ Responsible adult available to accompany patient at discharge
☐ TED Hose ☐ SCDs/plexi pulse
☐ Skin prep: _____ By: _____

Medication Given Prior to Procedure:

	Time:	Initials:
_____	_____	____
_____	Time: _____	Initials: ____
_____	Time: _____	Initials: ____
_____	Time: _____	Initials: ____
_____	Time: _____	Initials: ____
_____	Time: _____	Initials: ____
	Time: _____	Initials: ____

Douche/Enema: _____ Time: _____ Initials: ____
☐ IV gauge #: ____ Site: ____ Fluid: ____ Rate: ____ Initials: ____
☐ IV gauge #: ____ Site: ____ Fluid: ____ Rate: ____ Initials: ____

Completed by _____

Operating Room Checklist (initial when completed)

_____ ID Bracelet Correct   For Moderate Sedation and Anesthesia Patients:
_____ Informed Consent   _____ Preanesthesia Assessment
_____ H&P   _____ Anesthesia Plan of Care
_____ Operative Plan
_____ Site/Procedure Verified with Schedule/MD Order, Consent, and Patient/Representative
_____ Procedure Site Marked
_____ Procedure and Site Verified with Available Imaging Studies by MD, if Applicable (procedure
      staff)
_____ Patient, Procedure, and Site Verified Verbally Immediately prior to Start by Procedural Team
      (final "time out") (procedure staff)

Completed by: _____

Diagnostic Studies
(O if ordered, checkmark if on chart)
☐ CBC   ☐ Sed. Rate   ☐ Heme
☐ Chemistry ☐ Urine C&S   ☐ Potassium
☐ PT, PTT   ☐ U/A   ☐ Creatinine
☐ EKG   ☐ X-Rays   ☐ T+S
☐ T&C _____ Units Available

☐ Pregnancy ☐ _____

Bedside Glucose: _____

☐ Abnormal Results Called to MD

Completed by: _____

Assessment

Alert and Oriented: ☐ Yes ☐ No (see supplemental nurses' notes)
Suspected Abuse: ☐ No ☐ Yes (see supplemental nurses' notes)
Learning Barriers: ☐ No Barriers ☐ Physical ☐ Religious ☐ Cultural ☐ Cognitive ☐ Emotional ☐ Language (see supplemental nurses' notes)
Pain: ☐ No Pain ☐ Yes, Location: _____ ☐ Onset: _____ ☐ Duration: _____ ☐ Intensity: ____ (1–10) Qual/Characteristics/Pattern: _____
  Alleviating Factors: _____ Aggravating Factors: _____ Affects on ADL: _____ Relieved By: _____
Diabetic/Special Diet? ☐ No ☐ Yes (see supplemental nurses' notes)
Recent Mobility Limitation? ☐ No ☐ Yes (see supplemental nurses' notes)

Nursing Assessment (Inpatient) Initiated

Completed By: _____ **RN**

Plan of Care	Clinical Pathway Initiated
Potential for Fear and/or Anxiety **Goal: Reduction of Fear and Anxiety** ☐ **Goal Met**	**Potential for Injury** **Goal: Patient Is Free from Injury** ☐ **Goal Met**
☐ Procedures Explained to Patient and Family	Side Rails Up: ☐ × 2 ☐ × 4 Bed Position: ☐ Low ☐ High
☐ Patient and Family Encouraged to Verbalize Concerns and Questions	☐ Instructed Patient to Call for Assistance
☐ Patient and Family's Questions Answered	**Potential for Alteration in Fluid Volume** **Goal: Fluid Volume Is within Normal Limits** ☐ **Goal Met**
☐ Age-Appropriate Emotional Support Provided	☐ IV Access Present, No Infiltration Noted
Knowledge Deficit Relating to Procedure **Goal: Demonstrates and/or Verbalizes Knowledge** ☐ **Goal Met**	**Privacy/Confidentiality** **Goal: Privacy/Confidentiality Maintained** ☐ **Goal Met**
☐ Patient's Level of Learning Assessed and Instructions Modified to Meet Needs	☐ Confidentiality of Patient Records, Diagnosis, Procedure Maintained
☐ Reviewed Printed Discharge Instructions with Patient and Family	☐ Patient Minimally Exposed during Preparation
	Potential Alteration in Cardiovascular Function **Goal: Hemodynamically Stable** ☐ **Goal Met**
☐ Cough, Turn, Deep-Breathe	☐ Continuous Cardiac Monitoring ☐ Continuous Heart Rate Monitoring
☐ PRN Pain Medications/Pain Scale	**Potential Alteration in Gas Exchange** **Goal: Adequate Air Exchange** ☐ **Goal Met**
☐ Patient/Family Verbalize Understanding of Instructions	
☐ Age-Appropriate Approach Used in Education	☐ Continuous Pulse Oximetry in Use ☐ Oxygen Therapy Initiated as Ordered
Initials/Signature: _____ _____	Initials/Signature: _____ _____

PREPROCEDURE RECORD
000019 (11/2002)

Figure 3.36. (Continued)

University of Anystate Hospitals

PREPROCEDURE RECORD
PAGE 2 OF 2

PATIENT LABEL

Pediatrics (Neonate through 17 Years of Age)

☐ Grade in School _____   Feeding ☐ Breast ☐ Bottle/Formula ☐ Solids
☐ Developmental Milestones Appropriate for Age   Type of Formula _____
  ☐ Yes ☐ No
☐ Security Object/Toys _____   Primary Caregiver _____
☐ Immunizations Current ☐ Yes ☐ No

Signature: _____

Interaction between Caregiver and Child _____   Head Circumference _____
☐ Calming ☐ Agitative   (infants under 1 year of age only)
Signature: _____

Further Assessment

Cardiac Rhythm:

Preprocedure Peripheral Pulses (Absent, 1+, 2+, 3+, 4+, Doppler)
R DP: _____   L DP: _____   R PT: _____   L PT: _____   R Rad.:_____   L Rad.: _____   Other: _____

Other: _____
Signature: _____

Supplemental Nurses' Notes: _____
_____
_____
_____

Preprocedure Preparation

Type of Procedure: _____   Date Called: _____   Time Called: _____
Date of Procedure: _____   Time of Procedure: _____   Arrival Time: _____
Instructions Given To: _____
Via: ☐ Phone ☐ Appointment ☐ Left Phone Message   ☐ Unable to Reach
☐ No Makeup, Jewelry, Perfume, Nail Polish, or Valuables   ☐ Medications A.M. of Procedure with a Sip of Water
☐ NPO Status/Time _____
☐ Instructions for: _____
  _____   ☐ Bring Medications/Inhalers/List to Hospital
  _____   ☐ Preadmission Diagnostic Tests Done:
  _____   Date: _____ Location: _____
  _____   ☐ Date/Location Previous CXR: _____
  _____   ☐ Date/Location Previous EKG: _____
☐ Informed that responsible adult must accompany patient to hospital, transport home, and remain with patient after the procedure
Name of Responsible Person after Procedure: _____
Signature: _____ RN/LPN

PREPROCEDURE RECORD
000019 (11/2002)

Figure 3.37. Preoperative Checklist

University of Anystate Hospitals

PREOPERATIVE CHECKLIST

| PATIENT LABEL |

(It is the responsibility of the unit nurse to see that this is completed before the patient goes to the operating room.)

Vital Signs Taken prior to Transfer

Date: _____ Time: _____ BP: _____ T: _____ P: _____ R: _____ O_2Sat: _____ Weight: _____ Height: _____

	Yes	No	Initials		Yes	No	Initials		Yes	No	Initials
Side Rails Raised?	☐	☐	_____	Instructed Not to Smoke?	☐	☐	_____	Instructed to Stay in Bed?	☐	☐	_____

	Yes	No	N/A	Initials
Dentures Removed?	☐	☐	☐	_____
Contact Lens Removed?	☐	☐	☐	_____
Jewelry Removed?	☐	☐	☐	_____
Jewelry Disposition _____				
Hair Piece, Pins, Clamps Removed?	☐	☐	☐	_____
Hearing Aid(s) Removed?	☐	☐	☐	_____
Hospital Gown?	☐	☐		_____
ID Name Band on Patient?	☐	☐		_____
Fenwal ID Band on Patient?	☐	☐	☐	_____

Prep Site: _____
By Whom: _____ Checked By: _____
NPO Since: _____ a.m./p.m.
Voided: _____ cc Catheter: _____ cc
Bedside Glucose: _____ Time: _____

If Ordered to Operating Room with Patient

	Yes	No	N/A	Initials		Yes	No	N/A	Initials
X-Rays?	☐	☐	☐	_____	Meds?	☐	☐	☐	_____
Old Charts?	☐	☐	☐	_____					_____
SCDs/TEDs	☐	☐	☐	_____					_____

On Chart

	Initials
Site/procedure verified with schedule/MD order, consent, and patient/representative	_____
Procedure site marked	

	Yes	No	Initials
Informed Consent?	☐	☐	_____
History and Physical?	☐	☐	_____
Operative Plan?	☐	☐	_____
Patient Labels?	☐	☐	_____
MARS?	☐	☐	_____
Clinical Pathway, if applicable?	☐	☐	_____

OR/Procedure Staff Use Only

	Initials
Procedure and site verified with available imaging studies by MD, if applicable	_____
Patient, procedure, and site verified verbally immediately prior to start by procedural team (final "time out")	_____
Preanesthesia/moderate sedation assessment completed	_____
Anesthesia/moderate sedation plan completed	_____

Results on Chart: Preop Diagnostics

	Yes	No	N/A	Initials		Yes	No	N/A	Initials
T&C/T+S _____ Units available	☐	☐	☐	_____	EKG	☐	☐	☐	_____
CBC	☐	☐	☐	_____	X-ray reports	☐	☐	☐	_____
Chemistry	☐	☐	☐	_____	PT/PTT	☐	☐	☐	_____
Urinalysis	☐	☐	☐	_____	Physician notified of abnormal results?	☐	☐	☐	_____

Preop Medications/IV Therapy

☐ IV gauge # _____ Site _____ Fluid _____ Rate _____ Initials _____

☐ IV gauge # _____ Site _____ Fluid _____ Rate _____ Initials _____

Preop Meds _____ **Time Given/Initials** _____

Plan of Care	Clinical Pathway Initiated

Privacy/Confidentiality
Goal: Privacy/Confidentiality Maintained   ☐ Goal Met
☐ Patient Minimally Exposed during Preparation

Potential for Alteration in Fluid Volume
Goal: Fluid Volume Is within Normal Limits   ☐ Goal Met
☐ IV Access Present, No Infiltration Noted

Potential for Fear and/or Anxiety
Goal: Reduction of Fear and Anxiety   ☐ Goal Met
☐ Procedures Explained to Patient and Family
☐ Patient and Family Encouraged to Verbalize Concerns and Questions
☐ Patient and Family's Questions Answered
☐ Age-Appropriate Emotional Support Provided

Potential for Injury
Goal: Patient Is Free From Injury   ☐ Goal Met
Bed Position: ☐ Low   ☐ High
Side Rails Up   ☐ × 2   ☐ × 4
☐ Instructed to Call for Assistance

Knowledge Deficit Relating to Procedure
Goal: Demonstrates and/or Verbalizes Knowledge   ☐ Goal Met
☐ PEARLS for Progress Reviewed with Patient
☐ Cough, Turn, Deep Breath
☐ PRN Pain Medications/Pain Scale
☐ Patient/Family Verbalize Understanding of Instructions
☐ Age-Appropriate Approach Used in Education

Location of Family during Surgery _____

Report Called: Yes ☐   No ☐   N/A ☐   ☐ Called to:
Miscellaneous Information: _____

Signature of Nurse Transferring Patient to Operating Room

_____ Initials _____
_____ Initials _____

_____ Initials _____
_____ Initials _____

PREOPERATIVE CHECKLIST
000018 (11/2002)

Figure 3.38. Intraoperative Anesthesia Record in Paper Format

University of Anystate Hospitals

INTRAOPERATIVE RECORD

> PATIENT LABEL

OR #: _____   ☐ SDA   ☐ Outpatient   ☐ **Preoperative Assessment Reviewed**   ☐ **Patient Confirms Surgical Site**
Date: _____   ☐ Inpatient   ☐ Add-On (day of surgery)   ☐ Agree with Assessment   ☐ Yes
☐ See Additional Notes   ☐ See Additional Notes

Allergies: _____
_____

Preprocedure Diagnosis: _____
Postprocedure Diagnosis: _____
Procedure Performed: _____

Times: Room In/Room Out_____ / _____   **Transferred to/Discharge:** ☐ PACU ☐ ICU ☐ Room # _____ ☐ Home
Anesthesia Start _____ / _____   Method of Transfer: ☐ Stretcher ☐ Bed ☐ Other: _____ ☐ Report Called: _____
Procedure Start/Stop _____ / _____   Condition on Discharge: ☐ Satisfactory ☐ Other _____

Anesthesia: **Personnel Role:**
☐ General
☐ MAC   MD: _____   _____
☐ Regional   Circ.: _____   Relief: _____   Time: _____
  ☐ Epidural   Scrub: _____
  ☐ Spinal   Anes.: _____   Relief: _____
  ☐ Axillary Block   Other: _____   Rad. Tech.: _____
  ☐ Bier Block
☐ IV Sedation   Role: _____   Perfusionist: _____
☐ Local
☐ Other: _____

☐ **Potential for Fear and Anxiety** Goal: Reduction of Fear and Anxiety	☐ **Patient Privacy** Goal: Privacy Maintained
☐ Perioperative Events Explained ☐ Goal Met ☐ Intraop Family Communication Time: _____	☐ Patient Minimally Exposed during Positioning, Prepping, and Draping

☐ Potential for Injury Goal: Patient Free From Injury   **☐ Potential for Infection** Goal: Sterile Technique Maintained

Intraop Position: ☐ Goal Met
☐ Supine   Safety Strap =   **Skin Preparation:** ☐ None   **Prep:**   ☐ Goal Met
☐ Prone   Arm Position →   ☐ Shave _____   ☐ Iodophor Prep
☐ Lithotomy   ESU Pad ∅   ☐ Clip _____   ☐ Iodophor Scrub
☐ Lateral R   Padding #   ☐ Iodophor Gel
☐ Lateral L   Pulse Oximeter ☐   ☐ Dura-Prep
☐ Jackknife   EKG ●   **Skin Condition:**   ☐ Other: _____
☐ Beach Chair   BP Cuff **X**   Before Surgery: ☐ Normal ☐ Other: _____
☐ Other: _____   After Surgery: ☐ Normal ☐ Other: _____

Positional Aids: ☐ None   **Equipment:** ☐ None   **Cultures:** ☐ None   **Wound Class:**
☐ Donut   ☐ ESU #: _____ PAD #: _____   ☐ Aerobic—Site: ☐ I
☐ Pillow   Coagulation: _____ Cut: _____   ☐ Anaerobic—Site: ☐ II
☐ Eggcrate Pad   Post Op Site: _____   ☐ AFB—Site: ☐ III
☐ Bean Bag   ☐ Bipolar #: _____   ☐ Fungus—Site: ☐ IV
☐ Lami Rolls   Setting: _____   **Lines/Drains:** ☐ None   **Dressings:** ☐ Yes ☐ No
☐ Chest Roll   ☐ C-Arm/OEC   ☐ JP/Hemovac/Blake   _____
☐ Axilla Roll   ☐ Phaco #: _____   ☐ Chest Tube
☐ Shoulder Roll   ☐ Cryo #: _____   ☐ Foley   ☐ Splint _____
☐ Sand Bag   ☐ Laser #: _____   ☐ Arterial   ☐ Cast _____
☐ Stirrups   ☐ Ultrasound #: _____   ☐ CVP/Swanz   ☐ Other: _____
  ☐ Candy Cane   ☐ CUSA #: _____   ☐ NG Tube   ☐ **Packing:** ☐ Yes ☐ No
  ☐ Bierhoff   ☐ Bair Hugger #: _____   ☐ Other: _____
  ☐ Allen   ☐ Seq. Comp. Mach. #: _____
☐ Knee Holder   Settings _____   **☐**   **Miscellaneous**
☐ Mayfield Headrest   ☐ Tourniquet #: _____
☐ Lami-Frame   ☐ Arm ☐ Leg ☐ R ☐ L   Meds: _____   Irrigation Type: _____
☐ Shoulder Holder   Applied by: _____   _____   ☐ Heparin Amount: _____
☐ Beach Chair Attachment   Pressure: _____mm Hg   _____   ☐ NS Amount: _____
☐ Fracture Table   Time Up: _____   _____   ☐ LR Amount: _____
☐ Surgita Headrest   Time Down: _____   **Blood Products:** ☐ None   ☐ Triple Amount: _____
☐ Other: _____   ☐ PRC _____ Units   ☐ H_2O Amount: _____
Final Counts: ☐ FFP _____ Units   ☐ Glycerin Amount: _____
☐ Correct ☐ Incorrect   ☐ Cryo _____ Units   ☐ Other: _____
   ☐ Cell Saver _____   CCs Infused: _____
Circ. Signature: _____   **Specimens:** ☐ None
   ☐ Gross Only—Site: _____
   ☐ Frozen—Site: _____
   ☐ Fresh—Site: _____   INTRAOPERATIVE RECORD
   ☐ Routine—Site: _____   000020 (11/2002)

Figure 3.39.   Intraoperative Vital Signs Documentation in Graphic Format

University of Anystate Hospitals

ANESTHESIA RECORD
PAGE 1 OF 2

PATIENT LABEL

Date: _____   Time: _____

Age: ____ Sex: ____ Height: ____ Weight: ____ BP: ____ P: ____ R: ____ T: _____

Lab: _____   Status: _____

Allergies: _____   Last Intake: _____

Premedication: _____

☐ **Patient reassessed immediately prior to induction. Condition satisfactory for planned anesthesia.**

Vital Signs

Time		

Machine Check

Initials

Patient Position

☐ General
☐ Regional
☐ Local
☐ Monitored
☐ IVs (spinal/EPI needle)

Position

Prep

Site

Agent

Paresthesia

Catheter

Sensory Block TO

☐ Heat/Moisture Exchanger
☐ Warming Blanket
☐ Fluid Warmer
☐ Bair Hugger

Endotracheal Tube

Cuff Inflated

Laryngoscope Blade

Stylet

Direct Vision

Blind

Systolic
∨
Diastolic
∧
Pulse
∧⌣•
Respiration
○
Spon
●
Assist
⊙
Controlled

Surgery Start/End
⊗
Anesthesia Start/End
X
Anesthesia Start

Anesthesia End

240
220
200
180
160
140
120
100
80
60
40
20
15
10
5

Figure 3.39. (Continued)

University of Anystate Hospitals

ANESTHESIA RECORD
PAGE 2 OF 2

PATIENT LABEL

Monitors
☐ NIBP   ☐ R   ☐ L
☐ APB   ☐ R   ☐ L
☐ T (site): _____
☐ Pulse oximeter (site): _____
☐ ECG (lead): _____
☐ Airway gas monitor
☐ FiO$_2$ analyzer
☐ Pulmonary artery
☐ CVP
☐ EEG
☐ Stethoscope (site): _____
☐ SSEP
☐ Peripheral nerve stimulator
☐ Capnography

Remarks
_____

Fluid		Fluid		Fluid		Fluid		Fluid		Fluid	
Start	Finish	Start	Finish	Start	Finish	Start	Finish	Start	Finish	Start	Finish

Operation

Surgeon   Anesthesiologist   Date

Recovery Room
BP
P   T   °F   Endotracheal
                                   In ☐   Out ☐
Condition   SpO$_2$ %
Time: _____

Preanesthesia Evaluation

Review of Clinical Data

☐ Yes ☐ No   Patient Medical History Reviewed
☐ Yes ☐ No   Current Medications Reviewed
☐ Yes ☐ No   Allergies Reviewed
☐ Yes ☐ No ☐ N/A   Lab Results Reviewed
☐ Yes ☐ No ☐ N/A   CXR Results Reviewed
☐ Yes ☐ No ☐ N/A   EKG Results Reviewed

Pertinent Physical Exam

	Normal	Abnormal	Comments
EENT			
Respiratory			
Cardiac			
Mental Status			

Anesthesia History

☐ Yes ☐ No   Past Hx of Anesthesia Complications
☐ Yes ☐ No   Family Hx of Anesthesia Complications
☐ Yes ☐ No   History of Malignant Hyperthermia

ASA Classification

1   2   3   4   5   E

Airway Evaluation

Dentures: ☐ None ☐ Upper ☐ Lower
Capped Teeth: ☐ None ☐ Yes
Condition of Teeth: ☐ Good ☐ Fair ☐ Poor
Estimated Intubation Difficulty:
☐ Normal ☐ Moderately Difficult ☐ Difficult

Anesthesia Plan

☐ General   ☐ Rapid Sequence Intubation
☐ Spinal   ☐ MAC
☐ Epidural   ☐ Epidural for POPM
☐ Regional Block

☐ Alternatives, risks of anesthesia, and potential complications were discussed. Patient and/or guardian state understanding and acceptance of anesthesia plan.

Comments:

Anesthesiologist   Date

ANESTHESIA RECORD
000017 (11/2002)

Figure 3.40. Postanesthesia Record in Paper Format

Midwest Medical Center

POSTANESTHESIA RECORD
PAGE 1 OF 2

PATIENT LABEL

Date: _____
PACU Admission Time: _____ a.m./p.m.   Anesthesia End Time: _____ a.m./p.m.
Procedure: _____
Surgeon: _____   Anesthetist: _____
Anesthesia: ☐ General ☐ Regional ☐ Local Only ☐ Spinal ☐ Epidural ☐ Local w/Sedation
☐ Chart Orders Checked   Allergies: _____
Admitting Nurse(s): _____

Assessment

LOC: ☐ Drowsy ☐ Alert   ☐ Oriented ☐ Sleeping while
                                                                                     undisturbed
Respiratory Quality: ☐ Deep   ☐ Shallow ☐ Labored
Circulatory: ☐ Pink   ☐ Warm   ☐ Cool   ☐ Mottled
Circulation Check: ☐ N/A   ☐ Pink   ☐ Warm   ☐ Cool   ☐ Mottled
Operative: ☐ Pulse Palpable ☐ Unable to Palpate Due to Dressing
Extremity: ☐ Capillary Refill Adequate ☐ Other (see notes)
Dressing/Operative Site: _____ ☐ Dry and Intact ☐ Other (see notes)
IV Therapy: Fluid: _____ Site: _____ Amt.: _____ cc
☐ Patent, No Redness or Edema Noted   ☐ Other (see notes)
Level of Pain: _____ Init. _____

Vital Signs

Time	BP	Pulse	Resp.	Pain Level	Time	BP	Pulse	Resp.	Pain Level

Dressing Check: ☐ Time: ☐ Dry and Intact ☐ Other (see supplemental notes)
                           ☐ Time: ☐ Dry and Intact ☐ Other (see supplemental notes)

Medications

Medicine	Dosage	Route	Time Given	Initials

PACU Scoring

Time						
Activity						
R						
Circulation						
LOC						
Skin T						
Total						

Discharge Evaluation

☐ Vital Signs at Preoperative Level
☐ Meets PACU Score of 10 OR ☐ Return of Preoperative Level
☐ Minimal or No Pain
☐ Minimal or No Nausea
☐ Dressing Dry and Intact
☐ Ambulates with Minimal Assistance
☐ Responsible Adult Present to Accompany Patient Home

Initials: _____ Signature: _____
Initials: _____ Signature: _____
Initials: _____ Signature: _____

Plan of Care/Interventions

Potential Alteration in Mental Status   Goal: Return to Pre-Op Status
☐ Reoriented to time and place   ☐ Goal Met
☐ Other: _____

Potential for Fear and/or Anxiety   Goal: Reduction of Fear and Anxiety
☐ Oriented to Environment   ☐ Goal Met
☐ Encouraged to Verbalize Concerns
☐ Age-Appropriate Emotional Support Provided
☐ Family at Bedside
☐ Patients and/or Family's Questions Answered
☐ Other: _____

Potential Alteration in Comfort   Goal: Decrease Level of Pain
☐ Patient Repositioned for Comfort   ☐ Goal Met
☐ Pain Scale Used According to Verbal Communication Level
☐ Medication Given as Ordered
☐ Other: _____

Potential for Injury   Goal: Create a Safe Environment
☐ Siderails Elevated   ☐ Goal Met
☐ Ambulated with Assistance
☐ Family at Bedside
☐ Other: _____

Potential Alteration in Fluid Volume   Goal: Adequate I/O
☐ PO Fluids Given ☐ IV Discontinued ☐ Voided   ☐ Goal Met
☐ Antiemetic Medication Administered
☐ Other: _____

Knowledge Deficit/Potential   Goal: Exhibits Knowledge
for Post Op Complications at Home   of Post Op Care
☐ Need for home Care Assistance Assessed   ☐ Goal Met
Assistance Needed:
☐ No ☐ Yes If Yes: ☐ Physician ☐ Case Management Notified
☐ Written Discharge Instructions Given
☐ Prescriptions Given to Patient/Family
☐ Other: _____

Other Problems/Needs
_____
_____
_____

Discharge to		**Phase II Recovery**

Discharge _____ MD
Discharge to ☐ Home ☐ Room #: _____ Postop Contact #: _____
Discharged @: _____ Via ☐ Wheelchair ☐ Ambulance ☐ Stretcher
                                        ☐ Other _____

RN Signature: _____

Figure 3.40. (Continued)

Midwest Medical Center

POSTANESTHESIA RECORD
PAGE 2 OF 2

PATIENT LABEL

PACU Scoring Guide

Activity

2 = Able to move 4 extremities
1 = Able to move 2 extremities
0 = Able to move 0 extremities

Respirations

2 = Clear, unsupported
(strong cry, if pediatric)
1 = Obstructed, supported
(spontaneous respiration may
be shallow or slow)
0 = Apneic/mechanical ventilation/
Ambu

Circulation
(adults and children)

2 = BP ± 20 of preanesthesia level
1 = BP ± 20-50 of preanesthesia
level
0 = BP ± 50 or more of
preanesthesia level

Infants

2 = Radial pulse easy to palpate
1 = Axillary pulse palpable, radial
pulse weak
0 = Carotid is only palpable pulse

Consciousness

2 = Awake—Oriented to time
and place (preop level)
1 = Drowsy—Able to be aroused
on name calling or gentle
stimuli
0 = Unresponsive

Skin Temperature

2 = Warm, dry, pink
1 = Warm, dry, pale
0 = Cool, clammy, mottled

Supplemental Nursing Notes

_____
_____
_____
_____
_____
_____
_____
_____
_____
_____
_____
_____
_____
_____
_____
_____
_____

Postprocedure Followup

Date: _____ Time: _____

☐ Patient Contacted ☐ No Answer ☐ Answering Machine

Dressing: ☐ Dry and Intact ☐ Drainage Present (see comments)
☐ Redness Present (see comments)

Comfort: ☐ No Discomfort ☐ Mild Discomfort
☐ Moderate ☐ Severe Discomfort
Discomfort (any discomfort, see comments)

N/V: ☐ None ☐ Minimal ☐ Moderate ☐ Severe

Fever: ☐ No ☐ Yes:_____°F

Instructions: ☐ Easily Understood ☐ Further Instructions Needed
(see comments)

Comments:

_____
_____
_____
_____
_____
_____
_____
_____

Signature: _____

POSTANESTHESIA RECORD
000024 (11/2002)

Figure 3.41.   Postprocedure Record in Paper Format

University of Anystate Hospitals

POSTOPERATIVE RECORD
PAGE 1 OF 2

PATIENT LABEL

Type of Procedure: _____   Date: _____   Time Arrive on Unit: _____
Arrived Via: ☐ Bed   ☐ Stretcher   ☐ Wheelchair

Postprocedure Assessment

Level of Consciousness	☐ Alert ☐ Responds to Painful/Verbal Stimuli ☐ Drowsy ☐ Unresponsive
Oxygen	☐ Room Air ☐ Nasal Cannula ☐ Other @ _____ liter/min
Respiratory Quality	☐ Regular ☐ Irregular ☐ Other
Breath Sounds	☐ Clear all Fields ☐ Other: _____
Cardiac	☐ Regular ☐ Irregular ☐ Dysrhythmia
GI ☐ N/A	☐ Hypo Bowel Sound ☐ Hyper Bowel Sound ☐ Absent Bowel Sound
	☐ Firm ☐ Distended ☐ Tender ☐ Protuberant
Skin Color	☐ Pink ☐ Pale ☐ Mottled ☐ Cyanotic
Skin Condition	☐ Warm ☐ Dry ☐ Cold ☐ Clammy
Circ. √ Distal to Site	☐ N/A ☐ Warm ☐ Pink ☐ Cyanotic ☐ Mottled ☐ Cool

Peripheral Pulses (absent, +1, +2, +3, +4, Doppler)   _____ N/A
_____ R Rad   _____ R DP   _____ R PT   _____ Other
_____ L Rad   _____ L DP   _____ L PT

Dressing/Operative Site:_____   ☐ Dry and Intact
Dressing/Operative Site:_____   ☐ Dry and Intact

RN Signature: _____

IV Therapy
#1 Fluid: _____   Site: _____   Rate: _____
☐ No Redness or Swelling at Site   ☐ Other: _____
#2 Fluid: _____   Site: _____   Rate: _____
☐ No Redness or Swelling at Site   ☐ Other: _____
#3 Fluid: _____   Site: _____   Rate: _____
☐ No Redness or Swelling at Site   ☐ Other: _____

Drainage Tubes: ☐ N/A
Type: _____   ☐ Patency Checked Drainage: _____
Type: _____   ☐ Patency Checked Drainage: _____
Type: _____   ☐ Patency Checked Drainage: _____

Puncture Site: ☐ N/A
Location: _____
Sand Bag Intact: ☐ Yes ☐ No   Bleeding: ☐ Yes ☐ No
Hematoma: ☐ Yes ☐ No   Sheath Sutured: ☐ Yes ☐ No ☐ N/A

Sheath Removal   Date: _____   Time: _____   Initials: _____
Assessment Unchanged from Post Procedure   ☐ Yes   ☐ See Notes
Verbalizes Understanding of Sheath Removal   ☐ Yes   ☐ See Notes

Site Check Post Sheath Removal
Sandbag Intact	☐ Yes	☐ No
Hematoma	☐ Yes	☐ See Notes
Pain	☐ Yes	☐ See Notes
Loss of Distal Pulse	☐ Yes	☐ See Notes
Compression Device in Use	☐ Yes	☐ See Notes
Uncontrolled Bleeding	☐ Yes	☐ See Notes
Vasovagal Reaction	☐ Yes	☐ See Notes

Plan of Care   Clinical Pathway Continued

☐ **Potential for Alteration and Ventilation**
Goal: Adequate Air Exchange   ☐ Goal Met
   ☐ Continuous Pulse Oximetry in Use
   ☐ Coughing and Deep Breathing Encouraged
   ☐ O₂ Therapy Initiated as Ordered
   ☐ Incentive Spirometry Initiated as Ordered
   ☐ Other: _____

☐ **Potential Alteration Cardiovascular Function**
Goal: Hemodynamically Stable   ☐ Goal Met
   ☐ Continuous Cardiac Monitoring in Use
   ☐ Other: _____

☐ **Potential Alteration in Mental Status**
Goal: Return to Pre-Op Status   ☐ Goal Met
   ☐ Reoriented to Time and Place
   ☐ Other: _____

☐ **Potential for Fear and/or Anxiety**
Goal: Reduction of Fear and Anxiety   ☐ Goal Met
   ☐ Oriented to Environment
   ☐ Encouraged to Verbalize Concerns
   ☐ Age-Appropriate Emotional Support Provided
   ☐ Family at Bedside
   ☐ Patients/Families Questions Answered
   ☐ Other: _____

☐ **Potential for Injury**
Goal: Create a Safe Environment   ☐ Goal Met
   ☐ Side Rails Raised
   ☐ Ambulated with Assistance
   ☐ Family at Bedside
   ☐ Call Bell within Reach
   ☐ Bed in Low Position
   ☐ Other: _____

☐ **Knowledge Deficit/Potential for Postprocedure Complications at Home**
Goal: Exhibits Knowledge of Postprocedure Care   ☐ Goal Met
   ☐ Need for Home Care Assistance Assessed
   ☐ If Assistance Needed, Notify: ☐ Physician   ☐ Case Manager
   ☐ Written Discharge Instructions Reinforced. Copy to Patient.
   ☐ Prescription Given to Patient/Family with Instructions on Usage
   ☐ Explained Procedure for Transferring to Inpatient Unit
   ☐ Other: _____

☐ **Potential Alteration in Fluid Volume**
Goal: Adequate I/O   ☐ Goal Met
   ☐ IV Hydration Initiated
   ☐ Antiemetic Medication Administered
   ☐ PO Fluids Given without Nausea/Vomiting
   ☐ Other: _____

☐ **Potential Alteration in Comfort**
Goal: Decrease Level of Pain   ☐ Goal Met
   ☐ Patient Repositioned for Comfort
   ☐ Pain Level (0–10)
   ☐ Wong-Baker Face Scale for Pediatrics—Face Score: _____
   ☐ Reevaluation of Pain after Medication—Level of Pain: _____
   ☐ Medication Given as Ordered
   ☐ Other: _____

☐ **Other Problems/Needs**   ☐ Goal Met
_____
_____
_____

RN Signature: _____   Date: _____

Figure 3.41. (Continued)

University of Anystate Hospitals

POSTOPERATIVE RECORD
PAGE 2 OF 2

PATIENT LABEL

Postprocedure Record (page 2)

IV Site	Date	7–3	3–11	11–7	Date	7–3	3–11	11–7

Date: _____

0 NO HURT	2 HURTS LITTLE BIT	4 HURTS LITTLE MORE	6 HURTS EVEN MORE	8 HURTS WHOLE LOT	10 HURTS WORST

Pain Management (scale 0–10 for adults—Wong/Baker Faces for Pediatrics)

Time	Pain Scale	Medication/Dose	Initials	Response/Pain Scale	Time	Initials

Vital Sign Postprocedure/Sheath Removal

Time	LOC	T	BP	P	RR/O₂ Sat.	Pain Level	Peripheral Pulse	Site Check	Initials

Daily Care Record

Shift: Date	7–3	3–11	11–7	7–3	3–11	11–7
Bedrest						
Ambulating						
R or L Leg Straight						
SCD						
Antiembolism Hose						
PCA Pump						
Traction						
Telemetry						
Type of Diet						
Amount Eaten						
Bath/Shower/Bed						
Complete—Self/Assist.						
Oral Care/P.M. Care						
Other:						

Level of Consciousness (LOC) Scale
2 = Awake—Oriented to Preop Time and Place
1 = Drowsy—Able to Arouse with Name Calling or Gentle Stimuli
0 = Unresponsive—Unable to Arouse Except with Painful Stimuli

Date/Time	Notes:

Initials	Signature	Initials	Signature	Initials	Signature

POSTOPERATIVE RECORD
000022(11/2002)

Transfusion Records

Surgical and emergency patients sometimes require transfusions of whole blood and/or blood products. Blood transfusions carry an inherent risk for complications. Except in emergency situations, the patient's physician should discuss the relative risks and benefits with the patient and/or the patient's family before the procedure is performed. This discussion and patient consent must be documented in the patient's health record.

A **transfusion record** includes information on the type and amount of blood products the patient received, the source of the blood products, and the patient's reaction to the transfusion. The record also documents the blood group and Rh status of the patient and the donor, the results of cross-matching tests, and a description of the transfusion process. Every adverse reaction to a transfusion must be fully documented in the patient's health record.

Occasionally, hospitals receive information from area blood banks that a specific batch of blood products may have been contaminated with disease-causing organisms. In such cases, the Medicare *Conditions of Participation* require hospitals to notify the patients who received the tainted blood products and/or their physicians of the potential contamination. (The notification requirements are discussed in more detail in chapter 5.)

Postoperative Progress Notes

The surgeon primarily responsible for the case must write a brief postoperative progress note in the patient's record immediately after surgery and before the patient leaves the operative suite. The purpose of the note is to communicate postoperative care instructions to recovery room nurses. The note should also indicate the presence or absence of anesthesia-related complications or other postoperative abnormalities in addition to the patient's vital signs and general condition at the conclusion of the operation. Surgeons may also document postoperative orders in progress notes. (See figures 3.42 and 3.43, pp. 145–46.)

Recovery Room Records

Postsurgery patients are monitored in a dedicated recovery room until the effects of the anesthesia are completely reversed. Recovery room nurses monitor postsurgery patients very carefully until the patients are well enough to be moved to surgical intensive care or their regular rooms. (See figure 3.44, p. 147.) Same-day surgery patients receive the same level of care and observation as inpatients do until they are ready to leave the hospital.

Most hospitals have developed a **recovery room record** form that is used by nursing staff to document the patient's reaction to anesthesia and condition after surgery. Information on the patient's level of consciousness, overall medical condition, vital signs, and medications and intravenous fluids is documented by nurses when the patient enters the recovery room. The same information is documented when the patient is ready to be transferred or discharged. The status of any surgical dressings, catheters, tubes, and drains is also recorded.

The patient's surgical record should also include documentation that demonstrates that the patient met the facility's discharge criteria before being discharged or transferred. The name of the physician or surgeon who was responsible for the discharge must be included on the discharge order.

Operative Reports

Surgical procedures involve substantial medical, legal, and financial risks for patients, surgeons, and hospitals. For this reason, it is especially important that surgical documentation be complete, accurate, and timely. In addition to anesthesia and recovery room records, an operative report must be prepared for every surgical procedure performed outside the patient's room.

Figure 3.42. Postoperative Progress Note in Paper Format

Midwest Medical Center

POSTOPERATIVE PROGRESS NOTE

PATIENT LABEL

Procedure(s) Performed:
_____
_____
_____
_____
_____

Name of Primary Surgeon:
_____

Assistant(s):
_____

Findings:
_____
_____
_____
_____
_____

Technical Procedures Used:
_____
_____
_____
_____
_____

Specimens Removed:
_____
_____

Estimated Blood Loss:
_____

Postoperative Diagnosis:
_____
_____
_____
_____

Physician Signature: _____ Date: _____

POSTOPERATIVE PROGRESS NOTE
000025 (11/2002)

Figure 3.43.   Postoperative Orders in Paper Format

Midwest Medical Center

POSTOPERATIVE ORDERS

	PATIENT LABEL

Date: _____

Postoperative Diagnosis: _____

Operation: _____

Orders: Allergies:

Date/Time	RN Signature	Postop Orders Begin Here
		1. Position of Patient
		2. Ambulate
		3. Leg Exercises
		4. Medication for Pain
		5. Medication for Nausea
		6. Medication for Sleep
		7. Other Medications—Include Previous Orders to Be Continued
		8. Antibiotic
		9. Oral Intake
		10. IV Fluids (include blood)
		11. Tubes to Be Connected
		A. Nasogastric
		B. T Tube
		C. Thoracotomy
		D. Foley
		E. Other
		12. Catheterize
		13. Care of Dressing
		14. Drains
		15. Respiratory Care
		16. IPPB Freq. Duration Pressure Drug
		17. Vital Signs
		18. Intake and Output
		19. Lab Studies
		20. Other:

RN Signature: _____   Date: _____

Physician Signature: _____   Date: _____

POSTOPERATIVE ORDERS
000026 (11/2002)

Figure 3.44.   Postanesthesia Nursing Record in Paper Format

University of Anystate Hospitals

POSTANESTHESIA NURSING RECORD
PAGE 1 OF 4

PATIENT LABEL

Procedure: _____   Date: _____

Surgeon: _____ Anesthetist: _____   PACU Admission Time: _____ a.m./p.m.

Anesthesia: ☐ General ☐ Regional ☐ Local Only ☐ Epidural ☐ Local w/Sedation   Anesthesia End Time: _____ a.m./p.m.
☐ Chart Orders Checked   Allergies: _____

Phase I Assessment

Arrived Via: ☐ Stretcher   ☐ Bed   ☐ Infant Carried by Anesthetist   ☐ Crib
LOC: ☐ Drowsy   ☐ Reacting   ☐ Alert   ☐ Disoriented   ☐ Unresponsive
Circulatory:
  Skin: ☐ Pink   ☐ Warm   ☐ Cool   ☐ Mottled   ☐ Cyanotic
  Extremities: ☐ Pink   ☐ Warm   ☐ Cool   ☐ Mottled   ☐ Cyanotic   ☐ SCD _____
Airway Support: ☐ None   ☐ Oral   ☐ Nasal   ☐ Chin Lift   ☐ Jaw Thrust   ☐ ET Tube   ☐ Tracheostomy
Oxygen Ventilation: ☐ None   ☐ 40%   ☐ _____%   ☐ Mask   ☐ Cannula   ☐ T-Bar   ☐ LMA
                          ☐ Adequate Exchange   ☐ Ambu   ☐ Ventilator ☐ Other   ☐ Tent
Respiratory Quality: ☐ Deep   ☐ Shallow   ☐ Snoring   ☐ Stridor   ☐ Labored   ☐ Tachypnea
                          ☐ Regular   ☐ Irregular
Breath Sounds: ☐ Clear All Fields   ☐ Equal Bilat. ☐ Rates   ☐ Rhonchi   ☐ Wheezing   ☐ Other
Cardiac: ☐ Regular Rhythm: _____   ☐ Irregular Rhythm:_____
Abdomen: ☐ Soft   ☐ Firm   ☐ Distended

Dressing/Operative Site: _____ ☐ Dry and Intact   ☐ Other: _____
                          ☐ Peripad   ☐ Dry and Intact   ☐ Other:_____
                          ☐ Cast   ☐ Dry and Intact   ☐ Damp   ☐ Other: _____
                          ☐ Epidural   ☐ Dry and Intact   ☐ Other: _____
                          ☐ Packing   Site: _____

Drains: ☐ None   ☐ CBI Fluid: _____ Amt. on Admission: _____ ☐ Other: _____
☐ Foley Cath. ☐ Suprapubic   ☐ Patent Color of Drainage: _____   ☐ JP   Site: _____   ☐ Patent Color of Drainage: _____
☐ Hemovac Site: _____   ☐ Patent Color of Drainage: _____   ☐ NG   Site: _____   ☐ Patent Color of Drainage: _____
☐ Chest Tube Site: _____   ☐ Patent Color of Drainage: _____   ☐ Penrose Site: _____   ☐ Patent Color of Drainage: _____

IVs: ☐ None #1 Site: _____ Fluid: _____ Amount: _____   ☐ Patent, Dressing Dry and Intact, No Redness or Edema Noted   ☐ Other
          #2 Site: _____ Fluid: _____ Amount: _____   ☐ Patent, Dressing Dry and Intact, No Redness or Edema Noted   ☐ Other
          #3 Site: _____ Fluid: _____ Amount: _____   ☐ Patent, Dressing Dry and Intact, No Redness or Edema Noted   ☐ Other
          ☐ A-Line Site:_____ ☐ Calibrated to Monitor ☐ Heparin Flush ☐ Appropriate Waveform ☐ Other: _____
          ☐ Swan Site:_____   ☐ Calibrated to Monitor ☐ Heparin Flush ☐ Appropriate Waveform ☐ Other: _____

Physician Orders

PACU Orders	**Pain Control** **As Needed for Pain**
O₂ 3 LNC for O₂ Sat. < _____ for 24 hours	**Meperidine IV:** Dosage ☐ 6.25 mg ☐ 12.5 mg ☐ 25 mg ☐ Other: _____

PACU Orders

O$_2$ 3 LNC for O$_2$ Sat. < _____ for 24 hours
_____
_____
_____
_____
_____
_____

Diagnostic Studies
_____
_____
_____
_____
_____
_____
_____
_____
_____

Pain Control   **As Needed for Pain**

Meperidine IV: Dosage ☐ 6.25 mg ☐ 12.5 mg ☐ 25 mg ☐ Other: _____
                   Frequency ☐ q.5min. ☐ q.10min. ☐ q.15min. ☐ Other: _____
                   Maximum Dosage: _____ mg

Morphine IV: Dosage ☐ 1.0 mg ☐ 2.0 mg ☐ 5 mg ☐ Other: _____
                  Frequency ☐ q.5min. ☐ q.10min. ☐ q.15min. ☐ Other: _____
                  Maximum Dosage: _____ mg

Antiemetics   **As Needed for Nausea, Vomiting**

Phenergan IV: Dosage ☐ 6.25 mg ☐ 12.5 mg ☐ Other: _____
                  Frequency ☐ q.5min. ☐ q.10min. ☐ Other: _____
                  Maximum Dosage: _____ mg/h

Inapsine IV: Dosage ☐ 0.25 cc   ☐ Other: _____
                  Frequency: _____   Maximum Dosage: _____

Anzemet: Dosage ☐ 12.5 meq   ☐ Other: _____
                  Frequency: _____

Signature of MD: _____

Discharge after Score (≥) 8	**Discharge**
_____MD	_____MD

Figure 3.44.   (Continued)

University of Anystate Hospitals

POSTANESTHESIA NURSING RECORD
PAGE 2 OF 4

PATIENT LABEL

Ongoing Assessment/Evaluations/Documentation

Postop V/S: _____

Neurovascular/ Orthopedic Surgery Pulse Checks	R / L

Palpable=1+, 2+, 3+
√ = Yes X = No
B = Brisk S = Sluggish
W = Warm C = Cool
D = Doppler
U = Unable to palpate due to dressing/cast

Time			
Site			
Movement			
Sensation			
T			
Cap Refill			
P			

☐ See vascular flow sheet
☐ See neuro flow sheet

Sensory Chart
T-4 = Nipple line
T-6 = Xiphoid process
T-8 = Costal margin
T-10 = Umbilicus
T-12 = Iliac arrest
L-2, 3 = Thigh
S-2, 5 = Perineum

Site Code
A = L upper arm
B = R upper arm
C = L hip (LUOQ)
D = R hip (RUOQ)
E = L thigh
F = R thigh
G = Abdomen

IV Site Code
1 = R Extremity
2 = L Extremity
3 = Central Line
4 = Other (i.e., scalp)

Time, Activity, Respirations, Circulation, Consciousness, Temperature, Total, Pulse Oximetry, Temperature, CVP, Pap, Spinal Level, Epidural Level

Cuff ▽ BP △ A-Line ▼▲ NBP ∨∧ Pulse ● Warm Blanket B

BP scale: 250 240 230 220 210 200 190 180 170 160 150 140 130 120 110 100 90 80 70 60 50 40 30 20 10 0

Temperatures Tympanic, unless indicated:
R = Rectal
O = Oral
A = Axillary

Respirations
Dressing _____
Pain Level

Medication	Amount	Route	Site	Time/Initials				Time Started	Fluid, Amount, Additives	Initials

Activity
2 = Able to move 4 extremities
1 = Able to move 2 extremities
0 = Able to move 0 extremities

Respirations
2 = Clear, unsupported (strong cry if pediatric)
1 = Obstructed, supported (spontaneous respiration may be shallow or slow)
0 = Apneic/mechanical (ventilation/ambu)
Mandatory Score = 2 in Respiratory

Circulation
Adults and Children
2 = BP plus or minus 20 of preanesthesia level
1 = BP plus or minus 20-50 of preanesthesia level
0 = BP plus or minus 50 or more of preanesthesia level
Infants
2 = Radial pulse easy to palpate
1 = Axillary pulse palpable, radial pulse weak
0 = Carotid is only palpable pulse

Consciousness
2 = Awake—Oriented to time and Place (preop level)
1 = Drowsy—Able to be aroused with name calling or gentle stimuli
0 = Unresponsive

Temperature
2 = Tympanic T > 96° F, R= > 97°, 0= > 96°, A= >96°
1 = Tympanic T 95–96° F, R=96-97°, 0=95–96°, A=94–96°
0 = Tympanic T < 95°, R= < 96°, 0= < 95°, A= < 94°

Dressing
0 = Dry
* = See note

Miscellaneous
* = See note

Ongoing Assessment Nurse: _____ RN _____ RN _____ RN

Figure 3.44.   (Continued)

University of Anystate Hospitals

POSTANESTHESIA NURSING RECORD
PAGE 3 OF 4

PATIENT LABEL

Plan of Care/Interventions

☐ **Potential for Alteration in Ventilation**   **Goal: Adequate Air Exchange**
☐ Continuous pulse oximetry in use   ☐ Goal Met
☐ Coughing and deep breathing encouraged
☐ O₂ therapy initiated as ordered
☐ Airway out @ _____   ☐ Extubated @ _____
☐ O₂ discontinued @: _____
☐ O₂ reapplied @: _____ via mask @ _____ %
☐ O₂ reapplied @ _____ via nasal cannula @ _____ l/m
☐ Other: _____

☐ **Potential Alteration in Cardiovascular Function   Goal: Hemodynamically Stable**
☐ Continuous cardiac monitoring   ☐ Goal Met
☐ Other: _____

☐ **Potential Alteration in Mental Status**   **Goal: Return to Preop Status**
☐ Reoriented to time and place   ☐ Goal Met
☐ Other: _____

☐ **Potential for Fear and/or Anxiety**   **Goal: Reduction of Fear and Anxiety**
☐ Oriented to PACU environment
☐ Encouraged to verbalize concerns
☐ Age-appropriate emotional support provided
☐ Family at bedside
☐ Patient's and/or family's questions answered
☐ Other: _____

☐ **Potential for Injury**   **Goal: Create a Safe Environment**
☐ Side rails elevated   ☐ Goal Met
☐ Family at bedside
☐ Other: _____

☐ **Potential Alteration in Comfort**   **Goal: Decrease Level of Pain**
☐ Patient repositioned for comfort   ☐ Goal Met
☐ Medication given as ordered
☐ Scale used according to verbal communication level
☐ Other: _____

☐ **Potential Alteration in Body Temperature**   **Goal: Return to Preop Status**
☐ Bair hugger applied   ☐ Goal Met
☐ Warm blanket applied
☐ Warmed IV fluids given
☐ Other: _____

☐ **Potential Alteration in Tissue Perfusion   Goal: Adequate Vascular Perfusion**
☐ Capillary refill monitored on operative limb   ☐ Goal Met
☐ Circulation of operative limb monitored
☐ Other: _____

☐ **Potential Alteration in Fluid Volume**   **Goal: Adequate I/O**
☐ IV infusing   Goal Met
☐ Antiemetic medication administered
☐ Other: _____

☐ **Other Problems/Needs**
_____
_____
_____

Intake				Output				
Time	IV	Blood	PO	CBI	Urine ☐ Foley ☐ Voided	☐ NG ☐ CT	Emesis	☐ Hemovac ☐ JP	Other
OR I/O								
PACU I/O								
Total I/O								

Discharge IV Fluid

Type: _____   Amount: _____

Type: _____   Amount: _____

Type: _____   Amount: _____

Type: _____   Amount: _____

Phase I Discharge Assessment

LOC   ☐ Drowsy   ☐ Alert   ☐ Oriented   ☐ Sleeping While Undisturbed

Circulatory:
Skin   ☐ Pink   ☐ Warm   ☐ Cool   ☐ Mottled
Extremities   ☐ Pink   ☐ Warm   ☐ Cool   ☐ Mottled
Oxygen   ☐ Room Air   ☐ O₂ @ _____ %   _____   ☐ Vent
Respiratory Quality   ☐ Deep   ☐ Regular   ☐ Other: _____
Breath Sounds   ☐ Clear All Fields   ☐ Equal Bilat.   ☐ Rales
☐ Rhonchi   ☐ Wheezing
Cardiac   ☐ Regular Rhythm   ☐ Cardiac Monitoring   ☐ Rhythm: _____
Dressing/Operative Site: _____   ☐ Dry and Intact   ☐ Other: _____
Drains   ☐ None   ☐ Secure and Patent
IV Sites   ☐ Patent, Dressing Dry and Intact, No Redness or Edema Noted
☐ Other (see nurses' notes)
   ☐ A-Line: ☐ To Monitor   ☐ Heparin Flush   ☐ Appropriate Waveform
   ☐ Swan: ☐ To Monitor   ☐ Heparin Flush   ☐ Appropriate Waveform
Comfort   ☐ Comfortable   ☐ Other
Discharged To: ☐ Phase II Recovery   ☐ Room #: _____   ☐ Side Rails Up
☐ Prescription on Chart _____
_____

Discharge Time: _____ a.m./p.m.
☐ Family Notified   ☐ Unable to Reach
Report Called to: _____   Transported by: _____

RN Signature: _____

☐ Patient Reassessed—Agree with PACU Discharge   V/S: _____

_____ a.m./p.m.
RN Receiving Patient   Time

Figure 3.44. (Continued)

University of Anystate Hospitals

POSTANESTHESIA NURSING RECORD
PAGE 4 OF 4

PATIENT LABEL

Rhythm Strips

Supplemental Nursing Notes

POSTANESTHESIA NURSING RECORD
000023 (11/2002)

An **operative report** is a formal document prepared by the principal surgeon to describe the surgical procedure(s) performed for the patient. (See figures 3.45 and 3.46, pp. 152–54.) Each report includes the following information:

- Patient identification, including name and record number
- Patient's preoperative and postoperative diagnoses and indications for surgery
- Descriptions of the procedures performed
- Descriptions of all normal and abnormal findings
- Descriptions of any specimens removed
- Descriptions of the patient's medical condition before, during, and after the operation
- Estimated blood loss
- Descriptions of any unique or unusual events that occurred during the course of the surgery
- Names of the surgeons and their assistants
- Date and duration of the surgery
- Signature of principal physician, credentials, and date the report was written

Operating room nurses maintain a record of the number ligatures, sutures, packs, drains, sponges, instruments, and needles used during the procedure. This information may also be included in the surgeon's operative report.

The operative report should be written or dictated immediately after surgery and filed in the patient's health record as soon as possible. Some hospitals may require surgeons to include brief descriptions of the operations in their postoperative progress notes when delays in dictation or transcription are likely. The progress note can then be referred to by other caregivers until the final operative report becomes available.

Pathology Reports

Pathology examinations must be performed on every specimen or foreign object removed or expelled from a patient during a surgical procedure. Each examination includes a microscopic and macroscopic (or gross) evaluation of the specimen, which is fully described in a **pathology report.** Some hospitals have established medical staff rules that exempt some types of specimens from microscopic examination. Examples of such specimens include normal placentas, tonsils, and foreign bodies such as bullets.

Pathology reports must be prepared by pathologists, specialty physicians who analyze surgical specimens, perform autopsies, and supervise other laboratory services. Pathology reports on surgical specimens must be authenticated by the pathologist who performed the examination and then placed in the surgery section of the patient's health record. (See figures 3.47 and 3.48, pp. 155–56, for examples of pathology reports.) The following basic information is usually included in pathology reports:

- Patient identification, including name and record number
- Date of examination
- Description of the tissue examined
- Findings of the microscopic and macroscopic examination of the specimen
- Diagnosis or diagnoses
- Name, credentials, and signature of the pathologist

Figure 3.45.   Operative Report in Paper Format

Midwest Medical Center

OPERATIVE REPORT
PAGE 1 OF 2

PATIENT, TWEETY PYE
00555066
DOB: 02/18/1948

DATE: 06/02/2003

SURGEON: Douglas Default

ASSISTANT: Stanley Cutter

ANESTHETIC: Spinal

PREOPERATIVE DIAGNOSES:

1.   Intrauterine pregnancy, term, previous cesarean section, voluntary repeat cesarean section
2.   Multiparity, voluntary sterilization

POSTOPERATIVE DIAGNOSES:

1.   Intrauterine pregnancy, term, previous cesarean section, voluntary repeat cesarean section
2.   Multiparity, voluntary sterilization
3.   Delivery of viable unengaged 6 pound 2 ounce female, APGAR 8–9

OPERATION:

1.   Low-segment transverse cesarean section
2.   Bilateral partial salpingectomy

COMPLICATIONS: None

DRAINS: One Foley catheter in urinary bladder

ESTIMATED BLOOD LOSS: Approximately 500 to 600 cc

PACKS: None

DESCRIPTION OF OPERATION: After satisfactory level of spinal anesthesia was obtained, the patient was placed in the dorsal supine position with mild left lateral uterine displacement. The lower abdominal skin tissues were prepped with a Hibiclens solution. She was then draped with sterile drapes in a sterile manner.

There was a previous transverse skin scar on the lower abdominal skin. A repeat transverse skin incision was made very carefully with sharp dissection. The fascia of the anterior abdominal wall was incised in a lateral crescentic manner exposing the rectus muscles, which were then bluntly divided in the midline exposing the peritoneum, which was then carefully incised in a vertical manner. There was a wetting amount of peritoneal fluid. The peritoneum reflection over the lower anterior uterine segment was then incised in a superficial transverse manner, and the "bladder flap" was gently pushed off the lower segment without difficulty.

Figure 3.45.   (Continued)

Midwest Medical Center

OPERATIVE REPORT
PAGE 2 OF 2

PATIENT, TWEETY PYE
00555066
DOB: 02/18/1948

A transverse uterine incision was made very carefully with both sharp and blunt dissection. The myometrium was noted to be only 2 to 3 mm in thickness. The amniotic fluid was clear. The unengaged vertex was delivered through the uterine and abdominal incision without difficulty. The nasal and oropharynx were suctioned with bulb suction prior to the newborn's initial inspiration. The remainder of the delivery was accomplished without difficulty. The cord was clamped and severed, and the newborn was handed crying and in good condition to the awaiting nursery personnel.

The placenta was then manually removed from a fundal location showing a central insertion of a three-vessel cord. There were no visible extensions of the uterine incision. Both tubes and ovaries appeared normal for pregnant state. The uterine incision was then closed with a running interlocking #1 chromic suture.

With the patient's strong desire for permanent sterilization, approximately 1 to 1.5 cm segment of the isthmic portion of each fallopian tube was isolated with Babcock clamps, doubly ligated and excised, and sent to the laboratory labeled as portion of left and right fallopian tube, respectively. Hemostasis was deemed adequate. Both tubes appeared occluded.

The abdominal cavity was irrigated with copious amounts of warm normal saline. The first sponge, needle, and instrument counts were correct. The parietal peritoneum was then closed with a running 0 chromic suture. Hemostasis was deemed adequate in the subfascial space. The fascia was then approximated with running 0 PDS suture. Hemostasis was deemed adequate in the subcutaneous tissue. The skin was then approximated with running 3-0 Vicryl subcuticular suture. Sterile dressing was placed upon the incision.

The patient tolerated the procedure quite well and was sent to the recovery room in good condition. The newborn was taken to the nursery by the nursery personnel in good condition. The second and third sponge, needle, and instrument counts were corrected.

Signature:

Douglas D Default   6/2/03
Douglas D. Default, MD   Date

d: 06/02/2003
t: 06/04/2003
DDD, MD/sf

Figure 3.46. Operative Report in Electronic Format

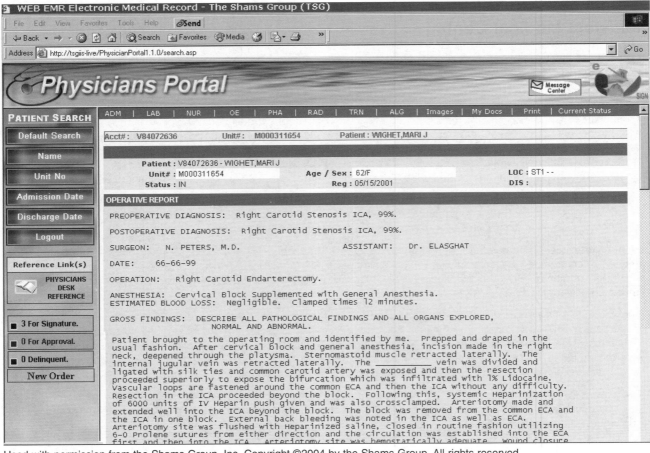

Preliminary pathology results are sometimes communicated to the surgical team while the procedure is still in progress. The purpose of the preliminary report is to provide information about the characteristics of any neoplasms or other abnormalities that have been removed for examination. The information allows the surgeons to modify their operative scope when the condition is more or less widespread than originally estimated.

Implant Information

Millions of Americans have undergone surgery for the implantation of artificial joints and heart valves, cardiac pacemakers, ocular lenses, and other types of medical devices in the past few decades. Although most of these devices are safe, there have been periodic product alerts and recalls.

The International Implant Registry was created in 1988. It collects information about patients who have received implants worldwide. Since 1991, federal regulations have required manufacturers to number and track many types of implantable devices so that patients and their physicians can be notified of potential safety concerns. In addition, hospitals and other health-care organizations are required to report deaths and serious illnesses that appear to have been the result of malfunctioning medical devices to the Food and Drug Administration. Some hospitals maintain their own implant registries in addition to taking part in the International Implant Registry.

Figure 3.47.   Surgical Pathology Consultation Report in Paper Format

Midwest Medical Center

SURGICAL PATHOLOGY CONSULTATION

PATIENT, SWEETPEA C.
007770021
DOB: 12/18/1931

ADMITTING PHYSICIAN: M. D. Doctor

CONSULT PHYSICIAN 1:

CONSULT PHYSICIAN 2:

ACCESSIONED IN LAB: 05/20/2003

ACCESSION #: S-03-010101

DATE OF SURGERY: 5/20/2003

SPECIMEN: A-Vag Mucosa

CLINICAL DATA: Cystocele/rectocele, stress incontinence

GROSS: Received are four wrinkled, variegated, pink/tan portions of vaginal mucosa, which are 7 × 6 × 1 cm in aggregate dimension. Representative portions of each are submitted for microscopic evaluation. M/1/pg.

MICROSCOPIC COMMENT: Sections are of squamous mucosa. There are no atypia.

DIAGNOSIS: Squamous mucosa, multiple portions exhibiting no atypia (vaginal)

Signature:

_____   _5/20/03_____
Walter Q. Pathman, MD   Date

d: 05/20/2003
t: 05/23/2003
WQP, MD/jt

Figure 3.48.   Surgical Pathology Consultation Report in Electronic Format

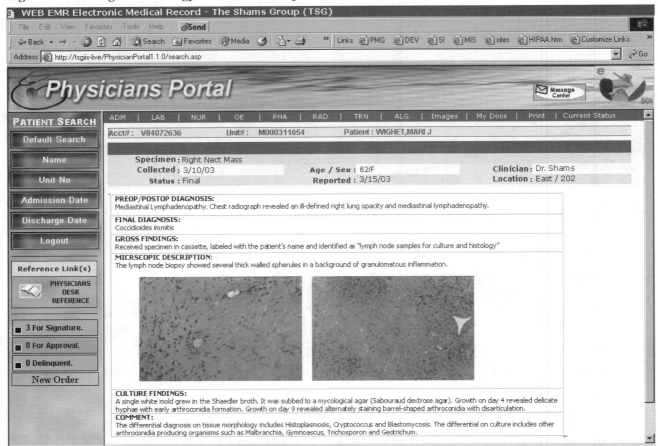

Information about the type of medical device, its manufacturer, and any product numbers on the device should be included in the operative report for the implantation procedure. In addition, for medical devices that require batteries, such as pacemakers, the operative reports should also indicate how often the devices must be replaced to ensure patient safety.

Transplantation and Organ Donation Records

Organ transplants have become increasingly common since the first attempts were made in the 1950s and 1960s. Today, thousands of patients every year receive kidneys, livers, hearts, and lungs salvaged from healthy patients who died from injuries and other causes. Organ donations from live donors have also become quite common, and it is not unusual for a family member to donate a kidney or part of his or her liver to a child or sibling. Bone marrow transplants from live donors have also saved the lives of thousands of cancer patients when other treatments failed.

Living donors must undergo surgery to remove bone marrow, kidneys, and other organs for transplantation to another patient. The surgical teams for the donor and the recipient must prepare operative reports for both patients, and the reports must follow the same standards as any other operative record.

Because of a shortage of transplantable organs and the difficulty of matching donors to recipients, transplantation entails a number of ethical problems. To ensure that the available organs are going to the most suitable recipients, the national Organ Procurement and Transplantation Network was implemented. Patients who need transplants are placed on a national waiting list. The application for the waiting list reports information about the patient, such as race, ethnicity, and geographic location.

The Medicare *Conditions of Participation* require hospitals to provide organ donation information to the families of potential organ donors. When a patient is near death and the family has decided to donate his or her organs, documentation that shows that the transplantation network has been notified must be placed in the patient's record. Arrangements should be made to harvest the patient's organs soon after death, and those procedures should also be documented in the patient's health record.

Discharge Summaries

The **discharge summary** is a concise account of the patient's illness, course of treatment, response to treatment, and condition at discharge. (Other terms for this type of documentation include *discharge abstract* and *clinical resume.*) The physician principally responsible for the patient's hospital care writes and signs the discharge summary. The discharge summary must be completed within thirty days after discharge for most patients but within twenty-four hours for patients transferred to other facilities. Discharge summaries are not always required for patients who were hospitalized for less than forty-eight hours.

The functions of the discharge summary include:

- Ensuring the continuity of future care by providing information to the patient's primary care physician and any consulting physicians
- Providing information to support the activities of the medical staff review committee
- Providing concise information that can be used to answer information requests from authorized individuals or entities

Hospitals are required to collect specific data elements at the time of discharge. (Standardized clinical data sets are discussed later in this chapter. See figures 3.49 through 3.51, pp. 158–60.) These data include:

- Name of the physician principally responsible for the patient's care
- Date and time of discharge
- Principal and secondary diagnoses
- ICD-9-CM code for the external cause of the patient's injury, if applicable
- Diagnostic and therapeutic procedures and the dates on which the procedures were performed
- Name of the surgeon or surgeons who performed the surgical procedures, if applicable
- Disposition of the patient (for example, transferred to a subacute facility or a rehabilitation facility or discharged to home)

Accreditation standards and the Medicare *Conditions of Participation* require that the patient's principal diagnosis be documented by the attending physician in the patient's health record no more than thirty days after discharge. The **principal diagnosis** is the condition established, after study, to have been the main reason for the patient's admission for inpatient treatment. The **principal procedure** is the procedure that was performed for the definitive treatment (rather than the diagnosis) of the main condition or a complication of the condition. A **complication** is defined as a condition that began after the patient was admitted for inpatient care. Pre-existing conditions that affected the patient's care are called **comorbidities.**

Figure 3.49. Discharge Summary in Paper Format

Midwest Medical Center

DISCHARGE SUMMARY

SAYLORMEN, POPEYE T.
333333333
DOB: 02/09/1961

PHYSICIAN/SURGEON: Philip P. Heartstopper, MD

DATE OF DISCHARGE: 05/18/2003

PRINCIPAL OPERATION AND PROCEDURE: OPCAB $\times$ 3, left internal mammary artery of the LAD, saphenous vein graft to D-1, and saphenous vein graft to OM-1

HISTORY OF PRESENT ILLNESS: Mr. Saylormen was seen at the request of Dr. Doctor regarding surgical treatment of ischemic heart disease. He is a 42-year-old male with a family history of coronary artery disease. He smokes a pipe and had a previous myocardial infarction approximately three years ago. His current status is postangioplasty. While working on a construction project, he developed anginal-type symptoms and was seen in the emergency room and then admitted to the hospital for further evaluation.

ADMITTING DIAGNOSIS: Coronary artery disease

HOSPITAL COURSE: The patient underwent cardiac catheterization and was found to have significant three-vessel coronary artery disease. It was felt that he would benefit from undergoing an OPCAB procedure. On 05/14/03, the patient underwent OPCAB $\times$ 3 as described above. The patient tolerated the procedure well and returned to the Cardiothoracic Intensive Care Unit hemodynamically stable. On postoperative day one, he was weaned from mechanical ventilation, extubated, and transferred to the Cardiothoracic Step-Down Unit, where he continued on a progressive course of recovery. On postoperative day four, he was up and about in his room and the halls without difficulty. Upon discharge, he was tolerating his diet well. His lungs were clear. His abdomen was soft, and his incisions were unremarkable. His vital signs were stable. He was in normal sinus rhythm. His heart rate was in the 70s and 80s. Blood pressure had been running consistently in the low 110s/60s. He was afebrile. Oxygen saturations on room air were reported at 97%.

LABORATORY DATA AT DISCHARGE: BUN 14, Creatinine 0.9, H&H 8.8 and 25.4

MEDICATIONS AT DISCHARGE: Lisinopril 5 mg q.d.; Lipitor 80 mg q.d.; metoprolol 50 mg q.d.; aspirin 81 mg q.d.; Darvocet-N 100—one to two tablets every 4–6 hours as needed for pain; iron sulfate 325 mg q.d. $\times$ 30 days; and Colace 100 mg b.i.d. $\times$ 30 days

DIET: He may follow a regular diet.

FINAL DIAGNOSIS: Coronary artery disease

DISPOSITION: No lifting greater than 10 pounds. No driving for 4–6 weeks. He may shower but he should not take a tub bath. Follow up with Dr. Doctor in 1–2 weeks.

_____   5/18/03
Philip P. Heartstopper, MD   _____
                                                              Date

d: 05/18/2003
t: 05/19/2003
PPH, MD/mb

Figure 3.50. Discharge Summary in Electronic Format

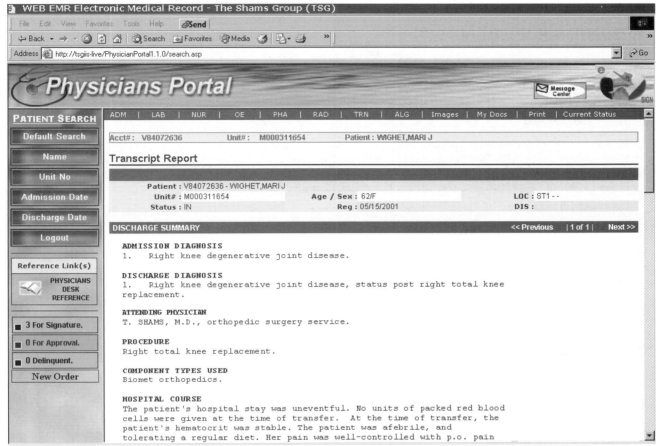

At patient discharge, hospitals are also required to collect and/or update the demographic and clinical data to be included on reimbursement claims. For inpatient services, as many as eight additional diagnostic codes can be reported in addition to the principal diagnosis. Up to five additional procedural codes can be reported along with the principal procedure. The additional diagnostic codes represent any comorbidities and/or complications that modified the course of the patient's illness and so should be considered in determining the amount of payment. The principal and additional procedural codes represent the most significant actions taken to diagnose and treat the patient's illness. The diagnostic and procedural codes are used for determining reimbursement for commercial third-party payers and diagnosis-related group assignments for Medicare patients.

Despite the best efforts of hospital caregivers and physicians, some patients die while they are hospitalized. In such cases, the principal physician should add a summary statement to the patient's health record to document the circumstances surrounding the patient's death. The statement can take the form of a final progress note, a discharge summary, or a separate report. The statement should indicate the reason for the patient's admission, his or her diagnosis and course in the hospital, and a description of the events that led to his or her death.

Discharge Instructions

The discharge summary usually includes specific instructions for patient care after discharge. The instructions for aftercare may be given directly to the patient or to his or her caregiver at

Figure 3.51.   Discharge Summary, Short Form, in Paper Format

Anytown Community Hospital

SHORT-FORM DISCHARGE SUMMARY

PATIENT LABEL

DATE OF DISCHARGE: _____

REASON FOR HOSPITALIZATION: _____

_____

_____

SIGNIFICANT FINDINGS: _____

_____

_____

CONDITION/CONCLUSIONS AT DISCHARGE: _____

_____

_____

PROCEDURES AND TREATMENT: _____

_____

_____

INSTRUCTIONS TO PATIENT/FAMILY: _____

_____

_____

DISCHARGE DIAGNOSIS(ES): _____

_____

_____

Physician Signature: _____   Date: _____

SHORT-FORM DISCHARGE SUMMARY
0034632 (02/2002)

the time of discharge. Discharge instructions usually include the primary physician's recommendations for diet and activity levels, prescriptions for any needed medications, and referrals for follow-up care. Many hospitals also provide standardized aftercare instructions to patients who underwent inpatient or outpatient surgical procedures or received other relatively common therapeutic services (for example, chemotherapy).

To ensure patient safety after hospital treatment, it is vital that the patient receive clear, concise discharge instructions. Ideally, patient instructions should be communicated both verbally and in writing. The healthcare professional (usually the patient's primary nurse) who delivers the instructions to the patient or the caregiver should also complete health record documentation that indicates that he or she explained the instructions before the patient left the facility. In addition, the person receiving the instructions should be asked to sign a form verifying that he or she understands the instructions. A copy of the written instructions should then be filed in the patient's health record. (See figure 3.52, pp. 162–63, for an example of patient instructions.)

When someone other than the patient assumes responsibility for the patient's aftercare, the record should indicate that the instructions were given to the party responsible. Documentation of patient education may be accomplished by using forms that prompt the person providing instruction to cover specific information.

Autopsy Reports

A hospital **autopsy report** is a description of the examination of a patient's body after he or she has died. Autopsies are usually conducted when there is some question about the cause of death or when information is needed for educational or legal purposes. The purpose of the autopsy is to determine or confirm the cause of death or to provide more information about the course of the patient's illness. (See figure 3.53, pp. 164–67, for an example of an autopsy report.)

When local authorities suspect that a patient's death may have been the result of a crime, a local medical examiner may conduct the autopsy rather than a hospital pathologist. In such cases, the patient's body is generally moved to a county facility for autopsy. In most states, medical examiners are required to issue provisional autopsy reports within three days of the autopsy and final reports within sixty days.

Authorizations for autopsy, signed by the patients' next of kin or by law enforcement officials, should also be filed in the patients' permanent health records. Copies of hospital autopsy reports should also be stored in the patients' records.

Specialty Care Documentation

Specialty care records often include information that is not required in general medical and surgical records. Government regulations, accreditation standards, and professional practice standards dictate unique content requirements for several types of specialty care records. However, the basic content and documentation guidelines that apply to general health records apply equally to specialty care records.

Obstetrical Services

The hospital records for pregnant women admitted for labor and delivery contain elements similar to general health records. The obstetrician's records of prenatal care constitute documentation of the patient's preadmission history and physical. At admission, the physician also prepares a note describing the patient's progress since he or she last saw her for prenatal care. (See figure 3.54, p. 168.) For normal deliveries, a **labor and delivery record** takes the place of an operative report. (See figure 3.55, pp. 169–73.)

Figure 3.52.   Example of Patient Discharge Instructions

University of Anystate Hospitals

PATIENT/FAMILY INSTRUCTIONS
PAGE 1 OF 2

PATIENT LABEL

This is a guide for your care. Call your doctor for any problems or changes that concern you.

Diet	Diet: _____ If on special diet and have questions, call dietitian.		**Managing Your Meds** Discussed (Place a checkmark if medication handouts given) ↓

Medications (list all medications)

Name/Dose	How to Take	

Activities/Special Care

Activities (Check as indicated)
- ☐ Crutches/walker
- ☐ Walk with assistance
- ☐ Gradually resume normal activity
- ☐ Bedrest
- ☐ Other _____

Dressing and Wound Care
(Report increased pain, redness, swelling, drainage, or fever)
- ☐ Doctor to change dressing
- ☐ Keep dressing dry
- ☐ If no dressing, keep incision clean and dry
- ☐ Clean wound and change dressing

Additional Instructions (PEARLS)

Follow-Up (appointments/equipment/referrals)

Agency	Phone	Arrangements (instructions provided by agency)

Dr. _____ Date/Time _____ ☐ Call for an appointment
Dr. _____ Date/Time _____ ☐ Call for an appointment
Dr. _____ Date/Time _____ ☐ Call for an appointment

I understand the above instructions and have the ability to carry these out after discharge. I am aware of the importance of medical follow-up with my doctor.

Patient/Patient Rep. Signature: _____ Date: _____

RN Signature: _____ Date: _____

Figure 3.52.   (Continued)

University of Anystate Hospitals

PATIENT/FAMILY INSTRUCTIONS
PAGE 2 OF 2

PATIENT LABEL

Discharge Date: _____   Time: _____   Mode: _____

_____

Discharged With:

☐ Family member   ☐ Friend   ☐ By self   ☐ Other: _____

_____

Escorted by: ☐ Hospital Attendant   ☐ Ambulance Attendant

_____

RN Discharge Assessment

_____

_____

_____

_____

_____

_____

Continuing Care Assessment	Care Plan	☐ All goals resolved on IPOC/clinical path/plan of care. Exceptions documented.
	Discharge with: ☐ Self/family care	• Patient and/or family verbalized an understanding of instructions. Person (s) to assist if needed: _____
	Discharge with: ☐ Support services	• Patient will receive follow-up with a referral agency or extended care facility. See front of form.
	Discharge to: ☐ Home ☐ Home with home health ☐ Extended care facility ☐ Other: _____	

☐ Patient Expired   Date: Time: Valuables Given to: ☐ Family   ☐ Funeral Home   ☐ Security

☐ Patient Left without Permission   Date: Time:

RN Signature: _____   Date: _____

PATIENT INSTRUCTIONS
5435680 (03/2002)

Figure 3.53.   Autopsy Report

Lincoln County Hospital

AUTOPSY REPORT
PAGE 1 OF 4

O'PATIENT, RENATA H.
4378802133524
DOB: 02/18/1958

ACCESSION NUMBER:	1-12132003
DATE OF DEATH:	12/13/2003
ADMITTING PHYSICIAN:	Nelda Oncodoct, DO
CONSULTING PHYSICIAN #1:	Leo Kardiovsky, MD
CONSULTING PHYSICIAN #2:	NA

DATE OF AUTOPSY: 12/15/2003
PATHOLOGIST: Frank Reeper, MD
PROSECTOR: Nelda Oncodoct, DO
ATTENDANT: Georges Helper

FINAL ANATOMICAL DIAGNOSES

CLINICAL DIAGNOSES:

1. Metastatic sarcoma

2. Possible sepsis

3. History of thyroid carcinoma

4. Hypocalcemia

5. Hypokalemia

PATHOLOGICAL DIAGNOSES:

1a. Possible primary osteosarcoma of superior sternum/anterior rib cage with superior mediastinal extension

1b. Metastatic osteosarcoma involving lungs extensively and T5 vertebral body with pathologic fracture

2a. Hemorrhagic bronchopneumonia

2b. Premortem sputum culture positive for Staphylococcus aureus (cocci identified in inflamed areas of lung at autopsy)

2c. Diffuse alveolar damage syndrome, lungs (shock lung)

3. No evidence of recurrent thyroid carcinoma, examination of neck not included

4. No anatomic correlate

5. No anatomic correlate

INCIDENTAL FINDINGS:

6. Cortical nodules, right adrenal gland

7. Angiolipoma, left kidney

8. Myocardial hypertrophy, left ventricle

9. Diverticulosis, colon

Signature: _Frank G Reeper, MD_   12/15/03
           PATHOLOGIST   DATE

Figure 3.53. (Continued)

Lincoln County Hospital

AUTOPSY REPORT
PAGE 2 OF 4

O'PATIENT, RENATA H.
4378802133524
DOB: 02/18/1958

CASE HISTORY: This 45-year-old, white female was admitted to the Medical ICU at County Hospital on 12/12/2003 after presenting earlier that day at Dr. Oncodoct's office with profound general weakness and difficulty breathing. The patient's past medical history indicated a history of thyroidectomy for tall-cell variant papillary carcinoma. She was treated postthyroidectomy with I-131 and external beam radiation because of multiple lymph node metastases. She had been diagnosed last month with metastatic sarcoma, which presented as a symptomatic T5 vertebral compression fracture. She had also developed progressive swelling of the legs, but a CT scan of the abdomen and pelvis performed several days before admission showed no evidence of venous thrombosis.

On admission, she had a potassium level of 2.5, calcium of 4.8, and phosphorus of 7.3. She was initially treated with two amps of calcium gluconate and potassium chloride administered intravenously. A chest X ray performed upon admission showed extensive masses within the lung fields, consistent with metastatic disease. Other studies performed after admission showed a free T-4 of 4.04 ng per deciliter (0.71 to 1.85). Shortly after admission, the patient was intubated and placed on a ventilator. A cardiology consultant noted pump failure secondary to tumor burden. The patient was febrile at admission, and her hypotension was thought to be secondary to sepsis. She was treated with antibiotics, but despite supportive measures, she died on the second hospital day (12/13) at 3:55 p.m. An autopsy limited to the chest and abdomen was performed on 12/15.

GROSS EXAMINATION

GENERAL INSPECTION: The body was that of a slightly malnourished female who looks like her stated age of 45 years. The body was identified at that of Renata H. O'Patient according to the ID band on her left wrist and the ID tag on her right big toe. The irides were hazel and the hair was brown, with normal female distribution. Oral and nasal tubes were present and in place. There was a single-lumen catheter in the right neck. A 9-cm, well-healed, longitudinal scar was also present on the anterior neck. There was also a full-lumen catheter in the right anticubital fossa. A Foley catheter was present. Postmortem lividity was present posteriorly, and marked edema was noted.

BODY CAVITIES: The organs of the thorax and abdomen were in their normal anatomic relationships. There was 10 ml of straw-colored serous fluid in the right and 15 ml of straw-colored serous fluid in the left pleural cavities. The pericardial sac contained 10 ml of serous fluid. The great vessels and chambers of the heart were in a normal anatomic relationship. Firm areas of gray and tan tumor involved the mediastinum. Tumor was identified and involved the upper sternum, skeletal muscle, anterior rib cage, and mediastinum. There was no fluid within the peritoneal cavity. The cranial cavity and neck organs were not examined due to permit restrictions.

CARDIOVASCULAR SYSTEM: The heart weighed 510 g and was of a normal configuration. The epicardium was normal. The heart was opened in the plan of the atrioventricular groove. Neither ventricle appeared dilated. The myocardium was reddish brown and firm. The right ventricular wall was 0.6 cm in thickness, and the left ventricular wall was 2.1 cm in thickness. The left ventricle appeared hypertrophic. No significant abnormalities were found in the valves, and the endocardium was normal. The coronary arteries had a normal anatomic distribution, with the right coronary artery being predominant. The arteries were sectioned in 0.2- to 0.3-cm intervals. The proximal right coronary artery, the main left coronary artery, the left anterior descending coronary artery, and the left circumflex coronary artery showed no calcific atherosclerosis. The aorta also showed no calcific atherosclerosis, ulceration, or mural thrombi.

RESPIRATORY SYSTEM: The mucosa of the trachea was unremarkable. The right lung weighed 1100 g and the left lung 1050 g. The pleura was glistening and nodular with multifocal gray and tan, firm lesions. The lung was fresh cut. The cut surfaces showed greater than twenty nodules within the parenchyma. The largest nodule was 8 by 6 by 3 cm, and it was located within the base of the left lower lobe. In addition, the parenchyma was congested and hemorrhagic. The bronchial walls were thickened and the mucosa reddened. The pulmonary arteries showed no atherosclerosis or thromboemboli. The hilar and bronchial lymph nodes had tumor and were enlarged.

Figure 3.53. (Continued)

Lincoln County Hospital

AUTOPSY REPORT
PAGE 3 OF 4

O'PATIENT, RENATA H.
4378802133524
DOB: 02/18/1958

DIGESTIVE SYSTEM: The esophagus was unremarkable. The stomach contained approximately 10 ml of semi-liquid, tan material. The mucosa was markedly reddened. The small intestine was unremarkable. The large intestine contained brown fecal material, and scant colonic diverticula were noted. The appendix was present and unremarkable. The liver weighed 2300 g, and the capsular surface was smooth and glistening. On section, the parenchyma was reddish brown with central lobular congestion. The gallbladder contained approximately 35 ml of brown-green bile. The mucosa showed prominent yellow streaks. No stones were identified. The common bile duct was unremarkable. The pancreas appeared normal and was normal in consistency.

GENITOURINARY SYSTEM: The right kidney weighed 210 g, and the left kidney weighed 220 g. The capsule was stripped with difficulty, and the underlying cortical surfaces were coarsely granular and pitted. A 0.3-cm, firm, tan-colored nodule was noted on the left kidney. On section, the cortex measured 0.8 cm in thickness. The cortex was markedly hyperemic. The renal arteries showed no atherosclerosis. The urinary bladder showed no mass lesions. Mucosal hemorrhages were absent. The endocervical canal and os appeared unremarkable. The endometrium was pale yellow. No leiomyomas were present. The myometrium was unremarkable. The ovaries were pale yellow and without cysts.

HEMATOPOIETIC SYSTEM: The thymus was not identified. The spleen weighed 250 g and had a dull-gray capsule. On section, the spleen was dark red and firm. Systemic lymph nodes were grayish tan and enlarged. The bone marrow was reddish brown.

ENDOCRINE SYSTEM: The adrenal glands were slightly enlarged. Two separate nodules were present within the right adrenal gland. Each nodule was about 1 cm in diameter.

MUSCULOSKELETAL SYSTEM: The vertebral column showed no osteopenia. A fracture was identified along the vertebral column at T5. The fracture site was surrounded by firm areas of tan to gray tumor.

CASSETTE SUMMARY: (1) Left lung, lower lobe and tumor; (2) left lung, upper and middle lobes and tumor; (3) right lung, upper lobe and tumor; (4) right lung, middle and lower lobes; (5) T5 soft-tissue mass; (6) upper sternum and mediastinal mass; (7) T5 vertebra; (8) liver and gallbladder; (9) spleen; (10) right kidney and adrenal gland with mass; (11) left kidney and adrenal gland with cortical nodule; (12) uterus, cervix, right tube and ovary; (13) pancreas and bladder; (14) stomach, small and large intestines; (15) right and left ventricles of heart.

MICROSCOPIC EXAMINATION

GENERAL TUMOR DESCRIPTION: Sections of the tumor masses show a neoplasm characterized by highly cellular proliferations of spindle cells with generally indistinct cytoplasm and marked nuclear pleomorphism. Best demonstrated in slide A1 from a metastatic site and A6, a possible primary site, there is prominent, irregular osteoid formation characteristic of osteosarcoma. Infiltration of subchondral bone is present in the latter area. Sections of the T5 vertebra show extensive necrosis of the neoplasm within the bone with no morphologically intact residual tumor seen. The adjacent soft-tissue mass, however, shows large zones of intact neoplasm associated with areas of necrosis.

RESPIRATORY SYSTEM: In addition to the metastatic osteosarcoma, the uninvolved lung tissue shows numerous areas of an exudate of neutrophils within the alveolar spaces associated with focal areas of hemorrhage. Numerous colonies of coccoid bacteria are present within these zones of inflammation. In addition to the extensive broncho-pneumonia, other areas show vascular congestion, prominent alveolar lining cells, and focal hyaline membrane formation consistent with shock lung (diffuse alveolar damage syndrome).

Figure 3.53. (Continued)

Lincoln County Hospital

AUTOPSY REPORT
PAGE 4 OF 4

O'PATIENT, RENATA H.
4378802133524
DOB: 02/18/1958

GENITOURINARY SYSTEM: Sections of the nodule in the left kidney show a lesion composed of spindle cells with a prominent vascular network mixed with fat cells. Spindle cells show fibrillar eosinophilic cytoplasm characteristic of smooth-muscle differentiation. This lesion represents an angiomyolipoma. There is no evidence of metastatic sarcoma. Elsewhere, the kidney shows pigment casts within tubules but no other significant findings.

ENDOCRINE SYSTEM: Sections confirm the presence of adrenal cortical nodules.

GENERAL: Sections of the other organs sampled show no additional significant findings or confirmed the gross impressions.

CASE SUMMARY: This 45-year-old white woman with a history of tall-cell variant of papillary carcinoma had been treated with I-131 and external beam radiation therapy because of multiple lymph node metastases and an aggressive primary tumor. Her course had been complicated by hypoparathyroidism. Recently, she had developed a compression fracture of the T5 vertebral body and on further evaluation was found to have a widely metastatic sarcoma involving the lungs and bones of the chest. Mediastinal tumor was noted on imaging studies. On the day before her death, the patient presented with a febrile illness and hypotension secondary to sepsis. Despite treatment, she died on the second hospital day.

Autopsy documented extensive metastatic sarcoma involving the lungs, and the large samples available at autopsy showed osteoid formation within several areas characteristic of osteosarcoma. A relatively large mass involving the superior sternum, anterior rib cage, and superior mediastinum suggested a possible primary tumor in this site. This finding raised the possibility of a postradiation sarcoma. Autopsy documented extensive pulmonary metastases involving nearly half of the lung parenchyma bilaterally. There was a large soft-tissue extension surrounding the vertebral body metastasis, and there was extensive necrosis of the bone tumor in this site consistent with recent radiation therapy.

The immediate case of death was hemorrhagic bronchopneumonia secondary to Staphylococcus aureus, which was cultured postmortem from the sputum. Other findings in the lungs were consistent with diffuse alveolar damage syndrome secondary to shock and sepsis (shock lung).

Other findings of an incidental nature are documented in the final diagnoses.

Figure 3.54. Maternal/Prenatal Care Summary in Paper Format

Anytown Community Hospital

MATERNAL/PRENATAL CARE SUMMARY

PATIENT LABEL

Mother's Name: _____

Mother's Age: _____ Gravida: _____ Term: ____

Premature: _____ Abnormal: ____ Living: ____

Expected Delivery Date: _____

Prenatal Labs: _____

Maternal/Prenatal/Family History: _____

_____

_____

Social Problems: _____

_____

Type of Delivery: ☐ Vaginal

                    ☐ C-Section

Type of Anesthesia: _____

Tubal Ligation: ☐ Yes   ☐ No

Apgars: 1 min __   5 min __   10 min __

Complications of Labor and Delivery: _____

_____

_____

Transfer From: _____

Date: _____

Delivery Weight: _____

Last Weight: _____

Service Notified: _____

Date and Time: _____

Person Notified: _____

Examined: _____

Void ☐

Stool ☐

Circumcision ☐ Yes ☐ No

Done: _____

Date: _____

Metabolic Screen: ☐ Yes ☐ No

Done: _____

Date: _____

Hearing Screen: ☐ Yes ☐ No

Done: _____

Date: _____

Pass/Refer:

Follow-up Appointment
Made: _____

Vitals: _____

Glucoses: _____

Breast: _____

Formula: _____

IVF _____ @ _____

UAC _____ @ _____

UVC _____ @ _____

Mother's Blood Type and RH: _____

Cord Blood: _____

COOMBS: _____

Cord Bili: _____

Baby Safe Signed: ☐

Gift Bags Given: ☐

Hepatitis B Vaccine:
☐ Yes   ☐ No

Orders:

_____

_____

_____

_____

_____

_____

_____

_____

_____

_____

_____

Medications: _____

_____

_____

Messages: _____

_____

Obstetrician	Delivery Date	Delivery Time	Baby's Gender
Mother's Room Number		Pediatrician	

Figure 3.55. Labor and Delivery Summary in Paper Format

Anytown Community Hospital

LABOR AND DELIVERY SUMMARY
PAGE 1 OF 5

PATIENT LABEL

LABOR SUMMARY

G	T	Pt	A	L	Blood Type and Rh	EDD
						/ /

Prenatal Events ☐ None

☐ No Prenatal Care

☐ Preterm Labor (≤37 Weeks)

☐ Postterm Labor (≥42 Weeks)

☐ Previous Cesarean

☐ Prenatal Complications

☐ Other _____

Maternal Intrapartal Events

☐ None

☐ Febrile (≥100.4°F/38°C)

☐ Bleeding—Site Undetermined

☐ Preeclampsia: ☐ Mild ☐ Severe

☐ Seizure Activity

☐ Medications: ☐ None

Date	Time	Medication	Dose	Route

☐ Transfusion _____ *units*

   Blood Component _____

☐ Other _____

Amniotic Fluid

☐ SROM ☐ AROM Date ____ Time ____

☐ Premature ROM ☐ Prolonged ROM

☐ Clear

☐ Meconium-Stained (Describe) _____

☐ Bloody

☐ Foul Odor

   ☐ Cultures Sent _____ Time _____

☐ Polyhydramnios

☐ Oligohydramnios

☐ Other _____

Placenta

☐ Placenta Previa

☐ Abruptio Placenta

☐ Other _____

Labor

☐ Precipitous Labor (<3 h)

☐ Prolonged Labor (≥20 h)

☐ Prolonged Latent Phase

☐ Prolonged Active Phase

☐ Prolonged 2nd Stage (>2.5 h)

☐ Secondary Arrest of Dilatation

☐ Induction:

   ☐ None   ☐ AROM

   ☐ Oxytocin   ☐ Other _____

☐ Augmentation:

   ☐ None   ☐ AROM

   ☐ Oxytocin   ☐ Other _____

Figure 3.55.   (Continued)

Anytown Community Hospital

LABOR AND DELIVERY SUMMARY
PAGE 2 OF 5

LABOR SUMMARY (Continued)

Fetus

Gestational Age (Weeks): _____ By Dates _____ By Ultrasound

Presentation: **Position:**

☐ Vertex ☐ Face/Brow

☐ Breech: ☐ Frank ☐ Complete ☐ Single Footing ☐ Double Footing

☐ Transverse Lie: ☐ Back Up ☐ Back Down

☐ Compound

☐ Unknown

☐ Cephalopelvic Disproportion (CPD)

☐ Cord Prolapse

Monitor: ☐ None ☐ External FHR ☐ External UC
                   ☐ Internal FHR ☐ Internal UC

STV: ☐ Present ☐ Absent

☐ LTV _____

☐ Fetal Bradycardia

☐ Fetal Tachycardia

☐ Sinusoidal Pattern

☐ Accelerations: ☐ Spontaneous ☐ Uniform

☐ Decelerations: ☐ Early ☐ Late ☐ Variable ☐ Prolonged

☐ Scalp pH ≤ 7.2

☐ _____

FM Discontinued _____ Time _____

FHR Prior to Delivery _____ bpm Time _____

Signature _____ Date _____

DELIVERY SUMMARY

Support Person Present: ☐ Yes ☐ No

Location: ☐ LDR ☐ LDRP ☐ DR ☐ OR ☐ Birthing Room ☐ Other _____

Method of Delivery: Vaginal

☐ VBAC (Number _____)

☐ Vertex

  ☐ Spontaneous

  ☐ Assisted   **Position:** to **Position:**

  ☐ Manual Rotation

  ☐ Forceps (Type) _____)

    ☐ Outlet ☐ Low ☐ Mid

  ☐ Vacuum Extraction Duration ___min.

    Degree of Suction _____kg/cm²

☐ Breech (Type _____)

  ☐ Spontaneous ☐ Partial Extraction (Assisted) ☐ Total Extraction

  ☐ Forceps Assist

    ☐ Piper ☐ Other _____

Episiotomy

☐ None ☐ Midline ☐ Mediolateral   L   R

Laceration/Episiotomy Extension:

☐ None ☐ Periurethral ☐ Vaginal ☐ Cervical ☐ Uterine

☐ Perineal ☐ 1" ☐ 2" ☐ 3" ☐ 4"

Repair Agent Used _____

☐ Vagina Free of Sponges

Placenta

☐ Spontaneous ☐ Expressed ☐ Manual Removal

☐ Adherent (Type _____)

☐ Uterine Exploration

☐ Curettage

Configuration

☐ Normal

☐ Abnormal _____

Weight _____ g

Disposition _____

Cord

☐ Nuchal Cord (× _____) ☐ True Knot Length _____ cm

☐ 2 Vessels ☐ 3 Vessels

Cord Blood ☐ To Lab ☐ Refrig ☐ Discard

Lab ☐ Type + Rh ☐ Cultures ☐ COOMBS

  ☐ pH   ☐ _____

Signature _____ Date _____

Figure 3.55. **(Continued)**

Anytown Community Hospital

LABOR AND DELIVERY SUMMARY
PAGE 3 OF 5

DELIVERY SUMMARY (Continued)

Method of Delivery: Cesarean

☐ Scheduled ☐ Emergency ☐ Primary ☐ Repeat (× ————) ☐ Other _____

Operative Indication: ☐ Previous Uterine Surgery ☐ Failure to Progress ☐ Placenta Previa ☐ Abruptio Placenta
☐ Fetal Malpresentation _____ ☐ Nonreassuring FHR Pattern _____
☐ Other_____

Uterine Incision: ☐ Low Cervical, Transverse ☐ Low Cervical, Vertical ☐ Classical

Hysterectomy: ☐ Yes ☐ No   **Tubal Ligation:** ☐ Yes ☐ No

Skin Incision: ☐ Vertical ☐ Pfannenstiel

Surgical Data

Sponge Counts Correct: ☐ NA ☐ Yes ☐ No _____
Needle Counts Correct: ☐ NA ☐ Yes ☐ No _____
Vaginal Pack Count Correct: ☐ NA ☐ Yes ☐ No _____
Estimated Blood Loss _____ *cc*

Anesthesia: ☐ None ☐ Local ☐ Pudendal ☐ General ☐ Epidural ☐ Spinal

Date	Time	Medication	Dose	Effect

Complications of Anesthesia: ☐ Yes _____ ☐ None

Medications: ☐ None

Date	Time	Medication	Dose	Route Site	Initials

Chronology

	Date	Time		
EDD				
Admit to Hospital				
Membranes Ruptured				
Onset of Labor			Total Time H/Min	
Complete Cervical Dilation				I
Delivery of Infant				II
Delivery of Placenta				III
				Total Labor

Signature _____ Date _____

Figure 3.55.   (Continued)

Anytown Community Hospital

LABOR AND DELIVERY SUMMARY
PAGE 4 OF 5

PATIENT LABEL

NEONATAL SUMMARY

Birth Data

Time of Birth _____   ☐ Male   ☐ Female

ID Band # _____

Condition: ☐ Alive   ☐ Antepartum Death   ☐ Intrapartum Death   ☐ Neonatal Death

Birth Order _____ of _____

Apgar Score	1 min	5 min	10 min
Heart Rate			
Respiratory Effort			
Muscle Tone			
Reflex Irritability			
Color			
Total			

Signature _____

Airway
☐ Bulb Suction
☐ Suction Catheter   Size _____ Fr
   ☐ Mouth   Pressure _____ mm Hg
   ☐ Nose   ☐ At Delivery
   ☐ Pharynx
☐ Endotracheal Tube Size _____ Fr
   ☐ Meconium Below Cords   Times _____

Breathing
☐ Spontaneous
☐ O$_2$ _____ Liters   Time Initiated
   ☐ Free Flow   _____
   ☐ PPV
      ☐ Bag/Mask   _____
      ☐ ET Tube Size ____ Fr   _____
      ☐ CPAP _____ *mm*
_____ Minutes to First Gasp
_____ Minutes to Sustained Respiration

Circulation
☐ Spontaneous
☐ External Cardiac Massage
   Time Initiated _____ Time Completed _____
   _____ Minutes for HR >100
      Heart Rate (bpm)
      _____ Time _____
      _____ Time _____
      _____ Time _____

IV Access
☐ Umbilical Catheter
☐ Peripheral Line

Person Managing Reuscitation

_____

Medications   ☐ None

Date	Time	Medication	Dose	Route Site	Initials

Laboratory Data: ☐ None

Blood Gases	Sent	Umb Art	Umb Vein
pH			
pO$_2$			
pCO$_2$			
HCO$_3$			

Test   **Result**
Dextrostix   _____

Figure 3.55. (Continued)

Anytown Community Hospital

LABOR AND DELIVERY SUMMARY
PAGE 5 OF 5

NEONATAL SUMMARY (Continued)

Initial Newborn Exam

Weight _____ g _____ lb _____ oz ☐ Deferred

Length _____ cm _____ in ☐ Deferred

Head _____ cm _____ in ☐ Deferred

Chest _____ cm _____ in ☐ Deferred

Abdomen _____ cm _____ in ☐ Deferred

T _____ ☐ Rectal   ☐ Axillary

AP _____ R _____ BP _____

☐ No Observed Abnormalities

☐ Abnormalities Noted

☐ Meconium Staining   ☐ Cephalhematoma

☐ Petechiae   ☐ Other

Describe _____

_____

_____

Intake ☐ None

   Breast Feed: ☐ Yes ☐ No

Output ☐ None

   ☐ Urine ☐ Stool (Type_____)

   ☐ Gastric Aspirate _____ cc

Examined By _____

Transfer   ☐ With Mother

    ☐ To Newborn Nursery

    ☐ To NICU

    ☐ Other_____

Date ___ / ___ / ___ Time _____

Mode of Transport_____

Delivery Personnel

RN (1)_____

   (2)_____

Anesthesiologist/CRNA_____

CNM _____

Physician—Attending _____

Physician—Assist (1) _____

    (2) _____

Pediatric Provider _____

☐ Notified ☐ Present at Birth

Remarks

_____   _____

        Signature   Date

LABOR AND DELIVERY SUMMARY
200366 (6/2004)

Caesarian deliveries are operative procedures, and as such they require documentation of the patient's informed consent. Obstetricians who perform Caesarian deliveries must prepare complete operative reports. Similarly, sterilization procedures performed after a Caesarian or normal delivery are considered separate procedures that must be fully documented.

Discharge summaries are not required for normal deliveries. A preprinted discharge form or discharge progress note is considered sufficient discharge reporting for mother and child. Complete discharge summaries, however, are required for surgical and complicated deliveries.

The health records of the mother and her newborn infant or infants must be maintained separately. An exception is made for cases of stillbirth. Information on the stillborn infant can be incorporated into the mother's record.

Every labor and delivery record should contain the following information:

- Patient's married and/or maiden name(s)
- Patient's record number
- Delivery date
- Gender of the infant
- Names and credentials of the physician and any assistants
- Descriptions of any complications that developed
- Type of anesthesia
- Name of the person who administered the anesthesia
- Names of other persons who witnessed the delivery

Neonatal Services

The health records of newborn infants are maintained separately from their mothers' records. For normal deliveries, the neonatal record usually duplicates much of the information documented in the mother's record in addition to a general assessment of the newborn's condition at birth. (See figure 3.56, pp. 175–76.) In some cases, a discharge progress note is acceptable for a normal newborn's record.

Much more extensive documentation is required for premature infants and other infants who require intensive care after birth. Some infants require months of treatment in the neonatal intensive care unit before they are strong enough to go home with their parents. The records of these babies require full documentation, including admission and discharge assessments, operative reports when applicable, and discharge summaries.

Some hospitals do not offer neonatal intensive care services. Infants born at these hospitals require immediate transfer to another facility equipped to handle their needs. In such cases, the neonatal record maintained by the hospital where the infant was born should include admission and discharge information and documentation of the reason for the child's transfer to the other facility.

Observation Services

Observation patients are considered outpatients, and they generally stay in the hospital for less than twenty-four hours. The health records for observation patients must include a physician's order for admission to an observation bed or unit as well as the time and date of the patient's admission and discharge. Other documentation should include vital signs and medication records as well as physicians' and nurses' progress notes. A discharge summary or note should describe the patient's condition and disposition at discharge.

Figure 3.56. Neonatal Assessment Record in Paper Format

Anytown Community Hospital

NEONATAL ASSESSMENT RECORD
PAGE 1 OF 2

> PATIENT LABEL

	Within Normal Anatomical Limits	
Development		Birth Date _____ Type of Delivery ☐ Vaginal ☐ C-Section Gender _____ Head Circumference _____ Birth Weight _____ Birth Length _____

Neurological/ Musculoskeletal

Pupil Size
R ___ L ___

Yes ☐ No ☐

LOC	Movement	Pupils
☐ Lethargic	☐ ↓ RA	☐ Nonreactive
☐ Unresponsive	☐ ↓ RL	☐ Sluggish
☐ Irritable	☐ ↓ LA	☐ Constricted
☐ Responds Only to Stimuli	☐ ↓ LL	☐ Fixed

Comments

Heart/Vascular

Yes ☐ No ☐

Heart	Edema	Vascular (0, 1, 3, 4)
☐ Skips	☐ Generalized	R Radial + _____ ☐ Dop ☐ Abs
☐ Palpitations	Location _____	L Radial + _____ ☐ Dop ☐ Abs
☐ Valve Click	Degree (1–4) _____	R Pedal + _____ ☐ Dop ☐ Abs
☐ Murmur		L Pedal + _____ ☐ Dop ☐ Abs
		R Brach + _____ ☐ Dop ☐ Abs
		L Brach + _____ ☐ Dop ☐ Abs

Comments

Pulmonary/ Lungs

Yes ☐ No ☐

Respirations		Breath Sounds	Right	Left
☐ Orthopnea	☐ Retractions	☐ Crackles	☐	☐
☐ Dyspnea	☐ Shallow	☐ Rhonchi	☐	☐
☐ Apnea	☐ Cough	☐ Wheezes	☐	☐
☐ Labored	☐ Nasal Flaring	☐ Diminished	☐	☐
☐ Tachypnea		☐ Absent	☐	☐

Comments

Gastrointestinal

Last BM _____
Pattern _____

Yes ☐ No ☐

Bowel Sounds	Abdomen	Bowel Habits
☐ Hypo	☐ Firm	☐ Frequency
☐ Hyper	☐ Protuberant	☐ Diarrhea
☐ Absent	☐ Distended	
	☐ Tender	

Comments

Nutritional

☐ Breast Feeding   Frequency _____ Feeding Length _____
☐ Bottle Feeding   Frequency _____ Formula _____ Amount _____

Genitourinary/ Reproductive

Yes ☐ No ☐

Urinary		Reproductive
☐ Hematuria	☐ Frequency	☐ Undescended testicles
☐ Oliguria	☐ Dysuria	R ☐ L ☐

Comments

EENT

Yes ☐ No ☐

Problem	Hearing	Sight
☐ Swallowing ☐ Choking	↓ ☐ R ↓ ☐ L	↓ ☐ R ↓ ☐ L

Comments

Figure 3.56. **(Continued)**

Anytown Community Hospital

NEONATAL ASSESSMENT RECORD
PAGE 2 OF 2

PATIENT LABEL

	Within Normal Anatomical Limits	

Skin Integumentary

Within Normal Anatomical Limits: Yes ☐ No ☐

Problem	Location	Problem	Location	Problem
☐ Bruise	_____	☐ Wound	_____	☐ Pale
☐ Burn	_____	☐ Ulcer	_____	☐ Jaundice
☐ Rash	_____	☐ Bleeding	_____	☐ Mottled
☐ Oral Mucosa	_____	☐ Other	_____	☐ Tugor
☐ Dry ☐ Thrush ☐ Lesions				☐ Tenting ☐ Dry

Comments:

Emotional/ Mental

Yes ☐ No ☐

☐ Lethargic ☐ Fussy ☐ Withdrawn ☐ Inconsolable Crying

Comments:

Sleep Pattern

Bedtime _____ Naptime _____

Family Information

Primary Caretaker _____

Siblings? How many and what are their ages? _____

Pain

Yes ☐ No ☐

Neonatal/Infant Pain Scale (NIPS) (A score greater than 3 indicates pain)

Observe	Criteria	Points
	Relaxed muscles—restful face, neutral expression	0
	Grimace—tight facial muscles, furrowed brow, chin, jaw (negative facial expression nose, mouth, and brow)	1
	No Cry—quiet, not crying	0
	Whimper—intermittent	1
	Vigorous Cry—loud scream, rising, shrill, continuous (note: silent cry may be scored if baby is intubated as evidenced by obvious mouth and facial movement)	2
	Relaxed—usual pattern for this infant	0
	Change in Breathing—indrawing, irregular, faster than usual, gagging, breath holding	1
Arms	Relaxed/Restrained—no muscular rigidity, occasional random movements of arms	0
	Flexed/Extended—tense, straight legs, rigid and/or rapid extension, flexion	1
Legs	Relaxed/Restrained—no muscular rigidity, occasional random leg movement	0
	Flexed/Extended—tense, straight legs, rigid and/or rapid extension, flexion	1
State of Arousal	Sleeping/Awake—quiet, peaceful sleeping or alert random leg movement	0
	Fussy—alert, restless, and thrashing	1
	Total Score	

Or
Nonverbal Assessment

Observe	Criteria	Points
	Anxious/Irritable	1
	Almost in Tears	2
	None	0
	Restless/Slow or Decreased Movement	1
	Immobile	2
Verbal Cues	Whining/Whimpering/Moaning	1
	Screaming, Crying Out	2
Facial Cues	Relaxed, Calm Expression	0
	Drawn Around Mouth and Eyes	1
	Facial Frowning, Wincing	2
Positioning/ Guarding	Relaxed Body	0
	Guarding/Tense	1
	Fetal Position/Jumps If Touched	2
	Total Points	

Comments

RN Initials: _____ RN Signature: _____ Date: _____ Time: _____ Unit: _____

RN Initials: _____ RN Signature: _____ Date: _____ Time: _____ Unit: _____

NEONATAL ASSESSMENT RECORD
000060 (10/2002)

Third-party payers have strict rules on reimbursement for observation services. Therefore, complete documentation of the medical necessity and length of observation services is particularly important.

Psychiatric Services

Inpatient psychiatric hospitals and psychiatric units within acute care hospitals maintain documentation similar to other inpatient units in addition to documentation unique to psychiatric care. The following list includes the elements of minimum documentation established by accreditation standards, federal regulations, and Medicare *Conditions of Participation:*

- Demographic data

- Source of referral

- Reason for referral

- Patient's legal status

- All appropriate consents for admission, treatment, evaluation, and aftercare

- Admitting psychiatric diagnoses

- Psychiatric history

- Record of the complete patient assessment, including the complaints of others regarding the patient as well as the patient's comments

- Medical history, report of physical examination, and list of medications

- Provisional diagnoses based on assessment that includes other current diseases as well as psychiatric diagnoses

- Written, individualized treatment plan

- Documentation of the course of treatment and all evaluations and examinations

- Multidisciplinary progress notes related to the goals and objectives outlined in the treatment plan

- Appropriate documentation related to special treatment procedures such as the use of physical and chemical restraints and seclusion techniques to control dangerous patient behavior

- Updates to the treatment plan as a result of ongoing assessments detailed in the progress notes

- Records of multidisciplinary case conferences and consultation notes, which include the dates of the conferences or consultations, the recommendations made, and the actions taken

- Information on any unusual occurrences such as treatment complications, accidents or injuries to the patient, death of the patient, and procedures that placed the patient at risk or caused unusual pain

- Correspondence related to the patient, including all letters and dated notations of telephone conversations relevant to the patient's treatment

- Discharge or termination summary

- Plan for follow-up care and documentation of its implementation

- Individualized aftercare or posttreatment plan

Rehabilitation Services

Rehabilitation services include a number of different therapies designed to build or rebuild the patient's ability to perform the activities of daily living. **Activities of daily living** (ADLs) include the basic activities of self-care, including the ability to communicate with others, feed oneself, bath and dress oneself, use the toilet, and move within one's environment. Rehabilitation services include physical therapy, occupational therapy, and speech therapy as well as treatment by physicians specializing in rehabilitation and the use of orthotics.

Physical therapists help patients to build or rebuild their muscle strength and respiratory and circulatory capacities. Physical therapists work with patients who have been disabled by illnesses (stroke and heart disease are the most common), injuries, and birth defects.

Occupational therapists help patients to restore their ability to read and write and to perform self-care activities after they have been disabled by illness or injury. Similarly, speech therapists conduct dysphasia evaluations and help disabled patients to regain their ability to communicate.

Inpatient rehabilitation hospitals and rehabilitation units within acute care hospitals are subject to a Medicare prospective payment system that is based on documentation. A standardized assessment tool called the **patient assessment instrument** (PAI) must be completed shortly after the patient's admission and upon discharge. Payment level is based on the patient's medical condition and diagnostic profile as well as the services provided.

The Joint Commission on Accreditation of Healthcare Organization's *Comprehensive Accreditation Manual for Hospitals and the Medicare Conditions of Participation for Hospitals* both require that the records of rehabilitation services include documentation of a preliminary patient assessment and a written rehabilitation plan. The plan must be developed by qualified professionals on the basis of the patient's needs. (See figure 3.57, pp. 179–82.)

Many rehabilitation facilities are accredited through the Commission on Accreditation of Rehabilitation Facilities (CARF). CARF requires rehabilitation facilities to maintain a single case record for every patient they admit. The documentation standard for health records includes the following requirements:

- Patient identification data

- Pertinent history

- Diagnosis of disability

- Rehabilitation problems, goals, and prognosis

- Reports of assessments and individual program planning

- Reports from referring sources and service referrals

- Reports from outside consultations and laboratory, radiology, orthotic, and prosthetic services

- Designation of a manager for the patient's program

- Evidence of the patient's or family's participation in decision making

- Evaluation reports from every service

- Reports of staff conferences

- Patient's total program plan

- Plans from each service

- Signed and dated service and progress reports

Figure 3.57.   Rehabilitation Care Plan in Paper Format

University of Anystate Hospital

REHABILITATION PLAN OF CARE
PAGE 1 OF 4

PATIENT LABEL

Date Developed/Updated:_____   Anticipated Discharge:_____

Rehab Diagnosis: _____   Prognosis: _____

Anticipated Discharge Disposition:_____

Patient/Caregiver Goals: _____

Medical Status:_____

Self-Care/Events	TD	RD	Interventions	Person(s) Responsible
1. Upper extremity dressing with: _____			1. ADL program	OT, Nursing
2. Lower extremity dressing with: _____			2. ADL program	OT, Nursing
3. Bathing with: _____			3. ADL program	OT, Nursing
4. Toileting with: _____			4. ADL program	OT, Nursing
5. Grooming with:_____			5. ADL program	OT, Nursing
6. Eating with: _____			6. ADL program	OT, Nursing, SLP

Discharge Outcome(s): ADLs with: _____

Mobility/Events	TD	RD	Interventions	Person(s) Responsible
1. Transfers with: _____			1. Transfer training	PT, Team
2. Tub/shower transfers with:_____			2. Transfer training	OT, Team
3. Toilet transfers with: _____			3. Transfer training	OT, Team
4. Bed mobility with:_____			4. Rolling, bridging, supine-sit	PT, Team
5. Wheelchair propulsion: _____ ft with: _____			5. Wheelchair skills training	PT, Team
6. Ambulation: _____ ft using: _____ with: _____			6. Gait training	PT, Team
7. Up and down: _____ stairs with: _____			7. Real-life room, flight of stairs	PT, TR
8. Community surfaces/barriers: _____			8. RLR, outing	TR, Team

Discharge Outcome(s): Transfer with: _____   Ambulation with: _____

Wheelchair propulsion with: _____   Up/down stairs with: _____

Figure 3.57. (Continued)

University of Anystate Hospital

REHABILITATION PLAN OF CARE
PAGE 2 OF 4

PATIENT LABEL

Communication/Events	TD	RD	Interventions	Person(s) Responsible

Discharge Outcome(s): Effective communication skills with: _____

Bio-Psycho-Social Functioning/Events	TD	RD	Interventions	Person(s) Responsible
Redirect pain complaints with: _____			Peer interaction, relaxation techniques	TR
Interact with peers/staff with: _____			Group and individual socialization	TR

Discharge Outcome(s): Adjust to lifestyle changes and to disability; to participate in community activities at level of functioning

Cognitive/Events	TD	RD	Interventions	Person(s) Responsible
Alert and oriented X: _____			Reorientation	SLP, Team
Adaptive leisure skills with: _____			Assistive devices, resources, body awareness	TR
				SLP, Team

Discharge Outcome(s): Increase cognition to within functional limits for basic self-care with good safety awareness and judgment

Patient/Caregiver Education/Events	TD	RD	Interventions	Person(s) Responsible
1. Patient/caregiver able to relate use and frequency of medications			1. Medication teaching	Nursing
2. Patient/caregiver able to assist patient with activities of daily living and transfers			2. ADL program, transfer training	Team
3. Patient/caregiver able to relate bowel and bladder programs			3. Bowel and bladder programs	Nursing
4. Patient/caregiver able to demonstrate skin care			4. Turning, pressure relief, skin assessment, skin care, signs of infection	Team
5. Patient/caregiver able to relate nutrition and hydration requirements			5. Dietary teaching	Nursing
6. Patient/caregiver able to relate safety issues/management precautions			6. Demonstration, discussion, activities of daily living, mobility	Team

Discharge Outcome(s): Caregiver able to safely and appropriately assist patient; patient able to manage own care

Figure 3.57. (Continued)

University of Anystate Hospital

REHABILITATION PLAN OF CARE
PAGE 3 OF 4

PATIENT LABEL

Environmental/Discharge Planning/Events	TD	RD	Interventions	Person(s) Responsible
Discharge planning			Patient/caregiver teaching, DME assessed and ordered, patient–caregiver conference, home healthcare	Team
Identify resources and complete appropriate applications			Leisure education, transportation resources	TR

Discharge Outcome(s): Safe discharge home with caregiver and support from community resource

Other Areas of Concern/Events	TD	RD	Interventions	Person(s) Responsible
1. Preadmission bowel status			1. Bowel program	Nursing
2. Preadmission bladder status			2. Bladder program	Team
3. Skin free of breakdown			3. Pressure relief measures	Nursing
4. Wound free of infection; facilitate healing			4. Wound care: per MD; D/C staple: per MD; ET consult PRN	Physician, Nursing,ET
5. Pain less than or equal to level 3			5. Medicate prior to therapy and PRN; cold pack PRN; relaxation techniques; position Δ	Team
6. Preadmission nutritional status			6. I&O, dietary consult, monitor caloric intake	Team
7. UE strength:			7. UE exercise program	OT
8. LE strength:			8. LE exercise program	PT
9. Endurance:			9. Endurance activities	Team

Discharge Outcome(s): No fall or injury during rehabilitation stay; reestablish appropriate bowel elimination; reestablish appropriate urinary elimination; skin intact; no signs of infection; patient/caregiver able to manage wound/skin care; adequate management of pain; adequate nutritional status; maximize UE/LE strength to perform ADLs

Figure 3.57.   (Continued)

University of Anystate Hospital

REHABILITATION PLAN OF CARE
PAGE 4 OF 4

PATIENT LABEL

Functional Independence Measure

	ADM	CURR		ADM	CURR			
Eating			Transfer: Tub/Shower					
Grooming			Locomotion: Walk		FT	SLS	US	FIM
Bathing			Locomotion: Wheelchair		FT	SLS	US	FIM
Dressing—Upper			Stairs					
Dressing—Lower			Comprehension					
Toileting			Expression					
Bladder Management			Social Interaction					
Bowel Management			Problem Solving					
Transfer: Bed, Chair, Wheelchair			Memory					
Transfer: Toilet								

Communication with patient/caregiver prior to team conference	NSG	OT	PT	PSY	SLP	TR	SW
Progress discussed with patient/caregiver							
Patient/caregiver input for treatment goals given and discussed							
Patient/caregiver input for treatment goals given/discussed; progress related							

N/A = Patient unable to provide input toward goals due to deficit

_____   _____
Physician Signature   Date

_____   _____
Patient/Caregiver Signature   Date

_____ Initials of person reviewing team conference with patient/caregiver

Signature	Date/Time	Signature	Date/Time

REHABILITATION PLAN OF CARE
0000205 (10/2002)

- Correspondence pertinent to the patient
- Release forms
- Discharge report
- Follow-up reports

Renal Dialysis Services

Renal failure is a relatively common illness among older people. The only cure for renal failure is a kidney transplant, but dialysis performed on a regular basis (for example, three times per week) can treat the illness's symptoms. Dialysis is the process of removing toxins from the blood directly or indirectly. Hemodialysis works by gradually removing the patient's blood and pumping it through an external filtering system before the blood is returned to the body via a vascular port. Peritoneal dialysis works by instilling an electrolyte solution into the patient's peritoneum. Periodically, the fluid is drained to remove the fluid and accumulated toxins.

Hemodialysis is performed in hospital-based units as well as in dedicated ambulatory care centers. Although it is less effective than hemodialysis, peritoneal dialysis is a simpler procedure and may even be performed in the patient's home.

The health records of dialysis patients include the following information (figure 3.58, p. 184):

- Patient identification, including name and record number
- Diagnosis
- Name of the procedure
- Duration of the procedure
- Date the procedure was performed
- Findings or results of the procedure
- Name, credentials, and signature of the nurse or physician who oversaw the procedure

Respiratory Services

Respiratory therapy is administered by respiratory therapists, nurses, and pulmonologists (physicians who specialize in the diagnosis and treatment of respiratory illness). Patients with acute and/or chronic respiratory conditions such as pneumonia and asthma often require respiratory therapy. Emergency respiratory therapy is often provided in hospital emergency departments when patient-administered treatments are not effective.

Basic treatments include the administration of aerosol medications and humidified oxygen. When breathing problems become life-threatening, physicians administer cardiopulmonary resuscitation and/or place the patient on mechanical ventilation.

Hospitals also provide a number of diagnostic services related to respiratory conditions. Common services include pulmonary function testing and blood gas analysis. Respiratory therapists and nurses work directly with patients to provide coughing and breathing exercises and therapeutic percussion and vibration to clear the lungs of fluid and mucus.

Respiratory therapy services must be ordered by the patient's physician. Respiratory assessments and treatment plans contain information about the patient's diagnosis, the services to be provided, and the goals of treatment. (An example of a respiratory therapy report is provided in figure 3.59, p. 185.)

Figure 3.58. Hemodialysis Record in Paper Format

Anycity General Hospital

HEMODIALYSIS RECORD

PATIENT LABEL

Machine Serial #: _____

Orders	Duration	Concentrate K+	Cell Type	Heparinization

Systemic: _____
ACT Range: _____

Blood Flow	Desired Weight Loss	BP Support		Blood
		Saline	Albumin	TXM: _____ Transfuse:_____

Predialysis Labs: Postdialysis Labs:

_____   _____
_____   _____
_____   _____

Assessment: _____ kg, Weight: _____ Time: _____

Abbreviations

ACT = Activated clotting time

Art   = Arterial

BF   = Blood flow

DLSC = Dual Lumen subclavian catheter

Pres = Pressure

Seq = Sequential

TMP = Transmembrane pressure

UF   = Ultrafiltration

Vital Signs	Post: ____	Pre: ____	Post: ____
Weight			
BP Supine			
BP Standing			
P			
T			
Edema			
Lungs/R			

Plan:

Time	BP	Blood Flow	Dialysate Flow	Arterial Pressure	Venous Pressure	Dialysate Pressure	UF / TMP	ACT / Heparin	NS / Albumin	Weight	Interventions/Comments:

Evaluation/Goal Achievement: _____ kg Weight: ____ Cell: ____   Total Heparin Dose: ____ units Total Saline: ____ cc Total Albumin: ____ g

☐ Goals and/or plan of care revised/reviewed with patient/family

Physician Signature: _____ Date: _____ RN Signature: _____ Date: _____

HEMODIALYSIS RECORD
000140 (10/2002)

Figure 3.59. Respiratory Therapy Record in Paper Format

Midwest Medical Center

VENTILATOR FLOW SHEET

PATIENT LABEL

Diagnoses: _____

Physician: _____

Current Settings: _____

DATE				
TIME				
INITIALS				
MODE				
SET VT				
ACTUAL VT				
PS/SPONT VT				
MINUTE VOLUME				
SET RATE/TOTAL RATE				
WAVE FORM/PF				
FIO_2/FIO_2 ACTUAL				
PRESSURE SUPPORT				
PEEP/CPAP				
PEAK PRESSURE				
SENSITIVITY				
PIP ALARM				
LIP ALARM				
LOW-PEEP ALARM				
LOW-VT ALARM				
LOW/SET VE ALARM				
HIGH-RR ALARM				
HME				
AMBU BAG/MASK				
HHN/MDI MED				
RESTRAINTS				
HR/PULSE O_2				
CUFF PRESSURE				
ET SIZE/PLACE CM				
BREATH SOUNDS R LUNG				
L LUNG				
SUCTION SITE				
SPUTUM AMOUNT				
COLOR				
APNEA ALARMS	Sec/VT	RR/PF/FIO_2	PIP/Itime	I:E/H PR

Breath Sounds:	1. Rhonchi	2. Rales	3. Wheezing	4. Diminished	5. Clear	6. Other _____
Sputum Amount:	1. Scant	2. Small	3. Moderate	4. Large	5. Copious	
Sputum Color:	1. Beige	2. Yellow	3. Blood-tinged	4. White	5. Clear	6. Other _____

Therapist Signature: _____ Date: _____

VENTILATOR FLOW SHEET
000035 (10/2002)

Chemotherapy Services

Chemotherapy involves the administration of oral and intravenous pharmaceuticals for the treatment of many forms of cancer. The type of disease determines the exact type of chemotherapeutic agent administered. Chemotherapy is performed as the primary treatment for diseases that are inoperable or cannot be treated surgically, for example, leukemia. Chemotherapy is also performed in combination with surgery alone, with radiotherapy alone, or with surgery and radiotherapy. The treatment goals of chemotherapy, like all treatments for cancer, may be to cure the disease, control it, or relieve its symptoms.

Intravenous forms of chemotherapy are usually performed in hospital oncology departments. Services may be performed on either an inpatient or an outpatient basis. Most patients, however, receive chemotherapy as outpatients either before or after surgical interventions to remove their tumors.

The health records of chemotherapy patients include the following information:

- Patient identification, including name and record number

- Diagnosis

- Name of the agent and method of administration

- Date the procedure was performed

- Findings or results of treatment procedure

- Date of report and signature of the oncologist who oversaw the treatment

Radiotherapy Services

Like chemotherapy, radiotherapy (also called radiation therapy) is performed as a primary or adjuvant (supporting) treatment for neoplastic disease and many forms of cancer. Physicians specializing in nuclear medicine work with oncologists and other specialty physicians to develop treatment plans targeted to reach specific types of lesions. Radiation therapy equipment is precisely calibrated to deliver radiation to the abnormal tissue while sparing the patient's normal tissue as much as possible. Individual patients may undergo weeks of daily radiation therapy to achieve partial or complete relief of their symptoms. Radiation therapy also prevents the recurrence of the disease in many cases.

Radiotherapy is usually performed in hospital nuclear medicine or radiology departments. Services may be performed on either an inpatient or an outpatient basis. Most patients, however, receive radiotherapy as outpatients either before or after surgical interventions to remove their tumors.

The health records of radiotherapy patients include the following information:

- Patient identification, including name and record number

- Diagnosis

- Name and site of the procedure

- Date the procedure was performed

- Findings or results of treatment procedure

- Date of report and signature of the radiologist who oversaw the treatment

Outpatient Services Provided in Acute Care Facilities

Acute care hospitals provide outpatient services in several departments. Outpatients receive treatment or undergo diagnostic procedures in hospital-based departments and then leave after the treatment or procedure is complete. The contents of outpatient records depend on the type of procedures provided.

Emergency and Trauma Care

Hospital emergency departments provide urgent diagnostic and therapeutic services to patients who have potentially life-threatening medical conditions or traumatic injuries that need immediate attention. The patients treated in emergency departments are considered hospital outpatients, although many emergency patients require inpatient care after their conditions have been diagnosed and stabilized in the emergency department. After being evaluated and treated in the emergency department, patients may be admitted to one of the hospital's inpatient units, discharged, or transferred to another facility.

Most states require emergency care facilities to maintain a chronological record of every patient who was treated at the facility, including those who were dead on arrival or left the facility against medical advice. The records in most states must include at least the patient's name, the date and time of arrival, and the patient's health record number.

Records of Emergency Services

The health records maintained for emergency services contain the same basic information as inpatient records. Emergency physicians take a medical history and perform a physical examination soon after each patient is admitted to the department. Nurses also perform a nursing assessment for each new patient. Physicians' orders, progress notes, and reports from ancillary services are documented throughout the patient's stay in the emergency department.

The content of the emergency health record usually includes:

- Patient identification, including name and record number
- Time of arrival
- Means of arrival (ambulance, private automobile, or police vehicle)
- Name of the person or organization that transported the patient to the emergency department
- Consent to treatment
- Pertinent history, including chief complaint and onset of injury or illness
- Significant physical findings
- Laboratory, X-ray, EEG, and EKG findings
- Treatment rendered and results
- Conclusions at termination of treatment
- Disposition of patient, including transfer, admission, or discharge home
- Condition of patient at discharge or transfer

- Diagnosis upon discharge

- Instructions given to the patient or family regarding care and follow-up

- Signatures and credentials of caregivers

Emergency services records may be filed separately or incorporated into the patient's inpatient record when the patient is admitted to the same facility. When the records are filed separately, the emergency record must be made available when the patient is readmitted or appears for care in the future.

Emergency Department Transfer Records

State regulations specifically require emergency facilities to maintain records of the screening examinations performed on patients who were subsequently transferred to other facilities. Similarly, federal legislation passed in 1986 and implemented in 1990 contains provisions intended to curtail the practice known as patient dumping. **Dumping** refers to the once-common practice of private hospitals to transfer indigent patients to the emergency departments of nearby public hospitals with the sole purpose of avoiding the cost of providing emergency treatment to patients who were uninsured or underensured and could not pay for the services themselves. Basically, state and federal regulations require emergency facilities to thoroughly document the reasons for patient transfers to confirm that the transfers were not related to the patients' ability to pay for treatment or the source of payment. (Antidumping regulations are also discussed in chapter 5.)

To avoid the appearance of dumping, it is particularly important that the records of emergency care patients include enough information to justify each patient's disposition after emergency treatment is complete or deemed unnecessary. In addition, when a decision is made to transfer a patient to another facility, the physician primarily responsible for the patient's care must document in detail the reason for the transfer and the results of the patient's screening examination. Specifically, the patient's record for the encounter must contain documentation that confirms that the following actions were taken (Glondys 1999, p. 215):

- The physician explained to the patient why the transfer was appropriate and what the risks and benefits of the transfer would be.

- Emergency department nursing and medical staff monitored the patient's medical condition from the time he or she came to the department for treatment until the time he or she was transferred.

- Emergency department staff recorded the patient's time of arrival and time of transfer.

- A screening examination was performed and clinical findings were analyzed to support the physician's initial diagnosis.

- Appropriate treatment was provided to stabilize the patient's medical condition before and during the transfer.

- On-call physicians were consulted as appropriate, the timing of the calls and responses was noted, and the on-call physicians' recommendations were documented.

- The hospital documented the patient's informed consent for the transfer if the patient decided to refuse the screening examination or the recommended care and treatment.

- If the patient requested a transfer, his or her request was documented and it was specifically noted that the transfer was not requested by a healthcare provider.

- The transferring hospital sent a copy of the patient's emergency record along with the patient to the second facility. The record described the reason why the patient sought treatment, the results of any diagnostic examinations or tests, and the treatments provided, including any medications that were administered. The record also included a copy of the patient's informed consent for the transfer or the physician's certification that the transfer was appropriate.

Ambulatory Surgery

The records of outpatients who receive surgical services in an ambulatory surgery unit of the hospital must meet the same documentation requirements as inpatient surgical cases. (See the discussion of surgical services earlier in the chapter.) The outpatient records of patients who require inpatient admission after ambulatory surgery should be combined with the patients' inpatient records.

Diagnostic and Therapeutic Services

Many patients receive diagnostic services in hospital departments on an outpatient basis. Their personal physicians send them to local hospitals for specialized tests such as colonoscopies and MRIs that require equipment that is not available in most physicians' offices. Similarly, because most physicians' offices are not equipped to perform procedures that require the use of anesthesia or sedation, patients go to local hospitals for such services. Physicians may also order diagnostic procedures that must be performed and/or interpreted by hospital specialists.

Many hospital-based therapeutic services can also be provided on an outpatient basis. Examples include renal dialysis, chemotherapy, and radiotherapy, which were discussed earlier in the chapter.

Accreditation standards require that the records of patients receiving ongoing ambulatory care services in hospital-based outpatient departments include at least a summary page that lists the patient's diagnoses, past procedures, medications, and allergies. The results of outpatient procedures are reported to the physicians who ordered the procedures, and copies of the reports are filed in the patients' outpatient records.

Standardized Clinical Data Sets

The concept of data standardization became widely accepted during the 1960s, when data sets were developed for a variety of healthcare settings. Data sets for acute care, long-term care, and ambulatory care were the first to be implemented. In healthcare, data sets have two purposes: to identify the data elements that should be collected for every patient and to provide uniform definitions for common terms. The use of standardized data with uniform definitions ensures that the data collected from similar healthcare facilities have comparable characteristics.

The standardization of data elements and definitions makes it possible to compare the data collected at different facilities. Comparative data are used for a variety of purposes, including external accreditation, internal performance improvement, and statistical and biomedical research studies. However, data sets are not meant to limit the number of data elements that can be collected. Most hospitals and other healthcare organizations collect additional data elements that apply to their specific administrative and clinical operations.

Uniform Hospital Discharge Data Set

The federal government adopted the **Uniform Hospital Discharge Data Set** (UHDDS) in 1974 for application to the Medicare and Medicaid programs. Subsequently, the UHDDS definitions were incorporated into the acute care prospective payment system implemented in 1983. The UHDDS is now used by all acute care organizations.

The UHDDS defines a set of common, uniform data elements to be collected in the health record of every hospital inpatient. The data elements then can be abstracted from inpatient records to create databases that describe the characteristics of the patients who receive inpatient care. (See figure 3.60, p. 191.)

Uniform Ambulatory Care Data Set

Hospitals provide ambulatory care services in their outpatient departments, for example, in same-day surgery units, diagnostic imaging services, and radiation therapy services. A data set similar to the UHDDS applies to ambulatory care services, but its use is voluntary.

The **Uniform Ambulatory Care Data Set** (UACDS) was adopted in 1989. Like the UHDDS, its purpose is to define a set of uniform data elements with common definitions so that data can be collected and compared. It includes optional data elements that describe the patient's living conditions, a factor that is more relevant to outpatient providers than to inpatient providers. (See figure 3.61, p. 192.)

Data Elements for Emergency Department Systems and Essential Medical Data Set

In 1997, the National Center for Injury Prevention and Control (NCIPC), a federal agency within the Centers for Disease Control and Prevention (CDC), published a data set applicable to emergency and trauma care. The purpose of the **Data Elements for Emergency Department Systems** (DEEDS), release 1, is to "foster greater uniformity among [the] individual data elements chosen for use" by decision makers within hospital-based emergency departments (National Center for Injury Prevention and Control 1997, p. 1). Participation is voluntary, and DEEDS was not designed to be used as a minimum data set.

The specifications for the data elements in the 1997 version of DEEDS are based on existing health data standards. The data elements were designed to be compatible with EHR and electronic data interchange systems, but many of the data elements are also relevant to traditional paper-based record systems.

DEEDS includes specifications for 156 data elements. The data elements are organized into sections and numbered sequentially within each section. The eight sections include:

- Patient identification data
- Facility and practitioner identification data
- Emergency department payment data
- Emergency department arrival and first-assessment data
- Emergency department history and physical examination data
- Emergency department procedural and outcomes data
- Emergency department medication data
- Emergency department disposition and diagnostic data

Figure 3.60. UHDDS Data Elements

Data Element	Definition/Descriptor
01. Personal identifier	The unique number assigned to each patient within a hospital that distinguishes the patient and his or her hospital record from all others in that institution.
02. Date of birth	Month, day, and year of birth. Capture of the full four-digit year of birth is recommended.
03. Sex	Male or female
04. Race and ethnicity	04a. Race American Indian/Eskimo/Aleut Asian or Pacific Islander Black White Other race Unknown 04b. Ethnicity Spanish origin/Hispanic Non-Spanish origin/Non-Hispanic Unknown
05. Residence	Full address of usual residence Zip code (nine digits, if available) Code for foreign residence
06. Hospital identification	A unique institutional number used across data collection systems. The Medicare provider number is the preferred hospital identifier.
07. Admission date	Month, day, and year of admission.
08. Type of admission	Scheduled: Arranged with admissions office at least 24 hours prior to admission Unscheduled: All other admissions
09. Discharge date	Month, day, and year of discharge
10 & 11. Physician identification • Attending physician • Operating physician	The Medicare unique physician identification number (UPIN) is the preferred method of identifying the attending physician and operating physician(s) because it is uniform across all data systems.
12. Principal diagnosis	The condition established, after study, to be chiefly responsible for occasioning the admission of the patient to the hospital for care.
13. Other diagnoses	All conditions that coexist at the time of admission or that develop subsequently or that affect the treatment received and/or the length of stay. Diagnoses that relate to an earlier episode and have no bearing on the current hospital stay are to be excluded.
14. Qualifier for other diagnoses	A qualifier is given for each diagnosis coded under "other diagnoses" to indicate whether the onset of the diagnosis preceded or followed admission to the hospital. The option "uncertain" is permitted.
15. External cause-of-injury code	The ICD-9-CM code for the external cause of an injury, poisoning, or adverse effect (commonly referred to as an E code). Hospitals should complete this item whenever there is a diagnosis of an injury, poisoning, or adverse effect.
16. Birth weight of neonate	The specific birth weight of a newborn, preferably recorded in grams.
17. Procedures and dates	All significant procedures are to be reported. A significant procedure is one that is: • Surgical in nature, or • Carries an anesthetic risk, or • Carries a procedural risk, or • Requires specialized training. The date of each significant procedure must be reported. When more than one procedure is reported, the principal procedure must be designated. The principal procedure is one that is performed for definitive treatment rather than one performed for diagnostic or exploratory purposes or was necessary to take care of a complication. If two procedures appear to be principal, the one most closely related to the principal diagnosis should be selected as the principal procedure. The UPIN must be reported for the person performing the principal procedure.
18. Disposition of the patient	• Discharged to home (excludes those patients referred to home health service) • Discharged to other healthcare facility • Discharged to acute care hospital • Left against medical advice • Discharged to nursing facility • Alive, other; or alive, not stated • Discharged home to be under the care of a home health service (including a hospice) • Died All categories for primary and other sources are: • Blue Cross/Blue Shield • Health maintenance organization (HMO) • Other health insurance companies • CHAMPUS • Other liability insurance • CHAMPVA • Medicare • Other government payers • Medicaid • Self-pay • Worker's Compensation • No charge (free, charity, special research, teaching) • Self-insured employer plan • Other
19. Patient's expected source of payment	Primary source Other sources
20. Total charges	All charges billed by the hospital for this hospitalization. Professional charges for individual patient care by physicians are excluded.

Figure 3.61. UACDS Data Elements

Data Element	Definition/Descriptor
Provider identification, address, type of practice	Provider identification: Include the full name of the provider as well as the unique physician identification number (UPIN). Address: The complete address of the provider's office. In cases where the provider has multiple offices, the location of the usual or principal place of practice should be given. Profession: • Physician, including specialty or field of practice • Other (specify)
Place of encounter	Specify the location of the encounter: • Private office • Clinic or health center • Hospital outpatient department • Hospital emergency department • Other (specify)
Reason for encounter	Includes, but is not limited to, the patient's complaints and symptoms reflecting his or her own perception of needs, provided verbally or in writing by the patient at the point of entry into the healthcare system or in the patient's own words recorded by an intermediary or provider at that time.
Diagnostic services	All diagnostic services of any type.
Problem, diagnosis, or assessment	Describes the provider's level of understanding and the interpretation of the patient's reasons for the encounter and all conditions requiring treatment or management at the time of the encounter.
Therapeutic services	List, by name, all services done or ordered: • Medical (including drug therapy) • Surgical • Patient education
Preventive services	List, by name, all preventive services and procedures performed at the time of encounter.

Disposition	The provider's statement of the next step(s) in the care of the patient. At a minimum, the following classification is suggested:
	
	1. No follow-up planned
	2. Follow-up planned
	  • Return when necessary
	  • Return to the current provider at a specified time
	  • Telephone follow-up
	  • Return to referring provider
	  • Refer to other provider
	  • Admit to hospital
	  • Other

According to the DEEDS user's manual (National Center for Injury Prevention and Control 1997, p. 2), a structured format is used to document each data element and includes the following information:

- A concise definition

- A description of uses

- A discussion of conceptual or operational issues

- A specification of the data type (and field length)

- A description of when data element repetition may occur

- Field values that designate coding specifications and valid data entries

- Reference to one or more data standards or guidelines used to define the data elements and its field values

- Other references considered in developing the data element

Data types and field lengths conform to Health Level Seven (HL7) electronic data exchange specifications and the American Society for Testing and Materials standard specification for transferring clinical observations between independent computer systems.

In addition to direct patient care and administrative functions, the data elements can be used for many secondary functions. For example, diagnostic data reported to public health agencies may make it possible to control or prevent future disease outbreaks. (Figure 3.62, pp. 194–95, provides an example of one of the DEEDS data elements.)

The **Essential Medical Data Set** (EMEDS) was designed to complement DEEDS. EMEDS is a data set developed specifically for use in collecting medical history data on emergency patients in an electronic health record environment. EMEDS data from emergency and trauma patients are sent to a regional data repository at the conclusion of their treatment. The database can then be analyzed to assess the effectiveness of the trauma care network in the region in terms of response time and patient survival rates.

Summary

Acute care health record documentation includes both administrative and clinical information. The clinical documentation includes a broad range of information and covers both medical and surgical services. Administrative documentation includes demographic information; financial and clinical data; and consents, authorizations, and acknowledgments. The most important function of the acute care health record is the collection of information on the patient's medical condition and progress throughout his or her stay in the hospital.

This chapter details the various types of clinical documentation that may be included in the acute care health record, including information collected specifically for specialty care such as obstetrics and psychiatry.

The importance of data sets in making it possible for multiple providers to compare data is also discussed. Common data sets include the Uniform Hospital Discharge Data Set, the Uniform Ambulatory Care Data Set, the Data Elements for Emergency Department Systems, and the Essential Medical Data Set.

Figure 3.62.   Example of a DEEDS Data Element

> ### 4.06 CHIEF COMPLAINT
>
> PART OF THE CHIEF COMPLAINT GROUP (4.06 AND 4.07)*
>
> #### Definition
>
> Patient's reason for seeking care or attention, expressed in terms as close as possible to those used by patient or responsible informant.
>
> #### Uses
>
> Data collected on the patient's chief complaint are pivotal to the clinical process and provide an important resource for measuring and evaluating health care services. The chief complaint figures prominently in triage decision making and is a key determinant of the direction and extent of history taking, physical examination, and diagnostic testing in the ED. When ED data on chief complaint are aggregated and linked with process, diagnosis, and financial data, they take on added value for clinical and epidemiologic research, practitioner training, quality management, and health care administration and finance.
>
> #### Discussion
>
> Chief complaints encompass more than reports of symptoms or complaints. A chief complaint may also be a request for:
> — a diagnostic, screening, or preventive procedure.
> — treatment or compliance with a practitioner's instructions to seek a specific treatment, procedure, or medication.
> — test results.
> — an examination required by a third-party.
> — a referral, such as follow-up initiated from this ED or elsewhere.
> — intervention for a stated diagnosis or disease.
>
> Although data describing the chief complaint are routinely and often repetitively recorded during a single ED visit, the data generally are not classified, coded, and stored in a form that facilitates aggregate analysis. Several established systems are candidates for classifying and coding ED chief complaints, but modifications or adaptations are likely to be needed for routine ED use. Among the candidate systems are the *International Classification of Primary Care (ICPC), Reason for Visit Classification and Coding Manual (RVC), Systematized Nomenclature of Human and Veterinary Medicine — SNOMED International, Read Codes Version 3,* and the *International Classification of Diseases, 9th Revision, Clinical Modification (ICD-9-CM).* In the interim, text descriptions or local codes can be used.
>
> #### Data Type (and Field Length)
>
> CE — coded element (200).
>
> #### Repetition
>
> Yes; if there is more than one chief complaint, the Chief Complaint Group repeats.
>
> _____
>
> *The Chief Complaint Group includes data elements 4.06 and 4.07. A single iteration of this group is used to report each chief complaint.

Figure 3.62. (Continued)

Field Values

Component 1 is the chief complaint code.
Component 2 is the chief complaint descriptor.
Component 3 is the coding system identifier.
Components 4–6 can be used for an alternate code, descriptor, and coding system identifier.

For example, to encode headache using the *International Classification of Primary Care* (ICP):
Component 1 = N01
Component 2 = Headache
Component 3 = ICP

Text data also can be entered without an accompanying code, as follows:
Component 1 = ""
Component 2 = Headache

If the chief complaint is unknown, enter data in the following manner:
Component 1 = Unknown

Data Standards or Guidelines

None.

Other References

ICPC (Lamberts and Wood, 1987), *RVC* (National Center for Health Statistics, 1994), *SNOMED International* (Cote et al., 1993), *Read Codes Version 3: A User Led Terminology* (O'Neill et al., 1995), and *ICD-9-CM* (U.S. Department of Health and Human Services, 1995).

References

Barnes, Catherine. 2002. Clinical quality management. In *Health Information Management: Concepts, Principles, and Practice*, edited by Kathleen LaTour and Shirley Eichenwald. Chicago: American Health Information Management Association.

Glondys, Barbara. 1999. *Documentation Requirements for the Acute Care Patient Record,* 1999 edition. Chicago: American Health Information Management Association. [Out of print.]

Kiger, Linda. 2002. Content and structure of the health record. In *Health Information Management: Principles and Organization for Health Information Services,* edited by Margaret Skurka. San Francisco: Jossey-Bass.

LaTour, Kathleen. 2002. Healthcare data sets. In *Health Information Management Technology: An Applied Approach,* edited by Merida Johns. Chicago: American Health Information Management Association.

McCain, Mary. 2002. Paper-based health records. In *Health Information Management: Concepts, Principles, and Practice,* edited by Kathleen LaTour and Shirley Eichenwald. Chicago: American Health Information Management Association.

National Center for Injury Prevention and Control. 1997. Data Elements for Emergency Department Systems, Release 1. Atlanta: Centers for Disease Control and Prevention.

National Guideline Clearinghouse. 2004. About NGC. Available at www.guideline.gov.

Shaw, Patricia, and others. 2003. *Quality and Performance Improvement in Healthcare,* revised edition. Chicago: American Health Information Management Association.

Teslow, Mary Spivey, and Wilde, Donna. 2001. Data collection standards. In *Health Information: Management of a Strategic Resource,* second edition, edited by Mervat Abdelhak and others. Philadelphia: W. B. Saunders.

Review Quiz

Directions: Choose the best answer for the following items.

1. ___ Personal information about patients such as their names, ages, and addresses is considered what type of information?
   A. Clinical
   B. Administrative
   C. Operational
   D. Accreditation

2. ___ Instructions on the use of restraints or seclusion are considered what type of documentation?
   A. Discharge orders
   B. Clinical observations
   C. Authentication requirements
   D. Special orders

3. ___ What type of order does this example represent: "Patient is to be transferred to Horizon Nursing Home in the morning"?
   A. Special
   B. Standing
   C. Discharge
   D. Verbal

4. ___ What is the purpose of clinical pathways?
   A. To coordinate clinical services
   B. To assist with case management reports
   C. To help case managers with preadmission planning
   D. To assess a patient's medical condition

5. ___ According to accreditation standards, which document must be placed in the patient's record before a surgical procedure may be performed?
   A. Admission record
   B. Physician's order
   C. Report of history and physical examination
   D. Discharge summary

6. ___ Which of the following is a multidisciplinary tool for organizing the diagnostic and therapeutic services to be provided to the patient?
   A. Initial assessment
   B. Discharge summary
   C. Progress notes
   D. Care plan

7. ___ When a patient collapses upon arrival at the entrance to an emergency department, what type of treatment authorization is in effect?
   A. Expressed consent
   B. Implied consent
   C. Informed consent
   D. Emergency consent

8. ___ What types of information make it easy for hospitals to compare and combine the contents of multiple patient health records?
   A. Administrative information
   B. Progress notes
   C. Demographic information
   D. Uniform data sets

9. ___ What category of services applies to tests related to cardiac and neurological functioning?
   A. Ancillary services
   B. Clinical procedures
   C. Specialty diagnostic services
   D. Principal procedures

10. ___ What name is used in reference to the formal document prepared by the principal surgeon to describe the surgical procedure(s) performed for the patient?
    A. Intraoperative anesthesia record
    B. Pathology report
    C. Recovery room record
    D. Operative report

11. ___ In which of the following types of health record documentation would you find statements like this one: "Specimen consists of normal fallopian tubes and ovaries and uterus showing submucus leiomyomas"?
    A. Postoperative progress notes
    B. Pathology reports
    C. Surgical consents
    D. Uniform data sets

12. ___ Which of the following is an example of demographic data?
    A. 125 Oak Street, Smallville, KS
    B. Temperature: 100 degrees F
    C. Mother died of heart disease
    D. History of appendectomy at age 4

13. ___ Which of the following data sets applies only to electronic health record systems?
    A. Uniform Ambulatory Care Data Set
    B. Data Elements for Emergency Department Systems
    C. Essential Medical Data Set
    D. Uniform Hospital Discharge Data Set

14. ___ "100 mg of penicillin per mouth administered at 8 a.m." is an example of what kind of documentation?
    A. Discharge assessment
    B. Progress note
    C. Medication record
    D. Initial assessment

15. ___ Why is patient financial information collected by healthcare providers?
    A. To confirm the identity of the patient
    B. To ensure that patients can afford healthcare
    C. To complete the claims forms submitted to third-party payers
    D. To conform to uniform data sets

16. ___ Under which circumstances may an interval note be added to a patient's health record in place of a complete history and physical?
    A. When the patient is readmitted a second time for the same condition
    B. When the patient is readmitted within thirty days of the initial treatment for a different condition
    C. When the patient is readmitted a third time for the same condition
    D. When the patient is readmitted within thirty days of the initial treatment for the same condition

17. ___ What type of documentation relates to the patient's condition and course of treatment?
    A. Financial
    B. Demographic
    C. Clinical
    D. Administrative

18. ___ Which of the following anesthesia reports would be used to document an unusual event or complication that occurred during surgery?
    A. Postoperative
    B. Recovery room
    C. Intraoperative
    D. Preoperative

19. ___ Which of the following types of documentation would be used to describe the process of surgically removing a shard of glass from a patient's foot?
    A. Operative report
    B. Pathology report
    C. Postoperative anesthesia record
    D. Intraoperative anesthesia record

20. ___ What type of information is exemplified by the insured party's member identification number?
    A. Demographic information
    B. Clinical information
    C. Certification information
    D. Financial information

21. ___ Why was the International Implant Registry created in 1988?
    A. To provide a support network for patients who have had implants
    B. To raise awareness of the availability of implantable devices
    C. To track patients who have had implants in order to notify them of potential safety concerns
    D. To raise awareness of the importance of organ donation

22. ___ Which of the following terms is used in reference to a written document that describes the patient's healthcare preferences in the event he or she becomes unable to communicate directly in the future?
    A. Interval note
    B. Rights statement
    C. Consent to treatment
    D. Advance directive

23. ___ Which of the following types of physician documentation is used to document the patient's own description of his or her present illness?
    A. History report
    B. Progress note
    C. Physician's order
    D. Demographic data

24. ___ What term is used in reference to the patient care instructions that physicians give to other healthcare providers?
    A. Medical history
    B. Physician's progress notes
    C. Physician's orders
    D. Discharge summary

25. ___ Which type of nursing documentation summarizes the date, time, and method of admission as well as the patient's current condition, symptoms, and vital signs?
    A. Discharge assessment
    B. Progress note
    C. Medication record
    D. Initial assessment

26. ___ What type of documentation represents a concise description of the patient's illness, course of treatment, response to treatment, and condition at the time he or she left the hospital?
    A. Medical history
    B. Discharge summary
    C. Physical examination
    D. Progress note

27. ___ Which data set would be used to document an elective surgical procedure that does not require an overnight hospital stay?
    A. Uniform Hospital Discharge Data Set
    B. Data Elements for Emergency Department Systems
    C. Uniform Ambulatory Care Data Set
    D. Essential Medical Data Set

28. ___ What type of information are consents and authorizations?
    A. Clinical
    B. Surgical
    C. Public
    D. Administrative

29. ___ What type of health record documentation represents a chronological record of the patient's condition and response to treatment throughout his or her hospital stay?
    A. Medical history
    B. Physical examination
    C. Operative report
    D. Progress notes

30. ___ What type of health record documentation would a physician use to give a nurse the following instructions: "Give 100 mg of penicillin, tid"?
    A. Patient instructions
    B. Medication report
    C. Physician's order
    D. Discharge order

31. ___ What type of health record documentation would a nurse use to document a patient's reaction to anesthesia and condition after surgery?
    A. Recovery room record
    B. Initial assessment
    C. Discharge assessment
    D. Nursing progress notes

32. ___ "Mother died of breast cancer; father still living but has heart disease" is an example of what type of health record documentation?
    A. Physician's progress note
    B. History report
    C. Physician's order
    D. Discharge summary

33. ___ What type of health record documentation includes aftercare instructions for the patient and/or his or her caregiver?
    A. Discharge summary
    B. Physical examination
    C. History
    D. Progress notes

34. ___ What type of report would be issued after a tilt-table test was performed?
    A. Laboratory
    B. Neurology
    C. Cardiology
    D. Imaging

35. ___ What type of report would be issued after an electroencephalogram was performed?
    A. Laboratory
    B. Neurology
    C. Cardiology
    D. Imaging

36. ___ What type of report would be issued after a CT scan was performed?
    A. Laboratory
    B. Neurology
    C. Cardiology
    D. Imaging

37. ___ What type of report would be issued after a urinalysis was performed?
    A. Laboratory
    B. Neurology
    C. Cardiology
    D. Imaging

Directions for Items 38–45: Match each of the following healthcare procedures with the hospital service that usually provides it.

38. ___ Caesarian delivery

39. ___ Assessment of a newborn's condition

40. ___ Assessment of a patient's mental health status

41. ___ Physical therapy for a stroke patient

42. ___ External filtering of blood to treat kidney disease

43. ___ Administration of aerosol medication to help breathing

44. ___ Administration of pharmaceuticals to treat cancer

45. ___ Administration of radiation to treat cancer

    A. Chemotherapy services
    B. Rehabilitation services
    C. Neonatal services
    D. Renal dialysis services
    E. Radiotherapy services
    F. Obstetrical services
    G. Psychiatric services
    H. Respiratory services

Chapter 4

Organization and Management of Acute Care Health Records

Learning Objectives

- Compare the features of the three different paper-based health record formats
- Describe the features of electronic health records
- Compare the benefits and drawbacks of EHRs and paper-based records
- Explain the types of technological systems that support EHRs
- Describe the basic types of health informatics standards
- Explain the functions of clinical decision support systems
- Describe and compare the different methods of health record numbering and filing
- Describe and compare the different methods of health record storage
- Outline the steps in record retrieval and tracking
- Explain the importance of the standardization of forms and views
- Explain the importance of the standardization of abbreviations and symbols
- Outline the process for correcting errors in health records
- Compare qualitative and quantitative health record analysis and explain the purposes of each
- Describe the four quality domains in the AHIMA data quality management model

Terminology

Alphabetic filing system
Alphanumeric filing system
American Society for Testing and Materials (ASTM)
Authentication
Average record delinquency rate
Clinical data repository
Clinical decision support (CDS)
Data exchange standards

Data quality management
Database
Database management system
Deficiency system
Digital signature
EHR Collaborative
Electronic document management system (EDMS)
Electronic health record (EHR)
Electronic signature
Health informatics standards
Health Level Seven (HL7)
Health record analysis
Health record number
Integrated health record
Messaging standards
Numeric filing system
Ongoing record review
Online analytical processing (OLAP)
Outguide
Privacy and security standards
Problem list
Problem-oriented health record
Prohibited abbreviations
Qualitative analysis
Quantitative analysis
Requisition
Serial numbering system
Serial–unit numbering system
Source-oriented health record
Structure and content standards
Telemedicine
Terminal-digit filing system
Unique identifier
Unit numbering system
Vocabulary standards

Introduction

Whether paper-based or computer-based, health records must include the same patient information and perform the same communications functions. (The functions of the health record were discussed in detail in chapter 2; the content in chapter 3.) All acute care facilities must develop and enforce policies that ensure the uniformity of health record content and format. Health record policies are based on a number of external and internal factors. Professional practice standards, reimbursement requirements, accreditation standards, state licensing requirements, federal regulations, and public health reporting requirements all must be considered. Each hospital's internal information requirements depend on its organizational structure, the type of care it provides, and the characteristics of the community it serves. For example, the health record policies of a public hospital in New York City might be quite different than those of a private psychiatric hospital in Spokane.

Early medical practitioners probably used handwritten notes to help them keep track of important information about their patients. A few of the handwritten records kept by field surgeons during the Civil War still survive in museums and private collections as examples. The first hospital in the British colonies of North America—Pennsylvania Hospital in Philadelphia—began maintaining paper health records on the day it opened, in 1752.

The standardization of medical and hospital care in the early twentieth century marked the beginning of modern medical record-keeping systems. For the first half of the century, all of the clinical, administrative, and financial records of hospitals and medical practitioners were maintained as handwritten notes, indexes, and registers and typewritten reports. The health information management profession grew out of the early efforts of medical record librarians to protect and organize those paper documents.

Hospitals, like other American businesses, began applying computer processing to operations and management in the 1960s. The first hospital applications of computer technology were implemented in the areas of financial management, admissions, and billing. By the year 2000, virtually every clinical laboratory in the United States had implemented computer-based diagnostic systems with automatic reporting capabilities. Many of today's sophisticated diagnostic, medical, and surgical procedures would not be possible without the support of accurate and reliable software systems.

In contrast, the application of computer technology to health record systems has progressed slowly. Most acute care organizations now depend on mixed-media health record systems made up of computer-generated laboratory reports, digital images, transcribed medical–surgical reports, and handwritten orders and progress notes. The cost of computer-based clinical documentation systems certainly has been one reason why progress has been slow. But the biggest factor delaying the universal implementation of electronic health records has probably been the lack of a shared vision. Healthcare organizations have been reluctant to undertake complex and expensive technology projects without national guidelines that establish what **electronic health record** (EHR) systems should include and how they should function.

Health Level Seven (HL7), a healthcare standards development organization, completed the initial work on a functional model for EHRs in late 2003. In early 2004, industry stakeholders led by the EHR Collaborative voted to adopt the proposed model. The **EHR Collaborative** is composed of several healthcare professional and trade associations, including the American Health Information Management Association, that support the universal implementation of EHRs. The model will be refined during a two-year trial period to begin in 2004. (A copy of the 2004 draft of the EHR model is provided in appendix L.) After the trial period is over and the model has been finalized, the model will become an HL7 standard. The American Health Information Management Association (AHIMA), along with the other healthcare organizations participating in the EHR Collaborative, believes that the adoption of a national EHR standard will stimulate the commercial development of more broadly applicable and less costly electronic health record systems.

The **American Society for Testing and Materials** (ASTM) has also developed a standard related to electronic health records. ASTM standard E1384-99el is entitled Standard Guide for Content and Structure of the Electronic Health Record. The new standard covers the content and structure of electronic health records and provides guidelines for healthcare organizations planning and implementing new systems.

The universal adoption of electronic health record systems may still be years off, but the change is inevitable. The primary goals of every health record system are to facilitate the sharing of clinical information and to ensure the quality and safety of patient care. Increasing demands for accurate, secure, and accessible health information will only be fully met through the application of advanced communications technology. (The AHIMA has published six practice briefs designed to guide hospitals and other healthcare organizations in the design and implementation of EHR systems. The briefs are reproduced in appendix M.)

Format of the Paper-Based Health Record

The traditional paper-based health record has several limitations. One limitation is the need to adhere to a strict record format, sometimes referred to as "chart order." Because paper-based records are lengthy and difficult to handle, healthcare organizations organize them according to a specific format that must be followed by every user. The greater the number of users, the more important it is that the records follow strict format guidelines.

Another limitation is the obvious fact that paper-based health records can be viewed by only one user at a time and in only one place at a time. Therefore, the valuable information documented in health records is often unavailable to individual users when and where they need it.

Paper-based health records also can be difficult to update. An active record of a patient receiving care moves from provider to provider within the healthcare facility. The individuals responsible for updating its content must hand-carry paper documents to wherever the record is located in order to file them or wait until the record is returned to them. Updates and reports may be delayed or misplaced as a result.

Finally, paper-based health records are fragile. They are susceptible to damage from water, fire, and the effects of daily use. For most hospitals, maintaining duplicate copies as backups for paper records would be prohibitively expensive. Consequently, paper-based health records are always at risk for being misplaced, misfiled, or damaged.

Most hospitals currently follow one of three formats for paper-based health records: the source-oriented health record, the problem-oriented health record, or the integrated health record. It is important to remember, however, that no hard-and-fast rules exist for arranging the elements of a health record. Hospitals are free to select the arrangement that best suits their needs as long as their systems fulfill the requirements of state laws, federal regulations, and accreditation standards.

Source-Oriented Health Records

In the **source-oriented health record,** documents are grouped together according to their point of origin. That is, laboratory records are grouped together, radiology records are grouped together, clinical notes are grouped together, and so on. Thus, physicians' progress notes for a single episode of patient care would be arranged, usually in reverse chronological order, and filed together in the patient's health record. Similarly, notes prepared by nursing services, social services, and other clinical services would be grouped separately.

Under this format, the individuals charged with filing reports in paper-based records can do so simply by looking at the source and date of the report. However, the users of information filed in this type of record have more trouble. To follow or document information on the patient's course of treatment, they must search by date of occurrence in each of the sections (that is, laboratory, radiology, and every group of clinical notes). The more departments a hospital has, the more sections the source-oriented health record can have. It is left to the end user to tie together information from the various sections of the record to get a full picture of the patient's course of treatment.

Problem-Oriented Health Records

The **problem-oriented health record** is easier for the patient's caregivers to use. The key characteristic of this format is that it is arranged according to a **problem list.** A problem list is an itemized description of the patient's past and present social, psychological, and medical problems. Each problem is indexed with a unique number, and reports and clinical documentation are keyed to the number of the problem they address. The documentation is then arranged in chronological or reverse chronological order within sections, each of which covers a specific problem. (See figure 4.1.)

In addition to the problem list, the problem-oriented health record contains a prescribed set of patient data, an initial care plan, and progress notes. The content of the problem-oriented health record is basically the same as the content of source-oriented records. Content includes:

- Chief complaint
- Present illness(es)
- Social history
- Medical history
- Physical examination
- Diagnostic test results

The initial care plan serves as an overall guide for addressing each of the patient's problems. The services described in the plan are numbered to correspond to the problems they address.

The patient's caregivers use progress notes to document how the patient's problems are being treated and how the patient is responding to treatment. Each progress note is labeled with the number of the problem it is intended to address. This problem-indexing system allows the clinician to easily follow the patient's course of treatment. Ideally, other elements of the health record (for example, physicians' orders) are also numbered according to the problems they address. The biggest shortcoming of problem-oriented records is the inconsistent application of problem numbers to every piece of documentation.

Integrated Health Records

The third format used for paper-based acute care records is the **integrated health record.** The integrated health record is arranged so that the documentation from various sources is intermingled and follows a strict chronological or reverse chronological order. The advantage of the integrated format is that it is easy for caregivers to follow the course of the patient's diagnosis and treatment. The disadvantage is that the format makes it difficult to compare related information. (See figure 4.2 for an example of a progress note page from an integrated health record.)

Format of the Electronic Health Record

The electronic health record can be considered the inevitable result of health record evolution. By design, the electronic health record addresses many of the problems that have troubled paper-based health record systems for years. For example, electronic health records are almost always accessible through a computer network, and so the availability problems characteristic of paper-based records do not affect electronic records. The other strengths of EHR systems are equally obvious. For example, EHR systems:

- Make it possible to access information quickly and easily
- Allow various levels of access and view customization

Figure 4.1. Example of a Problem List

Anytown Community Hospital

**INTERDISCIPLINARY PROBLEM LIST
AND PLAN OF CARE**

PATIENT LABEL

Category: Problem List:

Subcategory: ☐

                                             ☐

Discharge Outcomes

Target Date/ Initials	Key Interventions	Discipline	Start Date/ Initials	Stop Date/ Initials

Initials	Signature	Discipline	Initials	Signature	Discipline

Key

CM = Case Manager	NSG = Nursing	RD = Registered Dietitian
DTC = Diabetes Treatment Center	OT = Occupational Therapist	RT = Respiratory Therapist
ETN = Enterostomal Nurse	PC = Pastoral Care	SLP = Speech/Language Pathologist
FSR = Financial Services Representative	PHM = Pharmacy	SW = Social Worker
HCC = Home Care Coordinator	PT = Physical Therapist	

Origin:

INTERDISCIPLINARY PROBLEM LIST
000100 (10/2002)

Figure 4.2. Example of an Integrated Progress Note

University of Anystate Hospitals

PROGRESS NOTES
PAGE 1 OF 4

PATIENT LABEL

Barriers to Patient Education

☐ No Barriers ☐ Language
☐ Physical ☐ Reading Difficulties
☐ Cognitive ☐ Lacks Readiness
☐ Emotional ☐ Lacks Motivation
☐ Other _____

Patient/Family Instructions		Outcome	Initials	Discipline
☐ Nutrition	P/F			
☐ Medications	P/F			
☐ Activity/Rehabilitation	P/F			
☐ Safety	P/F			
☐ Signs/Symptoms	P/F			
☐ Wound/Skin Care	P/F			
☐ Pre/Postop Care	P/F			
☐ Equipment	P/F			
☐ Procedures	P/F			
☐ Treatments	P/F			
☐ Pain Management	P/F			
☐ Other	P/F			

Outcome Key:
1. Able to state understanding and/or return demonstration.
2. Unable to state understanding and/or return demonstration. Continue to reinforce. (See progress notes.)

Date	Time	Discipline	PROGRESS NOTES

Figure 4.2. **(Continued)**

University of Anystate Hospitals

PROGRESS NOTES
PAGE 2 OF 4

PATIENT LABEL

Date	Time	Discipline	PROGRESS NOTES

Key

CM = Case Manager	NSG = Nursing	RD = Registered Dietitian
CR = Cardiac Rehabilitation	NPSY = Neuropsychology	RT = Respiratory Therapy
DTC = Diabetes Treatment Center	OT = Occupational Therapy	SLP = Speech/Language Pathologist
ETN = Enterostomal Nurse	PC = Pastoral Care	SW = Social Worker
FSR = Financial Services Representative	PHM = Pharmacy	TR = Therapeutic Recreation
HCC = Home Care Coordinator	PT = Physical Therapy	

Figure 4.2. (Continued)

University of Anystate Hospitals

PROGRESS NOTES
PAGE 3 OF 4

PATIENT LABEL

DAILY RN REASSESSMENT

	Within Normal Anatomical Limits	

Neurological/ Musculoskeletal
Yes ☐ No ☐

Level of Consciousness
☐ Disoriented
☐ Lethargic
☐ Unresponsive
☐ Respond Only to Stimuli
Comments:

Speech
☐ Slurred
☐ Impediment
☐ Aphasic

Movement
☐ ↓RA
☐ ↓RL
☐ ↓LA
☐ ↓LL

Sensation
☐ Tingling
☐ Numbness

R/L Pupils
R ☐   L ☐ Nonreactive
☐   ☐ Sluggish
☐   ☐ Constricted
☐   ☐ Fixed
☐   ☐ Dilated

Heart/Vascular
Yes ☐ No ☐

Heart
☐ Skips   ☐ Murmur   ☐ Tachycardia
☐ Palpitations   ☐ Irreg. Rhythm   ☐ Bradycardia
☐ Valve Click
Comments:

Edema
☐ Generalized
Location _____
Degree (1–4) _____

Vascular (0,1,3,4)
R Radial + ____ ☐ Dop   R Pedal + ____ ☐ Dop
L Radial + ____ ☐ Dop   L Pedal + ____ ☐ Dop

Pulmonary/ Lungs
Yes ☐ No ☐

Respirations
☐ Orthopnea   ☐ Labored   ☐ Snoring
☐ Sputum Prod.   ☐ Shallow   ☐ Irregular
☐ Apnea   ☐ Retractions
Comments:

Breath Sounds   R   L
☐ Cracles   ☐   ☐   ☐ Diminished   R ☐   L ☐
☐ Rhonchi   ☐   ☐   ☐ Absent   ☐   ☐
☐ Wheezes   ☐   ☐

Gastrointestinal
Yes ☐ No ☐

Bowel Sounds
☐ Hypo
☐ Hyper
☐ Absent
Comments:

Abdomen
☐ Firm   ☐ Distended
☐ Protuberant   ☐ Tender

Bowel Habits
☐ Frequency   ☐ Diarrhea
☐ Hemorrhoids   ☐ Ostomy
☐ Constipation   ☐ Irregular

Recent Changes
☐ Bleeding   ☐ Color Change
☐ Incontinent   ☐ Nausea
☐ Vomiting

Skin Integumentary
Yes ☐ No ☐

Problem   **Location**
☐ Bruise   _____
☐ Burn   _____
☐ Rash   _____
☐ Cyanotic
Comments:

Problem   **Location**
☐ Wound   _____
☐ Ulcer   _____
☐ Other

Problem
☐ Cold & Clammy
☐ Diaphoretic
☐ Pale
☐ Jaundice

Genitourinary Reproductive
Yes ☐ No ☐

Urinary
☐ Urgency   ☐ Hematuria   ☐ Frequency   ☐ Nocturia
☐ Oliguria   ☐ Incontinent   ☐ Hesitancy   ☐ Dysuria
Comments:

Reproductive
☐ Discharge   ☐ Breast Problems
☐ Bleeding   ☐ Prostate Problems

Emotional Mental
Yes ☐ No ☐

☐ Anxious   ☐ Combative   ☐ Upset   ☐ Suicidal Ideations   ☐ Withdrawn   ☐ Multiple Life Crises
☐ Uncommunicative   ☐ Uncooperative
Comments:

Pain
Yes ☐ No ☐

Location: _____
Onset: _____
Duration: _____
Intensity (0–10): _____
Quality/Characteristics/Pattern: _____
Comments:

Alleviating Factors: _____
Aggravating Factors: _____
Affects on ADL: _____
Relieved by: _____

Plan of Care	Interdisciplinary plan of care/clinical pathway/clinical guidelines ☐ **Reviewed** ☐ **Revised** Discussed with patient/family? ☐ **Yes** ☐ **No**	Referral recommended (yes) requires date and initial of person entering dept. consult/information into Star
Risk for Falls/ Injury	Patient is on falls/injury precautions ☐ **Yes** ☐ **No** If no, proceed with falls/injury reassessment: Altered mobility=2 Altered mental status=2 Fall or near fall=2 **TOTAL** Within 24 hrs postop=2 Altered elimination pattern=2 Fails to follow directions=1 **SCORE** ☐	High risk for falls/injury (3 or more falls) _____ Initials
Advance Directives	If patient has an advanced directive, is a copy on the chart?	☐ No ☐ Yes Date:_____ Initials:_____ ☐ N/A
Integument	One or more (√) checks indicates a reevaluation of the plan of care is needed. ☐ Does patient demonstrate a decrease in mobility? ☐ Does patient have any reddened areas on bony prominences? If (√) checked, refer to the ETN ☐ Is there a loss of previously intact skin?	☐ No ☐ Yes Date:_____ Initials:_____
Diabetic Treatment	If (√) checked, refer to the DTC ☐ Patient ordered insulin or oral agents in the past 24 hours	☐ No ☐ Yes Date:_____ Initials:_____
Nutrition	One or more (√) checks, refer to the RD ☐ Change in functional status (i.e., difficulty swallowing, ↓LOC) ☐ New procedure affecting nutrition (i.e., chemotherapy, dialysis) ☐ Altered diet or inadequate nutrition (i.e., TF, TPN, PPN) ☐ Patient on special diet for first time (i.e., ↓ cholesterol, ADA)	☐ No ☐ Yes Date:_____ Initials:_____
Discharge Planning	One or more (√) checks, refer to the CM ☐ Current discharge plan is not appropriate for patient	☐ No ☐ Yes Date:_____ Initials:_____
Spiritual Needs	One or more (√) checks, refer to PC ☐ Patient/family needs spiritual or emotional support from hospital chaplain, personal clergy, or religious community	☐ No ☐ Yes Date:_____ Initials:_____
Functional	One or more (√) checks, refer to OT/SLP/PT ☐ Has there been a surgical procedure or other condition change resulting in change in function? ☐ Change in ADLs ☐ Change in communication ☐ Change in mobility ☐ Change in swallowing	☐ No ☐ Yes Date:_____ Initials:_____

RN Initials: _____   RN Signature: _____   Date: _____   Time: _____   Unit: _____

Figure 4.2. (Continued)

University of Anystate Hospitals

PROGRESS NOTES
PAGE 4 OF 4

PATIENT LABEL

DAILY CARE RECORD

DATE: _____

Activity	7–3	3–11	11–7
Activity Ad Lib			
Bedrest			
Dangle			
Ambulating			
Up in Chair			
Turning Time			
Position: Right Left Back			
Bedside Commode/Bathroom Privileges			
ROM/Leg Exercise			
Incentive Spirometry			
Cough, Deep Breath			
Other:			

Hygiene	7–3	3–11	11–7
Bathtub/Shower/Bed			
Complete/Self/Assist			
Skin Care			
Oral Care/Nasal Care			
Perineal Care			
Other:			

Nutrition	7–3	3–11	11–7
Type of Diet			
Amount Eaten			
HS Snack			
Calorie Count			
Tube Feeding/Supplement			
Other:			

Risk Management	7–3	3–11	11–7
Side Rails (×2 or ×4)			
Call Light in Reach			
Name Band On			
Bed in Low Position			
Fall Precaution Protocol			
Seizure Precautions			
Isolations			
*Self-Injury Precaution			
Other:			

Equipment	7–3	3–11	11–7
Telemetry/Traction			
Ventilator			
IV Pump			
Antiembolism Hose			
O₂ Amount ____ Device ____			
Feeding Pump/Bag Changed			
Suction-Gastric/Thoracic/Oral			
Special Matress/Bed			
Skin Protectors			
Sequential Compression Device			
Pulse Oximeter			
Other:			

√=Maintained entire shift   *Refer to interdisciplinary progress notes (for equipment that is ordered and recorded in notes).

Maintenance Record

		Site Port	Time Int.

Cap/Δ
Site Care
Site Start/Δ
Size

Primary Caregiver Signatures

7–3	
3–11	
11–7	

Initials	Additional Signatures

Specimen/Tests/Procedures

Specimen	Results
Type	
Blood	
Urine	
Stool/Wound	
X Ray	
Scan	
Diagnostic Test	

Respiratory Care Services

Therapy: ☐ HHN ☐ MDI ☐ CPT ☐ Other_____
Frequency: ____ Hour ____ ID ☐ A/C ☐ WA

7 a.m. 8   9   10   11   12   1   2   3   4   5   6

7 p.m. 8   9   10   11   12   1   2   3   4   5   6

Special Instructions:

Medication & Dose:

Comments:

Site Check: (IV/INT/AV Fistula = q. 8. h.)

Initials = No evidence of redness, swelling, or drainage; rate and fluid checked; and/or presence of bruit and thrill. *Refer to IPN

Site	7–3	3–11	11–7

Sites

SC = Subclavian (R or L)   PC = Portacath
RAV = Right AV Fistula   LAV = Left AV Fistula
H = Hickman   PB = Piggyback
LA = Left Arm   RA = Right Arm
LH = Left Hand   RH = Right Hand
O= _____

PROGRESS NOTES
000009 (11/2002)

- Allow multiple users to access the same information simultaneously

- Perform complex or difficult tasks quickly

- Permit ready access to volumes of professional resource information such as practice standards and medical literature

Another benefit of electronic health records is the ease with which they can be updated and maintained. In addition, because EHRs can be copied and stored in a variety of electronic media, computer files can be backed up frequently and stored at off-site locations or in secure storage areas within the facility. Thus, they can be more easily protected from damage, loss, and tampering than paper-based records.

EHR systems also have one obvious drawback: They are very expensive to design, implement, and maintain. But like all technological advances, the cost of EHR systems is probably the highest now, when the technology is still relatively new. As national standards are accepted and more customers want the technology, more vendors will begin marketing uniform systems that meet industry standards. Prices should go down dramatically after the original development costs have been recouped and manufacturing processes have been refined.

EHR systems are also expensive to implement because of the extensive training required for health record users. The need to make process changes, redevelop health record policies and procedures, convert existing paper records to electronic formats, and recruit information system support staff also adds to the total cost of implementing a new system.

For individual hospitals, the implementation of an EHR system is likely to yield significant and lasting improvements in both operations and patient care. On the national level, the potential value of enhanced information sharing among policy makers and public health experts is obvious. The dollar value of these benefits, however, is impossible to quantify. There is no way to place a price tag on improved outcomes for patients, reduced levels of medical error, or more efficient healthcare delivery systems. Still, in spite of the complexity and cost of implementing EHR systems, few healthcare experts doubt that the electronic health record will become the industry standard in the near future.

Definition of the Electronic Health Record

In its landmark report, *The Computer-Based Patient Record: An Essential Technology for Health Care,* the Institute of Medicine (Dick et al. 1997, p. 55) defined the computer-based health record as follows:

> A computer-based patient record (CPR) is an electronic patient record that resides in a system specifically designed to support users by providing accessibility to complete and accurate data, alerts, reminders, clinical decision support systems, links to medical knowledge, and other aids.

A number of different terms have been used to refer to health records created and maintained in digital environments. Computer-based patient record (CPR), electronic medical record (EMR), and electronic patient record (EPR) are some of the most common. Currently, the AHIMA prefers to use the term electronic health record, or EHR. The AHIMA reserves the term EHR for record systems that fulfill the Institute of Medicine's vision for computer-based records. (The IOM of the National Academies, an entity of the National Academy of Sciences, provides health and science policy guidance to all sectors of society.)

True EHRs are not simply digitized versions of traditional paper records. Rather, they incorporate sophisticated data capture and retrieval technology as well as fully functional decision support systems. In addition, the infrastructure of EHRs automatically protects the security and integrity of clinical documentation and makes it available instantaneously to multiple users.

Many hospitals and other healthcare organizations are currently using computerized health record systems that store whole files as images rather than as individual data elements. In other words, many existing computer-based records are storage mechanisms for electronic versions of paper documentation. For example, a record in this type of system might contain a scanned digital image of a physician's history and physical report, but the clinical content stored within the history and physical report would only be accessible visually. Therefore, it would still function in the same way a paper-based record would, and it would still have many of the paper-based record's limitations.

Current computer-based record systems do make patient information more widely accessible, but most lack the decision support capabilities and links to expert medical resources that are characteristic of fully functional EHRs. In today's healthcare environment, few organizations have implemented fully functional EHRs as envisioned by the Institute of Medicine. However, the implementation of electronic imaging technology in mixed-media records stored electronically is probably the first step toward more widespread adoption of true EHRs.

Technological Support for EHRs

Electronic health record systems are very complex. They are not like other digital systems currently used in hospitals to perform relatively narrow functions such as admitting and administration or laboratory reporting. EHRs fulfill a number of interrelated communications functions that involve virtually every area of the hospital.

Communications technology has evolved quickly over the past fifteen years, and EHR developers and administrators often find it challenging to keep up with new developments. System administrators also must develop ways to make existing information systems work with new technological devices.

A number of communications technologies support EHR systems. The most important are databases, database management systems, image processing and storage systems, data capture and retrieval technology, and servers and networks. (See figures 4.3 and 4.4.)

Figure 4.3.   EHR Data Types and Their Sources

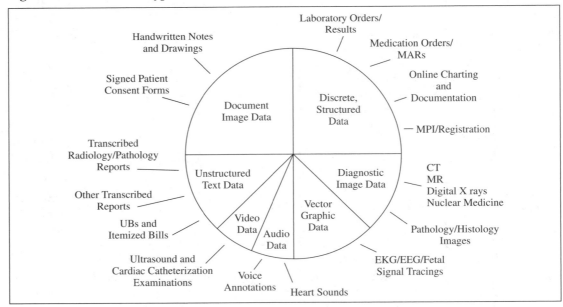

Figure 4.4. Conceptual Model for a Health Information Management System

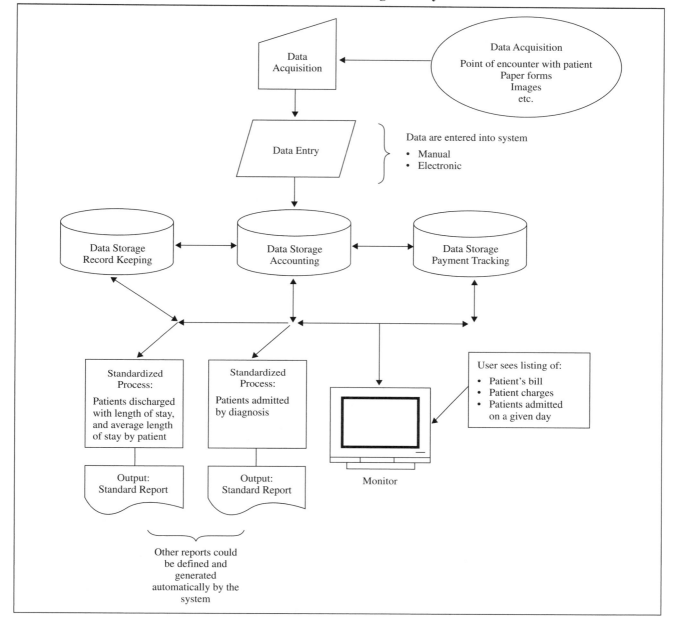

Databases and Database Management Systems

A **database** is an organized collection of data that have been stored electronically for easy access. **Database management systems** make it possible to create, modify, delete, and view the data in a database.

Most EHRs are organized according to one of two database models—the centralized EHR and the distributed EHR—or in a hybrid of the two models. In the centralized EHR, all of the organization's patient health information and data are stored in a single EHR system. In the distributed EHR, patient health information and data are distributed in department-based systems or subsystems that are able to exchange information with one another.

The centralized EHR system is built around a clinical data repository. A **clinical data repository** is a centralized database that captures, sorts, and processes patient data and then sends them back to the user. These functions demand specialized database management capabilities. The most common type of database management system in use today is the relational database, which uses data tables to organize information. New types of database management systems are in development and will probably speed up processing time in the future. (See figure 4.5.)

In decentralized EHR systems, health record information is retained in separate departmental computer systems or databases. Data are then exchanged among departmental systems as needed (for example, between the clinical laboratory's system and the obstetrics unit's system). The decentralized system can work relatively well when all or most of the facility's computers were manufactured using the same proprietary operational system. However, all of the organization's departments must follow established **data exchange standards,** which ensure that all of the organization's data are structured and formatted in the same way (Amatayakul 2002, p. 180).

Image Processing and Storage Technology

Traditional paper-based health records included few photographs and diagnostic images. With the introduction of clinical imaging devices, it has become possible to combine health record text files with digital diagnostic images (X rays, CT scans, and so on) as well as digital photographs. This technology makes it possible for clinicians at different locations to view the same images at the same time and then compare their diagnostic interpretations.

Many hospitals have incorporated document image processing technology into their health record systems. Digital scanners create images of handwritten and printed documents that are then stored in health record databases as electronic files. Using scanned images solves many of the problems associated with traditional paper health records. Digital files can be backed up frequently, which helps solve the problem of lost paper and microfilm records. In addition, because digital files are always under the control of a system administrator, access and confidentiality can be protected simultaneously. Digital imaging also makes it possible for more than one clinician to view the same document at the same time from distant locations. However, as noted previously, clinical documentation stored as digital images can only be accessed visually; that is, it cannot be searched electronically.

Data Retrieval Technology

Retrieving a single piece of information from a paper record can require a lot of time and effort. Many organizations have attempted to improve retrieval processes by using color-coded file folders, flags, and tabs as well as automated record-tracking systems. Although such methods are helpful, they have not completely resolved the problem of inefficient information retrieval.

Figure 4.5. Physical and Logical Data Repositories for EHR Systems

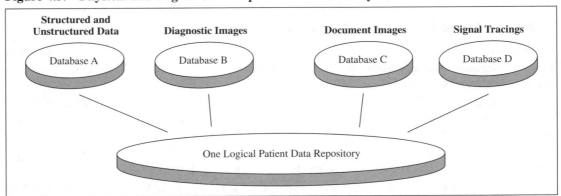

The ultimate goal of every EHR system is the fast and secure delivery of accurate and complete health information to authorized recipients when and where they need it. To be effective, data retrieval systems must be based on the needs of the users.

Database systems that use query language applications allow users to perform text searches of electronic health record data. The ability to identify key words and phrases in textual data makes it easier to find and retrieve key pieces of patient information from health records.

Unfortunately, the usefulness of text search technology in healthcare applications has been limited by the lack of standardization in medical terminology. Currently, several different medical terms can be used to describe the same condition. For example, angiohemophilia may also be called von Willebrand's disease, von Willebrand's syndrome, constitutional thrombopathy, or vascular hemophilia. As a result, text searches using one of the synonyms for this condition would likely yield only a small portion of the information that is actually available.

To address this problem, healthcare industry groups are working together to develop standardized vocabularies. Of these, the Systematized Nomenclature of Medicine Clinical Terms® (SNOMED CT®) is the most likely to be adopted universally. (SNOMED CT and other clinical vocabularies are discussed in more detail in chapter 5.)

Data Capture Technology

Creating a workable data capture process has proved to be one of the biggest challenges in EHR development and implementation. Ideally, the individual responsible for providing each service would enter the documentation for the service into the health record database at or near the time the service was performed. Once recorded, the information would become available immediately to all authorized users who needed access.

Unfortunately, many clinicians who graduated from medical school before the widespread use of personal computers have been very reluctant to learn how to input data directly into electronic records. As a result, transcription of dictated reports is still the most common type of data input for hospital EHRs.

Although continuous voice recognition technology is now available, the level of error is still too high for most medical applications unless the digital output is checked against the dictation and corrected. However, the reliability of voice recognition systems is steadily improving, and the technology may become a viable clinical documentation tool in the future.

Optical character readers (OCRs) have also been developed. These devices work like digital scanners and can be used to convert handwritten data into digital data. Like voice recognition technology, however, optical character readers yield poor results when used in medical applications.

Additional data capture tools are being developed to address the challenge of creating a workable data capture process for clinical documentation. Structured data entry screens are one type of alternative data capture tool. (Figure 4.6 provides examples.)

Text processing software applies very sophisticated formulas to narrative text in order to convert the text into structured data. Text processing can be considered a type of data entry, but it is not yet a practical tool for application to EHRs (Amatayakul 2002, p. 181).

Healthcare Information System Standards

In the current healthcare environment, there are hundreds of healthcare information system (HIS) vendors but only limited standardization of products. The use of proprietary software and technology is widespread. Healthcare professionals, managers, policy makers, regulators, and educators often struggle to locate and share information among incompatible computer information systems.

Figure 4.6.   Examples of Data Capture Tools

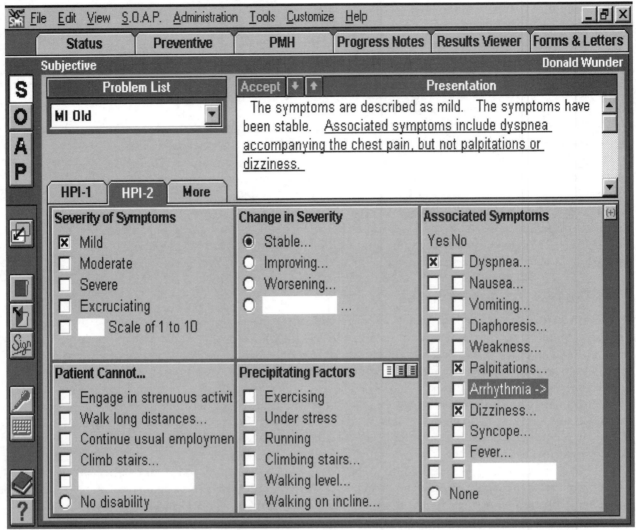

Source: Amatayakul 2004.

Unlike other industries such as banking and air travel, the healthcare industry has been slow to develop and accept IS standardization. Even in areas where IS standards do exist, non-compliance remains a problem. The slow progress toward industry standardization was a major contributing factor behind the passage of Health Insurance Portability and Accountability Act (HIPAA) in 1996. (HIPAA regulations are discussed in chapter 5.)

Recent efforts toward the development of healthcare standards have gained momentum. Today, the following standards development organizations are working to develop HIS standards for healthcare organizations:

- Health Level Seven (HL7)

- American Society for Testing and Materials (ASTM)

- The Institute of Electronic and Electrical Engineers (IEEE)

- American College of Radiologists/National Electrical Manufacturers Association (ACR/NEMA)

- International Standards Organization (ISO)

- Systematized Nomenclature of Medicine (SNOMED)

- National Library of Medicine (NLM)

- Unified Medical Language System (UMLS)

For EHR systems to function beyond one healthcare facility, several types of HIS standards must be established and followed (LaTour 2002, pp. 122–24):

- **Health informatics standards:** General standards that describe acceptable methods for collecting, maintaining, and transferring health-related data and information

- **Vocabulary standards:** Standards that establish the medical terms to be used in health record documentation as well as common definitions for those terms

- **Structure and content standards:** Standards that establish the data elements to be collected in health records as well as clear definitions for those data elements

- **Messaging standards:** Standards that facilitate the electronic interchange of data between two or more separate computer systems

- **Privacy and security standards:** Standards that ensure the confidentiality and integrity of patient-identifiable information

(Standards development is discussed in more detail in chapter 5.)

Network and Server Technology

EHR systems are made up of a complex configuration of computer hardware and software. A computer system's architecture includes the configuration and structure of the system's components as well as the interrelationships of the components. Three main types of system architecture form the basis of an EHR system (Amatayakul 2002, p. 182):

- Mainframe architecture uses a single, large computer that processes the data received from input devices. The mainframe generally has limited analytical capacity.

- Client/server architecture uses a combination of smaller computers to process and capture data. Server computers are powerful processors that support multiple client computers, which have specialized data capture capabilities.

- Web-based architecture uses the latest browser and network technology to capture data and move it through the system. Network devices connect computers to the main network and to other networks. Network devices also direct data traffic.

Clinical Decision Support Systems

Clinical decision support (CDS) systems help physicians and other clinicians make diagnostic and treatment decisions. A CDS system automatically analyzes health record data and searches for unusual patterns. When a potential problem is identified (for example, a drug interaction), the system issues an alert or a reminder that includes a recommendation for specific corrective action.

CDS systems rely on **online analytical processing** (OLAP) technology and an elaborate set of rules. OLAP technology includes statistical analysis and search capabilities that match health record data to facts, rules, and other data stored in an electronic knowledge base. The information in the knowledge base is based on biomedical research, medical literature, clinical guidelines, and other advice from expert physicians (Amatayakul 2002, p. 182).

Links to Secondary Databases

Clinical indexes and registries have been compiled by acute care hospitals and other healthcare organizations for decades. These secondary databases are a valuable source of information for healthcare policy makers, researchers, and educators. In the past, the information in secondary databases was compiled directly from paper-based health records, and so maintaining the databases was labor intensive and expensive.

Today, the availability of clinical information in digital format has made it easier and less expensive to create secondary databases. (For example, information on diagnoses and procedures is routinely collected in the form of ICD-9-CM codes, which are recorded electronically during the coding and billing process.) As a result, the number, size, and complexity of clinical registries, indexes, and other databases have grown rapidly. Database development, however, has not been without its problems. Organizations that manage clinical databases have had to deal with a number of complex issues, including patient confidentiality, health information ownership and control, and data quality and accuracy.

Health Record Identification and Storage Systems

Record identification and storage are integral parts of electronic health record systems. But there are a number of different options for identifying and storing paper and mixed-media records.

In hospitals that use paper-based clinical documentation systems, it is not unusual for the record of one inpatient encounter to include 100 or more pages of computer-generated and transcribed reports and handwritten documentation. The reports and documents generated by various departments and caregivers must be sorted into individual health records for each patient. The content of each record then must be arranged according to the facility's accepted record format. Each health record is labeled as belonging to a specific patient and placed in some sort of folder. The folder is used by caregivers and stored on the nursing unit until the patient is discharged. The record is then brought to the health information management (HIM) department for coding and quality assessment. Once physicians have provided any missing documentation and the record is complete, it can be moved to permanent storage. When the patient returns to the facility for inpatient or outpatient services some time in the future, his or her record will be retrieved and updated. Eventually, inactive paper records will be destroyed according to state and federal record retention guidelines. (The AHIMA's guidelines on health record retention and destruction are provided in appendix H.)

Health Record Identification and Filing Systems

Acute care facilities assign a **unique identifier** to each patient's health record during the process of admission and registration. The unique identifier in virtually all hospitals is a number referred to as the **health record number** or medical record number. In general, alphabetical identification using a form of the patient's name is not practical for large healthcare facilities such as hospitals.

Hospital HIM departments are usually responsible for ensuring that no two patients receive the same health record number. However, caregivers must still confirm that they are looking at the correct record before making documentation entries or using health record information for patient care purposes. In both paper and electronic health record systems, the process for confirming patient identification is usually stipulated in the hospital's policies and procedures.

Electronic health records can be accessed using the patient's name or health record number. However, it is still very important that caregivers verify that the correct record has been accessed by checking the patient's full name, date of birth, Social Security number, and other identifiers before making entries or using information in electronic records (Johns 2002, pp. 760–70).

In hospitals that use paper-based record systems, the system of health record identification is coordinated with the record filing and storage system. The patient's name and health record number must be included on every page of documentation to ensure that every record is up-to-date and complete during and after the patient's stay.

Health Record Numbering Systems

Acute care facilities use several different systems of health record numbering. However, most acute care hospitals use some version of the unit numbering system. Three types of health record numbering systems are common: serial, unit, and serial–unit.

Serial Numbering System

Under the **serial numbering system,** patients are assigned a different but unique numerical identifier for every admission. In other words, each patient receives the next available number in a series of predetermined health record numbers.

For example: A patient admitted to the hospital at 8:00 a.m. on October 12 would be assigned number 786544. The next patient, who registered at 8:05 a.m. on the same day, would be assigned the next available number, 786545. If the same patient were admitted to the hospital on three separate occasions, three different health record numbers would be assigned. Therefore, three completely separate health records would be created and maintained for the same patient.

The serial numbering system has one obvious shortcoming: Having three separate records for the same patient makes it difficult to retrieve and compare information on the patient's three admissions. The serial numbering system is also more costly than other systems because it requires more materials, labor, and storage space.

Unit Numbering System

In the **unit numbering system,** the health record for every new patient is assigned a unique health record number the first time the patient is admitted as an inpatient or outpatient. The health record number assigned for the first admission is then used for every subsequent admission. The records of every one of the patient's admissions are then filed together. Consequently, the unit numbering system is more cost and labor efficient. But using this system does involve an extra step in the admissions process: checking the facility's master patient index to ensure that the patient was not assigned a record number during a previous admission.

Serial-Unit Numbering System

The **serial-unit numbering system** combines the features of the serial and unit numbering systems. Under this system, health record numbers from a predetermined numerical series are assigned by admitting staff, just as in the serial numbering system. However, the health records of the patient's previous admissions are then retrieved from storage and combined with the record of the current admission. After the episode of care is finished, the complete unit record is then filed according to the most recent number. This system has the merits of the other two systems without the drawbacks.

Health Record Filing Systems

Few hospitals use an **alphabetic filing system** for paper-based health records, because the system is inadequate for heavy patient volume. Some small facilities and specialty clinics, however, may still use some form of the patient's name as a unique identifier on health records. Under this system, the patient's last name is used as the first component of identification, and his or her first name and middle name or initial provide further definition. The obvious shortcoming of this system is the likelihood of duplicate or similar names. Facilities that use alphabetic identification and filing systems usually use the patients' dates of birth to distinguish duplicate records. But duplicate dates of birth are still a possibility, and the identification of the patient must always be confirmed before the record is used.

All but the smallest hospitals use a numeric or alphanumeric filing system. In a **numeric filing system,** records are filed by health record number. Numeric filing systems rely on the use of a master patient index to match each patient's name with his or her health record number. (The master patient index is discussed in chapter 2. Maintenance guidelines for the master patient index are provided in appendix F.) Three types of numeric filing systems are common (Johns 2002):

- **Straight numeric filing systems,** in which records are arranged consecutively in ascending numerical order according to the health record number

- **Terminal-digit filing systems,** in which the last digit or group of digits (terminal digits) in the health record number determines file placement

- **Alphanumeric filing systems,** in which a combination of alphabetic letters (usually the first two letters of the patient's last name) and the health record number are used

The terminal-digit system is preferred by most hospitals. In a typical terminal-digit system, records are filed according to a three-part number made up of two-digit pairs. The typical system contains 10,000 divisions within each section, with 100 sections numbered from 00 to 99 and 100 divisions within each section numbered from 00 to 99.

Terminal-digit filing is different from straight numeric filing: In straight numeric filing, the first numbers (those farthest to the left) are considered first. The number itself can be a permanent unit number or a serial number. In terminal-digit filing, the record number is placed into terminal-digit order when the health record is ready for filing. The number is broken down into two-digit pairs and read from right to left. For example, the number 670187 would be written as 67-01-87:

- The first pair of digits on the right (87) is called the primary number or the terminal-digit number.

- The second pair of digits (01) is called the secondary number.

- The third pair of digits (67) is called the tertiary or final number.

The primary number is considered first for filing. Because many records are filed in each section of the file, each section is further subdivided, first according to the secondary number and then according to the tertiary number. In this example, the record numbered 67-01-87 would be filed in section 87, in subsection 01, and then in numerical order for 67 (after 66-01-87 and before 68-01-87). All records with the tertiary and secondary numbers of 01-87 would be filed within the same part of the file.

One advantage of terminal-digit filing is that file shelves fill equally rather than at the end, as is the case with conventional straight numeric filing. Another advantage is that the department's workload can be evenly distributed among filing personnel because specific sections can be assigned to each employee.

Health Record Storage Systems

As discussed earlier in the chapter, electronic health records are stored digitally in centralized or departmental clinical data repositories. The storage options for paper and mixed-media records include paper-based storage systems, microfilm-based storage systems, and digital image-based storage systems.

Paper-Based Storage Systems

No matter what type of identification system the hospital uses, most use color coding on health record folders to make storage and retrieval more efficient. Color-coded file folders are available from suppliers, but color-coded labels can also be used to organize records.

Paper-based health record files can be stored in vertical or lateral filing cabinets, open-shelf files, or compressible file systems. Vertical file cabinets are difficult to access and so are rarely used to store health records. Lateral file cabinets are easier to access but would only be used in low-volume areas of the hospital.

Hospitals usually use open-shelf or compressible files for housing paper-based health records. Open-shelf filing units resemble open bookshelves. Some are always open, and others have recessed doors that can be closed and locked.

Compressible file systems take up less space than fixed storage units. Compressible file systems are similar to open-shelf systems. The difference is that the shelving units are not fixed. In one type of compressible system, the units are mounted on permanent tracks in the floor so that they can be moved. Another type of compressible system is made up of horizontal or vertical carousels. The horizontal carousel contains open-shelf files that revolve around a central spine or track. The vertical carousel brings all files or records directly to a workstation. Vertical carousel systems are often used to store master patient indexes.

Microfilm-Based Storage Systems

Paper-based health records require a huge amount of storage space, but alternative storage options can reduce space needs significantly. Storing images of paper reports and documentation on microfilm is an effective option for inactive or infrequently used health records. Microfilm records are also acceptable as courtroom evidence, because they are difficult to alter (Johns 2002, pp. 786–87).

The process of microfilming involves making special photomicrographs of the original paper documents. These tiny negative film images are then archived for long-term storage. Anyone who is interested in accessing the stored records must use a special microfilm reader, which magnifies the images.

Image-Based Storage Systems

Another storage solution for health records is based on digital scanning technology. In **electronic document management systems** (EDMs), source documents are scanned to create digital images of the documents that can be stored electronically on optical disks. Some digital scanners can process hundreds or even thousands of documents per day. Access to images stored on optical disks is fast and easy, and scanned information can be made available to any number of users simultaneously. Document scanning is also being used to convert stored health record information into images that can be loaded onto new electronic health record systems.

Retrieval and Tracking Systems

In paper-based health record systems, tracking and retrieving records is an important process. In most acute care facilities, there is usually only one copy of each complete health record but many potential users. One of the HIM department's biggest responsibilities is ensuring that paper-based health records are available when and where they are needed.

In traditional paper-based systems, authorized users sent a written requisition to the HIM department whenever they needed to access a health record in storage. However, most hospitals today use electronic record request systems, and written requisitions are used mostly by small facilities. Whether in written or electronic format, the record **requisition** asks the HIM department to retrieve a specific health record from storage and deliver it to the department that needs it. The information contained on the requisition usually includes:

- Patient's name

- Health record number

- Date of the request

- Date and time the record is needed

- Name of the person making the request

- Delivery location

Electronic requisition and tracking systems make it easy to monitor how many records are charged out of the HIM department at any time. The systems also provide information on each record's location and when it is due back to the department.

Paper-based requisition and tracking systems use multiple copies of paper requisition forms. The first copy becomes the routing slip that arrives with the health record. The second copy is used to mark the record's place in the file. The third copy may be used as a transfer notice when the health record is subsequently transferred to another location rather than being returned to storage. Using outguides is probably the most common type of tracking system for paper-based requisition systems. An **outguide** is a durable sheet of paper or vinyl that is inserted into a file to replace a health record that has been removed from storage.

Standardization of Forms and Views

Forms management is critical in both electronic data management systems and traditional paper-based record systems. The standardization of data capture tools ensures the quality and completeness of health record content in both paper-based and computer-based environments. Most acute care organizations have established forms committees to oversee the development, review, and control of the facilities' data capture tools, including all paper forms and computer views and screens. The committee should include information users from the following departments (Johns 2002, p, 780):

- Health information management

- Medical staff

- Nursing staff

- Purchasing

- Information services

- Performance improvement

- Support and ancillary departments

The forms committee or a representative of the committee usually works directly with commercial vendors to develop health record forms or electronic data capture systems that fulfill the information needs of the organization.

The design of computer views and data entry screens is one of the most important considerations in developing EHR systems. Electronic systems allow individual users to choose the way data are presented, and so designers should understand how clinicians and other users prefer to receive information. For example, physicians generally prefer to find all of the information they need in one place. Therefore, putting as much information as possible in each view would meet their needs better than creating less crowded views that require users to scroll down into the document or view multiple pages.

In both electronic and paper-based health record systems, the most important step in the standardization of forms and views is to establish the information needs of health information users. In other words, every form or view must fulfill its intended purpose by including all of the data required in an appropriate and easy-to-use format.

For example: When the purpose of a form is to provide patient instructions for aftercare, the data elements on the form must provide all of the information the patient will need in language that the patient can understand. Similarly, when the form is meant to be completed by hand, the response areas on the form must allow enough space for handwritten information. When the purpose of a view is to provide clinicians with an update on the patient's condition, the view should contain all of the pertinent information in a format that can be reviewed at a glance. (Complete principles of form and screen design are provided in appendix D.)

Following thoughtful design practices may not always ensure the overall effectiveness of the organization's documentation and data entry tools. Duplication and redundancy can also frustrate users and yield conflicting information. Forms design and management processes should ensure that only one version of each form is available for use at any one time. Processes should also look at the number of different forms in use to determine whether the same information is being collected on multiple forms or views in more than one way.

For example: The admissions form might ask for the name of the patient's next of kin while the patient assessment form asks for the name of the patient's spouse. If the patient's spouse were deceased, the information on the patient's next of kin would be inconsistent.

Standardization of Acronyms, Abbreviations, and Symbols

To avoid ambiguity, acute care facilities should standardize the abbreviations, acronyms, and symbols that may be used in health record documentation. Hospital health record policies and medical staff rules should determine which symbols, acronyms, and abbreviations may be used by the clinicians who author health record entries, and the rules should be enforced. As an alternative method, some hospitals develop lists of prohibited acronyms, symbols, and abbreviations rather than approved lists.

In 2003, the JCAHO published six patient safety goals, one of which was to require healthcare organizations to designate the abbreviations that should never be used in health records (JCAHO 2003). In general, **prohibited abbreviations** are those that have more than one meaning or can easily be misinterpreted in handwritten form, with potentially dangerous results for patients. The JCAHO now requires hospitals to prohibit the use of the following abbreviations in all handwritten, patient-specific documentation:

U (for unit)
IU or iu
QD or qd
QOD or qod
Zero after decimal point
No zero before decimal point
MS, MSO_4, $MgSO_4$

Symbols, acronyms, and abbreviations should be limited to those that are the most widely applicable and unambiguous. The list of abbreviations, acronyms, and symbols should include the accepted definition of each entry, and ideally, each abbreviation, acronym, or symbol should have only one meaning. When illustrations, forms, or other complex materials use numerous or unusual abbreviations, the author should provide a legend to explain what the abbreviations mean.

Because of space limitations, the use of symbols, acronyms, and abbreviations in EHR data entry screens may create problems in interpretation. To solve this problem, developers should consider creating a feature whereby definitions are made available when users click on an abbreviation, symbol, or acronym.

Authentication of Health Record Entries

In the context of health records, **authentication** is the process of providing proof of the authorship of health record documentation. Authentication can be performed in several different ways, depending on the health record environment. Some types of health record documentation require an original handwritten signature as authentication, for example, physicians' orders for drugs and other substances. (Most states also require that prescriptions include the prescribing physician's original signature.) Computer-generated documentation generally does not require authentication, for example, routine reports of laboratory test results.

State laws dealing with the authentication of health record entries vary widely. Some states have no requirements at all, while others outline specific procedures for authentication, including acceptable methods and time frames (Welch 2000a). Many state laws apply exclusively to physicians' orders for drugs and services (Dougherty 2001).

According to Medicare regulations and accreditation standards, only qualified individuals as specified in hospital and medical staff policy may enter information in health records. Entries must be written by the clinicians who personally provided, ordered, or interpreted the services, and the entries should be made at the time the services were delivered or as soon as possible afterward. Entries must also be authenticated and dated by the authors of the entries, never by their surrogates. Specifically, physicians must personally authenticate their reports of history and physical examinations, surgical procedures, and medical consultations as well as discharge summaries. When an unlicensed physician's surrogate, such as a physician's assistant, authors a record entry, the surrogate should sign his or her own name, not the physician's name. In some cases, state regulations and hospital policies may require physicians to countersign the record entries made by their surrogates.

In general, most hospital policies allow only physicians, nurses, social workers, dietitians, psychologists, and allied health professionals to author and authenticate health record entries. Routine diagnostic reports such as laboratory results, however, usually do not require authentication.

Authentication requirements are most stringent in the area of physicians' orders for pharmaceuticals and biological substances such as blood products. In general, every physician's order for drugs or biologicals must be documented in writing and signed by the physician responsible for the care of the patient. Physicians' telephone and verbal orders for drugs and biologicals may be accepted only by clinical personnel authorized to do so by medical staff policies and procedures. In most hospitals, only registered nurses and licensed pharmacists are allowed to accept and execute verbal and telephone orders for pharmaceuticals. Federal Medicare regulations and some state laws require that the prescribing physician authenticate verbal and telephone orders as soon as possible after issuing them. Physicians' orders permitting the use of restraints in medical and psychiatric units also must meet specific authentication and time-frame requirements.

Paper-Based Records

In paper-based records, authentication includes the author's signature along with the author's credentials and the date the entry was made. Handwritten authentication must be made in permanent ink. Some hospitals accept caregivers' initials on specific types of reports, such as records of vital signs. Hospitals may also permit rubber-stamp signatures but should have strict rules that disallow the use of rubber stamps by anyone other than the person represented by the signature.

Entries written by medical, nursing, and allied health students and clinical staff who are working under the supervision of licensed healthcare professionals usually require a supervisor's countersignature. Depending on state law and hospital policy, documentation authored by physician's assistants and nursing assistants may require countersignature. Teaching hospitals generally require an attending physician to countersign all of the reports completed by unlicensed physicians in resident training programs. The countersignatures are meant to confirm that the supervisors have reviewed and approved the documentation prepared by those working under their supervision.

Electronic Records

Authentication in electronic health record systems is accomplished through the use of electronic signatures or digital signatures. An **electronic signature** is a unique personal identifier that is entered by the author of EHR documentation via electronic means. The unique personal identifier may be in the form of a code or password, or it may be a biometric identifier such as a fingerprint or retinal scan. Each unique personal identifier must be assigned exclusively to a specific clinician, and a master list of the electronic identifiers must be maintained in a secure environment. Electronic signatures are permitted under Medicare regulations and accreditation standards as well as most state laws (AHIMA E-HIM Task Force 2003a).

Digital signatures use the same technology as automated credit card authentication systems. A **digital signature** is a digitized version of a handwritten signature. The author of the documentation signs his or her name on a pen pad, and the signature is automatically converted to a digital signature that is affixed to the electronic document (AHIMA E-HIM Task Force 2003a). (More information on electronic and digital signatures is provided in appendix M.)

Corrections in Clinical Documentation

Health record documentation is considered a legal business record, and so all entries in health records must be permanent. Entries must never be erased, removed, or obliterated even when they are found to contain incorrect information. Any corrections to entries should be added as notes to the original entries so that the entries remain intact and in chronological order. This requirement is the same for both paper-based and computer-based records. Only clinicians authorized to enter information into health records should be permitted to make health record corrections.

Patients are permitted to access their own health records and to correct or add information under the provisions of the HIPAA regulations. (See chapter 5.) Any information or corrections added to health records by patients should be inserted as separate notes, or addenda. Patients' changes must never be made in original health record entries. Any information added to the health record by the patient should be clearly identified as an addendum authored by the patient.

Paper-Based Records

Errors in paper-based records should be corrected according to the following process (Smith 2001):

1. The clinician making the correction should draw a single line in ink through the incorrect entry.

2. The clinician should then print the word error at the top of the entry.

3. The clinician should authenticate the error notation by signing or initialing the notation and noting the date and time. The signature should include the individual's credentials and title. The reason why the change is needed should also be noted.

4. The correct information should then be added to the entry as a notation. Late entries should be labeled as such; that is, entries must never be antedated (assigned a date earlier than the current date).

Electronic Records

Making corrections in EHRs is essentially the same as making corrections in paper-based records (Welch 1999). Data capture methods for EHRs must include a mechanism for adding corrections to electronic documentation without changing or deleting the originals. The process of error correction in EHRs should include the same basic steps as the process for paper-based records, namely:

*   The original entries must remain unchanged. (EHRs automatically protect earlier entries from change and deletion.)

*   Corrections must be added as notations to the original entries.

*   Corrections must be dated and authenticated by the author of the changes at the time the changes are entered. (EHRs automatically disallow antedating of entries.)

Inclusion of Other Types of Documentation in Acute Care Records

The basic function of the health record is to collect and store documentation of the services provided to patients by a healthcare practitioner or facility. Health records are considered legal business records, and so the information stored in them must relate exclusively to the services provided by the facility maintaining the records. Therefore, information provided by patients (for example, copies of personal health records) and health information furnished by independent healthcare practitioners (for example, copies of past diagnostic results) should not be stored as part of a hospital's official health record. There is, however, one important exception: copies of records provided by patients or outside providers that are used directly in the current course of hospital care.

In general, federal regulations and rules of evidence allow the use of copies in legal business records, including health records. State laws vary. Accreditation standards allow the use of copies as long as there is no question of their authenticity. Common methods of making copies include computer printing, digital imaging, photocopying, and facsimile transmission.

Telephones have been in common use for more than 100 years. Telephone conversations between patients and providers as well as between providers engaging in consultations related to the care of a specific patient should be documented in the patient's health record. (Verbal and telephone orders were discussed earlier in the chapter.)

Use of Copies from Outside Providers

In general, the legal health record should not include copies of health record information created by other providers and furnished directly by the patient. Similarly, personal health records created or controlled by the patient should not be included in the legal health record. However, if any of these materials (for example, a patient's glucose/insulin-tracking records) are actually used by the provider organization in delivering care, they may be included in the legal health record (Amatayakul and others 2001; Dougherty 2002).

Use of Facsimiles and Photocopies

Federal regulations do not specifically address the use of photocopies and facsimile (fax) copies in health records, although federal rules of evidence do permit the use of copies in general (Hughes 2001). State laws vary and may address the use of fax copies in licensing or health information laws or in laws related to specific types of disease, such as sexually transmitted infections and psychiatric disorders. The fax transmission of physicians' orders is permissible under Medicare regulations, and the regulations do not require the prescribing physician to countersign the orders at a later date.

Use of Electronic Communications

Web-based communications technology has partially replaced the use of telephones and regular mail in healthcare communications. E-mail communications between patients and their healthcare providers and online consultations between providers are becoming more and more common.

Patient–Provider Communications

Patient–provider electronic communications include e-mail messages and PDA text messages. Electronic communications between patients and healthcare providers are considered business records, and so they are subject to the same policies and protections as any other patient-identifiable documentation (AHIMA E-HIM Task Force 2003c).

Obviously, the use of e-mail communications between providers and patients in inpatient settings is very limited, but such communications are relatively common in outpatient settings. In outpatient clinics, e-mail applications include appointment scheduling, patient education, requests for prescription refills, and discussions of test results. Ensuring the confidentiality, authenticity, and integrity of electronic messages is critical. The AHIMA E-HIM Task Force has developed policy and technology guidelines for managing e-mail and other electronic communications between patients and providers (AHIMA E-HIM Task Force 2003c).

For paper-based health record systems, physicians and other clinicians should print out paper copies of e-mail communications for inclusion in the patient's health record. Both the patient's original message and the provider's reply should be copied and authenticated. Similarly, in EHR systems, all messages and replies should be copied to the patient's record (AHIMA E-HIM Task Force 2003c).

Provider–Provider Communications

Communications between healthcare practitioners should be documented in the health record when they apply to a specific patient, because such discussions constitute medical consultations. Consultations may be accomplished through a variety of communications systems, including telephones, regular mail, e-mail, video, and online "chats."

Telemedicine incorporates medical consultations that are conducted between providers or between providers and patients located in different geographic locations. Telemedical consultations can be interactive; that is, they can be conducted via Web-based conferencing technology. Alternatively, they can be static; that is, they can be conducted through the use of video, or one physician can send diagnostic images to another via the Internet. As telecommunications technology has become more sophisticated and reliable, some healthcare providers are even providing treatment to patients through telemedical applications.

For example, in October 2001, surgeons in New York City successfully performed gallbladder surgery on a patient in France. They sent instructions to surgical robots in a Strasbourg clinic via high-speed fiber-optic cables under the Atlantic Ocean (Kohn 2002, p. 53).

Best Practices in Acute Care Documentation

In 1998, the AHIMA's House of Delegates approved a resolution that called for "Advocating Quality and Cost-Efficient Health Information Documentation Requirements" (Fletcher 1999). The resolution noted that documentation is an important, dynamic form of communication that provides a clinical treatment record for healthcare practitioners and an historical medical–legal document for use in future patient care, education, research, and reimbursement. The resolution also stated that documentation guidelines should reflect both current practice and modern technology.

A subsequent practice brief (Fletcher 1999) published in 1999 described a process for making improvements in health record documentation. The practice brief also provided a list of best practices in health record documentation. (See figure 4.7.)

Health Record Analysis and Management

In many acute care hospitals, health information management (HIM) professionals are responsible for assembling and/or evaluating every health record after the patient has been discharged. In addition, HIM professionals may also perform a concurrent or ongoing review of health record content while the patient is still receiving inpatient services. These assessments are often grouped together under the term **health record analysis,** health record review, or discharge review.

The purpose of health record analysis is to ensure the quality and completeness of clinical documentation. The process is not an evaluation of the clinical care provided to the patient. However, quality improvement and accreditation organizations do look to health record documentation for evidence that appropriate and effective care is being provided to patients in the facility. In addition, the quality of clinical documentation has a very significant impact on the coding and billing processes that lead to reimbursement.

Figure 4.7. Recommended Best Practices in Health Record Documentation

1. **Consistent and standardized documentation requirements**

   a. Advocate consistent and standardized documentation requirements by working with stakeholders and accrediting and regulatory bodies, including but not limited to the JCAHO, the National Committee for Quality Assurance, the Centers for Medicare and Medicaid Services, the ASTM, and HL7.

      • Eliminate physician attestation requirement.

      • Streamline regulatory activities.

      • Change laws or legislation that requires physician signatures on verbal orders.

2. **Innovative, high-quality, and cost-efficient clinical documentation practices**

   a. Utilize authentication and authorship mechanisms that use available technology.

   b. Reduce record completion time frames. The time from patient discharge to record completion should bas as short as possible. Develop policies and practices to facilitate completing records in a timely manner.

      • Collect records of discharged patients quickly.

      • Ensure that incomplete records remain available to physicians for completion. When the record is needed for purposes unrelated to patient care, have the record reviewed in the department.

      • Establish the physician's preferred appointment day and time to complete records and make them available at the appointed time.

      • Develop an equal-access system so that every physician who has deficiencies in the same record can have access to the record.

      • Apply record completions policies uniformly to all physicians without exception.

      • Withhold the paychecks of residents or do not allow them to graduate when they have incomplete records outstanding.

      • Use quality improvement techniques to improve record completion timeliness.

      • Reduce documentation requirements to those required to fulfill accreditation standards, federal regulations, and state laws.

      • Monitor and graphically report improvement efforts.

      • Redesign forms to ensure that they are user-friendly.

      • Decentralize record completion.

      • Work with other hospitals in the system or geographic area to standardize record completion requirements.

      • Analyze records for deficiencies on a concurrent basis.

      • Levy fines, suspend privileges, or otherwise punish physicians who do not complete records in a timely manner.

      • Utilize positive incentive programs for timely record completion.

      • Reduce reliance on paper-based sources of information to reduce or eliminate routine delivery and maintenance requirements.

      • Standardize billing process so that claims are derived exclusively from electronic documentation to reduce or eliminate the need to release paper-based information for reimbursement purposes, claim audits, and record handling.

      • Streamline health record completion guidelines.

      • Minimize the number of unsigned verbal orders.

      • Reduce loose filing backlogs.

      • Allow medical staff to take responsibility for record completion timeliness.

   c. Utilize new and improved technology for documentation.

      • Use speech recognition technology to supplement transcription services.

      • Develop a standardized format for policies and procedures that are accessible electronically.

      • Utilize e-mail to transmit information.

      • Implement telemedical record documentation processes.

(Continued on next page)

Figure 4.7. (Continued)

3. **Appropriate measures and monitors to assess health record documentation quality**

   a. Develop documentation processes that reflect the organization's uniqueness.

   b. Organize an ongoing records review program and monitor its effectiveness using performance improvement techniques.

   c. Streamline health record completion guidelines.

   d. Educate practitioners and others on the importance of innovate, high-quality, and cost efficient documentation practices.

   e. Recruit a physician to act as a liaison to improve documentation.

4. **Strategic Planning**

   a. Develop and implement an electronic health record system.

   b. Develop processes to accommodate the emergence of integrated health delivery systems and transition of patient care to nonacute settings.

   c. Prepare for the implementation of ICD-10-CM and ICD-10-PCS.

Source: Fletcher 1999.

Traditional health record analysis comprises two separate but related processes: quantitative analysis and qualitative analysis. Many hospitals are applying a new quality review technique that combines quantitative and qualitative review. Ongoing record review is performed while the patient is still hospitalized.

In hospitals that use traditional, paper-based health record systems, the HIM department is responsible for ensuring that the health records of discharged, transferred, and deceased patients are returned to the department (Coffman-Kadish 2002a). Department personnel may also update the master patient index at this time. Depending on the hospital's health record policies, HIM personnel may also reassemble the contents of the record in a specific order for storage. (This order is sometimes referred to as chart order.) These processes are not necessary in facilities that use electronic health record systems. (See figure 4.8.)

Quantitative Analysis

The purpose of **quantitative analysis** is to assess the completeness and accuracy of patient health records. Quantitative evaluations are based on the regulatory, accreditation, licensing, and reimbursement requirements that apply to the hospital. Therefore, the timing and extent of quantitative health record analysis depend on policies developed by individual organizations. Both paper-based and computer-based records are subject to quantitative review.

For inpatient records, quantitative analysis may be performed concurrently (while the patient is still hospitalized) or retrospectively (after the patient has been discharged). For outpatient records, quantitative analysis usually takes place after the patient encounter is complete. The benefit of concurrent review is that content or authentication issues can be addressed before the patient has been released, when it is still possible to address clinical quality issues.

The value of retrospective health record review is not universally accepted. Many hospitals feel that concurrent review is a much more effective way to ensure that documentation is completed at the time patient services are performed. The implementation of electronic health record systems should make concurrent review more universal.

Whether performed concurrently or retrospectively, quantitative review may include an evaluation of any or all of the following factors (Johns 2002; Coffman-Kadish 2002a):

- All of the necessary reports and data entry forms or screens have been completed.

Figure 4.8. Steps in the Flow of the Paper-Based Health Record after Discharge

1. Records of discharged patients arrive or are delivered to HIM department.

2. Receipt of records is verified by comparing discharge lists to actual charts received.

3. Folder corresponding to records is pulled.

4. Record is assembled according to prescribed format ensuring that all pages belong to the correct patient and that forms are in correct date order.

5. Deficiencies such as signatures, reports needing completion, and so on are assigned to the responsible provider.

6. Diagnoses and procedures are coded.

7. Record is held for final completion by providers either in incomplete chart area or some other filing area.

8. Charts are rechecked after the providers have done their work to ensure that all have been completed.

9. The complete record is filed in the permanent filing area.

- All of the reports and data entry forms or screens include accurate patient identification information (name, health record number, gender, attending physician, and so on).

- All of the necessary consents and authorizations have been signed by the patient or the patient's legal representative.

- All of the diagnostic tests ordered by the patient's physician have been performed, and the results have been documented.

- All of the medical consultations ordered by the patient's physician have been performed, and the consultants' reports are complete.

- All of the entries and reports that require authentication have been signed and dated according to hospital policy.

- The history and physical examination report is complete and includes documentation of all admission diagnoses.

- The discharge summary is complete.

- The physician's documentation includes all of the principal and additional diagnoses and principal and additional procedures.

- For surgical patients, all preoperative, intraoperative, and postoperative anesthesia reports are complete.

- For surgical patients, all operative reports, pathology reports, and postoperative progress notes are complete.

- For surgical patients, all recovery room reports and progress notes are complete.

- For patients who died while under hospital care, preliminary and final autopsy reports are complete if an autopsy was ordered.

When record analysis identifies missing or incomplete information, the reviewer may first attempt to find the missing documentation. When the materials cannot be located, the HIM department issues deficiency notifications to the appropriate caregivers.

Deficiency systems may be paper based or computer based. Paper-based deficiency systems use a checklist to indicate missing orders, progress notes, reports, consents, and other documentation. (See figure 4.9 for an example of a paper deficiency slip.) Computer-based deficiency systems provide logs for reporting and tracking health record deficiencies. Most HIM departments periodically remind physicians that they need to complete their patients' records for past admissions.

Figure 4.9. Sample Deficiency Slip

| Physician/Practitioner's Name: _____ |
| Health Record Number: _____ |
| Patient's Name: _____ |
| Discharge Date:_____ |
| Analyzed by:_____ |
| Date: _____ |

Signatures Required	Dictation Required	Missing Reports
_____ History	_____ History	_____ History
_____ Physical	_____ Physical	_____ Physical
_____ Consultation	_____ Consultation	_____ Consultation
_____ Operative Report	_____ Operative Report	_____ Operative Report
_____ Discharge Summary	_____ Discharge Summary	_____ Discharge Summary
		_____ Radiology Report
Other	Other	_____ Pathology Report
		_____ Progress Notes
_____ _____	_____ _____	
_____ _____	_____ _____	Other
_____ _____	_____ _____	
		_____ _____
		_____ _____
		_____ _____

Accreditation standards require hospitals to track the number of deficient records and to report the **average record deficiency rate** at least quarterly (JCAHO 2003). The delinquency rate is calculated by dividing the monthly average number of discharges by the monthly average number of delinquent records.

Qualitative Analysis

Qualitative analysis is the systematic review of sample health records to determine whether patient care and record documentation standards are being met. Qualitative record analysis may be performed at the point of care by clinical or HIM professionals or after discharge when the record is returned to the HIM department. The goal of qualitative analysis is to determine the adequacy of the health record as documentation of the quality of care provided to the patient. For example, HIM professionals look for evidence in the record that indicates that caregivers followed clinical practice guidelines, performed adequate patient assessments, and so on.

The results of qualitative analyses are usually reported to the health records committee or performance improvement manager for action. Common problems identified during qualitative reviews include the following:

- Obvious inconsistencies in documentation related to the diagnostic information recorded on admissions records, history and physical reports, operative and pathology reports, care plans, and discharge summaries
- Inconsistencies between the patient's pharmacy profile and the medication record

- Inconsistencies in the documentation related to test results, treatment plans, and follow-up instructions

- Ambiguities in documentation resulting from the use of unapproved symbols and abbreviations

- Inconsistencies in nursing documentation related to the patient's pain status compared to physician's orders for analgesics

- Inadequacies in nursing documentation related to interdepartmental transfers that result in time gaps during which the patient's location is not accounted for

Ongoing Record Review

Ongoing record review is a continuous health record quality review process. Clinical and/or HIM professionals review the records of current inpatients daily as well as closed records after the patients have been discharged or transferred. The goal of ongoing record review is to ensure that inpatient health records are complete and accurate and that the facility's clinical documentation practices meet relevant accreditation standards, state licensing laws, and federal regulatory requirements. (See figures 4.10 and 4.11 [pp. 236–37] for examples of record review checklists.)

Data Quality Management Model

In 1998, the AHIMA spearheaded a task force to study data quality management. **Data quality management** is a process that ensures the integrity of data during data collection, application, warehousing, and analysis. The task force developed a data quality management model, which is based on four quality domains (Cassidy and others 1998):

- Data applications: The purposes for which data are collected
- Data collection: The processes whereby data are collected
- Data warehousing: The processes and systems whereby data are archived (saved for future use)
- Data analysis: The processes whereby data are translated into information that can be used for a designated application

The data quality management model applies the following basic characteristics to the four quality management domains:

- Accuracy: The correctness of the data
- Accessibility: The easy availability of the data
- Comprehensiveness: The completeness of the data
- Consistency: The reliability of the data
- Currency: The immediacy of the data in relation to the events they describe
- Definition: The meaning of the data
- Granularity: The level of detail in the data
- Precision: The acceptable value ranges in the data
- Relevancy: The usefulness of the data
- Timeliness: The availability of the data at the time they are needed

The AHIMA data quality management model is explained in more detail in appendix E.

Figure 4.10. Open Record Review Checklist: Initial Assessments

Information/Indicator	Record Number	Record Number	Record Number	Record Number	Record Number	Record Number	Record Number
	004303	193847					
1. Nursing unit	11B	12B					
2. Admission date	04/06/04	04/06/04					
3. Primary physician	Jones	Smith					
4. Was the history and physical report available within 24 hours of the admission?	**No**	Yes					
5. Does the history and physical report include information of the patient's the past history, examination of heart, lungs, and mental status and other body systems related to the condition for which the patient was admitted?	Yes	Yes					
6. Is the nursing initial assessment complete and free of blanks?	Yes	Yes					
7. Was the nursing initial assessment completed within 24 hours of the admission?	Yes	Yes					
8. Was a functional status screen completed when warranted by the patient's condition?	Yes	Yes					
9. Was a nutritional status screen completed when warranted by the patient's condition?	Yes	Yes					
10. Was the need to plan for discharge or transfer determined?	Yes	Yes					
11. Was the patient's level of pain assessed?	Yes	Yes					
12. Did the patient sign the consent to treatment?	Yes	Yes					
13. Was it determined whether the patient had an advance directive?	**No**	Yes					
Comments							

Actions Needed	Who	When Due
Supply missing report of history and physical.	Dr. Jones	04/08/2004

Figure 4.11.   Closed Record Review Checklist: Discharge Summary

Information/Indicator	Record Number	Record Number	Record Number	Record Number	Record Number	Record Number	Record Number
	000011	000026	001000	000090	000087	000560	000777
1. Nursing unit	10A	12B	10A	10A	10A	12B	10A
2. Primary physician	Smith	Green	Jones	Smith	Black	White	Jones
3. Discharge date	04/04/04	04/04/04	04/04/04	04/04/04	04/04/04	04/04/04	04/04/04
4. Was the discharge summary in the record within 30 days of discharge?	Yes	Yes	Yes	Yes	Yes	Yes	Yes
5. Does the discharge summary include the reason for the patient's hospitalization?	Yes	Yes	Yes	Yes	Yes	Yes	Yes
6. Does the discharge summary include documentation of significant findings?	Yes	Yes	Yes	Yes	Yes	Yes	Yes
7. Does the discharge summary include documentation of all of the procedures performed and the other care, treatment, and services provided?	Yes	Yes	Yes	Yes	Yes	Yes	Yes
8. Does the discharge summary include documentation of the patient's condition at discharge?	Yes	Yes	Yes	**No**	Yes	Yes	Yes
9. Does the discharge summary include documentation of the patient aftercare instructions?	Yes	Yes	Yes	Yes	Yes	Yes	Yes
10. Is the discharge summary readable, complete, and free of blanks?	Yes	Yes	Yes	Yes	Yes	Yes	Yes
11. Is the discharge summary free of abbreviations from the prohibited list?	**No**	Yes	Yes	Yes	Yes	Yes	Yes
12. Is the discharge summary signed and dated by the author or otherwise authenticated?	Yes	Yes	Yes	Yes	Yes	Yes	Yes
Comments	Trend						

Actions Needed	Who	When Due
Send Dr. Smith another reminder about the use of prohibited abbreviations from the JCAHO list, specifically SO4.	Tilly	Today
Ask Dr. Smith to add specific information about the patient's condition at discharge.	Dr. Smith	04/10/2004

Summary

Every acute care facility must develop and enforce policies that ensure the uniformity of health record content and format in both paper-based and computer-based health record systems. Most hospitals currently use one of three formats for paper-based health records: the source-oriented health record, the problem-oriented health record, or the integrated health record. In addition, there are several options for storing paper-based or mixed-media records.

The organization of electronic health records is accomplished through the application of various types of technological support, including database management, image processing and storage technology, data capture and retrieval technologies, and information system standards.

References

AHIMA E-HIM Task Force. 2003a. Practice Brief: Implementing electronic signatures. *Journal of the American Health Information Management Association* 74(10). Available at www.ahima.org.

AHIMA E-HIM Task Force. 2003b. Practice Brief: Speech recognition in the electronic health record. *Journal of the American Health Information Management Association* 74(10). Available at www.ahima.org.

AHIMA E-HIM Task Force. 2003c. Practice Brief: E-mail as a provider–patient electronic communication medium and its impact on the electronic health record. *Journal of the American Health Information Management Association* 74(10). Available at www.ahima.org.

Amatayakul, Margret. 2002. Computer-based patient records. In *Health Information Management: Concepts, Principles, and Practice,* edited by Kathleen LaTour and Shirley Eichenwald Maki. Chicago: American Health Information Management Association.

Amatayakul, Margret, and others. 2001. Practice Brief: Definition of the health record for legal purposes. *Journal of the American Health Information Management Association* 72(10). Available at www.ahima.org.

American Osteopathic Association. 2004. *Accreditation Requirements for Healthcare Facilities.* Chicago: AOA.

American Society for Testing and Materials. 2004. Standard Guide for Content and Structure of the Electronic Health Record. Available at www.astm.org.

Burrington-Brown, Jill, and Hughes, Gwen. 2003. Practice Brief: Provider–patient e-mail security. *Journal of the American Health Information Management Association* 74(6). Available at www.ahima.org.

Cassidy, Bonnie, and others. 1998. Practice Brief: Data quality management model. *Journal of the American Health Information Management Association* 69(6). Available at www.ahima.org.

Centers for Medicare and Medicaid Services. 2004. *Medicare Conditions of Participation for Hospitals.* Washington, D.C.: CMS.

Coffman-Kadish, Nancy. 2002a. Health record analysis. In *Health Information Management: Principles and Organization for Health Information Services,* fifth edition, edited by Margaret Skurka. San Francisco: Jossey-Bass.

Coffman-Kadish, Nancy. 2002b. Numbering and filing systems. In *Health Information Management: Principles and Organization for Health Information Services,* fifth edition, edited by Margaret Skurka. San Francisco: Jossey-Bass.

Dick, Richard, and others, editors. 1997. *The Computer-Based Patient Record: An Essential Technology for Health Care,* revised edition. Washington, D.C.: National Academy Press.

Dougherty, Michelle. 2001. Practice Brief: Verbal/telephone order authentication and time frames. *Journal of the American Health Information Management Association* 72(2). Available at www.ahima.org.

Dougherty, Michelle. 2002. Practice Brief: Maintaining a legally sound health record. *Journal of the American Health Information Management Association* 73(9). Available at www.ahima.org.

EHR Collaborative. 2004. EHR Functional Model. Available at www.ehrcollaborative.com.

Fletcher, Donna. 1997. Practice Brief: Telemedical records. *Journal of the American Health Information Management Association* 68(4). Available at www.ahima.org.

Fletcher, Donna. 1999. Practice Brief: Best practices in medical record documentation and completion. *Journal of the American Health Information Management Association* 70(10). Available at www.ahima.org.

Hjort, Beth, and others. 2001. Practice Brief: Patient photography, videotaping, and other imaging. *Journal of the American Health Information Management Association* 72(6). Available at www.ahima.org.

Hughes, Gwen. 2000. Practice Brief: Authentication of health record entries. *Journal of the American Health Information Management Association* 71(3). Available at www.ahima.org.

Hughes, Gwen. 2001. Practice Brief: Facsimile transmission of health information. *Journal of the American Health Information Management Association* 72(6). Available at www.ahima.org.

Johns, Merida. 2002. Supervision of health information technology functions. In *Health Information Management Technology: An Applied Approach,* edited by Merida Johns. Chicago: American Health Information Management Association.

Joint Commission on Accreditation of Healthcare Organizations. 2004. *2004 Comprehensive Accreditation Manual for Hospitals.* Oakbrook Terrace, Il.: JCAHO

Kiger, Linda. 2002a. Content and structure of the health record. In *Health Information Management: Principles and Organization for Health Information Services,* fifth edition, edited by Margaret Skurka. San Francisco: Jossey-Bass.

Kiger, Linda. 2002b. Information-capture design and principles. In *Health Information Management: Principles and Organization for Health Information Services,* fifth edition, edited by Margaret Skurka. San Francisco: Jossey-Bass.

Kohn, Deborah. 2002. Informatics in healthcare. In *Health Information Management: Concepts, Principles, and Practice,* edited by Kathleen LaTour and Shirley Eichenwald. Chicago: American Health Information Management Association.

LaTour, Kathleen. 2002. Healthcare data sets. In *Health Information Management Technology: An Applied Approach,* edited by Merida Johns. Chicago: American Health Information Management Association.

Mancilla, Desla. 2002. The emergence of electronic patient record systems. In *Health Information Management: Principles and Organization for Health Information Services,* fifth edition, edited by Margaret Skurka. San Francisco: Jossey-Bass.

McCain, Mary. 2002. Paper-based health records. In *Health Information Management: Concepts, Principles, and Practice,* edited by Kathleen LaTour and Shirley Eichenwald. Chicago: American Health Information Management Association.

Smith, Cheryl. 2001. Practice Brief: Documentation requirements for the acute care inpatient record. *Journal of the American Health Information Management Association* 72(3). Available at www.ahima.org.

Welch, Julie. 1999. Practice Brief: Correcting and amending entries in a computerized patient record. *Journal of the American Health Information Management Association* 70(8). Available at www.ahima.org.

Welch, Julie. 2000a. Practice Brief: Authentication of health record entries. *Journal of the American Health Information Management Association* 71(3). Available at www.ahima.org.

Welch, Julie. 2000b. Practice Brief: Storage media for health information. *Journal of the American Health Information Management Association* 71(6). Available at www.ahima.org.

Review Quiz

Directions: Select the best answer for the following items.

1. ___ What is the term used in reference to the systematic review of sample health records to determine whether documentation standards are being met?
   A. Qualitative record review
   B. Legal record review
   C. Quantitative record review
   D. Ongoing record review

2. ___ George Johnson was admitted to the hospital on July 1 and assigned the health record number 334567. On August 9, George was readmitted to this same hospital and assigned the health record number 334975. All of the health record information for each admission is filed under its respective health record number. What type of numbering system does this case exemplify?
   A. Serial
   B. Unit
   C. Terminal-digit
   D. Serial-unit

3. ___ What type of signature is created when a person signs his or her name on a pen pad and the signature is automatically converted and affixed to a computer document?
   A. Identification
   B. Digital signature
   C. Electronic signature
   D. Standardization

4. ___ What technology creates images of handwritten and printed documents that are then stored in health record databases as electronic files?
   A. Clinical data repository
   B. Data exchange standards
   C. Central processor
   D. Digital scanner

5. ___ Which type of computer system architecture uses a single, large computer that processes the data received from input devices?
   A. Web-based
   B. Mainframe
   C. Client/server
   D. Desktop

6. ___ Which type of computer system architecture uses a combination of smaller computers to process and capture data?
   A. Web-based
   B. Mainframe
   C. Client/server
   D. Desktop

7. ___ Which type of computer system architecture uses the latest browser and network technology to capture data and move it through the system?
   A. Web-based
   B. Mainframe
   C. Client/server
   D. Desktop

8. ___ Which health record format is in use when documents are grouped together according to their point of origin?
   A. Electronic
   B. Source-oriented
   C. Problem-oriented
   D. Integrated

9. ___ What term is used for a centralized database that captures, sorts, and processes patient data and then sends it back to the user?
   A. Clinical data repository
   B. Data exchange standard
   C. Central processor
   D. Digital system

10. ___ In health record documentation, the use of approved symbols, acronyms, and abbreviations is usually limited to those that:
   A. Have more than one meaning and are never used
   B. Are approved by the JCAHO
   C. Are the most widely applicable and unambiguous
   D. Are approved by the CMS

11. ___ Which type of numbering system assigns a unique health record number to every new patient the first time he or she is admitted and then uses the number for all subsequent admissions?
   A. Serial
   B. Unit
   C. Terminal-digit
   D. Serial-unit

Directions for items 12–20: Match the definition with the type of filing or storage system.

12. ___ Records are arranged consecutively in ascending numerical order according to the health record number.

13. ___ The patient's last name is used as the first component of identification and his or her first name and middle name or initial provide further definition.

14. ___ This record storage system would only be used in low-volume areas of the hospital.

15. ___ Source documents are scanned to create digital images of the documents that can then be stored electronically on optical disks.

16. ___ The last digit or group of digits in the health record number determines file placement.

17. ___ This type of record storage takes up less space and is mounted on permanent tracks in the floor so that the shelves can be moved.

18. ___ A combination of letters and health record numbers are used to file patient records.

19. ___ This type of record storage resembles bookshelves.

20. ___ This type of record storage involves storing images as special photographs.

   A. Alphabetic
   B. Alphanumeric
   C. Compressible units
   D. Digital image
   E. Lateral file cabinets
   F. Microfilm
   G. Open-shelf
   H. Straight numeric
   I. Terminal digit

21. ___ In which EHR database model is all of the organization's patient health information stored in one system?
    A. Distributed
    B. Centralized
    C. Hybrid
    D. Traditional

22. ___ The process of providing proof of the authorship of health record documentation is called what?
    A. Authentication
    B. Standardization of data capture
    C. Standardization of abbreviations
    D. Identification

23. ___ What is the key characteristic of the problem-oriented health record?
    A. Problem list
    B. Chief complaint
    C. Initial care plan
    D. Physical examination

24. ___ Sue Smith was admitted to General Hospital on June 10 and assigned the health record number 334685. Sue was readmitted to General Hospital on October 20 and assigned the health record number 339124. Sue's previous records for the June admission were combined with this current admission and filed under the health record number 339124. This is an example of what numbering system?
    A. Serial
    B. Unit
    C. Terminal-digit
    D. Serial-unit

25. ___ What mechanism allows two or more databases to transfer data between them?
    A. Clinical data repository
    B. Data exchange standards
    C. Central processor
    D. Digital scanner

26. ___ What process helps to ensure the quality and completeness of health record content in both paper-based and computer-based environments?
    A. Standardization of data capture tools
    B. Data exchange standards
    C. Standardization of abbreviations
    D. Authentication of health record entries

27. ___ A unique personal identifier that is entered by the author of EHR documentation via computer technology is called what?
    A. Digital signature
    B. Identification
    C. Electronic signature
    D. Standardization

28. ___ Dr. Smith orders 500 mg of penicillin by mouth tid for Jane Doe in the hospital emergency department. The computer sends an alert to Dr. Smith to tell her that the patient, Jane Doe, is allergic to penicillin. What type of computer system is Dr. Smith using?
    A. Clinical data repository
    B. Data exchange standard
    C. Clinical decision support
    D. Health informatics standard

29. ____ Which health record format is arranged in chronological order with documentation from various sources intermingled?
   A.   Electronic
   B.   Source-oriented
   C.   Problem-oriented
   D.   Integrated

30. ____ Which of the following represents one of the biggest challenges in EHR development and implementation?
   A.   Images of handwritten and printed documents
   B.   Data exchange standards
   C.   A workable data capture process
   D.   A clinical data repository

31. ____ Which of the following technologies would allow surgeons in Dallas to perform an appendectomy on a patient in Italy?
   A.   Facsimiles
   B.   Telemedicine
   C.   Provider-provider communication
   D.   Provider-patient communication

32. ____ What type of health record analysis assesses the completeness and accuracy of patient health records?
   A.   Qualitative record review
   B.   Legal record review
   C.   Quantitative record review
   D.   Ongoing record review

33. ____ Which area of hospital operations was the first to utilize computer technology?
   A.   Financial management
   B.   Order-entry
   C.   Clinical laboratory
   D.   Computer-based diagnostic systems

34. ____ HIM professionals sometimes monitor the records of current inpatients as well as closed records after the patients have been discharged or transferred. What is this process called?
   A.   Qualitative record review
   B.   Legal record review
   C.   Quantitative record review
   D.   Ongoing record review

35. ____ What term is used to refer to an organized collection of data that have been stored electronically to facilitate easy access?
   A.   Digital formatting
   B.   Database
   C.   Telemedicine
   D.   Data capture

Chapter 5

Accreditation and Regulatory Requirements for the Acute Care Record

Learning Objectives

- List and explain the sources of regulations, legal doctrine, and standards that apply to acute care health records

- Describe the difference between subpoenas and court orders

- Explain why health records are considered legal documents

- Describe the patient's rights relative to his or her own health records and identify the sources of patient's rights

- Describe the process of release and disclosure as prescribed by the HIPAA privacy standard

- Explain why hospitals and other healthcare organizations establish health record retention policies

- Describe the basic hospital licensure process

- List the sources of information on Medicare and Medicaid regulations

- List and explain the documentation standards in the Medicare *Conditions of Participation for Hospitals*

- Explain the concept of deemed status

- List and explain the HIPAA privacy requirements relevant to health information disclosure

- Explain the minimum necessary standard

- Discuss the HIPAA security and administrative requirements

- Explain the regulatory requirements relevant to records of psychotherapy and other psychiatric care

- Explain the regulatory requirements relevant to records of substance abuse treatment

- Discuss the confidentiality issues related to records of HIV/AIDS diagnosis and treatment

- Explain the difference between regulatory standards and accreditation standards

- Briefly outline the JCAHO accreditation process

- Explain the JCAHO's sentinel event policy

- Explain the purpose of tracer methodology

- Briefly outline the AOA HFAP accreditation process

- Briefly outline the CARF accreditation process

- Discuss the purpose of medical staff credentialing and privileging processes

- Explain the concept of corporate negligence

- List the data elements collected in incident reports

- Explain the purpose of incident reporting and risk management

- Explain the purpose of establishing uniform data sets

- List and define the five types of health informatics standards

- Describe the status of the HL7 standard on electronic health records

- Describe the purpose of developing health record policies and procedures and explain the difference between a policy and a procedure

Terminology

Accreditation
Accreditation Association for Ambulatory Healthcare (AAAHC)
Accreditation organizations
American Osteopathic Association (AOA)
American Society for Testing and Materials (ASTM)
Board certification
Centers for Medicare and Medicaid Services (CMS)
Certificate of destruction
Clinical privileges
Code of Federal Regulations (CFR)
Commission on Accreditation of Rehabilitation Facilities (CARF)
Conditions of Participation (COPs) *for Hospitals*
Corporate negligence
Court order
Credentialing
Deemed status
Destruction
EHR Collaborative
Electronic data interchange (EDI)
Federal Register
Health informatics standards
Health Insurance Portability and Accountability Act (HIPAA)
Health Level Seven (HL7)
Healthcare Facilities Accreditation Program (HFAP)
Healthcare Integrity and Protection Data Bank (HIPDB)
Identifier standards
Incident

Incident report
Joint Commission on Accreditation of Healthcare Organizations (JCAHO)
Judicial decision
Jurisdiction
Liability
Licensure
Medical staff bylaws, rules, and regulations
Minimum necessary standard
Municipal ordinance/code
National Committee for Quality Assurance (NCQA)
National Practitioner Data Bank (NPDB)
Notice of privacy practices
Periodic performance review (PPR)
Policies
Priority focus areas (PFAs)
Priority focus process (PFP)
Privileged communication
Procedures
Professional certification organizations
Psychotherapy notes
Redisclosure
Regulation
Release and disclosure
Retention
Risk management
RxNorm
Security standards
Sentinel event
Shared Visions—New Pathways
Standards
Standards development organizations (SDOs)
Statute
Statute of limitations
Structure and content standards
Subpoena
Subpoena duces tecum
Systematized Nomenclature of Medicine Clinical Terms® (SNOMED CT®)
Tracer methodology
Transaction and messaging standards
Vocabulary standards

Introduction

Acute care hospitals are subject to a number of complex operating requirements. These requirements are established by federal, state, and local branches of government; accreditation organizations; professional medical societies and associations; and national and international standards development organizations. Some of the requirements are mandatory; others are voluntary.

The mandatory rules that apply to hospitals and other healthcare organizations come from several different sources:

- Federal statutes and regulations, which apply throughout the United States

- State statutes and regulations, which apply only within individual states

- County and municipal ordinances and codes, which apply only to local communities

- State and federal judicial decisions, which apply only to the geopolitical areas that fall under the jurisdiction of the court that made the decision

A **statute** is a piece of legislation written and approved by a state or federal legislature and then signed into law by the president or the state's governor. The Health Insurance Portability and Accountability Act (HIPAA) of 1996 is an example of a federal statute. (Table 5.1 provides a list of the other federal legislation relevant to acute care records.)

A **regulation** is a rule established by an administrative agency of government. Administrative agencies are responsible for implementing and managing the programs instituted by state and federal statutes. The Centers for Medicare and Medicaid Services (CMS) is an example of an administrative agency. The CMS is the federal agency charged with developing and implementing Medicare and Medicaid regulations, such as the Medicare *Conditions of Participation for Hospitals.*

A **municipal ordinance** or **code** is a rule established by a local government. The Cook County, Illinois, ordinance prohibiting smoking in public buildings is an example. In compliance with the ordinance, smoking is not permitted in Chicago-area hospitals. In general, although not universally, federal laws take precedence over state laws and state laws over local laws.

A **judicial decision** is a ruling handed down by a court to settle a legal dispute. Judges base their decisions on constitutional laws, state and federal statutes, and previous judicial decisions. In the United States, the court system is organized according to a pyramidal hierarchy, with municipal and county courts at the bottom and the U.S. Supreme Court at the top. The higher the court, the broader is its authority, or **jurisdiction.**

Private court cases are named after the two main parties in the dispute: the plaintiff and the defendant. (In criminal cases, the parties are known as the prosecution, which represents the public's interests in the case, and the defendant.) One of the most famous judicial decisions was handed down by the U.S. Supreme Court in *Roe v. Wade.* This decision declared state laws that prohibited the voluntary termination of pregnancy to be in violation of the U.S. Constitution. As a consequence, state antiabortion laws were invalidated throughout the United States.

Other examples of the legal requirements that individual acute care organizations must fulfill include the following:

- State licensure requirements

- State health record regulations

- State public health regulations

- State rules on Medicaid qualifications

- County and municipal building safety codes

- Federal health information privacy and security standards

- Legal doctrines of medical liability based on judicial decisions

Table 5.1. Federal Laws That Affect Acute Care Documentation

Legislation	Date	Impact on Documentation
False Claims Act Amendment	1863 1986	Established federal penalties for cheating the federal government by supplying inferior goods and services Established federal penalties for filling false or fraudulent Medicare and Medicaid claims
Social Security Act Amendments (Public Law 89-97) Amendment (Public Law 98-21)	1935 1965 1983	Established the Social Security program Established the Medicare and Medicaid Programs Established the prospective payment system for inpatient care
Freedom of Information Act	1966	Established public's right to access information maintained by branches of the federal government
Alcohol Abuse and Alcoholism Prevention, Treatment and Rehabilitation Act Amendment	1970 2000	Established patient's right to control the release of information related to his or her treatment for alcoholism Established strict confidentiality requirements for treatment records maintained by facilities that receive federal funding
Drug Abuse Prevention, Treatment and Rehabilitation Act Amendment	1970 2000	Established patient's right to control the release of information related to his or her treatment for drug addiction Established strict confidentiality requirements for treatment records maintained by facilities that receive federal funding
Comprehensive Drug Abuse Prevention and Control Act	1970	Established strict federal controls on the dispensing of narcotics, depressants, stimulants, and hallucinogens
Privacy Act	1974	Established requirements for obtaining written consent before disclosure of confidential personal information
Food, Drug and Cosmetics Act, Medical Device Amendments	1976	Established controls on the testing, manufacturing, labeling and distribution of drugs and medical devices,
Utilization Review Act	1977	Established Medicare and Medicaid requirement for continued-stay reviews of acute care services
Tax Equity and Fiscal Responsibility Act	1982	Established efforts to control Medicare spending through the gradual implementation of prospective payment systems
Peer Review Improvement Act	1982	Established Medicare and Medicaid requirements for medical necessity and quality reviews of acute care services
Emergency Treatment and Active Labor Act	1985	Established "antidumping" regulations under the Consolidated Omnibus Reconciliation Act; prohibits hospital emergency departments from transferring medically unstable patients to other facilities because they have no health insurance coverage
Consolidated Omnibus Budget Reconciliation Act	1985	Established reimbursement penalties for providing substandard healthcare services to Medicare and Medicaid patients
Omnibus Budget Reconciliation Act	1986	Established reporting requirements for peer review organizations that identify facilities providing substandard healthcare
Health Care Quality Improvement Act	1986	Established the National Practitioner Data Bank
Omnibus Budget Reconciliation Act	1989	Established the Agency for Health Care Policy and Research
Omnibus Budget Reconciliation Act	1990	Established reporting requirements for peer review organizations that identify practitioners providing substandard healthcare
Americans with Disabilities Act	1990	Established the equal opportunity and physical access rights of people with physical and mental disabilities
Patient Self-Determination Act	1990	Established the rights of patients to refuse medical treatment, make healthcare decisions, and establish advance directives
Safe Medical Devices Act	1993	Established reporting requirements for hospitals that identify potential safety problems with medical equipment and implantable devices
Health Insurance Portability and Accountability Act	1996	Established privacy and security rules to protect the confidentiality and integrity of patient-identifiable information; also established the Healthcare Integrity and Protection Data Bank
Balanced Budget Act	1997	Established Medicare requirement that physicians provide diagnostic information to support orders for services under certain limited circumstances; led to general practice of including diagnostic information on physicians' orders

The voluntary rules that apply to acute care organizations also come from a variety of sources:

- **Accreditation organizations,** professional organizations that set the standards against which healthcare organizations are measured to ensure the quality and safety of their services

- **Professional certification organizations,** private societies and membership organizations that establish professional qualification requirements and clinical practice standards for specific areas of medicine, nursing, and allied health professions

- **Standards development organizations,** private or governmental agencies that develop scientifically based models against which structures, processes, and outcomes can be measured

Although following the recommendations of standards-setting organizations is voluntary, it is generally in the best interest of healthcare organizations and clinical professionals to adopt them as uniform practice. For example, hospitals that have been accredited by the **Joint Commission on Accreditation of Healthcare Organizations** (JCAHO) or the **American Osteopathic Association** (AOA) are automatically granted deemed status by the Medicare program. **Deemed status** means that the hospitals are allowed to claim reimbursement for services provided to Medicare beneficiaries without having to provide further evidence that they meet the Medicare *Conditions of Participation* (COPs) *for Hospitals.*

Similarly, physicians and other clinical professionals who have earned **board certification** through a professional certification organization are generally assumed to be fully qualified to practice in their area of specialty. In addition, the professional practice guidelines developed by a certification organization are generally accepted as the established standard of care for that specialty. A specific procedure performed by a board-certified physician or surgeon according to the practice guidelines established for that procedure, therefore, would be considered to have met the established standard of care.

Hospitals are legally responsible for the quality of nursing and medical care as well as other clinical services provided to inpatients and outpatients in their facilities. When a patient is harmed by an unqualified or negligent clinician in one of the hospital's departments, the hospital as well as the clinician may be held jointly accountable for the patient's injury.

The governing board of every hospital is responsible for establishing policies and procedures to ensure that only qualified clinical practitioners are allowed to provide patient services in the facility. These policies and procedures guide the process of credentialing. **Credentialing** is the process of verifying the educational qualifications, licensure status, and experience levels of healthcare professionals who have applied for the privilege of practicing within a healthcare facility.

Standards development organizations such as the **American Society for Testing and Materials** (ASTM) and **Health Level Seven** (HL7) work with professional and trade associations and governmental agencies to establish uniform operating practices. It is in the interest of hospitals to follow the national standards established by such organizations, especially the standards relevant to data transmission and healthcare informatics. Efficient information sharing is critical to many areas of healthcare operations but especially to reimbursement and performance improvement. The current work being done to establish healthcare informatics standards will be critical to the future implementation and success of electronic health record systems.

Each hospital's location, services, and organizational structure are unique. Therefore, every hospital must design and follow its own operating policies and procedures to ensure that its services and health records fulfill all of the standards and regulations that apply to its situation. In designing health record policies, it is also important to remember that regulatory and accreditation agencies rely heavily on the information documented in health records to determine whether patient care standards are being met.

State and federal regulations, national accreditation standards, and clinical practice standards are created, updated, and changed frequently. Therefore, health information managers must make reviewing the sources of regulations and standards a routine part of their responsibilities. Although this chapter cannot describe all of the requirements that acute care records must fulfill, it will provide general background information as a starting point for health record policy and procedure development. (Tables 5.2 through 5.5 list sources of more specific information on health record regulations and standards.)

Table 5.2. Resources for Health Record Policy Making: State Regulations

Resource	Web Site
Manuals covering state regulations on confidentiality and release of information	State and local HIM associations
State health record retention and destruction regulations	Individual state government Web sites and www.alllaw.com
State hospital licensure regulations	State departments of health Web sites and www.astho.org/index.php?template=regional_links.php

Source: Rhodes and Burrington-Brown 2002.

Table 5.3. Resources for Health Record Policy Making: Federal Regulations

Resource	Federal Agency and Web Site
Health Insurance Portability and Accountability Act, privacy and security standards	U.S. Department of Health and Human Services, http://aspe.hhs.gov/admnsimp
Patient Self-Determination Act (advance directives)	The Office of the Law Revision Counsel, http://uscode.house.gov/uscode-cgi/fastweb.exe?getdoc+uscview+t41t42+1960+0++%28%29%20%20A
Office of Inspector General, compliance program guidance	Department of Health and Human Services, Office of the Inspector General, http://oig.hhs.gov/authorities/docs.cpghosp.pdf
Privacy Act of 1974	U.S. Department of Justice, www.usdoj.gov/04foia/privstat.htm
Protection of Human Subjects (45 CFR46)	National Archives and Records Administration, *Code of Federal Regulations,* www.access.gpo.gov/nara/cfr/waisdx_01/45cfr46_01.html
Recording and Reporting Occupational Injuries and Illnesses (29 CFR1904)	National Archives and Records Administration, *Code of Federal Regulations,* www.access.gpo.gov/nara/cfr/waisdx_01/29cfr1904_01.html

Source: Rhodes and Burrington-Brown 2002.

Table 5.4.   Resources for Health Record Policy Making: Medicare/Medicaid Regulations

Resource	Web Site
Centers for Medicare and Medicaid Services, program manuals, memorandums, and transmittals	www.cms.hhs.gov/cop/1.asp
Medicare *Conditions of Participation for Comprehensive Outpatient Rehabilitation Facilities* (42 CFR488)	www.cms.hhs.gov/cop/1.asp
Medicare *Conditions of Participation for Drug, Alcohol, and Substance Abuse Treatment Facilities* (42 CFR2)	www.cms.hhs.gov/cop/1.asp
Medicare *Conditions of Participation for Hospitals* (42 CFR482)	www.cms.hhs.gov/cop/1.asp
Medicare *Conditions of Participation for Specialized Providers* (42 CFR485) (inpatient rehabilitation facilities)	www.cms.hhs.gov/cop/1.asp
Medicare inpatient prospective payment system	www.cms.hhs.gov/providers/hipps/default.asp
Medicare interpretive guidelines	www.cms.hhs.gov/cop/1.asp
Medicare inpatient rehabilitation facility prospective payment system	www.cms.hhs.gov/providers/irfpps/default.asp
Medicare outpatient prospective payment system	www.cms.hhs.gov/regulations/hopps/default.asp
Medicare patient's rights	www.cms.hhs.gov/cop/2b.asp

Source: Rhodes and Burrington-Brown 2002.

General Legal Requirements for the Acute Care Record

The legal requirements for acute care records are generally established by the laws and regulations of individual states. (Federal regulatory requirements related to health records are discussed in detail in subsequent sections of this chapter.) The legal requirements of individual states can be broken down into three general areas (Johns 2002a):

- Requirements related to the use of health records and confidential healthcare information in legal proceedings

- Requirements related to the form and content of health records and confidential healthcare information

- Requirements related to the ownership and control of health records and confidential healthcare information

Health Records as Legal Documents

As chapter 1 explained, the health record is generally considered a business record, and as such its contents are admissible as evidence in legal proceedings. Patients who have been treated for

Table 5.5.   Resources for Health Record Policy Making: Accreditation Standards

Resource	Web Site
American Correctional Association, *Agency Manual of Accreditation Policy and Procedure*	www.aca.org/standards/index.html
American Healthcare Accreditation Commission, *Health Network Accreditation Standards*	www.urac.org/urac.asp?id=65
American Healthcare Accreditation Commission, Healthcare Provider Credentialing Standards	www.urac.org/urac.asp?id=6
American Accreditation Healthcare Commission, Healthcare Utilization Management Standards	www.urac.org/docs/standards/Health%20UM%20v4-1%20Standards%20020725.pdf
American Healthcare Accreditation Commission, Workers' Compensation Utilization Management Standards	www.urac.org/urac.asp?id=69
American Osteopathic Association, *Accreditation Requirements for Healthcare Facilities*	www.aoa-net.org/Accreditation/HFAP/HFAP.htm
Commission on Accreditation of Rehabilitation Facilities, *Behavioral Health Standards Manual*	www.carf.org
Commission on Accreditation of Rehabilitation Facilities, *Medical Rehabilitation Standards Manual*	www.carf.org
Joint Commission on Accreditation of Healthcare Organizations, *Comprehensive Accreditation Manual for Ambulatory Surgery*	www.jcaho.org
Joint Commission on Accreditation of Healthcare Organizations, *Comprehensive Accreditation Manual for Behavioral Health Care*	www.jcaho.org
Joint Commission on Accreditation of Healthcare Organizations, *Comprehensive Accreditation Manual for Critical Access Hospitals*	www.jcaho.org
Joint Commission on Accreditation of Healthcare Organizations, *Comprehensive Accreditation Manual for Healthcare Networks*	www.jcaho.org
Joint Commission on Accreditation of Healthcare Organizations, *Comprehensive Accreditation Manual for Hospitals*	www.jcaho.org
National Commission on Correctional Health Care, *Standards for Health Services in Jails*	www.ncchc.org/pubs_catalog.html
National Commission on Correctional Health Care, *Standards for Health Services in Juvenile Detention and Confinement Facilities*	www.ncchc.org/pubs_catalog.html
National Commission on Correctional Health Care, *Standards for Health Services in Prisons*	www.ncchc.org/pubs_catalog.html
National Committee for Quality Assurance, *Standards for the Accreditation of Managed Behavioral Healthcare Organizations*	www.ncqa.org

Source: Rhodes and Burrington-Brown 2002.

injuries related to automobile accidents or violent crimes often become involved in private liability lawsuits or criminal court cases. Patients suffering from employment-related injuries or illnesses may file worker's compensation claims. And patients or their families who believe they have been harmed by medical mistakes sometimes file malpractice lawsuits against physicians, hospitals, and other healthcare providers. In all of these legal proceedings, the information documented in the health record plays a critical part in the decisions eventually handed down by judges and juries. Because many court cases do not go to trial until years after the original events, the written documentation in health records may be the only reliable information available. For this reason, the importance of complete and accurate health records cannot be overemphasized.

In order for healthcare information to be considered admissible in court, it must represent the health record of one of the persons involved in the legal proceedings. In other words, the contents of the record must be relevant to the issue being decided. In most instances, patient authorization or notification is not required for disclosures related to legal proceedings.

When the court has determined that a health record is relevant to a particular case, the judge will issue a subpoena or a court order to the owner of the record. A **subpoena** is a direct command that requires an individual or a representative of an organization to appear in court and/or to present an object to the court. In the healthcare context, a **subpoena duces tecum** directs a hospital's representative (usually the director of health information management) to submit a specific health record or other business record to the court that holds jurisdiction over the pending proceedings. With the advice of legal counsel, an HIM director may decide that it is inappropriate for the hospital to release a subpoenaed record. In such cases, a **court order** must be issued in place of a subpoena when the disclosure of the material would otherwise be prohibited by state or federal statutes and regulations (McWay 2002, pp. 139 and 142).

The method used to respond to subpoenas and court orders depends on the regulations in force for the state in which the court is located. Some states allow hospitals to make certified copies of the health records in question and then mail the copies to the clerk of the court or to another designated individual. In other states, a representative of the hospital must deliver the original records in person and then testify to their authenticity.

Form and Content of Health Records

State laws and regulations establish legal requirements related to the form and content of health records for facilities located within the covered geopolitical area. Health record regulations are usually developed by the state administrative agency responsible for licensing hospitals and other healthcare organizations. Some state regulations are very simple and only require that clinical records be maintained by hospitals. Other state regulations require that the clinical records must be complete and accurate. In a few states, health record regulations spell out the specific categories of information that hospitals must collect. In addition, some state regulations incorporate the health record requirements of the Medicare *Conditions of Participation* or pertinent accreditation standards (McWay 2002, p. 69).

Public health regulations in many states require hospitals to routinely report some types of confidential health-related information that is collected directly from health records. Specifically, public health regulations often require the reporting of vital statistics information (births and deaths) and other information related to the public's health, safety, and welfare. For example, many states require reporting of communicable diseases and injuries that were the result of violent crime. In addition, most states now require hospitals and other healthcare providers to report cases of suspected child abuse or neglect to the appropriate legal authorities.

Failure to comply with state health record or public health regulations may result in some type of penalty for noncompliant hospitals. Examples include forfeiture of operating licenses, fines, and criminal sanctions.

Ownership and Control of Health Records

Acute care health records and other documentation related to patient care are generally considered to be the property of the hospital or healthcare provider that maintains the records. To ensure their validity and confidentiality, the records must remain under the facility's physical control except in certain legal situations explained earlier in the chapter.

Nonetheless, patients have the right to control how the personal information in their health records is used and to review, copy, and correct the records when necessary. Outside healthcare providers, third-party payers, clinical researchers, and others who have a legitimate interest in the contents of health records must also be allowed access. To meet the growing demand for healthcare information, hospitals and other healthcare providers must develop processes for fulfilling legitimate requests for health information while at the same time protecting the confidentiality of health records and the privacy of patients. Hospitals must also make sure that acute care records remain accessible for legitimate purposes for a reasonable period of time after the original healthcare episode is complete.

The processes that make health record information available to legitimate users are known collectively as **release and disclosure.** The processes entailed in storing health information and destroying it when it is no longer needed are called **retention** and **destruction.** These processes are subject to specific regulations in many states. Federal regulations and accreditation standards also include specific guidelines on the release and retention of patient-identified health information. (The national guidelines are discussed in detail later in the chapter. Appendix G reproduces the AHIMA's general guidelines on health record release and disclosure. Appendix H provides general guidelines on health record retention and destruction.)

Patient's Right to Health Record Access

More than half of the states have statutes that address the patient's right to view, copy, and/or correct his or her health record (Johns 2002b). The Medicare *Conditions of Participation for Hospitals* also establish the individual's right to access his or her health information, as does the HIPAA privacy standard. In addition, the privacy standard describes the limited situations in which patient access may be denied. In those states that have instituted regulations on the patient's right to access his or her record, hospital policies need to address the requirements of applicable state laws as well as the HIPAA privacy standard and the *Conditions of Participation.*

Release and Disclosure of Confidential Health Information

Until the HIPAA privacy standard was implemented in 2002, there were no generally applicable federal statutes or regulations to protect the confidentiality of health records. The privacy rights of patients and the confidentiality of health records were addressed in a patchwork of state and federal regulations, professional practice standards, and individual facility policies.

When the Medicare program was established in the late 1960s, the *Conditions of Participation* included a general requirement regarding the confidentiality of health records maintained for Medicare beneficiaries. In the 1970s, federal legislation was implemented to ensure the privacy of patients in some types of treatment programs operated or supported by the federal government. However, the regulations applied exclusively to federally supported or operated programs. The drug and alcohol treatment legislation passed in 1970 and amended in 2000 established strict confidentiality requirements for substance abuse treatment records but only for records maintained by facilities that receive federal funding. Similarly, the provisions of the Privacy Act of 1974 apply only to facilities operated by the federal government.

In contrast, the HIPAA privacy standard is widely applicable. It has established a consistent set of rules that apply to virtually every healthcare facility, healthcare professional, healthcare information clearinghouse, and health plan in the United States. The standard also supersedes state regulations that permitted less stringent privacy practices. (The HIPAA privacy and security standards are discussed in more detail later in the chapter.)

Although the federal privacy standard has preempted some state health record regulations, many state regulations must still be observed. The federal regulations constitute a minimum standard for protecting confidential records. When state regulations require stricter privacy practices, hospitals and other healthcare organizations must continue to follow state regulations in addition to the federal privacy standard. Healthcare organizations must also continue to comply with public health reporting regulations and licensure/certification requirements in their geopolitical area (Hughes 2002b).

Many states base the confidentiality rights of patients on the concept of **privileged communication.** According to this concept, medical practitioners, like lawyers and other professionals, are not allowed to disclose the confidential information that they learn in their capacity as professional service providers. There are very few exceptions to this basic rule for medical practitioners.

The HIPAA privacy standard does not require healthcare organizations to obtain the patient's formal consent to use health information for routine therapeutic, reimbursement, operational, and reporting purposes. However, in some states, hospitals and other healthcare providers may still be required to obtain a written consent from the patient or the patient's legal representative before they can share the patient's confidential health information with external healthcare providers and third-party payers.

Even in the absence of state and federal requirements, many hospitals choose to document the patient's consent for routine uses and disclosures of confidential information. Patients are usually asked to sign general consents during the admissions process. (See figure 5.1 for an example of a general consent form.) Consents relevant to information are treated as separate documents rather than as elements of the general consent to treatment, which is also obtained at admission (Hjort and Hughes 2002).

State regulations governing the release and disclosure of confidential medical information take a variety of approaches. Implicitly or explicitly, however, all grant patients or their legal representatives two basic rights: the right to limit access to their records under certain circumstances and to waive their confidentiality rights when they choose.

In general, healthcare facilities and practitioners are required to obtain the patient's explicit, written permission before disclosing information for any purpose that is not related to treatment, reimbursement, operations, or public health reporting. Federal and state regulations, accreditation standards, and professional practice guidelines dictate the specific form and content of such consents and authorizations. (The requirements stipulated in the HIPAA privacy standard are discussed later in the chapter.)

Rediscdosure of Confidential Health Information

Acute care records sometimes include clinical information originally collected by other healthcare providers. For example, surgeons often supply copies of preadmission laboratory test

Figure 5.1.   Example of a General Consent for Use and Disclosure of Health Information

---

Consent to the Use and Disclosure of Health Information for Treatment, Payment, or Healthcare Operations

I understand that as part of my healthcare, this organization originates and maintains health records describing my health history, symptoms, examination and test results, diagnoses, treatment, and any plans for future care or treatment. I understand that this information serves as:

- A basis for planning my care and treatment

- A means of communication among the many health professionals who contribute to my care

- A source of information for applying my diagnosis and surgical information to my bill

- A means by which a third-party payer can verify that services billed were actually provided

- A tool for routine healthcare operations such as assessing quality and reviewing the competence of healthcare professionals

I understand and have been provided with a Notice of Information Practices that provides a more complete description of information uses and disclosures. I understand that I have the right to review the notice prior to signing this consent. I understand that the organization reserves the right to change its notice and practices and prior to implementation will mail a copy of any revised notice to the address I've provided. I understand that I have the right to object to the use of my health information for directory purposes. I understand that I have the right to request restrictions as to how my health information may be used or disclosed to carry out treatment, payment, or healthcare operations and that the organization is not required to agree to the restrictions requested. I understand that I may revoke this consent in writing, except to the extent that the organization has already taken action in reliance thereon. Therefore, I consent to the use and disclosure of my healthcare information.

☐ I request the following restrictions to the use or disclosure of my health information.

Signature of Patient or Legal Representative

_____

Witness _____

Date Notice Effective _____

Date or Version _____

☐ Accepted   ☐ Denied

Signature _____

Title _____

Date _____

---

results for patients scheduled to undergo elective surgery in the hospital. Such documents become a permanent part of the patient's acute care record only when they are actually used during the patient's course of treatment in the hospital.

The process of disclosing health record documentation originally created by a different provider is called **redisclosure.** Federal and state regulations provide some specific redisclosure guidance. In general, however, redisclosure guidelines follow the same principles as the release and disclosure guidelines for other types of health record information (Rhodes and Hughes 2003).

Retention of Health Records

Hospitals and other healthcare facilities develop health record retention policies to ensure that health records comply with all applicable state and federal regulations and accreditation standards as well as meeting future patient care needs. Establishing and following consistent record retention and destruction policies also helps control the cost of record storage space and equipment as well as labor.

Most states have established regulations that address how long health records and other healthcare-related documents must be maintained before they can be destroyed. Although the Medicare *Conditions of Participation for Hospitals* stipulate a five-year minimum, many states require longer retention periods. Some states base their retention guidelines on the type of services represented in the record. A few state laws also specify the length of time that health records must be retained in their original form before they can be converted to less accessible storage media such as microfilm. In many states, retention guidelines require facilities to retain the records of infants and children longer than the records of adults.

For example: The state of South Carolina includes the following health record retention requirements in its hospital licensure regulations:

> The records shall be treated as confidential and shall not be disposed of under 10 years. Records may be destroyed after 10 years provided that: (1) Records of minors must be retained until after the expiration of the period of election following achievement of majority as prescribed by statute. (2) The hospital retains an index, register, or summary cards providing such basic information as dates of admission and discharge, name of responsible physician, and record of diagnoses and operations for all records so destroyed.

In states that do not stipulate how long health records must be retained, healthcare providers generally maintain records for the period established by the state's statute of limitations (Rhodes and Fletcher 2002). A **statute of limitations** is a law that dictates the maximum period of time that may elapse between an event (for example, an injury or a crime) and any consequent legal action. In most states, the statute of limitations requires legal action in less than ten years. Therefore, in the absence of other state retention guidelines, hospitals and other healthcare providers may decide to maintain health records for a minimum of ten years (Kiger 2002, p. 218).

Similarly, the AHIMA recommends that health records should be retained for at least ten years. It also recommends that several other records of patient care should be maintained permanently, namely (Rhodes and Fletcher 2002):

- Master patient index
- Register of births

- Register of deaths

- Register of surgical procedures

(See appendix H for more information on the retention guidelines recommended by the American Health Information Management Association.)

Although the Medicare *Conditions of Participation for Hospitals* and various accreditation standards provide some guidance, every hospital should establish its own health record retention policies to reflect its unique regulatory climate. As a matter of law, retention policies must comply with the local, state, and federal regulations that apply to the facility. However, hospital retention policies must also consider the facility's internal information needs because hospitals use health records for a number of purposes in addition to patient care (for example, in medical staff credentialing and performance improvement activities). Hospital health record retention policies should also take into account the advice of the facility's malpractice insurance carrier and legal counsel.

In addition to patient care records, hospitals and other healthcare organizations maintain huge amounts of administrative information. The hospital's board of directors, executive staff, legal counsel, and medical staff should work together to develop retention guidelines for all of the facility's records, and not just patient records. State and federal regulations on taxation and business reporting must also be considered in drafting information retention policies.

Destruction of Health Records

Because of cost and space limitations, permanently storing paper- and microfilm-based health record documents is not an option for most hospitals. The question of how to dispose of original records in a way that protects their confidentiality usually comes up in one of four situations:

- The retention period for a set of paper-based or micrographic records has elapsed, and the hospital needs to free up storage space for more recent records.

- The hospital routinely copies paper-based records onto microfiche or optical disks for long-term storage and needs to dispose of the original paper documents.

- The hospital is in the process of implementing a new electronic health record system and needs to dispose of paper records that have been scanned and loaded onto the new system.

- The hospital is being sold or is closing permanently and needs to arrange for the disposition of its health records.

The destruction of patient-identifiable clinical documentation should be carried out in accordance with relevant federal and state regulations and hospital policy. Obviously, health records related to any open investigations, audits, or court cases should not be destroyed for any reason (Hughes 2002a).

Some states require hospitals and other providers to complete certain preparatory activities before the health records are destroyed. Examples include creating health record abstracts or notifying the patients so that they have enough time to request copies before their original records are destroyed. Some states also establish specific requirements for the method of destruction.

According to AHIMA practice standards, acceptable destruction methods include the following (Hughes 2002a):

- Paper documents: burning, shredding, pulping, and pulverizing

- Micrographic film: recycling and pulverizing

- Optical disks: pulverizing

- Electronic documents: magnetic degaussing (demagnetizing)

- Magnetic tapes: magnetic degaussing (demagnetizing)

Some facilities engage record destruction services to process obsolete health records. In such cases, the facility's contract with the vendor must fulfill the requirements of the HIPAA privacy standard.

Appropriate documentation of health record destruction must be maintained permanently no matter how the process is carried out. This documentation usually takes the form of a **certificate of destruction** (Hughes 2002a), which should include the following information:

- Date of destruction

- Method of destruction

- Description of the record(s) destroyed, including heath record number(s)

- Statement that the record(s) was destroyed during the normal course of business

- Signatures of the individuals who authorized and witnessed the destruction

Maintaining such documentation in a permanent file provides the facility legal protection in any future liability actions (McWay 2002, pp. 78–80). (See figure 5.2 for an example of a destruction record.) (Appendix H provides additional information on health record destruction.)

State and federal record retention requirements continue to apply to health records maintained by facilities that have been sold or closed permanently. Well in advance of sales and closures, hospitals should develop plans for ensuring that the health records of former patients will continue to be stored appropriately and made available for legitimate access over the required retention period. (An AHIMA practice brief provides specific guidance on handling patient information after a facility closure [Rhodes and Brandt 2003].)

State and Local Licensure Requirements

All states require hospitals and other healthcare facilities to undergo licensure. **Licensure** is the mandatory process whereby state governments grant individual facilities permission to operate within a specific geopolitical area and provide a specific range of healthcare services. All fifty states also require physicians, dentists, and nurses to undergo an individual licensure process. Some states license other groups of clinical professionals as well, for example, clinical psychologists and social workers.

The state agencies charged with administering hospital licensure programs have a variety of names; the most common is the department of health. Elements of the licensure program are

Figure 5.2.   Example of a Certificate of Destruction

Anytown General Hospital

CERTIFICATE OF HEALTH
RECORD DESTRUCTION

PATIENT LABEL

The information described below was destroyed in the normal course of business pursuant to a proper retention schedule and destruction policies and procedures.

Date of destruction: _____

Description of records or record series disposed of:_____

_____

_____

Inclusive dates covered: _____

Method of destruction: _____

☐ Burning   ☐ Shredding   ☐ Pulping

☐ Demagnetizing   ☐ Overwriting   ☐ Pulverizing

☐ Other: _____

Records Destroyed By: _____
                                          Signature   Date

Witness Signature:_____
                                          Signature   Date

Department Manager: _____
                                          Signature   Date

CERTIFICATE OF HEALTH RECORD DESTRUCTION
0943217 (08/2003)

similar in most states. The state departments of health are usually charged with performing the following activities (Johns 2002a, p. 203):

- Developing hospital operating standards

- Issuing licenses to hospitals that meet the standards

- Monitoring hospital compliance with the standards

- Sanctioning hospitals that do not comply with the standards

In general, state licensure regulations are modeled after the Medicare *Conditions of Participation* and JCAHO accreditation standards. Typical hospital licensure standards address minimum operating requirements in the areas of operational procedures, staffing, and environmental safety. Some states also require hospitals to maintain additional licenses for specific services such as laboratory, radiology, renal dialysis, and substance abuse treatment. Most states have separate licensure requirements for pharmacies.

The documentation in health records is an important source of information in licensure surveys. States conduct annual surveys to determine the hospital's continued compliance with licensure standards. Surveys are often unannounced and generally focus on clinical services and the care environment. In addition, state surveyors conduct reviews in response to specific complaints from consumers. State surveys are also used to validate compliance with Medicaid regulations.

Medicare and Medicaid Administrative Policies and Regulations

In 1965, amendments to the Social Security Act of 1935 established the Medicare and Medicaid programs. The federal healthcare programs were originally administered by the U.S. Department of Health, Education, and Welfare. The Health Care Financing Administration (HCFA) was established in 1977 to coordinate Medicare and Medicaid benefits on the federal level. The agency was renamed in 2001. Today, Medicare and the federal portion of Medicaid are administered by the **Centers for Medicare and Medicaid Services** (CMS), an agency of the U.S. Department of Health and Human Services. Local Medicaid programs are administered by agencies within individual state governments.

The health records of Medicare beneficiaries are subject to federal Medicare regulations and policies. Similarly, the records of Medicaid beneficiaries must fulfill the requirements of state medical assistance programs. However, the health records of Medicaid and Medicare patients are also subject to other state laws and regulations as well as to national privacy, security, and accreditation standards.

Like other third-party payers, state Medicaid agencies and Medicare fiscal intermediaries may request information from patient records to support reimbursement claims. Patients give their permission for the release of information as a condition of Medicaid or Medicare coverage, and so providers are not required to specifically ask for the patient's permission to release information for reimbursement purposes.

Medicaid Participation

The federal Medicaid program helps pay for the healthcare services provided to individuals and families with low incomes and limited financial resources. Medicaid funding is provided through state-run medical assistance programs, which set the requirements for Medicaid eligibility in their geopolitical regions. In order to receive federal funding, state programs must meet specific minimum requirements as established by federal regulations and CMS policies. However, states decide specific service coverage and reimbursement levels.

Medicaid eligibility and services vary significantly among states, and local providers are subject to complex administrative requirements as defined by state regulations. Participation in state Medicaid programs is voluntary for healthcare professionals and organizations. Hospitals that choose to participate must apply to the state agency that administers the Medicaid program in their local area. Hospitals then supply services to Medicaid beneficiaries under contractual arrangements with the state.

Annual surveys are conducted by most states to confirm hospital compliance with Medicaid regulations. The state agency responsible for conducting annual licensure activities is also responsible for ensuring compliance with Medicaid participation requirements.

Medicare *Conditions of Participation*

The Medicare program provides healthcare coverage for about 40 million retired and/or disabled Americans (CMS 2004). It is the largest single payer for healthcare services in the United States. Although participation in the Medicare program is voluntary, few acute care facilities would be able to survive economically if they did not provide services to Medicare beneficiaries.

Hospitals supply services to Medicare beneficiaries under contractual arrangements with the U.S. Department of Health and Human Services. To qualify for Medicare participation, hospitals must fulfill the Medicare *Conditions of Participation for Hospitals.* Providers of other types of healthcare services are required to follow the Medicare *Conditions of Participation* that apply specifically to them.

Conditions of Participation for Hospitals

The Medicare *Conditions of Participation for Hospitals* are published under title 42, part 482, of the *Code of Federal Regulations.* The **Code of Federal Regulations (CFR)** is updated whenever statutes or regulations are added or changed. Final changes and updates and proposed changes and updates are also published in the **Federal Register,** a daily publication of the U.S. Government Printing Office. Up-to-date information is also available in other print and online resources provided by the Government Printing Office.

The current version of the Medicare *Conditions of Participation for Hospitals* became effective on January 1, 2003. The sections of the regulation that are relevant to acute care documentation are reproduced in figure 5.3.

The CMS works directly with accreditation organizations to coordinate the Medicare *Conditions of Participation* with national accreditation standards. As a result, the Medicare acute care standards are similar to the acute care standards published by the Joint Commission on Accreditation of Healthcare Organizations and the American Osteopathic Association. (Appendix C of this book provides a crosswalk between the requirements of the Medicare program and acute care accreditation standards.)

Section 482.24 of the Medicare regulation deals exclusively with health information management. According to this section, every "hospital must have a medical record service that has administrative responsibility for medical records. A medical record must be maintained for every individual evaluated or treated in the hospital." The first standard in this section addresses the organization and staffing of the health information (medical record) department. Specifically, it requires that the organization of the health information management function must be appropriate to the scope and complexity of the services provided by the hospital. It also requires that the staffing of the department must be adequate to ensure the efficient performance of health record functions.

Figure 5.3. Medicare *Conditions of Participation for Hospitals:* Sections Relevant to Acute Care Clinical Documentation

Section 482.13. Condition of Participation: Patients' Rights
A hospital must protect and promote each patient's rights.

(a) **Standard: Notice of Rights**
  (1) A hospital must inform each patient, or when appropriate, the patient's representative (as allowed under state law), of the patient's rights, in advance of furnishing or discontinuing patient care whenever possible.
  (2) The hospital must establish a process for prompt resolution of patient grievances and must inform each patient whom to contact to file a grievance. The hospital's governing body must approve and be responsible for the effective operation of the grievance process and must review and resolve grievances, unless it delegates the responsibility in writing to a grievance committee. The grievance process must include a mechanism for timely referral of patient concerns regarding quality of care or premature discharge to the appropriate utilization and quality control quality improvement organization. At a minimum:
    (i) The hospital must establish a clearly explained procedure for the submission of a patient's written or verbal grievance to the hospital.
    (ii) The grievance process must specify time frames for review of the grievance and the provision of a response.
    (iii) In its resolution of the grievance, the hospital must provide the patient with written notice of its decision that contains the name of the hospital contact person, the steps taken on behalf of the patient to investigate the grievance, the results of the grievance process, and the date of completion.

(b) **Standard: Exercise of Rights**
  (1) The patient has the right to participate in the development and implementation of his or her plan of care.
  (2) The patient or his or her representative (as allowed under state law) has the right to make informed decisions regarding his or her care. The patient's rights include being informed of his or her health status, being involved in care planning and treatment, and being able to request or refuse treatment. This right must not be construed as a mechanism to demand the provision of treatment or services deemed medically unnecessary or inappropriate.
  (3) The patient has the right to formulate advance directives and to have hospital staff and practitioners who provide care in the hospital comply with these directives, in accordance with Section 489.100 of this part (definition), Section 489.102 of this part (requirements for providers), and Section 489.104 of this part (effective dates).
  (4) The patient has the right to have a family member or representative of his or her choice and his or her own physician notified promptly of his or her admission to the hospital.

(c) **Standard: Privacy and Safety**
  (1) The patient has the right to personal privacy.
  (2) The patient has the right to receive care in a safe setting.
  (3) The patient has the right to be free from all forms of abuse or harassment.

(d) **Standard: Confidentiality of Patient Records**
  (1) The patient has the right to the confidentiality of his or her clinical records.
  (2) The patient has the right to access information contained in his or her clinical records within a reasonable time frame. The hospital must not frustrate the legitimate efforts of individuals to gain access to their own medical records and must actively seek to meet these requests as quickly as its recordkeeping system permits.

(e) **Standard: Restraint for Acute Medical and Surgical Care**
  (1) The patient has the right to be free from restraints of any form that are not medically necessary or are used as a means of coercion, discipline, convenience, or retaliation by staff. The term "restraint" includes either a physical restraint or a drug that is being used as a restraint. A physical restraint is any manual method or physical or mechanical device, material, or equipment attached or adjacent to the patient's body that he or she cannot easily remove that restricts freedom of movement or normal access to one's body. A drug used as a restraint is a medication used to control behavior or to restrict the patient's freedom of movement and is not a standard treatment for the patient's medical or psychiatric condition.
  (2) A restraint can only be used if needed to improve the patient's well-being and less restrictive interventions have been determined to be ineffective.
  (3) The use of a restraint must be—
    (i) Selected only when other less restrictive measures have been found to be ineffective to protect the patient or others from harm

Figure 5.3. (Continued)

      (ii)   In accordance with the order of a physician or other licensed independent practitioner permitted by the state and hospital to order a restraint. This order must: (A) never be written as a standing or on an as needed basis (that is, PRN) and (B) be followed by consultation with the patient's treating physician, as soon as possible, if the restraint is not ordered by the patient's treating physician;

      (iii)   In accordance with a written modification to the patient's plan of care;

      (iv)   Implemented in the least restrictive manner possible;

      (v)   In accordance with safe and appropriate restraining techniques; and

      (vi)   Ended at the earliest possible time.

  (4)   The condition of the restrained patient must be continually assessed, monitored, and reevaluated.

  (5)   All staff who have direct patient contact must have ongoing education and training in the proper and safe use of restraints.

(f)   ***Standard: Seclusion and Restraint for Behavior Management***

  (1)   The patient has the right to be free from seclusion and restraints, of any form, imposed as a means of coercion, discipline, convenience, or retaliation by staff. The term "restraint'" includes either a physical restraint or a drug that is being used as a restraint. A physical restraint is any manual method or physical or mechanical device, material, or equipment attached or adjacent to the patient's body that he or she cannot easily remove that restricts freedom of movement or normal access to one's body. A drug used as a restraint is a medication used to control behavior or to restrict the patient's freedom of movement and is not a standard treatment for the patient's medical or psychiatric condition. Seclusion is the involuntary confinement of a person in a room or an area where the person is physically prevented from leaving.

  (2)   Seclusion or a restraint can only be used in emergency situations if needed to ensure the patient's physical safety and less restrictive interventions have been determined to be ineffective.

  (3)   The use of a restraint or seclusion must be—

      (i)   Selected only when less restrictive measures have been found to be ineffective to protect the patient or others from harm;

      (ii)   In accordance with the order of a physician or other licensed independent practitioner permitted by the state and hospital to order seclusion or restraint. The following requirements will be superseded by existing state laws that are more restrictive: (A) Orders for the use of seclusion or a restraint must never be written as a standing order or on an as needed basis (that is, PRN). (B) The treating physician must be consulted as soon as possible, if the restraint or seclusion is not ordered by the patient's treating physician. (C) A physician or other licensed independent practitioner must see and evaluate the need for restraint or seclusion within 1 hour after the initiation of this intervention. (D) Each written order for a physical restraint or seclusion is limited to 4 hours for adults; 2 hours for children and adolescents ages 9 to 17; or 1 hour for patients under 9. The original order may only be renewed in accordance with these limits for up to a total of 24 hours. After the original order expires, a physician or licensed independent practitioner (if allowed under state law) must see and assess the patient before issuing a new order.

      (iii)   In accordance with a written modification to the patient's plan of care;

      (iv)   Implemented in the least restrictive manner possible;

      (v)   In accordance with safe appropriate restraining techniques; and

      (vi)   Ended at the earliest possible time.

  (4)   A restraint and seclusion may not be used simultaneously unless the patient is—

      (i)   Continually monitored face-to-face by an assigned staff member; or

      (ii)   Continually monitored by staff using both video and audio equipment. This monitoring must be in close proximity the patient.

  (5)   The condition of the patient who is in a restraint or in seclusion must continually be assessed, monitored, and reevaluated.

  (6)   All staff who have direct patient contact must have ongoing education and training in the proper and safe use of seclusion and restraint application and techniques and alternative methods for handling behavior, symptoms, and situations that traditionally have been treated through the use of restraints or seclusion.

  (7)   The hospital must report to CMS any death that occurs while a patient is restrained or in seclusion or where it is reasonable to assume that a patient's death is a result of restraint or seclusion.

(Continued on next page)

Figure 5.3. (Continued)

Section 482.22. Condition of Participation: Medical Staff

The hospital must have an organized medical staff that operates under bylaws approved by the governing body and is responsible for the quality of medical care provided to patients by the hospital.

(a) *Standard: Composition of the Medical Staff.* The medical staff must be composed of doctors of medicine or osteopathy and, in accordance with state law, may also be composed of other practitioners appointed by the governing body.

    (1) The medical staff must periodically conduct appraisals of its members.

    (2) The medical staff must examine credentials of candidates for medical staff membership and make recommendations to the governing body on the appointment of the candidates.

(b) *Standard: Medical Staff Organization and Accountability.* The medical staff must be well organized and accountable to the governing body for the quality of the medical care provided to patients.

    (1) The medical staff must be organized in a manner approved by the governing body.

    (2) If the medical staff has an executive committee, a majority of the members of the committee must be doctors of medicine or osteopathy.

    (3) The responsibility for organization and conduct of the medical staff must be assigned only to an individual doctor of medicine or osteopathy or, when permitted by state law of the state in which the hospital is located, a doctor of dental surgery or dental medicine.

(c) *Standard: Medical Staff Bylaws.* The medical staff must adopt and enforce bylaws to carry out its responsibilities. The bylaws must:

    (1) Be approved by the governing body.

    (2) Include a statement of the duties and privileges of each category of medical staff (e.g., active, courtesy, etc.).

    (3) Describe the organization of the medical staff.

    (4) Describe the qualifications to be met by a candidate in order for the medical staff to recommend that the candidate be appointed by the governing body.

    (5) Include a requirement that a physical examination and medical history be done no more than 7 days before or 48 hours after an admission for each patient by a doctor of medicine or osteopathy, or, for patients admitted only for oromaxillofacial surgery, by an oromaxillofacial surgeon who has been granted such privileges by the medical staff in accordance with state law.

    (6) Include criteria for determining the privileges to be granted to individual practitioners and a procedure for applying the criteria to individuals requesting privileges.

(d) *Standard: Autopsies.* The medical staff should attempt to secure autopsies in all cases of unusual deaths and of medical–legal and educational interest. The mechanism for documenting permission to perform an autopsy must be defined. There must be a system for notifying the medical staff, and specifically the attending practitioner, when an autopsy is being performed.

Section 482.23. Condition of Participation: Nursing Services

The hospital must have an organized nursing service that provides 24-hour nursing services. The nursing services must be furnished or supervised by a registered nurse.

(a) *Standard: Organization.* The hospital must have a well-organized service with a plan of administrative authority and delineation of responsibilities for patient care. The director of the nursing service must be a licensed registered nurse. He or she is responsible for the operation of the service, including determining the types and numbers of nursing personnel and staff necessary to provide nursing care for all areas of the hospital.

(b) *Standard: Staffing and Delivery of Care.* The nursing service must have adequate numbers of licensed registered nurses, licensed practical (vocational) nurses, and other personnel to provide nursing care to all patients as needed. There must be supervisory and staff personnel for each department or nursing unit to ensure, when needed, the immediate availability of a registered nurse for bedside care of any patient.

    (1) The hospital must provide 24-hour nursing services furnished or supervised by a registered nurse and have a licensed practical nurse or registered nurse on duty at all times, except for rural hospitals that have in effect a 24-hour nursing waiver granted under Section 405.1910(c) of this chapter.

    (2) The nursing service must have a procedure to ensure that hospital nursing personnel for whom licensure is required have valid and current licensure.

    (3) A registered nurse must supervise and evaluate the nursing care for each patient.

    (4) The hospital must ensure that the nursing staff develops, and keeps current, a nursing care plan for each patient.

    (5) A registered nurse must assign the nursing care of each patient to other nursing personnel in accordance with the patient's needs and the specialized qualifications and competence of the nursing staff available.

    (6) Nonemployee licensed nurses who are working in the hospital must adhere to the policies and procedures of the hospital. The director of nursing service must provide for the adequate supervision and evaluation of the clinical activities of non-employee nursing personnel which occur within the responsibility of the nursing service.

Figure 5.3. (Continued)

(c)   ***Standard: Preparation and Administration of Drugs.*** Drugs and biologicals must be prepared and administered in accordance with federal and state laws, the orders of the practitioner or practitioners responsible for the patient's care as specified under Section 482.12(c), and accepted standards of practice.

    (1)   All drugs and biologicals must be administered by, or under supervision of, nursing or other personnel in accordance with federal and state laws and regulations, including applicable licensing requirements, and in accordance with the approved medical staff policies and procedures.

    (2)   All orders for drugs and biologicals must be in writing and signed by the practitioner or practitioners responsible for the care of the patient as specified under Section 482.12(c) with the exception of influenza and pneumococcal polysaccharide vaccines, which may be administered per physician-approved hospital policy after an assessment for contraindications. When telephone or oral orders must be used, they must be—

        (i)   Accepted only by personnel who are authorized to do so by the medical staff policies and procedures, consistent with federal and state law;

        (ii)   Signed or initialed by the prescribing practitioner as soon as possible; and

        (iii)   Used infrequently.

    (3)   Blood transfusions and intravenous medications must be administered in accordance with state law and approved medical staff policies and procedures. If blood transfusions and intravenous medications are administered by personnel other than doctors of medicine or osteopathy, the personnel must have special training for this duty.

    (4)   There must be a hospital procedure for reporting transfusion reactions, adverse drug reactions, and errors in administration of drugs.

Section 482.24. Condition of Participation: Medical Record Services
The hospital must have a medical record service that has administrative responsibility for medical records. A medical record must be maintained for every individual evaluated or treated in the hospital.

(a)   ***Standard: Organization and Staffing.*** The organization of the medical record service must be appropriate to the scope and complexity of the services performed. The hospital must employ adequate personnel to ensure prompt completion, filing, and retrieval of records.

(b)   ***Standard: Form and Retention of Record.*** The hospital must maintain a medical record for each inpatient and outpatient. Medical records must be accurately written, promptly completed, properly filed and retained, and accessible. The hospital must use a system of author identification and record maintenance that ensures the integrity of the authentication and protects the security of all record entries.

    (1)   Medical records must be retained in their original or legally reproduced form for a period of at least 5 years.

    (2)   The hospital must have a system of coding and indexing medical records. The system must allow for timely retrieval by diagnosis and procedure, in order to support medical care evaluation studies.

    (3)   The hospital must have a procedure for ensuring the confidentiality of patient records. Information from or copies of records may be released only to authorized individuals, and the hospital must ensure that unauthorized individuals cannot gain access to or alter patient records. Original medical records must be released by the hospital only in accordance with federal or state laws, court orders, or subpoenas.

(c)   ***Standard: Content of Record.*** The medical record must contain information to justify admission and continued hospitalization, support the diagnosis, and describe the patient's progress and response to medications and services.

    (1)   All entries must be legible and complete and must be authenticated and dated promptly by the person (identified by name and discipline) who is responsible for ordering, providing, or evaluating the service furnished.

        (i)   The author of each entry must be identified and must authenticate his or her entry.

        (ii)   Authentication may include signatures, written initials, or computer entry.

    (2)   All records must document the following, as appropriate:

        (i)   Evidence of a physical examination, including a health history, performed no more than 7 days prior to admission or within 48 hours after admission.

        (ii)   Admitting diagnosis.

        (iii)   Results of all consultative evaluations of the patient and appropriate findings by clinical and other staff involved in the care of the patient.

        (iv)   Documentation of complications, hospital-acquired infections, and unfavorable reactions to drugs and anesthesia.

        (v)   Properly executed informed consent forms for procedures and treatments specified by the medical staff, or by federal or state law if applicable, to require written patient consent.

        (vi)   All practitioners' orders, nursing notes, reports of treatment, medication records, radiology and laboratory reports, and vital signs and other information necessary to monitor the patient's condition.

        (vii)   Discharge summary with outcome of hospitalization, disposition of case, and provisions for follow-up care.

        (viii)   Final diagnosis, with completion of medical records within 30 days following discharge.

(Continued on next page)

Figure 5.3. (Continued)

Section 482.43. Condition of Participation: Discharge Planning

The hospital must have in effect a discharge planning process that applies to all patients. The hospital's policies and procedures must be specified in writing.

(a) *Standard: Identification of Patients in Need of Discharge Planning.* The hospital must identify at an early stage of hospitalization all patients who are likely to suffer adverse health consequences upon discharge if there is no adequate discharge planning.

(b) *Standard: Discharge Planning Evaluation*

    (1) The hospital must provide a discharge planning evaluation to the patients identified in paragraph (a) of this section, and to other patients upon the patient's request, the request of a person acting on the patient's behalf, or the request of the physician.

    (2) A registered nurse, social worker, or other appropriately qualified personnel must develop, or supervise the development of, the evaluation.

    (3) The discharge planning evaluation must include an evaluation of the likelihood of a patient needing posthospital services and of the availability of the services.

    (4) The discharge planning evaluation must include an evaluation of the likelihood of a patient's capacity for self-care or of the possibility of the patient being cared for in the environment from which he or she entered the hospital.

    (5) The hospital personnel must complete the evaluation on a timely basis so that appropriate arrangements for posthospital care are made before discharge and to avoid unnecessary delays in discharge.

    (6) The hospital must include the discharge planning evaluation in the patient's medical record for use in establishing an appropriate discharge plan and must discuss the results of the evaluation with the patient or individual acting on his or her behalf.

(c) *Standard: Discharge Plan*

    (1) A registered nurse, social worker, or other appropriately qualified personnel must develop, or supervise the development of, a discharge plan if the discharge planning evaluation indicates a need for a discharge plan.

    (2) In the absence of a finding by the hospital that a patient needs a discharge plan, the patient's physician may request a discharge plan. In such a case, the hospital must develop a discharge plan for the patient.

    (3) The hospital must arrange for the initial implementation of the patient's discharge plan.

    (4) The hospital must reassess the patient's discharge plan if there are factors that may affect continuing care needs or the appropriateness of the discharge plan.

    (5) As needed, the patient and family members or interested persons must be counseled to prepare them for posthospital care.

(d) *Standard: Transfer or Referral.* The hospital must transfer or refer patients, along with necessary medical information, to appropriate facilities, agencies, or outpatient services, as needed, for follow-up or ancillary care.

(e) *Standard: Reassessment.* The hospital must reassess its discharge planning process on an ongoing basis. The reassessment must include a review of discharge plans to ensure that they are responsive to discharge needs.

Section 482.51. Condition of Participation: Surgical Services

If the hospital provides surgical services, the services must be well organized and provided in accordance with acceptable standards of practice. If outpatient surgical services are offered, the services must be consistent in quality with inpatient care in accordance with the complexity of services offered.

(a) *Standard: Organization and Staffing.* The organization of the surgical services must be appropriate to the scope of the services offered.

    (1) The operating rooms must be supervised by an experienced registered nurse or a doctor of medicine or osteopathy.

    (2) Licensed practical nurses (LPNs) and surgical technologists (operating room technicians) may serve as "scrub nurses" under the supervision of a registered nurse.

    (3) Qualified registered nurses may perform circulating duties in the operating room. In accordance with applicable state laws and approved medical staff policies and procedures, LPNs and surgical technologists may assist in circulatory duties under the supervision of a qualified registered nurse who is immediately available to respond to emergencies.

    (4) Surgical privileges must be delineated for all practitioners performing surgery in accordance with the competencies of each practitioner. The surgical service must maintain a roster of practitioners specifying the surgical privileges of each practitioner.

Figure 5.3. **(Continued)**

(b) ***Standard: Delivery of Service.*** Surgical services must be consistent with needs and resources. Policies governing surgical care must be designed to assure the achievement and maintenance of high standards of medical practice and patient care.

    (1) There must be a complete history and physical work-up in the chart of every patient prior to surgery, except in emergencies. If this has been dictated, but not yet recorded in the patient's chart, there must be a statement to that effect and an admission note in the chart by the practitioner who admitted the patient.

    (2) A properly executed informed consent form for the operation must be in the patient's chart before surgery, except in emergencies.

    (3) The following equipment must be available to the operating room suites: call-in system, cardiac monitor, resuscitator, defibrillator, aspirator, and tracheotomy set.

    (4) There must be adequate provisions for immediate postoperative care.

    (5) The operating room register must be complete and up-to-date.

    (6) An operative report describing techniques, findings, and tissues removed or altered must be written or dictated immediately following surgery and signed by the surgeon.

Section. 482.52. Condition of Participation: Anesthesia Services

If the hospital furnishes anesthesia services, they must be provided in a well-organized manner under the direction of a qualified doctor of medicine or osteopathy. The service is responsible for all anesthesia administered in the hospital.

(a) ***Standard: Organization and Staffing.*** The organization of anesthesia services must be appropriate to the scope of the services offered. Anesthesia must be administered only by—

    (1) A qualified anesthesiologist;

    (2) A doctor of medicine or osteopathy (other than an anesthesiologist);

    (3) A dentist, oral surgeon, or podiatrist who is qualified to administer anesthesia under state law;

    (4) A certified registered nurse anesthetist (CRNA), as defined in Section 410.69(b) of this chapter, who, unless exempted in accordance with paragraph (c) of this section, is under the supervision of the operating practitioner or of an anesthesiologist who is immediately available if needed; or

    (5) An anesthesiologist's assistant, as defined in Section 410.69(b) of this chapter, who is under the supervision of an anesthesiologist who is immediately available if needed.

(b) ***Standard: Delivery of Services.*** Anesthesia services must be consistent with needs and resources. Policies on anesthesia procedures must include the delineation of preanesthesia and postanesthesia responsibilities. The policies must ensure that the following are provided for each patient:

    (1) A preanesthesia evaluation by an individual qualified to administer anesthesia under paragraph (a) of this section performed within 48 hours prior to surgery.

    (2) An intraoperative anesthesia record.

    (3) With respect to inpatients, a postanesthesia followup report by the individual who administers the anesthesia that is written within 48 hours after surgery.

    (4) With respect to outpatients, a postanesthesia evaluation for proper anesthesia recovery performed in accordance with policies and procedures approved by the medical staff.

(c) ***Standard: State Exemption.***

    (1) A hospital may be exempted from the requirement for physician supervision of CRNAs as described in paragraph (a)(4) of this section, if the state in which the hospital is located submits a letter to CMS signed by the governor, following consultation with the state's boards of medicine and nursing, requesting exemption from physician supervision of CRNAs. The letter from the governor must attest that he or she has consulted with state boards of medicine and nursing about issues related to access to and the quality of anesthesia services in the state and has concluded that it is in the best interests of the state's citizens to opt out of the current physician supervision requirement and that the opt-out is consistent with state law.

    (2) The request for exemption and recognition of state laws and the withdrawal of the request may be submitted at any time and are effective upon submission.

Source: 2003 *Code of Federal Regulations*, Title 42, Part 482 [42 CFR482, volume 3], effective 1/1/2003.

The second standard addresses health record format and retention requirements. Specifically:

- The hospital must maintain a health record for every inpatient and outpatient it treats or evaluates.

- Health records must be accurately written, promptly completed, properly filed and retained, and easily accessible.

- The hospital must follow an effective system for authenticating the authorship of health record documentation.

- The hospital must have an effective system for protecting the integrity of health information and maintaining the security of health records.

- Health records must be retained for a minimum of five years.

- The hospital must have a system for coding and indexing the content of health records so that information on diagnoses and procedures can be quickly retrieved for evaluations of medical effectiveness.

- The hospital must have an effective system for ensuring the confidentiality of health records.

- The hospital must have a system for releasing confidential health record information to authorized users but preventing unauthorized access.

- Original health records must not be removed from the hospital except in response to federal or state laws, court orders, and subpoenas.

The third standard describes the content requirements for acute care documentation. The standard requires that the information in the health record must justify the patient's admission to the hospital as well as his or her continued hospitalization. The standard further stipulates that acute care documentation must support the patient's diagnosis and describe the patient's progress and response to services. In addition:

- All health record entries must be legible and complete.

- All services must be promptly documented and dated by the individual who is responsible for ordering, performing, or evaluating the services provided.

- The author of every entry must be identified by name and discipline, and the author must authenticate the entries by signing his or her full name or initials or by using an electronic verification entry.

- The health record must be completed within thirty days after the patient's discharge, transfer, or death.

- All acute care records must include the following types of clinical information:

  —Documentation that a physical examination and medical history were performed no more than seven days before the patient's admission or forty-eight hours after the admission

  —Documentation of the patient's admitting diagnosis or diagnoses

  —Results of any clinical consultations

—Documentation of clinical evaluations performed by the clinical staff involved in the patient's care

—Documentation of any complications, hospital-acquired infections, or negative reactions to medications or anesthesia

—Fully executed informed consent forms for procedures, as required by medical staff rules, state laws, or federal regulations

—All physicians' orders, nursing notes, treatment reports, medication records, diagnostic results, vital signs logs, and other information gathered in evaluating and monitoring the patient's condition

—A discharge summary that includes the outcome of hospitalization, the disposition of the case, and the provisions for follow-up care

—Documentation of the patient's final diagnosis or diagnoses

Section 482.13 of the Medicare *Conditions of Participation* requires hospitals to protect the personal and medical rights of patients. This section of the regulation lists the patient's rights provisions of the Medicare program. It also requires that hospitals provide a notice of rights to patients or their legal representatives. Specifically:

Section 482.13, Patient's Rights: (1) A notice of the rights of patients must be provided to patients or their legal representatives, and the notice should be furnished in advance of providing or discontinuing services whenever possible. (2) The notice must describe the facility's procedures for receiving and resolving patients' grievances. (3) The patient's rights notice must include the following provisions:
—The patient's right to participate in the development and implementation of his or her care plan
—The patient's right to accept or refuse treatment
—The patient's right to formulate advance directives and expect caregivers to follow those directives
—The patient's right to have a family member or personal representative as well as his or her personal physician notified promptly of his or her hospital admission
—The patient's right to personal privacy and safety
—The patient's right to be free from all forms of abuse and harassment
—The patient's right to the confidentiality of his or her clinical records
—The patient's right to access his or her clinical records within a reasonable time frame
—The patient's right to be free from restraints of any form (physical or chemical) that are not medically necessary and established by a physician's order (specifically, to be free of restraints applied as a means of coercion, discipline, convenience, or retaliation by staff)

The hospital should ask patients or their representatives to sign acknowledgment forms to document the fact that information about patient's rights was provided.

Several other sections of the Medicare *Conditions of Participation for Hospitals* also include documentation requirements. These sections can be summarized as follows:

Section 482.22, Medical Staff: The hospital must have a system for documenting the family's (or legal representative's) permission to perform an autopsy on a patient who died while under the hospital's care.

Section 482.23, Nursing Services: (1) A registered nurse must supervise, and ensure the documentation of, the development and maintenance of a care plan for every patient. (2) All orders for drugs and biologicals must be made in writing and signed by the physician responsible for the patient's care. (3) Telephone and verbal orders must be accepted only by personnel authorized by medical staff rules, consistent with applicable state and federal regulations. (4) Telephone and verbal orders must be signed or initialed by the prescribing practitioner as soon as possible. (5) The hospital must have a procedure in place for reporting transfusion reactions, adverse drug reactions, and medication errors.

Section 482.26, Radiology Services: (1) The radiologist responsible for interpreting diagnostic images must authenticate the reports of his or her findings. (2) The hospital must maintain records of radiology procedures, consultations, and interpretations for at least five years.

Section 482.27, Laboratory Services: The hospital must have a system in place for notifying patients who may have been exposed to infectious diseases through contaminated blood transfusions.

Section 482.43, Discharge Planning: (1) Hospital personnel must complete a discharge evaluation for every patient who is likely to require posthospital services. (2) The discharge evaluation and plan must be completed in time to avoid unnecessary delays in arranging posthospital services. (3) The discharge plan must be documented in the patient's health record.

Section 482.51, Surgical Services: (1) A complete history and physical must be documented in the patient's health record before surgery begins, except in emergencies. (2) A fully executed consent form must be placed in the patient's health record before surgery begins, except in emergencies. (3) The operating room register must be complete and up to date. (4) An operative report that describes surgical techniques, surgical findings, and any tissues removed or altered must be written or dictated and authenticated by the surgeon immediately following surgery.

Section 482.52, Anesthesia Services: (1) A preanesthesia patient evaluation must be performed and documented no more than forty-eight hours before surgery. (2) An intraoperative record must be maintained while the procedure is in progress. (3) For inpatients, a postanesthesia follow-up report must be written within forty-eight hours after surgery. (4) For outpatients, a postanesthesia evaluation must be performed and documented according to medical staff policy.

Section 482, Nuclear Medicine Services: (1) The practitioner approved by the medical staff to interpret the results of diagnostic procedures that use nuclear materials must sign and date the reports of his or her interpretation of the findings. (2) The hospital must maintain records of nuclear medicine procedures, consultations, and interpretations for at least five years.

Medicare Compliance Surveys

Hospitals that are accredited through the JCAHO hospital accreditation program or the AOA's Healthcare Facilities Accreditation Program (HFAP) are granted deemed status by the Medicare program. Deemed status means that accredited facilities are automatically considered to be in compliance with the Medicare *Conditions of Participation for Hospitals.*

Most acute care hospitals are accredited through a survey process conducted by the Joint Commission on Accreditation of Healthcare Organizations (JCAHO) or the American Osteopathic Association (AOA). Consequently, they are not required to undergo annual Medicare certification surveys. However, CMS policy requires that a sample of hospitals with deemed status (approximately 10 percent each year) must undergo a Medicare validation survey soon after the JCAHO or AOA accreditation survey is completed (Shaw and others 2003, p. 247).

Medicare/Medicaid certification programs are conducted by state licensure agencies working under contract with the CMS. Those few hospitals that do not qualify for deemed status are required to undergo a Medicare certification survey annually. Such facilities may have chosen not to participate in one of the accreditation programs, or they may have lost their accreditation temporarily because of compliance deficiencies.

As noted earlier in the chapter, the JCAHO and other accreditation organizations work with the CMS in an attempt to coordinate their accreditation standards with the Medicare *Conditions of Participation.* However, some inconsistencies still exist. For example, the Medicare health record regulation requires that every health record entry must be authenticated, but the JCAHO standard on maintaining patient-specific information (IM.6.10) establishes a more lenient minimum requirement (JCAHO 2004b, p. IM-15):

> Every medical record entry is dated, the author identified and, when necessary according to law or regulation and hospital policy, is authenticated.
>
> At a minimum, the following are authenticated either by written signature, electronic signature, or computer key or rubber stamp:
> * The history and physical examination
> * Operative report
> * Consultations
> * Discharge summary

In contrast, section 482.24(c)(1)(i) of the 2003 Medicare *Conditions of Participation for Hospitals* indicates that "the author of each entry [in the medical record] must be identified and must authenticate his or her entry." Section 482.24(c)(1)(ii) of the regulation goes on to define *authentication* as "signatures, written initials, or computer entry."

As the preceding example shows, the Medicare *Conditions of Participation,* accreditation standards, HIPAA standards, state health record and licensure regulations, and hospital policies can, and often do, present conflicting guidelines. In such cases, the hospital must develop health record policies based on the strictest regulatory and accreditation requirements that apply. In this way, the hospital can ensure that it fulfills the requirements of all the regulatory and accreditation agencies (Shaw and others 2003, p. 246).

Federal Privacy and Security Regulations and Standards

As noted earlier in the chapter, before the implementation of the final HIPAA privacy and security standards in 2003, the confidentiality and integrity of health records were protected by a number of different regulations, standards, and policies. As a standard of professional practice, healthcare organizations generally obtained the patient's formal, written permission to release information from his or her health record only when the information was requested by parties outside the organization. In acute care facilities, the process of release and disclosure was managed by the health information management (HIM) department.

In addition to recently implemented privacy and security regulations, several other federal regulations apply to the confidentiality of healthcare treatment records. These include the Privacy Act of 1974 and the substance abuse treatment legislation initially implemented in 1970 and amended in 2000.

Health Insurance Portability and Accountability Act

The **Health Insurance Portability and Accountability Act** (HIPAA) was signed into law by President Clinton in 1996. The regulations instituted to fulfill the provisions of the act were fully implemented for all but a few covered entities in April 2003. (The final privacy and security standards are established under title 45, parts 160, 162, and 164, of the *Code of Federal Regulations.*) HIPAA compliance activities are managed by the Office of Civil Rights, a federal agency within the Department of Health and Human Services.

HIPAA regulations apply specifically to healthcare facilities, professionals, health plans, and healthcare information clearinghouses that transmit healthcare information electronically. In practical terms, because virtually every healthcare provider and payer in the United States processes reimbursement claims electronically, the regulations apply universally.

The HIPAA regulations define *health information* as any information that is created or received by a healthcare provider in relation to:

- The past, present, or future physical or mental health of an individual

- The provision of healthcare services to an individual

- The past, present, or future payment for healthcare services provided to the individual

The definition applies to all types of information in any form or medium, including verbal and recorded communications.

The HIPAA regulations have had a broad impact on healthcare providers and payers in the United States. Nowhere is this fact more evident than in the area of health information management. Protecting the privacy of patients and the confidentiality of health records have long been the central focus of HIM professionals and the American Health Information Management Association (AHIMA). However, the specific reporting and record-keeping requirements of the new regulations have necessitated significant policy and procedure changes for most healthcare organizations, particularly acute care hospitals.

HIPAA Privacy Standard

Under HIPAA regulations, patients are assumed to have given healthcare providers implied permission to use and disclose personal information about them by virtue of their voluntary submission to medical services. In order to ensure efficient healthcare operations, therefore, healthcare providers are allowed to access, use, and disclose personally identifiable information for healthcare purposes without first obtaining the patient's expressed (written) permission. Specifically (Hjort and Hughes 2002):

- A healthcare organization can use confidential patient information for purposes related to the patient's care and treatment.

- A healthcare organization can disclose confidential patient information to another healthcare provider for purposes related to the patient's treatment.

- A healthcare organization can use confidential patient information for purposes related to reimbursement for the services provided to the patient.

- A healthcare organization can disclose confidential patient information to another healthcare provider or covered organization for purposes related to reimbursement for services provided to the patient.

- A healthcare organization can use confidential patient information for purposes related to healthcare operations.

- A healthcare organization can disclose confidential patient information to another covered organization for purposes related to the healthcare operations of the other organization when both organizations have or had a relationship with the individual who is the subject of the protected information to be disclosed.

- A healthcare organization that is part of an organized healthcare delivery system can disclose confidential health information to another organization within the system for purposes related to the healthcare operations of the system.

Under the regulations, healthcare operations include quality and performance improvement activities, medical staff credentialing activities, review activities related to fraud and abuse detection, business planning and development, and general administrative activities.

The HIPAA privacy standard preempts state laws that are not consistent with federal privacy protections except under the following specific circumstances:

- An exception is made by the secretary of Health and Human Services.

- A provision in state law is more stringent than the federal standard.

- The state law relates to public health surveillance and reporting.

- The state law relates to reporting for the purpose of management or financial audits, program monitoring and evaluation, and licensure or certification of facilities or individuals.

Notice of Privacy Practices

To comply with the HIPAA privacy standard, hospitals and other healthcare providers are required to make a notice of privacy practices available to every new patient. The **notice of privacy practices** is a written description of the facility's procedures related to the use and disclosure of protected health information. The notice also explains the privacy rights of individual patients and the facility's legal responsibility for protecting private health information. Providers are also required to obtain a signed acknowledgment that indicates that the patient received such a notice. (A sample notice of privacy practices is shown in figure 5.4.)

Patient's Privacy Rights

According to HIPAA regulations, individual patients have specific rights in relation to how their confidential health information is used:

- Patients may opt out of the facility's patient directory.

- Patients may request restrictions on the use of their health information.

- Patients may ask that communications from the facility be sent by alternative means or to an alternative address.

- Patients may request an accounting of any disclosures of their health information. (See figure 5.5, p. 280.)

Figure 5.4.   Example of a Notice of Privacy Practices

PATIENT: This notice describes how information about you may be used and disclosed and how you can get access to this information. Please review it carefully.

Understanding Your Health Record/Information

Each time you visit a hospital, physician, or another healthcare provider, a record of your visit is made. Typically, this record contains symptoms, examination and test results, diagnoses, treatment, and the plan for future care or treatment. This has the following functions:

- It serves as the basis for planning your care and treatment.

- It serves as the means of communication among the various health professionals who contribute to your care.

- It becomes the legal document that describes the care you received.

- It serves as the means by which you or a third-party payer representing you can verify that billed services were actually provided.

- It is used as a tool in the education of healthcare professionals.

- It is a source of data for medical research.

- It is a source of information for the public health officials charged with improving the health of the nation.

- It is a source of data for facility planning and marketing.

- It serves as a tool for assessing and continually improving the care we render and the outcomes we achieve.

Understanding what is in your record and how your health information is used helps you to ensure its accuracy; better understand who, what, when, where, and why others may access your health information; and make more informed decisions about authorizing the disclosure of your healthcare information to other parties.

Figure 5.4.   (Continued)

Your Health Information Rights

Although your health record is the property of the healthcare practitioner or facility that compiled it, the information in the record belongs to you. You have certain rights in connection with your health information. You have the right to:

- Request a restriction on certain uses and disclosures of your information as provided by 45 CFR164.522.

- Obtain a paper copy of the notice of information practices upon request.

- Inspect and copy your health record as provided for in 45 CFR164.524.

- Amend your health record as provided in 45 CFR164.528.

- Obtain an accounting of disclosures of your health information as provided in 45 CFR164.528.

- Request communications of your health information by alternative means or at alternative locations.

- Revoke your authorization to use or disclose health information except to the extent that action has already been taken.

Our Responsibilities

This organization has certain responsibilities in connection with your health record. We are required to:

- Maintain the privacy of your health information.

- Provide you with a notice as to our legal duties and privacy practices with respect to information we collect and maintain about you.

- Abide by the terms of this notice.

- Notify you if we are unable to agree to a requested restriction.

- Accommodate reasonable requests you may have to communicate health information by alternative means or at alternative locations.

We reserve the right to change our practices and to make the new provisions effective for all of the protected health information we maintain. Should our information practices change, we will mail a revised notice to the address you have supplied to us. We will not use or disclose your health information without your authorization, except as described in this notice.

For More Information or to Report a Problem

If you have questions and would like additional information, you may contact the director of health information management at [telephone number]. If you believe that your right to privacy has been violated, you can file a complaint with the director of health information management or with the secretary of Health and Human Services. There will be no retaliation for filing a complaint.

(Continued on next page)

Figure 5.4. (Continued)

Examples of Disclosures for Treatment, Payment, and Health Operations

1. We will use information about you for the purposes of diagnosis and treatment.

   For example, information obtained by a nurse, physician, or other member of your healthcare team will be recorded in your record and used to determine your course of treatment. Your physician will also document his or her expectations of the members of your healthcare team in the same record. Members of your healthcare team will then record the actions they took and their observations in your health record. In that way, the physician will know how you are responding to treatment.

   We will also provide your physician or a subsequent healthcare provider with copies of various reports to assist him or her in treating you once you have been discharged from this hospital.

2. We will use your health information to request payment for the services you receive.

   For example, a bill may be sent to you or a third-party payer. The information on or accompanying the bill may include information that identifies you, as well as your diagnosis, procedures, and supply usage.

3. We will use your health information for regular health operations in our facility.

   For example, members of the medical staff, the risk or quality improvement manager, or members of the quality improvement team may use information from your health record to assess the care and clinical outcomes in your case and others like it. This information will then be used in an effort to continually improve the quality and effectiveness of the healthcare services we provide.

4. We will share your health information with our business associates only when necessary to conduct operations or provide services.

   For example, outside business associates sometimes provide physician services in the emergency department and for radiology and certain laboratory tests. In addition, we may use a copy service for making copies of your health record. When these services are contracted, we may disclose your health information to our business associates so that they can perform the job we have asked them to perform and then bill you or your third-party payer for services rendered. To protect your health information, however, we require the business associate to appropriately safeguard your information.

5. We will share limited personal information about you in our directory of patients unless you notify us that you object.

   For example, your name, location in the facility, general condition, and religious affiliation may be used for directory purposes. This information may be provided to members of the clergy and, except for religious affiliation, to other people who ask for you by name.

6. We will share limited personal information about you (your location and general condition) for the purpose of notifying your family members, personal representatives, or other people responsible for your care.

Figure 5.4. (Continued)

7. We will share limited personal information about you for the purpose of communication with your family or other designated individuals.

   For example, using their best judgment, healthcare professionals may disclose to a family member, relative, close personal friend, or any other person you designate health information relevant to that person's involvement in your care or payment.

8. We may disclose information to researchers when their research has been approved by an institutional review board that has reviewed the research proposal and established protocols to ensure the privacy of your health information.

9. Consistent with applicable law, we may disclose health information to funeral directors so that they can carry out their duties.

10. Consistent with applicable law, we may disclose health information to organ procurement organizations or other entities engaged in the procurement, banking, or transplantation of organs for the purpose of tissue donation and transplantation.

11. We may contact you to provide appointment reminders or information about treatment alternatives or other health-related benefits and services that may be of interest to you.

12. We may contact you as part of a fund-raising effort.

13. We may disclose to the FDA health information relative to adverse events with respect to food, supplements, product and product defects, or postmarketing surveillance information to enable product recalls, repairs, or replacement.

14. We may disclose health information to the extent authorized by, and to the extent necessary to comply with, laws relating to workers' compensation or other similar programs established by law.

15. As required by law, we may disclose your health information to public health or legal authorities charged with preventing or controlling disease, injury, or disability.

16. If you are an inmate of a correctional institution, we may disclose to the institution or agents thereof health information necessary for your health and the health and safety of other individuals.

17. We may disclose health information for law enforcement purposes as required by law or in response to a valid subpoena.

Federal law makes provision for your health information to be released to an appropriate health oversight agency, public health authority, or attorney, provided that a workforce member or business associate believes in good faith that we have engaged in unlawful conduct or have otherwise violated professional or clinical standards and are potentially endangering one or more patients, workers, or the public.

Effective Date: [DATE]

Figure 5.5. Example of a Request for Accounting of Disclosures

Anytown Community Hospital

REQUEST FOR ACCOUNTING OF DISCLOSURES

PATIENT LABEL

Date of Request: _____

Patient Name: _____

Date of Birth: _____ Health Record Number: _____

Patient Address: _____

Address to Send Disclosure Accounting (if different from above):

_____

Dates Requested

I would like an accounting of all disclosures for the following time frame.

From: _____ To: _____

(Please note: The maximum time frame that can be requested is six years prior to the date of request.)

Fees

First request in a 12-month period: Free

Subsequent requests: (Insert cost-based fee per entity)

The fee for this request will be: _____

I understand that there is a fee for this accounting and wish to proceed. I also understand that the accounting will be provided to me within 60 days unless I am notified in writing that an extension of up to 30 days is needed.

_____   _____
      Signature of Patient or Legal Representative   Date

For Healthcare Organization Use Only:

Date Received: _____ Date Sent: _____

Extension Requested: ☐ No ☐ Yes, Reason _____

Patient Notified in Writing on This Date: _____

Staff Member Processing Request: _____

REQUEST FOR ACCOUNTING OF DISCLOSURES
300252 (10/2002)

Patient's Right to Health Record Access

Under the federal privacy standard, patients also have the right to access their own health information. Specifically:

- Patients must be allowed to review their own health records.

- Patients must be allowed to obtain copies of their own protected health information.

- Patients must be allowed to request that their health information be corrected or amended. (The process for making patients' amendments in health records was discussed in chapter 4.)

The individual's rights extend for as long as the information is maintained.

According to the standard, patients or their legal representatives are required to submit requests for access in writing. Hospitals and other healthcare providers must respond in a timely manner, usually within thirty days. Under the regulations, providers are allowed to request a thirty-day extension as long as the person making the request is notified of the reason for the delay. The time frame for responding to requests for records stored off site is sixty days. Patients or their representatives must be allowed to make convenient arrangements for reviewing original records. They must also be able to obtain photocopies. Providers may charge a reasonable cost-based fee for providing copies.

There are, however, some exceptions to the patient's right to access his or her health information:

- Patients are not allowed to access information compiled in anticipation of, or for use in, civil, criminal, or administrative actions or proceedings.

- Patients are not entitled to access information subject to the Clinical Laboratory Improvements Act (that is, reference laboratory records and research laboratory records).

- Patients are not allowed to review psychotherapy notes prepared by counselors and psychiatric practitioners for their own use.

In addition, any licensed healthcare professional may deny patients access to their records under either of two circumstances: (1) when access would likely endanger the life or physical safety of the individual or another person or (2) when access would endanger the life or physical safety of another person mentioned in the protected health information.

Release and Disclosure Practices

The HIPAA privacy standard specifies the following requirements related to the hospital's information use and disclosure processes:

- Hospital policy must identify the uses and disclosures for which authorization is required.

- Hospital policy must specify who may authorize disclosure on behalf of an individual patient.

- Hospital policy must provide special protections for psychotherapy notes.

- Hospital policy must establish limitations on the use of protected health information for fund-raising and must provide a mechanism that allows individuals to opt out of fund-raising communications.

- Hospital policy must establish the requirements for the deidentification of protected health information before it can be released without the patient's authorization.

- Hospital policy must establish a standard to limit the amount of information used or disclosed to the minimum necessary to accomplish the intended purpose.

- Hospital policy must establish classes of personnel who need access to protected health information, the specific categories of information each class needs, and the conditions under which access is appropriate.

The **minimum necessary** standard was not meant to require the implementation of inflexible restrictions. Rather, it is meant as a best practice guideline. Specifically, the minimum necessary standard does not apply to information requested by healthcare providers for purposes related to the patient's treatment or to requests made or authorized by the patient. The standard also does not apply to information requests related to compliance investigations conducted by the Department of Health and Human Services.

The minimum necessary standard does require covered healthcare facilities to identify individuals or classes of individuals in their workforce who need access to protected health information. The types of information needed by each class of individuals are then identified along with any conditions related to access. For routine and recurring disclosures, the facility is required to implement standardized procedures that limit the disclosures to the amount needed to accomplish the purposes of the requests. For other requests for disclosure, the facility is required to develop criteria that limit the amount of information disclosed to the minimum amount necessary. Similarly, the standard also recommends that facilities limit the amount of protected information they request from other providers (Amatayakul and others 2002).

Authorizations for Disclosure

Disclosures of patient-identifiable health information for purposes that are not related to patient treatment, reimbursement, reporting, or healthcare operations require authorization from the patient or the patient's legal representative. The HIPAA privacy standard establishes federal guidelines for the content and use of authorization forms. It states that, to be valid, an authorization form must be written in plain language and it must pertain to one specific request. It must also contain the following elements (Hughes 2002d):

- A specific and meaningful description of the information to be used or disclosed

- The name or other specific identification of the person(s) or class of persons to whom the information will be disclosed

- The name or other specific identification of the person(s) or class of persons authorized to disclose the information

- An expiration date or event that relates to the individual or the purpose of the disclosure

- A statement of the individual's right to revoke the authorization

- A statement describing the exceptions to the right of revocation

- A description of how the individual may revoke the authorization

- A statement that information disclosed according to the authorization may be subject to redisclosure by the recipient and so would no longer be protected

- The signature of the individual

- The date

When the authorization is signed by a personal or legal representative acting on the patient's behalf, it should include a description of the representative's relationship to the patient. (See figure 5.6 for an example of a valid authorization.)

An authorization that has any of the following defects would be considered invalid:

- The expiration date or event has already passed.

- The authorization has not been filled out completely.

- The covered party knows that the authorization has been revoked.

- The authorization lacks one or more of the required elements.

- The authorization is a prohibited type of authorization; that is, it covers more than one request.

- The covered entity knows that part or all of the information in the authorization is false.

The hospital must retain the original signed authorization or an electronic copy of the signed authorization and a written or electronic record of the action taken in response to the authorization. (See figure 5.7 for an example of a disclosure tracking log.)

An individual may revoke any previous authorization at any time by submitting a written statement that specifies that he or she has revoked the authorization. There are two exceptions to the right to revoke existing authorizations. An authorization cannot be revoked (1) when the covered entity has already taken action or (2) when the authorization was obtained as a condition of obtaining insurance coverage and the insurer has the right to contest a claim under the policy.

The HIPAA privacy rule requires special handling for psychotherapy notes. Special protection requirements for records of psychotherapy and other types of sensitive information are discussed later in the chapter.

Security Standard

HIPAA also established a federal baseline requirement for health information security. The standard allows healthcare providers and other covered organizations flexibility in choosing security methods to address their own operational needs and climate. In sum, it requires that hospitals and other healthcare organizations conduct systematic risk analyses to serve as the basis for instituting effective security programs (Amatayakul 2004, pp. 188–90).

Specifically, the standard calls for providers to develop security policies, procedures, contracts, and plans. It also requires the implementation of physical and technical safeguards to protect confidential health record and information. Physical safeguards include:

- Environmental safety systems such as fire alarms, smoke detectors, and sprinkler systems

- Surveillance systems and other methods of controlling and monitoring access to the facility

- Media control systems that prevent unauthorized access to computer equipment and work stations

Figure 5.6. Example of a HIPAA-Compliant Authorization Form

Midwest Medical Center

CONSENT FOR DISCLOSURE
OF HEALTH INFORMATION

PATIENT LABEL

(1)   I hereby authorize (name of provider) to disclose the following information from the health records of:

Patient Name: _____ Date of Birth: _____

Address: _____

Telephone: _____ Patient Number: _____

Covering the period(s) of healthcare:

From (date) _____ to (date) _____

From (date) _____ to (date) _____

(2)   Information to be disclosed:

    ☐ Complete health record(s)

        ☐ Discharge summary   ☐ Progress notes

        ☐ History and physical examination   ☐ Laboratory test results

        ☐ Consultation reports   ☐ X-ray reports

    ☐ Photographs, videotapes, digital or other images

    ☐ Other (please specify) _____

I understand that this will include information relating to (check if applicable):

    ☐ AIDS (acquired immunodeficiency syndrome) or HIV (human immunodeficiency virus) infection

    ☐ Psychiatric care

    ☐ Treatment for alcohol and/or drug abuse

(3)   This information is to be disclosed to _____ for the purpose of

_____.

(4)   I understand this authorization may be revoked in writing at any time, except to the extent that action has been taken in reliance on this authorization. Unless otherwise revoked, this authorization will expire on the following date, event, or condition: _____

_____

(5)   The facility, its employees, officers, and physicians are hereby released from any legal responsibility or liability for disclosure of the above information to the extent indicated and authorized herein.

_____   _____

Signature of Patient or Legal Representative   Date   Signature of Witness   Date

CONSENT FOR DISCLOSURE OF HEALTH INFORMATION
000089 (9/2001)

Figure 5.7.   Example of a Disclosure Tracking Log

Anytown Community Hospital

DISCLOSURE TRACKING LOG

PATIENT LABEL

Date Received	Name of Requestor	Address (if known)	Authorization or Written Request (Y/N)	Purpose*	PHI Disclosed*	Date Disclosed*	Disclosed By	Fee Billed	Fee Received	Date Received

Fields required by HIPAA privacy standards. Note: Fields can be incorporated into a computerized tracking system.

Requests for Accounting of Disclosures

Requested By (individual/legal rep):	Date Requested	Date Range Requested	Staff Completing Request	Date Provided

(Use this section to document accounting requests when a copy of this disclosure log is provided to the individual.)

Key

Date received: The date request is received to disclose or release information when applicable

Name of requestor: Name of entity or person requesting information to be disclosed or released

Address: If known, the address of the entity or person requesting information to be disclosed or released

Authorization or written request (yes/no): Identify if there is a written request or authorization; if there is not, indicate how request was received (for example, verbal)

Purpose: Brief description of the purpose of the disclosure to reasonably inform the individual of the basis of the disclosure; if documented on authorization or written request, state "see authorization/written request"

PHI disclosed: Brief description of the information disclosed/released

Date disclosed: Date the information was released or disclosed

Sent by: Staff member processing the request and disclosing the information

Amount billed: If applicable, the copy fee charged for records released

Amount received: Copy fee received

Date received: Date the fee was received

DISCLOSURE TRACKING LOG
300251 (10/2002)

The standard also calls for technical security mechanisms and procedures to protect health record data during transmission and storage. Examples include access control technology based on the user's identity or role and/or the specific information being accessed. Data authentication, audit trails, and encryption technology can also be implemented to protect the security of clinical information systems (Quinsey and Brandt 2003).

Administrative Requirements

HIPAA regulations also establish specific administrative requirements in relation for confidential health record information:

- Every facility must designate a specific individual to manage its privacy program.

- Every facility must designate a specific individual to answer requests for privacy information and respond to privacy-related complaints.

- Every facility must designate a specific individual to oversee its information security program.

- Every facility must train its employees and medical staff on the provisions of its privacy and security policies.

- Every facility must establish appropriate administrative, technical, and physical safeguards to protect confidential health information.

- Every facility must develop contingency plans that address information system backup, disaster recovery, and emergency operating procedures.

- Every facility must establish health record content and clinical documentation policies and procedures.

- Every facility must specify policies and procedures related to privacy notifications, authorizations for disclosure, health record corrections and amendments, disclosure documentation, complaint handling, and overall HIPAA compliance.

- Every facility must establish the copying fees to be charged for disclosures.

Federal Requirements for Special Health Record Protection

The confidentiality of all patient-identifiable health information must be protected, but several types of health-related information are particularly sensitive. The inappropriate disclosure of information related to substance abuse treatment or psychiatric care can have devastating consequences for patients and their families. Similarly, information about a patient's HIV status or sexually transmitted illness can lead to discrimination in employment and housing. Concerns related to the release genetic information and the potential for discrimination based on genetic profiles are a relatively new area of concern. Several federal regulations supplement state laws and voluntary accreditation standards to provide special protection to particularly sensitive health information.

Records of Psychiatric Care and Psychotherapy

Psychiatric records are unique in that they include two separate records: an official or legal record, which documents the patient's care and treatment, and a personal record, which documents the clinician's experience and conversations with the patient (McWay 2002, p. 164).

(In the language of the HIPAA privacy standard, a psychiatric practitioner's personal record is referred to as *psychotherapy notes.*)

The HIPAA privacy standard provides specific guidance regarding psychotherapy notes. Psychotherapy notes may not be released unless specifically identified on an authorization form signed by the patient or the patient's legal representative. HIPAA defines **psychotherapy notes** as documentation recorded in any medium by a mental health professional to record or analyze the contents of conversations with patients during private treatment sessions or group, joint, or family counseling sessions. As noted in the preceding paragraph, such notes are usually separated from the rest of the individual's health record. When the notes are included in the patient's health record, however, the special protection afforded by the HIPAA privacy standard does not apply.

Not all psychotherapy documentation requires special handling. Some psychotherapy documentation may be released with a valid authorization from the patient or his or her legal representative. Such documentation includes the following:

- Records of the prescription and monitoring of medications

- Start and stop times for counseling sessions

- Modalities and frequency of treatment

- Results of clinical tests

- Any summary of the patient's diagnoses, functional status, treatment plan, symptoms, prognosis, and progress to date

Many states have laws and regulations that address the use and disclosure of behavioral health and psychotherapy records. The federal privacy standard does not preempt state laws and regulations that protect individual health information more stringently or provide the individual greater access or control over protected health information.

Individual states may also institute regulations that define the content of authorizations. When such laws or regulations exist, the facility should consider the HIPAA privacy standard in determining how to apply the state requirements (Hughes 2002c and 2002d).

Records of Substance Abuse Treatment

Two federal statutes apply specifically to the health records of patients undergoing substance abuse treatment. The Alcohol Abuse and Alcoholism Prevention, Treatment, and Rehabilitation Act and the Drug Abuse Prevention, Treatment, and Rehabilitation Act were passed in 1970 and amended in 2000. The regulations apply specifically to programs operated, regulated, or directly or indirectly funded by the federal government. Because most substance abuse treatment programs receive some type of federal funding, even if only by virtue of Medicaid and Medicare participation, the regulatory requirements apply to virtually all of the programs in the United States (McWay 2002, p. 152).

The regulations prohibit the disclosure and redisclosure of treatment records that include the identity, diagnosis, prognosis, and treatment outcomes of patients without the written permission of the patient. A special notice must be included with every authorized disclosure (Rhodes and Hughes 2003):

> The information has been disclosed to you from records protected by federal confidentiality rules (42 CFR2). The federal rules prohibit you from making any further redisclosure of this

information unless further disclosure is expressly permitted by the written consent of the person to whom it pertains or as otherwise permitted by 42 CFR, Part 2. A general authorization for the release of medical or other information is not sufficient for this purpose. The federal rules restrict any use of the information to criminally investigate or prosecute any alcohol or drug abuse patient.

(An example of a valid notice is provided in figure 5.8.)

The regulations permit the release of information without the patient's consent in three situations: when medical personnel need the information to address a genuine medical emergency, for research and audit activities, and in response to a legitimate court order. Patients also have the right to access their own records. The HIPAA privacy standard preempts the provisions of the substance abuse treatment regulations only insofar as the substance abuse information regulations call for measures less strict than those of the privacy standard.

The substance abuse regulations establish the following content requirements for authorizations to disclose patient-identifiable health information maintained by alcohol or drug abuse programs (title 42, chapter 1, part 2 of the *Code of Federal Regulations*):

- Specific name or general designation of the program or person permitted to make the disclosure

- Name or title of the individual or name of the organization to which disclosure is to be made

- Name of the patient

- Purpose of the disclosure

- Quantity and nature of the information to be disclosed

- Signature of the patient

- Date the authorization was signed

- Statement that the authorization is subject to revocation at any time

- The date, event, or condition upon which the authorization will expire if not revoked (this date, event, or condition must ensure that the authorization will last no longer than reasonably necessary to serve the purpose for which it is given)

Records of HIV/AIDS Diagnosis and Treatment

The illness caused by the human immunodeficiency virus (HIV) (acquired immunodeficiency disease, or AIDS) has been a worldwide public health concern for more than two decades. In response to the AIDS epidemic in the United States, most state legislatures have enacted laws that require HIV/AIDS reporting. Because individuals infected with HIV often face discrimination in housing, employment, and healthcare services, many state regulations also specifically address confidentiality issues related to HIV testing and AIDS treatment.

HIV Testing
HIV testing has become a common practice. Many individuals at risk for contracting HIV voluntarily choose to be tested. However, individuals may also be compelled by court order to undergo involuntary testing. In addition, many states have enacted statutes that require specific groups of individuals to undergo routine HIV testing, most commonly healthcare workers.

Figure 5.8.   Example of a Confidentiality Notice for Records of Alcohol and Drug Abuse Treatment

Anytown Community Hospital

CONFIDENTIALITY OF ALCOHOL AND
DRUG ABUSE PATIENT RECORDS

PATIENT LABEL

The confidentiality of alcohol and drug abuse patient records maintained by this program is protected by federal law and regulations. Generally, the program may not say to a person outside the program that a patient attends the program or disclose any information identifying a patient as an alcohol or drug abuser unless:

1. The patient consents in writing.
2. The disclosure is allowed by a court order.
3. The disclosure is made to medical personnel in a medical emergency or to qualified personnel for research, audit, or program evaluation.

Violation of the federal law and regulations by a program is a crime. Suspected violations may be reported to appropriate authorities in accordance with federal regulations.

Federal law and regulations do not protect any information about a crime committed by a patient either at the program or against any person who works for the program or about any threat to commit such a crime.

Federal laws and regulations do not protect any information about suspected child abuse or neglect from being reported under State law to appropriate state or local authorities.

(Approved by the Office of Management and Budget under control number 0930-0099)

Source: "Confidentiality of Alcohol and Drug Abuse Patient Records," *Code of Federal Regulations,* 2000.42 CFR, chapter I, part 2.

CONFIDENTIALITY OF ALCOHOL AND DRUG ABUSE PATIENT RECORDS
003226 (11/2002)

Most HIV testing in the United States is performed on a voluntary basis. Some states have even developed anonymous HIV testing programs to encourage individuals at risk of infection to be tested without identifying themselves by name. In addition, many individuals undergo routine voluntary testing when they donate blood, plasma, semen, and other human tissue to blood and tissue banks. HIV testing has also become a routine element in prenatal care, and infants are usually tested shortly after birth when their mothers are known or suspected to be HIV positive.

Involuntary HIV testing, however, may be required for specific groups of individuals by state statute or for individuals by court order. Where they exist, state regulations mandating HIV testing generally apply to specific groups whose infection would present the greatest potential threat to public health. Examples of such groups include convicted sex offenders and prison inmates entering or leaving correctional facilities (McWay 2002, pp. 198–99).

Some states also require mandatory testing of specific groups of employees. Others permit only voluntary employee-testing programs. And still others prohibit mandatory employee testing or allow it only under specific circumstances, that is, when health status affects the employees' ability to perform their jobs safely. Healthcare workers who perform invasive procedures are one common example.

Court orders for mandatory HIV testing of individuals must demonstrate two things: (1) that the individual is likely to be infected with HIV and (2) that the individual's HIV status presents a serious threat to the health of other individuals.

Discrimination based on disability status is prohibited by law in some states as well as by the federal Americans with Disabilities Act of 1990. Therefore, the collection of information about an employee's HIV status is a serious issue. The federal regulations in this area also apply to applicants for employment. Hospitals and other healthcare facilities must consult legal counsel before establishing policies and procedures related to human resources issues.

Confidentiality Issues Related to HIV/AIDS

In general, most state regulations developed to protect the identity of HIV-positive individuals address confidentiality practices in three areas: consent for testing, general information on testing, and reporting of test results. Individuals must sign a formal informed consent before testing. Most states also require healthcare providers to provide information about HIV testing and AIDS to patients before they perform the test. The provider's method of communicating test results to patients is also covered in many state HIV testing regulations (McWay 2002, pp. 197 and 199).

Virtually every state requires providers to report cases of positive HIV results to the state's public health department. Some counties and municipalities may also require reporting. In general, reporting involves the identification of the infected individual. Therefore, the communication of public health reports containing HIV/AIDS information should be accomplished through a confidential medium, specifically, not via telephone, e-mail, or facsimile transmission (Carpenter 1999).

The AHIMA has recommended the following procedures for managing health information related to HIV infection and AIDS (Carpenter 1999):

- HIV employee-screening programs should protect the confidentiality of test results.

- Specific, written informed consent should be obtained from the individual or the individual's legal representative before voluntary testing.

- When state regulations permit the mandatory testing of patients after healthcare workers have been exposed to blood or bodily fluids, the need for testing should be discussed with the patient or his or her legal representative before testing.

- Counseling provided before or after testing should be performed by a qualified health-care professional.

- The records of HIV-positive patients should not be subject to special handling procedures because special procedures are more likely to draw attention than routine security measures. In states where special handling is required for the records of HIV-positive individuals or HIV test results, the records should be identified with an obscure code or symbol to avoid inadvertent release of HIV-related information.

- Facilities should implement, and monitor compliance with, clear policies and procedures on the disclosure of health information related to HIV/AIDS. Policies should dictate that HIV/AIDS information must be used only for diagnosis, treatment, and patient care management. Other disclosures, including disclosures for billing and claims purposes, must be allowed only with the patient's written consent and should be limited to the minimum amount needed for the authorized purpose. Authorized disclosures of HIV/AIDS information should include a notice that redisclosure is prohibited except when required by law.

- HIV/AIDS-related information should only be discussed via telephone in emergency situations.

- Clinical coding should be based only on the diagnoses verified in patient records and not on the basis of laboratory results alone.

- Information related to the HIV-positive status of healthcare workers, including information on any restrictions to their practice, should be protected according to all applicable state and federal regulations. Such information should only be disclosed to patients upon the advice of legal counsel.

Records That Contain Genetic Information

In 2003, the Human Genome Project completed the mapping of the genetic structure of humans. The project was jointly sponsored by the U.S. Department of Energy and the National Institutes of Health. The project was one of the largest scientific projects ever undertaken. Its research identified the function of every human gene. This information promises to revolutionize the future of medicine. (The DOE promotes scientific and technological innovation, and the NIH supports medical research.)

Genetic information can be used to predict an individual's risk of eventually contracting many types of illness, including diabetes, heart disease, cancer, and even mental health disorders such as alcoholism and schizophrenia. For this reason, the potential for using genetic information as the basis of discrimination against individuals cannot be ignored.

Although genetic information is extremely sensitive, it is usually afforded no special protection under state health record regulations. In addition, the results of genetic tests and genetic information based on family history may be referred to in any part of the health record, and so it is difficult to protect such information from inadvertent disclosure.

HIPAA addressed the issue of health insurance discrimination based on genetic information. The act specifically prohibits healthcare insurance plans from basing coverage decisions and premiums on genetic information alone. Several states have enacted similar health insurance and genetic testing regulations, including Missouri, California, Arizona, Maryland, and Wisconsin (McWay 2002, p. 170). In 2004, the U.S. House of Representatives was also working on legislation that would ban other types of discrimination based on the genetic profiles of individual Americans.

Federal Patient Safety Legislation

In July 2004, the U.S. Senate passed the Patient Safety and Quality Improvement Act. Similar legislation was passed by the U.S. House of Representatives in March 2003. The two versions of the legislation will be reconciled to create the final provisions of the act, which is an amendment of the Public Health Service Act. One of the outcomes of the legislation will be the creation of a confidential and voluntary system for reporting medical errors. The overall goal of the national reporting system will be to improve patient safety and reduce the number of medical errors nationwide.

Accreditation Requirements for Acute Care Hospitals

Acute care facilities must fulfill the various regulatory requirements of federal, local, and state governments, but most also choose to participate in one or more voluntary accreditation programs. One of the benefits of accreditation is that it enhances the hospital's public reputation for providing high-quality clinical services. In some cases, it also satisfies eligibility requirements for hospitals that participate in programs that affect their financial status, such as Medicare and Medicaid. In addition, many state licensure agencies base their licensure requirements for hospitals on the JCAHO standards.

Accreditation is a systematic quality review process that evaluates the healthcare facility's performance against preestablished, written criteria, or **standards.** Healthcare organizations voluntarily seek accreditation from a variety of private, not-for-profit accreditation organizations. Different types of healthcare organizations and services are accredited by different accreditation organizations.

Most acute care hospitals are accredited by either the Joint Commission on Accreditation of Healthcare Organizations or the American Osteopathic Association's Healthcare Facilities Accreditation Program. Psychiatric and rehabilitation specialty hospitals and hospital departments devoted to psychiatric and rehabilitation services may also be accredited through the Commission on Accreditation of Rehabilitation Facilities. Managed care programs that provide acute care services may be accredited through the National Committee for Quality Assurance. Ambulatory surgery centers and outpatient diagnostic imaging and radiation oncology treatment facilities may be accredited through the Accreditation Association for Ambulatory Health Care.

Joint Commission on Accreditation of Healthcare Organizations

The **Joint Commission on Accreditation of Healthcare Organizations** (JCAHO) is a not-for-profit, standards-setting organization whose primary mission is "to continuously improve the safety and quality of care provided to the public through the provision of health care accreditation and related services that support performance improvement in health care organizations" (JCAHO 2004a). Currently, it accredits over 17,000 healthcare organizations in the Unites States. The JCAHO also has an international branch that accredits healthcare facilities in Spain and Saudi Arabia.

A number of healthcare organizations are eligible for accreditation by the JCAHO, including:

- Acute care hospitals
- Critical access hospitals

- Children's hospitals

- Psychiatric hospitals

- Rehabilitation hospitals

- Ambulatory care organizations

- Behavioral health organizations

- Home care agencies

- Long-term care (or skilled nursing) facilities

- Healthcare networks

- Clinical laboratories

In addition, several specialty settings are eligible for JCAHO certificate programs. Examples include assisted living, office-based surgery, and disease-specific programs.

The JCAHO began implementing a new accreditation process in January 2004. The new process is called **Shared Visions—New Pathways.** It focuses on systems critical to the safety and quality of patient care, treatment, and services. With the implementation of the new process, the emphasis in JCAHO accreditation has shifted away from triennial survey preparation to a continuous improvement philosophy that applies to every area of the facility. Implementation began with acute care organizations in 2004. Gradual implementation for other settings is planned over the next two years. The ultimate goal is complete implementation for all of the JCAHO's programs by 2006 (Shaw and others 2003, p. 247).

JCAHO Documentation Standards for Hospitals

Organizations seeking JCAHO accreditation must meet standards in every area of patient care, including clinical documentation and health records. Periodic accreditation surveys test the adequacy of documentation through detailed health record reviews.

The JCAHO has developed a number of documentation standards that apply to every healthcare setting. These core standards are supplemented by standards that address the additional documentation requirements of specialty settings and specific clinical services. For example, a teaching hospital that hosts medical education programs would be evaluated on its compliance with authentication requirements for documentation created by medical students and unlicensed physicians in addition to other acute care documentation standards.

As part of the Shared Visions—New Pathways project, the JCAHO reviewed and streamlined its hospital standards to eliminate redundancies and to clarify the language used. The project also reduced the amount of paperwork facilities need to prepare as documentation of their compliance with the standards.

The format of the 2004 hospital accreditation manual was also changed to make it easier to use. Like previous manuals, the new manual is formatted in sections, but each section is now organized into the same three elements (JCAHO 2004b):

- The *standard,* which is a concise statement of the goal

- The *rationale for the standard,* which explains why achieving the goal is important

- The *elements of performance* (EPs), which describe the steps to be followed in meeting the goal

The numbering system for the standards was also simplified. For example:

Standard IM.5.10: Knowledge-based information resources are readily available, current, and authoritative.

Rationale for IM.5.10: Hospital practitioners and staff have access to knowledge-based information to do the following:
- Help them acquire and maintain the knowledge and skills needed to maintain and improve compliance
- Help with clinical/service and management decision making
- Provide appropriate information and education to patients and families
- Support performance improvement and patient safety activities
- Support the institution's education and research needs

Elements of Performance for IM.5.10:
1. Library services are provided by cooperative or contractual arrangements with other institutions, if not available on site.
2. The hospital provides access to information resources needed by staff in print, electronic, Internet, audio, and/or other appropriate form.
3. Knowledge-based resources are available at all times to clinical/service staff, through electronic means, after-hours access to an in-house collection, or other methods.
4. The hospital has a plan to provide for access to information during times when electronic systems are unavailable.

The scoring method is also new. A score is assigned to each element of performance to determine whether the hospital is in compliance with the standard. Scoring uses the following scale:

0	Insufficient compliance
1	Partial compliance
2	Satisfactory compliance
NA	Not applicable

The JCAHO's standards on the management of information concentrate on organization-wide information planning and management in the following areas:

- Identification of the hospital's information needs

- Structure of the hospital's information management system

- Processes for capturing, organizing, storing, retrieving, processing, and analyzing clinical data and information

- Processes for transmitting, reporting, displaying, integrating, and using clinical data and information

- Processes for safeguarding the confidentiality and integrity of clinical data and information

Thirteen JCAHO standards organized in five parts apply specifically to health information management processes. The first part, Information Management Planning, includes the following standard:

IM.1.10 The hospital plans and designs information management processes to meet internal and external information needs.

The next set of standards pertains to confidentiality and security:

IM.2.10 Information privacy and security are maintained.
IM.2.20 Information security, including data integrity, is maintained.
IM.2.30 The hospital has a process for maintaining continuity of information.

The standard on information management processes reads as follows:

IM.3.10 The hospital has a process in place to effectively manage information, including the capturing, reporting, processing, storing, retrieving, disseminating, and displaying of clinical/service and nonclinical data and information.

There are two standards on information-based decision making:

IM.4.10 The information management system provides information for use in decision making.
IM.5.20 Knowledge-based information resources are readily available, current, and authoritative.

The last six standards in the management of information section apply to patient-specific information:

IM.6.10 The hospital has a complete and accurate medical record for every patient assessed or treated.
IM.6.20 Records contain patient-specific information, as appropriate, to the care, treatment, and services provided.
IM.6.30 The medical record thoroughly documents operative or other procedures and the use of moderate or deep sedation or anesthesia.
IM.6.40 For patients receiving continuing ambulatory care services, the medical record contains a summary list of all significant diagnoses, procedures, drug allergies, and medications.
IM.6.50 Designated qualified personnel accept and transcribe verbal orders from authorized individuals.
IM.6.60 The hospital can provide access to all relevant information from a patient's record when needed for use in patient care, treatment, and services.

Other sections of the hospital accreditation manual also include standards relevant to health records and health information. The section on the ethics, rights, and responsibilities of hospitals provides standards on the individual rights of patients, including their right to privacy. The standards in this section also apply to the documentation of informed consent, advance directives, and authorizations to disclose patient information. (See figure 5.9 for a list of the JCAHO's patients' rights standards.)

The section on patient care includes a number of elements of performance related to health record documentation. Performance standards from this section apply to the following areas:

- Patient assessments

- Timing of initial physical examinations and histories

- Nutritional screening and planning

- Functional status screening

- Care planning

- Discharge planning

- Appropriateness of care

- Patient education

- Preoperative assessments

- Anesthesia records

- Operative reports

- Use of restraints

Specific patient care standards also apply to documentation for psychiatric and addiction treatment services. The documentation standards for critical access hospitals are the same as the documentation standards for acute care hospitals.

Figure 5.9.   JCAHO Standards on Patients' Rights and Responsibilities

RI.2.10	The hospital respects the rights of patients.
RI.2.20	Patients receive information about their rights.
RI.2.30	Patients are involved in decisions about care, treatment, and services provided.
RI.2.40	Informed consent is obtained.
RI.2.50	Consent is obtained for recording or filming made for purposes other than the identification, diagnosis, or treatment of the patients.
RI.2.60	Patients receive adequate information about the person(s) responsible for the delivery of their care, treatment, and services.
RI.2.70	Patients have the right to refuse care, treatment, and services in accordance with the law.
RI.2.80	The hospital addresses the wishes of the patient relating to end-of-life decisions.
RI.2.90	Patients and, when appropriate, their families are informed about the outcomes of care, treatment, and services, including unanticipated outcomes.
RI.2.100	The hospital respects the patient's right to and need for effective communication.
RI.2.120	The hospital addresses the resolution of complaints from patients and their families.
RI.2.130	The hospital respects the needs of patients for confidentiality, privacy, and security.
RI.2.140	Patients have a right to an environment that preserves dignity and contributes to a positive self-image.
RI.2.150	Patients have the right to be free from mental, physical, sexual, and verbal abuse, neglect, and exploitation.
RI.2.160	Patients have the right to pain management.
RI.2.170	Patients have a right to access protective and advocacy services.
RI.2.180	The hospital protects research subjects and their rights during research, investigation, and clinical trials involving human subjects.
RI.2.190	In hospitals that provide opportunities for work, a defined policy addresses situations in which patients work.
RI.3.10	Patients are given information about their responsibilities while receiving care, treatment, and services.

Source: JCAHO 2004a, pp. RI-2 and RI-3.

Several standards in the medication management section of the manual address the health record documentation required for ordering and administering medications and monitoring their effects. Individual sections also pertain to the responsibilities of the hospital's medical staff and nursing staff. (Appendix C provides more detailed information on the JCAHO documentation standards.)

JCAHO Sentinel Event Policy

The JCAHO also recommends that accredited hospitals and other healthcare facilities implement systems for identifying and addressing what the JCAHO calls *sentinel events*. A **sentinel event** is "an unexpected occurrence involving death or serious physical or psychological injury, or the risk thereof" (JCAHO 2004b, p. SE-1). The JCAHO defines a serious injury as one that results in the loss of a limb or the loss of bodily function. A sentinel event is not the same thing as a medical error, because many sentinel events are not the result of mistakes. Sentinel events are simply events that call for immediate investigation and appropriate response. The goal of sentinel event reporting is to reduce the risk of similar events happening again in the future. One example of a sentinel event might be the unintentional amputation of the wrong leg during cancer surgery. Another might involve the correct administration of a medication that caused an unanticipated allergic reaction in the patient that led to near-fatal anaphylactic shock. The unexpected death of an infant during the delivery process would also be a reportable sentinel event.

Several standards in the performance improvement section of the 2004 hospital accreditation manual pertain to sentinel events. Standard PI.2.30 specifically requires that "processes for identifying and managing sentinel events are defined and implemented." The rationale for this standard states that (JCAHO 2004b, p. PI-9):

> Identifying, reporting, analyzing, and managing sentinel events can help the hospital to prevent such incidents. Leaders define and implement such a program as part of the process to measure, assess, and improve the hospital's performance.

Hospitals and other facilities are encouraged to submit a sentinel event report to the JCAHO when the event resulted in an unanticipated death or a permanent loss of significant function that was not related to the natural course of the patient's illness or an underlying condition. In other words, the event should be reported when it was related to the patient's treatment rather than to his or her illness (JCAHO 2004b, p. SE-3). The JCAHO also asks that hospitals report the following types of events:

- Abductions of infants or discharges of infants to the wrong families

- Cases of nonconsensual sexual contact involving patients with other patients, staff members, or other attackers

- Hemolytic transfusion reactions involving the administration of blood or blood products with major blood-group incompatibilities

- Surgical procedures performed on the wrong patient or the wrong body part

- Unanticipated deaths of full-term infants

- Suicides of patients in settings where patients receive twenty-four-hour care

Examples of reportable sentinel events include (JCAHO 2004b, p. SE-4):

- Cases of death, paralysis, and coma associated with medication errors

- Cases of death among women in labor from causes related to the birth process

- Assaults, homicides, and other crimes committed in the facility that result in the death or permanent impairment of patients

- Patient falls that result in death or permanent functional impairment

Events such as medication errors and unsuccessful suicides that do not result in death or a permanent loss of significant function need not be reported to the JCAHO. However, such events should be investigated as part of the facility's routine sentinel event investigation and management program.

JCAHO National Patient Safety Goals

The JCAHO also evaluates hospital performance against a set of goals designed to complement its longstanding patient safety standards. The most recent revision of the patient safety goals was released in July 2004 and is available on the commission's Web site (JCAHO 2004c).

JCAHO Survey Process

In 2001, a JCAHO task force examined the commission's accreditation standards and processes. Ultimately, the task force's work resulted in the publication of a significantly revised *Comprehensive Accreditation Manual for Hospitals* in 2004. The 2004 revision also brought the information management standards and other related standards into compliance with the HIPAA privacy and security regulations.

As noted earlier in this section, the JCAHO's new hospital accreditation process focuses on continuous compliance with quality and patient safety standards. The goal of the new process is to encourage hospitals and other healthcare organizations to follow best practice standards consistently rather than waiting to implement improvements in anticipation of a scheduled survey. Currently, the JCAHO's survey process is scheduled well in advance of the site visit, and every hospital receives an accreditation review at least once every three years. The JCAHO's goal is to move its accreditation programs to completely unannounced surveys by 2006 (JCAHO 2004b, pp. SV-1 through SV-34).

Midcycle Performance Review

The JCAHO's new accreditation process initially required every accredited organization to complete an additional step in the accreditation cycle called the periodic performance review (PPR). The **periodic performance review** is based on a self-assessment conducted by the organization at the halfway point between triennial on-site accreditation surveys. Part of the PPR process called for the organization to submit the results of its review to the JCAHO by using an electronic tool provided by the commission.

Subsequently, healthcare organizations expressed serious concerns about the possible legal ramifications of this reporting requirement. Specifically, hospitals and other healthcare organizations feared that they might be forced to reveal the contents of the confidential PPR reports as part of the legal discovery process in future court cases. In response to these concerns, the JCAHO decided to allow organizations to choose one of three additional options to fulfill the midcyle performance review requirement.

For organizations that choose to follow the original PPR design, the process begins with an organizational self-assessment. The organization evaluates itself on its compliance with the standards and elements of performance that apply to the services it provides. The results of the evaluation are reported to the JCAHO, and the hospital develops an action plan for correcting any deficiencies identified. The action plan is then to be implemented during the second half of the accreditation cycle, and outcome measures are to be evaluated as part of the regular survey visit. The goal of the PPR process is to encourage continuous compliance with the JCAHO's standards and to provide additional opportunities for continuing quality education and performance improvement.

The PPR assessment tool is made available in electronic format on the JCAHO's private Internet site. Hospitals access the site using a password provided by the JCAHO. The PPR tool created for each hospital is designed to assess the hospital's compliance with all relevant standards and EPs, accreditation participation requirements, and national patient safety goals. The self-assessment is completed online and submitted electronically to the JCAHO.

After the PPR is complete, a representative of the JCAHO discusses the results with the hospital's representatives via telephone. The outcome of these conversations is a final plan of action that addresses any shortcomings that were identified during the PPR process. During the regular on-site survey about eighteen months later, the surveyors validate the hospital's execution of the action plan and evaluate its success.

As an alternative to completing the full PPR process, acute care organizations can choose one of the following three options (JCAHO 2004d):

- **Option 1:** The organization would perform a midcycle self-assessment and develop a plan of action and measures of success as originally required. However, it would not be required to submit the PPR results to the JCAHO at the midcycle point. Instead, the organization would attest to the fact that it completed the assessment on time and developed the plan but has been advised not to submit the results to the JCAHO. The organization would still have the opportunity to discuss performance-related information with JCAHO staff but without identifying its level of standards compliance. Then, in anticipation of the regular on-site survey eighteen months later, the organization would provide its measures of success to JCAHO for evaluation during the survey.

- **Option 2:** The organization would not perform a midcycle self-assessment or develop an action plan. Instead, the organization would choose to undergo an on-site survey at the midpoint of its accreditation cycle. The survey would be much shorter than a full survey, and the organization would pay an additional fee to cover the cost of the additional survey. The JCAHO then would provide a written report that detailed the results of the survey. After analyzing the survey report, the organization would submit a plan of action for correcting the areas of noncompliance. JCAHO staff would work with the organization to refine the action plan. Finally, in anticipation of the regular on-site survey eighteen months later, the organization would provide its measures of success to the JCAHO for evaluation during the survey.

- **Option 3:** As in option 1, the organization could choose to undergo a short midcycle survey instead of the PPR process. However, the JCAHO would not provide a written report of the survey results to the organization. Instead, the surveyors' findings would be discussed verbally with the organization so that there would be no possibility of disclosure issues. Then, during the subsequent full survey conducted eighteen months later, there would be no mention of the midcycle survey. The survey would concentrate on the organization's compliance at the time of the triennial survey.

No matter which of the four options the organization chooses to follow, the results of the midcycle review will have no effect on the organization's current accreditation status or the JCAHO's ultimate accreditation decision at the beginning of the next three-year cycle. The purpose of the midcycle review is to encourage the adoption of continuous improvement processes, improve clinical quality, and ensure patient safety.

Triennial Site Survey

When a hospital is nearing the end of its three-year accreditation cycle or has not been accredited in the past, it initiates the process of renewal or initial accreditation by submitting an application to the JCAHO. The application requires the hospital to provide information about its state licensure status, corporate structure, and clinical services as well as commonly computed statistical information (total admissions, occupancy rate, average length of stay, and so on).

Presurvey accreditation activities also include a priority focus process (PFP). According to the hospital accreditation manual, the **priority focus process** "converts presurvey data into information that focuses survey activities, increases consistency in the accreditation process, and customizes the accreditation process to make it specific to [the] hospital. Surveyors will receive enhanced information and insight about a hospital before the on-site survey" (JCAHO 2004b, p. SV-5). Sources of PFP information include the following:

- Core measure data

- Previous survey findings

- Sentinel event data

- Complaints about the hospital submitted to the JCAHO

- Data submitted by the hospital

- External, publicly available data

Priority focus areas (PFAs) include processes, systems, and structures that have the most substantial effect on patient care services. The JCAHO designates health information management as one of fourteen PFAs vital to successful operation in hospitals (JCAHO 2004b, p. SV-6).

The length of JCAHO on-site surveys for acute care and critical access hospitals depends on the individual hospital's size and scope of services. (Critical access hospitals are very small, rural hospitals that provide short-term inpatient services to communities in isolated areas of the country.) Under the new accreditation process, the on-site survey agenda generally includes the following elements (JCAHO 2004b, pp. SV-21 through SV-22):

- Opening conference and orientation to the hospital

- Survey planning meeting

- Unit visits guided by priority focus information and patient tracers

- Assessment of the medical staff credentialing process

- Assessment of environments of care

- System tracer conferences

- Interviews with staff

- Interviews with hospital leaders

- Assessment of standards compliance

- Environment-of-care issues resolution

- Exit conference

Reviewing the health records of current and past patients has always been a component of the JCAHO on-site survey process, but it has even greater importance under the JCAHO's new system for evaluating compliance. The new system is called **tracer methodology**. Tracer methodology involves an evaluation that follows (traces) the hospital experiences of specific patients (JCAHO 2004b, pp. SV-22 and SV-23). By tracing the services provided to a sample of patients, surveyors .e able to evaluate how well the hospital's processes and departments work with each other. As part of the process, surveyors interview the physicians and staff involved in each patient's care as well as the patients themselves when possible.

The number of tracer evaluations conducted during each on-site survey depends on the size of the hospital and the duration of the survey. The JCAHO estimates that tracer activities are likely to fill 50 to 60 percent of survey time. On average, a three-person team of surveyors conducting a three-day site survey might complete about eleven tracer evaluations (JCAHO 2004b, p. SV-23).

Because no two hospitals are exactly alike, no two tracer evaluations can be the same. Tracers are specific to the hospital being surveyed and the type of care the organization provides. However, the hospital accreditation manual does provide the following hypothetical example (JCAHO 2004b, pp. SV-23 through SV-24):

A hospital tracer activity might take place if the hospital's data from various sources indicate that the hospital has received type I recommendations in the past related to medication use. Medication Management is identified as one of the PFAs for the hospital.

To begin the tracer methodology, the surveyor [might] ask the hospital to identify active files for pediatric patients receiving multiple medications. The surveyor then [might] randomly choose several charts that meet these criteria and follow each patient's care, treatment, and services. . . . By examining the different areas where patients are cared for, the survey can [reveal] systems issues specifically relevant to [the] hospital. . . . If the surveyor identifies a standards compliance issue while tracing one patient, he or she [might] pull other records, active or closed, of similar patients to determine if the problem represents an isolated issue or a pattern. As multiple cases are examined throughout [the] actual care process, the surveyor [might] identify performance-issue trends in one or more of the processes.

JCAHO Accreditation Decision Process

According to the 2004 hospital accreditation manual (JCAHO 2004b, p. SV-24), "the goal of the new accreditation decision and reporting approach is to move hospitals away from focusing on achieving high scores . . . [and toward] achieving and maintaining safe, high-quality systems of care, treatment, and services." Beginning with surveys conducted in 2005, the JCAHO will no longer calculate numerical scores nor disclose scores to the public. Instead, performance on individual standards will be identified as being compliant or not compliant. Recommendations will be considered requirements for improvement. In addition, each hospital's accreditation report will be issued electronically about forty-eight hours after the survey is complete (JCAHO 2004b, pp. SV-24 through SV-25).

Under the new accreditation process, the number of standards determined to be partially or insufficiently compliant will be used to determine the hospital's accreditation category. Effective

January 2004, the JCAHO's accreditation decision categories are the following (JCAHO 2004b, p. SV-25):

- *Accredited:* The hospital was in substantial compliance with all standards at the time of the on-site survey or has successfully addressed all requirements for improvement within 90 days after the survey.

- *Provisional accreditation:* The hospital was in substantial compliance with all standards at the time of the on-site survey but has not successfully addressed all requirements for improvement within 90 days after the survey.

- *Conditional accreditation:* The hospital was not in substantial compliance with standards at the time of the on-site survey and must address identified problem areas and then undergo another follow-up on-site survey.

- *Preliminary denial of accreditation:* The hospital was not in compliance with enough standards to warrant a denial of accreditation, but the decision is subject to an appeal process before a final decision will be issued.

- *Denial of accreditation:* The hospital has been denied accreditation, and all appeals have been exhausted.

- *Preliminary accreditation:* The hospital that has not been accredited by the JCAHO in the past has complied with selected standards in the first of two on-site surveys.

American Osteopathic Association

The American Osteopathic Association (AOA) is a professional membership association that represents approximately two-thirds of the 52,000 osteopathic physicians (DOs) in practice in the United States. The AOA is also the primary certification agency for osteopathic physicians and the accreditation agency for all osteopathic medical colleges and many osteopathic healthcare facilities (AOA 2004a).

The practice of osteopathic medicine began at the end of the nineteenth century. Osteopathy is a therapeutic approach to the practice of medicine that uses all the usual forms of medical therapy and diagnosis, including drugs and surgery. However, it places greater emphasis on the influence of the relationship between the organs and the musculoskeletal system than traditional medical science does. Osteopathic physicians recognize and correct structural problems by using manipulation techniques in both diagnostic and therapeutic processes. The manipulation techniques used by osteopathic physicians are similar to the techniques employed by doctors of chiropractic. The difference is that osteopaths attempt to address structural problems within the body through physical manipulation; chiropractors are attempting to address abnormal nerve function. (Unlike osteopaths, however, chiropractors are not considered medical physicians, and their practices are limited to spinal manipulation and other skeletal "adjustments.")

The AOA first initiated its hospital accreditation program in 1945 to ensure the quality of residency training programs for doctors of osteopathy. Today, the association's **Healthcare Facilities Accreditation Program** (HFAP) accredits a number of healthcare facilities and services, including laboratories, ambulatory care clinics, ambulatory surgery centers, behavioral health and substance abuse treatment facilities, physical rehabilitation facilities, acute care hospitals, and critical access hospitals.

Healthcare facilities that have been accredited by the AOA earn deemed status from the Centers for Medicare and Medicaid Services (CMS). Like hospitals accredited by the JCAHO,

AOA-accredited hospitals are not required to undergo yearly Medicare certification surveys, although a sample of accredited osteopathic hospitals is designated to undergo a Medicare survey each year. State licensure agencies conduct Medicare certification surveys under contracts with the CMS. The CMS has also granted the AOA accreditation program deeming authority for hospital laboratory services under the Clinical Laboratory Improvements Act (CLIA) of 1988.

HFAP Documentation Standards

The HFAP's acute care accreditation standards are tied closely to the Medicare *Conditions of Participation for Hospitals* (AOA 2004b). The AOA's documentation standards pertain broadly to common documentation requirements, but specific guidelines apply to specialty services such as psychiatric care. (The Medicare *Conditions of Participation for Hospitals* were discussed in detail earlier in the chapter. Appendix C provides a crosswalk between the AOA's HFAP standards, the JCAHO's standards, and the Medicare *Conditions of Participation for Hospitals*.)

The most recent revision of the AOA's accreditation manual for hospitals is still under development and will probably be released in late 2004. Most of the AOA's documentation standards are very similar to the JCAHO's standards except in the area of osteopathic medical practice. According to the HFAP's standards, osteopathic physicians are required to perform musculoskeletal examinations in addition to traditional physical examinations shortly before or after a patient's admission to the hospital unless the patient's condition contraindicates such an examination. One standard specifically requires osteopathic physicians to document the results of such examinations in the patient's health record or to document the reason why an osteopathic examination was not performed. Failure to meet this standard is one of the most common deficiencies cited during the survey process (AOA 2004a).

The AOA reports that several health record deficiencies in other areas have also been relatively common. Many osteopathic hospitals demonstrate high levels of record completion delinquency. According to the AOA's Web site (AOA 2004a), inadequate clinical documentation is also evident in three specific areas:

- Authentication of informed consent for surgical procedures

- Progress note documentation by allied health professionals and physicians

- Care plans and care-planning documentation

HFAP Survey and Accreditation Processes

Like JCAHO-accredited hospitals, hospitals requesting initial accreditation or renewed accreditation from the AOA initiate the process by submitting an application. The HFAP application asks for the same types of information that the JCAHO application requires. Also like the JCAHO, the HFAP conducts on-site surveys at accredited hospitals at least once every three years, and accreditation decisions are based on compliance with the HFAP standards and participation requirements (AOA 2004a).

Commission on Accreditation of Rehabilitation Facilities

The **Commission on Accreditation of Rehabilitation Facilities** (CARF) is a private, not-for-profit organization that offers healthcare accreditation programs in the areas of medical rehabilitation, behavioral health, adult day care and assisted living, and employment and community services. CARF currently accredits about 38,000 facilities in the United States, Canada, and

Europe. CARF's mission is "to promote the quality, value, and optimal outcomes of services through accreditation that centers on enhancing the lives of the persons served" (CARF 2004a).

CARF offers accreditation programs for inpatient services in two areas: behavioral health and medical rehabilitation. The accreditation programs emphasize the importance of continuous performance improvement and customer satisfaction (CARF 2004a).

CARF Documentation Standards

The standards in the *Behavioral Health Standards Manual* (CARF 2004b) are organized in sections. Sections cover business practices, leadership and management, and delivery of services. The manual covers numerous core program areas that apply throughout the continuum of care and to all age-groups. Similarly, the standards in the *Medical Rehabilitation Standards Manual* (CARF 2004c) apply to facilities that provide services to patients in the areas of medical and occupational rehabilitation. The standards are organized in three sections: business practices, delivery of services, and specific core program areas.

Like JCAHO and HFAP standards, CARF inpatient documentation standards require accredited facilities to maintain a separate health record for every patient who receives services and to guard the confidentiality and security of those records. Standards for record content, completeness, and authentication are basically the same as those for other types of inpatient care except that rehabilitation and psychiatric documentation places more emphasis on interdisciplinary treatment planning and consultations.

The standards for psychiatric records also provide special provisions for the documentation of restraint and seclusion procedures. The documentation requirements for specialized psychiatric treatments such as electroconvulsive therapy and psychosurgery emphasize the importance of the meticulous documentation of informed consent.

CARF Survey Process

CARF accreditation reviews are accomplished through on-site surveys conducted by volunteer surveyors. Survey teams include professionals from other CARF-accredited organizations that offer services similar to those of the organization under review. For example, for an inpatient psychiatric department, the surveyors assigned to perform the review would generally have experience as administrators or clinicians in the psychiatric inpatient setting. Surveyors undergo extensive training in CARF accreditation processes before they are assigned to a survey team.

Most CARF surveys are scheduled in advance. Typically, CARF-accredited organizations go through an on-site survey at least once every three years. Like other accreditation programs, the CARF accreditation process begins with an application that describes the facility and its services and provides statistical and textual descriptions of its characteristics and the names of its leaders.

Unlike the JCAHO process, the CARF accreditation process is relatively flexible. The process is customized to reflect the facility's patient care services and patient population. The agenda for the survey depends in large part on the characteristics of the organization applying for accreditation.

CARF surveys are usually conducted by three-person teams. The on-site visit begins with an opening conference. Participants may include representatives from third-party payers, staff members, referral agencies, members of the community, and patients. Participants are usually encouraged to voice concerns and issues during the opening conference. The survey team then outlines the agenda for the on-site portion of the review, which usually lasts two or three days. The rest of the survey includes the following activities (Shaw and others 2003, p. 252):

- *Document review:* an examination of the facility's policies and procedures, administrative rules and regulations, administrative records, human resources records, and patient health records.

- *Interviews with program staff and patients:* discussions aimed at validating the information gathered during the document review and determining whether there are any concerns related to patient care services.

- *Exit interview with the organization's leaders:* discussions of any deficiencies that have been identified and a summary of the survey's findings.

CARF Accreditation Decision Process

CARF accreditation decisions are based on an objective assessment of the facility's performance compared to CARF's accreditation standards. Performance currently is designated as fulfilling (with a rating of *recommendation*) or not fulfilling *(no recommendation)* each standard.

CARF is currently in the process of implementing a new rating system known as the Standards Conformance Rating System. The new system is based on a Likert-type rating scale. Scores are assigned to the facility's performance on each standard as follows (CARF 2004a):

0   Nonconformance
1   Partial conformance
2   Conformance
3   Exemplary conformance

Accreditation Association for Ambulatory Healthcare

The **Accreditation Association for Ambulatory Healthcare** (AAAHC) establishes standards for outpatient documentation that are similar to acute care documentation practices. The ambulatory care standards emphasize the use of clinical summaries to enhance the continuity of care, which are especially important in outpatient records. For example, summaries of past surgeries, diagnoses, and problems are helpful in transferring medical history information to new treatment settings, especially for complex cases.

National Committee for Quality Assurance

The **National Committee for Quality Assurance** (NCQA) is a private, not-for-profit organization dedicated to improving healthcare quality by conducting assessments of managed care and other healthcare programs in the United States. The NCQA began accrediting managed care organizations in 1991. Today, it provides accreditation programs and related services for health maintenance organizations, preferred provider organizations, managed behavioral health programs, and physician organizations. The NCQA's standards focus on patient safety, confidentiality, member satisfaction, access to services, service quality, and continuous improvement.

Hospital Liability Issues

As the preceding sections of this chapter have shown, numerous private and governmental organizations work with acute care providers to ensure the safety and quality of patient services and the accuracy and confidentiality of health record information. Acute care organizations also implement and maintain internal systems to protect their patients' health, safety, and privacy. Three of these internal systems—medical staff credentialing and privileging, incident reporting, and risk management—depend at least in part on the use of patient-identifiable health record information.

Medical Staff Appointments and Privileges

Virtually all of the medical care provided to patients in acute care settings is either performed directly or managed by physicians and surgeons. Except in teaching hospitals, most of the physicians and surgeons who provide medical services in hospitals are independent practitioners; that is, they are not employees or agents of the hospital. Nonetheless, hospitals are held accountable for the quality of all the medical treatment provided to inpatients and outpatients in their facilities.

For example: Suppose a physician who was not qualified to perform orthopedic surgery treated a patient with a broken leg in the emergency department of a hospital. If the physician injured that patient by providing substandard care, both the physician and the hospital would be held jointly liable (the legal term for responsible) for the patient's injury.

This hypothetical case represents an example of the doctrine of **corporate negligence.** This legal doctrine was established by a judicial decision handed down in a 1965 court case. In *Darling v. Charleston Community Hospital,* the court ruled specifically that hospital governing boards have a "duty to establish mechanisms for the medical staff to evaluate, counsel, and when necessary, take action against an unreasonable risk of harm to a patient arising from the patient's treatment by a personal physician" (Pozgar 1999, p. 198). The court's ruling established the hospital's obligation to appoint only highly qualified practitioners to the medical staff. Owing to that obligation, hospitals may be held liable when a member of the medical staff fails to meet established standards of patient care.

Most states have also instituted statutes that regulate medical staff appointment processes. In addition, accreditation programs generally require hospitals to confirm the qualifications of practitioners before clinicians are given the right to practice in the facility.

Hospital governing boards (sometimes called boards of directors or trustees) are legally responsible for the overall operation of acute care facilities. Therefore, every hospital governing board has a duty to establish medical staff policies to ensure that unqualified practitioners are not allowed to provide medical services in the facility. The hospital's medical staff qualification criteria and processes are based on these policies.

Physicians and other clinical practitioners who wish to practice in a hospital must first become members of that hospital's medical staff. Although the governing board considers the recommendations of medical staff leaders in making medical staff appointments, the ultimate responsibility for such decisions rests with the board.

The governing board generally relies on the hospital's medical staff leaders to manage independent clinical practitioners by setting medical staff bylaws. **Medical staff bylaws** describe the rights and responsibilities of individual members as well as the means by which medical staff leaders govern the conduct of members.

Credentialing Process

Before making medical staff appointments and reappointments, hospitals evaluate the qualifications of physicians, surgeons, podiatrists, dentists, clinical psychologists, and other practitioners through a systematic process called credentialing. **Credentialing** involves the review and validation of an individual practitioner's qualifications to practice medicine. (See figure 5.10.)

Figure 5.10. Credentialing and Privileging Processes

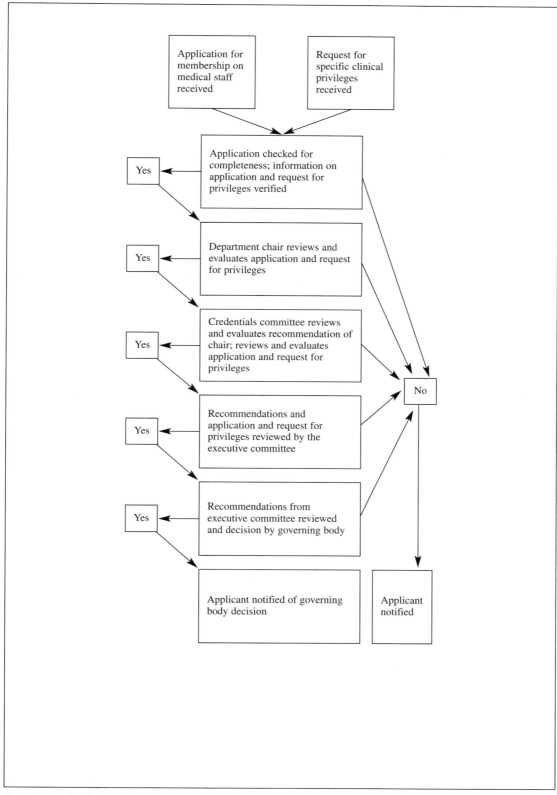

Source: Zeman 2002.

Initial credentialing reviews typically include the following types of information:

- Verifications of the applicant's undergraduate, medical, and postdoctoral education
- Verifications of the applicant's residency and fellowship training as well as continuing medical education
- Past and current medical staff appointments at other facilities
- Current state licenses to practice medicine
- Current specialty board certifications
- Current Drug Enforcement Administration registration
- Documentation of professional liability insurance
- References and recommendations from the applicant's professional peers
- Information on the applicant's health status
- Past and current liability status

As part of every medical staff appointment process, hospitals and other healthcare organizations are also required by federal law to send inquiries to two national databases: the **National Practitioner Data Bank** (NPDB) and the **Healthcare Integrity and Protection Data Bank** (HIPDB). The NPDB collects information on medical malpractice settlements, clinical privilege actions, and medical society actions taken against licensed healthcare providers in the United States. The HIPDB collects information on legal actions taken against licensed healthcare providers, including both civil judgments and criminal convictions.

When the practitioner's credentials have been verified and it has been determined that the practitioner meets the medical staff qualification criteria, the practitioner's application is reviewed by the hospital's medical staff executive committee. The committee then submits its recommendations to the governing board for final action.

Privileging Process

With the board's approval, the hospital then grants the practitioner medical staff privileges. These **clinical privileges** authorize the practitioner to provide patient services in the hospital but only those specific services that fall within his or her area of medical expertise. (For example, a cardiovascular surgeon's clinical privileges would allow her to perform cardiac bypass surgery but not cataract surgery.) Medical staff appointments are granted on a time-limited basis, and so members of the medical staff must routinely apply for reappointment, typically every two years.

Reappointments are based on another review of the practitioner's current qualifications and require new queries to the NPDB and HIPDB. Hospitals also consider how often the practitioner used his or her privileges during the preceding period to determine whether the practitioner is still proficient in the clinical services for which he or she is seeking privileges. They also look at outcomes data for the practitioner's patients as well as peer review information.

Reappointment decisions also consider whether the practitioner has fulfilled his or her administrative responsibilities as specified in the hospital's medical staff bylaws. For example, medical staff bylaws may require members to attend a specific percentage of medical staff meetings or to participate on medical staff committees.

Medical staff reappointments also review the practitioner's health record delinquency status. Practitioners who have consistently high delinquency rates may lose their medical staff privileges as a result.

Risk Management and Incident Reporting

Acute care services are by their nature technologically and medically complex, and hospitals can sometimes prove to be dangerous places. Although hospitals and caregivers make every effort to ensure the safety of patients, visitors, and staff, unforeseen events can occur. Whether the consequence of accidents or mistakes, some of these unforeseen events inevitably result in serious and sometimes fatal injuries.

Hospitals devise systems for responding to such events and taking steps to prevent similar problems in the future. Several terms are used to describe unforeseen events that lead to injuries and other losses, including *incidents, adverse events, potentially compensable events,* and *adverse occurrences.* The JCAHO uses the term *sentinel event* to describe such events and requests that the most serious events be reported to the JCAHO as well as to government agencies as required by federal or state law. Hospitals also develop internal reporting procedures. Internal and external reporting procedures are part of every hospital's risk management program.

Risk management is the process of overseeing the hospital's internal medical, legal, and administrative operations with the goal of minimizing the hospital's exposure to liability. In this context, risk is a formal insurance term referring to situations that may lead to liability claims. **Liability** is the legal responsibility to compensate individuals for injuries and losses sustained as the result of negligence.

As previous chapters have explained, health records constitute the hospital's legal record of the services provided to individual patients from the time they are admitted until the time they are discharged. Health record documentation, therefore, must be completely objective; that is, documentation must be based on actual observations rather than on private opinions and conjecture.

Like other events and outcomes during the patient's stay in the hospital, adverse events must be completely and accurately described in the patient's health record. But it is extremely important that the health record documentation of adverse events remain entirely objective, with no comments from caregivers that suggest blame or speculate on causation.

Hospital internal risk management policies usually define the circumstances that constitute a reportable **incident** (an event that is considered to be inconsistent with accepted standards of care). Policies also address the steps to be taken in response to an incident. Most hospitals institute policies that call for the preparation of incident reports. (Some facilities use the terms *occurrence* and *occurrence report* in this context.)

An **incident report** describes the occurrence (and its time, date, and location), the identity of the individual or individuals involved (patients, visitors, and/or staff), and the current condition of the individual(s) who were affected. The report should also include statements from witnesses. The report should be completed as soon as possible after the incident to ensure its accuracy and completeness.

Incident reports are prepared for risk management, performance improvement, and staff education purposes and not direct patient care. They also contain subjective information from witnesses and the individuals involved in the incident. For these reasons, incident reports must never be included or mentioned in a patient's legal health record. Instead, incident reports should be stored in separate, secure databases or files in the facility's risk management or performance improvement department. In anticipation of possible court action in the future, incident reports should also be marked as confidential and addressed to the hospital's attorney. Incident reports should not be disseminated internally or externally to anyone other than the individuals designated in the hospital's risk management policies (McWay 2002, pp. 181–82). (An example of an incident report is provided in figure 5.11. A health record progress note for the same incident is shown in figure 5.12, p. 316.)

Figure 5.11. Example of an Incident Report

Med Rec # *00-05-45*
Name: *Jackson, Julia*
Date of Birth: *06-22-23*
Street: *6401 Fremont Ave*
City: *Western City, CA*

Risk Management use only_____

Patient ID/name of individual involved.
Use addressograph for patient.

INSTRUCTIONS: (1) Fill out the first page of the Incident Report Form. (2) Select the type of incident from the bottom of page 2. (3) Fill out all appropriate sections as directed. The report must be dated and filled out by the end of the shift in which the incident occurred or was discovered. **DO NOT COPY THIS FORM.** Please print, this report must be legible. **Please fill out all applicable parts of this form.** Upon completion of this form route it to your Nurse Manager or Supervisor. Do not leave this form in the patient's chart.

Date of incident: *05* / *29* / *03*   Time (2400 Clock): ____*1645*____   Hospital Unit: *Med/Surg*

What day of the week did it occur on?

				Did the incident occur during:		Employee involved worked a(n)	
Sun	[ ]	Thurs	[√]	Day 0701–1500	[ ]	8 Hour shift	[√]
Mon	[ ]	Fri	[ ]	Evening 1501–2300	[√]	10 Hour shift	[ ]
Tues	[ ]	Sat	[ ]	Night 2301–0700	[ ]	12 Hour shift	[ ]
Wed	[ ]					Double shift	[ ]
						Other_____	

Where did the incident occur? *patient room*_____

Description of incident. Include: follow-up care given, i.e., vital signs, X-Ray, laboratory tests, etc.
Pt. developed a macular rash over trunk and extremities after 10 mg
dose of Compazine given for postop nausea. Compazine stopped
and Benadryl given IM.

IMMEDIATE EFFECT OF THE INCIDENT: ___*Severe macular rash over trunk*___
and extremities

Involved Person Data

Date of Admission *05* / *29* / *03*

What sex is the person?
Male   [ ]
Female   [√]

What is the person's age? ____*79*____

Inpatient	[√]
Outpatient	[ ]
Student	[ ]
Employee	[ ]
Visitor	[ ]
Volunteer	[ ]
Other_____	

Current Diagnosis/Reason for visit: *Bowel Obstruction*_____

Is the involved person aware of the incident?	Yes	[√]	No	[ ]
Is the family aware of incident?	Yes	[ ]	No	[√]
Did the incident involve equipment?	Yes	[ ]	No	[√]
If Yes, was Bioengineering notified?	Yes	[ ]	No	[ ] N/A [ ]

CONFIDENTIAL: This material is prepared pursuant to Code Annotated, §26-25-1, et seq., and 58-12-43(7, 8, and 9), for the purpose of evaluating health care rendered by hospitals or physicians and is NOT PART of the medical record.

Figure 5.11. **(Continued)**

DO NOT COPY

**** PLEASE PRINT ****

Person preparing report (Signature): _Gwen Nelson, R.N._ Print _Gwen Nelson, R.N._

Name of individual witnessing incident (Print): _Bob Patterson, R.N._

Dept/Address: _Med/Surg Team Leader_

Name of employee involved in incident: _Gwen Nelson, R.N._ Dept/Address _Med/Surg_

Name of employee discovering incident: _Gwen Nelson, R.N._ Dept/Address _Med/Surg_

**** STAFF TO NOTIFY ATTENDING PHYSICIAN AND/OR DESIGNATED RESIDENT/NURSE PRACTITIONER OF INCIDENT ****

I notified Dr./NP _Jeff Cook_ at _1650_ (time).

M.D./NP responded ☐ in person ☑ by phone at _1705_ (time).

Was the attending physician notified?

Yes [ ] Date: _05 / 29 / 03_ Time: _1650_

No [√] Why not? _____

Examining Physician/Nurse Practitioner statement regarding condition/outcome of person involved:

Pt. was examined by me at 1700 hours. Trunk and extremities show a macular
rash on them. One dose of Benadryl given IM to pt. and rash began to subside.
Compazine stopped.

Examining MD/NP signature: _Tom Lander, M.D. House Staff_

Examining MD/NP name (print): _Tom Lander, M.D._

Date: _05 / 29 / 03_ Time: _1700_ Clinical Service: _Medicine_

CHOOSE THE TYPE OF INCIDENT YOU ARE REPORTING. Use the index below to locate the type of incident you are reporting, go to that section and mark the appropriate box(es). THERE MAY BE MORE THAN ONE ITEM APPLICABLE IN A SECTION. CHECK BOX(ES) IN APPROPRIATE SECTIONS.

Medication/IV Incident	Page 3, Section 1	Patient Behavioral Incident	Page 5, Section 6
Blood/Blood incident	Page 3, Section 2	Safety Incident	Page 5, Section 9
Burn	Page 5, Section 7	Security Incident	Page 5, Section 8
Equipment Incident	Page 5, Section 10	Surgery Incident	Page 5, Section 4
Fall	Page 4, Section 3	Treatment/Procedure Incident	Page 5, Section 5
Fire Incident	Page 5, Section 11		

CONFIDENTIAL: This material is prepared pursuant to Code Annotated, §26-25-1, et seq., and 58-12-43(7, 8, and 9), for the purpose of evaluating health care rendered by hospitals or physicians and is NOT PART of the medical record.

(Continued on next page)

Figure 5.11.   (Continued)

SECTION 1 MEDICATION/IV INCIDENT

1A. TYPE OF MEDICATION

Fill in specific medication/solution on the adjacent line.

Analgesic _____
Anesthetic agent _____
Antibiotic _____
Anticoagulant _____
Anticonvulsant _____
Antidepressant _____
Antiemetic _*Compazine*_____
Antihistamine _____
Antineoplastic _____
Bronchodilator _____
Cardiovascular _____
Contrast media _____
Diuretic _____
Immunizations _____
Immunosuppressive _____
Insulin _____
Intralipids _____
Investigational drug _____
IV solution _____
Laxative_____
Narcotic_____
Oxytocics _____
Psychotherapeutic _____
Radionuclides _____
Sedative/tranquilizer _____
TPN _____
Vasodilator _____
Vasopressor _____
Vitamin _____
Other _____

1B. TYPE OF MEDICATION OR IV INCIDENT

Adverse reaction	[√]	1B01
Allergic/contraindication	[ ]	1B02
Delayed stat order	[ ]	1B03
Improper order (MD/NP)	[ ]	1B04
Incompatible additive	[ ]	1B05
Incorrect additive	[ ]	1B06
Incorrect dosage	[ ]	1B07
Incorrect drug	[ ]	1B08
Incorrect narcotic count	[ ]	1B09
Incorrect patient	[ ]	1B10
Incorrect rate of flow	[ ]	1B11
Incorrect route	[ ]	1B12
Incorrect schedule	[ ]	1B13
Incorrect solution/type	[ ]	1B14
Incorrect time	[ ]	1B15
Incorrect volume	[ ]	1B16
Infiltration	[ ]	1B17
Given before culture taken	[ ]	1B18
Medication given before lab results returned	[ ]	1B19
Medication missing from cart	[ ]	1B20

Not documented	[ ]	1B21
Not prescribed	[ ]	1B22
Omitted	[ ]	1B23
Outdated	[ ]	1B24
Out-of-sequence	[ ]	1B25
Patient took unprescribed medication	[ ]	1B26
Repeat administration	[ ]	1B27
Transcription error	[ ]	1B28
Other_____	[ ]	1B29

1C. ROUTE OF MEDICATION ORDERED:

IM	[ ]	1C01
IV	[ ]	1C02
PO	[ ]	1C03
Other_*Suppository*_____	[√]	1C04

1D. MEDICATION DISPENSING INCIDENT

Meds not sent/delayed from pharmacy	[ ]	1C01
Incorrectly labeled	[ ]	1C02
Incorrect dose	[ ]	1C03
Incorrect drug sent	[ ]	1C04
Incorrect IV additive	[ ]	1C05
Incorrect IV fluid	[ ]	1C06
Incorrect route (IV, PO, IM, PR)	[ ]	1C07
Mislabeled	[ ]	1C08
Other_____	[ ]	1C09

SECTION 2
BLOOD/BLOOD COMPONENT INCIDENT

2A. BLOOD/BLOOD COMPONENT TYPE

Albumin	[ ]	2A01
Cryoprecipitate	[ ]	2A02
Factor VIII (AHF)	[ ]	2A03
Factor IX (Konyne)	[ ]	2A04
Fresh frozen plasma	[ ]	2A05
Packed red blood cells (PRBC)	[ ]	2A06
Plasmanate	[ ]	2A07
Platelets	[ ]	2A08
Rhogam	[ ]	2A09
Washed red blood cells (WRBC)	[ ]	2A10
Whole blood	[ ]	2A11
Other_____	[ ]	2A12

2B. TYPE OF BLOOD/BLOOD COMPONENT INCIDENT

Crossmatch problem	[ ]	2B01
Improper unit verification	[ ]	2B02
Inappropriate IV fluids administered with blood components	[ ]	2B03
Inappropriate documentation	[ ]	2B04
Inappropriate storage	[ ]	2B05
Incomplete patient ID	[ ]	2B06
Incorrect patient	[ ]	2B07
Incorrect rate	[ ]	2B08
Incorrect type	[ ]	2B09
Incorrect volume	[ ]	2B10
Patient refused	[ ]	2B11
Other_____	[ ]	2B12

Figure 5.11. (Continued)

DO NOT COPY

SECTION 3
FALLS

3A. FALL CODE STATUS OF PATIENT

Attended	[ ] 3A01
Unattended	[ ] 3A02

3B. LOCATION OF FALL

Bathroom in patient's room	[ ] 3B01
Bathroom (other location)	[ ] 3B02
Elevator	[ ] 3B03
Examining/treatment room	[ ] 3B04
Hallway/corridor	[ ] 3B05
Nursing station	[ ] 3B06
Parking lot	[ ] 3B07
Patient's room	[ ] 3B08
Recreation area	[ ] 3B09
Shower/tub room	[ ] 3B10
Stairs	[ ] 3B11
Waiting room	[ ] 3B12
Walkway/sidewalk	[ ] 3B13
Other_____	[ ] 3B14

3C. FALL OCCURRED IN CONJUNCTION WITH:

Bedside commode	[ ] 3C01
Chair	[ ] 3C02
Due to toy	[ ] 3C03
During transfer	[ ] 3C04
Exam table	[ ] 3C05
Fainting/dizzy	[ ] 3C06
Fall/slip	[ ] 3C07
From bed	[ ] 3C08
Improperly locked device	[ ] 3C09
Recreational activity	[ ] 3C10
Scales	[ ] 3C11
Stretcher	[ ] 3C12
Table	[ ] 3C13
Tripped	[ ] 3C14
While ambulating unattended	[ ] 3C15
While ambulating with assist	[ ] 3C16
While entering or leaving bed	[ ] 3C17
While using ambulatory device	[ ] 3C18
Other_____	[ ] 3C19

3D. PATIENT ACTIVITY PRIVILEGES
(As per medical order)

Ambulate with assistance	[ ] 3D01
Ambulate with walker	[ ] 3D02
Ambulate without assistance	[ ] 3D03
Bathroom privileges with assistance	[ ] 3D04
Bathroom privileges without assistance	[ ] 3D05
Bedrest	[ ] 3D06
Up Ad lib	[ ] 3D07
Up in chair/wheelchair	[ ] 3D08
Other_____	[ ] 3D09

3E. PATIENT MENTAL CONDITION AT THE TIME
OF THE FALL

Confused/poor judgment	[ ] 3E01
Language barrier	[ ] 3E02
Oriented	[ ] 3E03
Unconscious	[ ] 3E04
Uncooperative	[ ] 3E05
Unresponsive/medicated	[ ] 3E06
Other_____	[ ] 3E07

3F. PATIENT'S CALL LIGHT WAS:

On	[ ] 3F01
Off	[ ] 3F02
Not within reach	[ ] 3F03
Patient unable to use	[ ] 3F04
Not applicable	[ ] 3F05

3G. POSITION OF BED

High	[ ] 3G01
Low	[ ] 3G02
Intermediate	[ ] 3G03
Not applicable	[ ] 3G04

3H. BED ALARM

On	[ ] 3H01
Off	[ ] 3H02
Not applicable	[ ] 3H03

3I. POSITION OF SIDE RAILS
(At the time of the fall)

Half Rails	[ ] 3I01	Full Rails	[ ] 3I06
1 Up	[ ] 3I02	1 Up	[ ] 3I07
2 Up	[ ] 3I03	2 Up	[ ] 3I08
3 Up	[ ] 3I04		
4 Up	[ ] 3I05		

Not applicable   [ ] 3I09

3J. PATIENT RESTRAINTS

Removed by patient	[ ] 3J01
Restraints intact	[ ] 3J02
Not applicable	[ ] 3J03
Other_____	[ ] 3J04

3K. CONDITION OF AREA WHERE FALL
OCCURRED

Normal/dry	[ ] 3K01
Wet floor	[ ] 3K02
Ice condition	[ ] 3K03
Other_____	[ ] 3K04

3L. FALLS IN CONJUNCTION
WITH MEDICATION

Narcotic or sedative received by patient in the past 12 hours?	[ ] 3L01
When was the last dose? _____	[ ] 3L02
What was the drug? _____	[ ] 3L03
What was the route of administration? _____	[ ] 3L04

(Continued on next page)

Figure 5.11.   (Continued)

<table>
<tr><td colspan="2" align="center">DO NOT COPY</td></tr>
</table>

SECTION 4
SURGERY INCIDENT

Anesthesia occurrence	[ ] 0401
Contamination	[ ] 0402
Incorrect needle count	[ ] 0403
Incorrect sponge count	[ ] 0404
Informed consent absent	[ ] 0405
Informed consent incorrect	[ ] 0406
Instrument lost/broken	[ ] 0407
Retained foreign body	[ ] 0408
Other_____	[ ] 0409

SECTION 5
TREATMENT/PROCEDURE INCIDENT

Adverse reaction	[ ] 0501
Allergic response	[ ] 0502
Application/removal of cast/splint	[ ] 0503
Cancellation of procedures	[ ] 0504
Catheter or tube related	[ ] 0505
Delay	[ ] 0506
Dietary problem	[ ] 0507
Dressing/wound occurrence	[ ] 0508
Informed consent absent	[ ] 0509
Informed consent incorrect	[ ] 0510
Injection site	[ ] 0511
Invasive procedure/placement	[ ] 0512
Mislabeled specimen	[ ] 0513
Missing specimen	[ ] 0514
Not documented	[ ] 0515
Omitted	[ ] 0516
Patient/site identification	[ ] 0517
Positioning	[ ] 0518
Prep problem	[ ] 0519
Repeat procedure	[ ] 0520
Reporting of test results	[ ] 0521
Thermoregulation problem	[ ] 0522
Transcription error	[ ] 0523
Transfer/moving of patient	[ ] 0524
Other_____	[ ] 0525

SECTION 6
PATIENT BEHAVIORAL INCIDENT

Attempted AWOL	[ ] 0601
AWOL	[ ] 0602
Inappropriate sexual behavior	[ ] 0603
Injured by other patient	[ ] 0604
Patient altercation	[ ] 0605
Self-inflicted injury	[ ] 0606
Suicide gesture	[ ] 0607
Other_____	[ ] 0608

SECTION 7
BURNS

Chemical	[ ] 0701
Electrical	[ ] 0702
Inhalation	[ ] 0703
Radioactive	[ ] 0704
Thermal	[ ] 0705

SECTION 8
SECURITY INCIDENTS

Bomb threat	[ ] 0801
Breaking and entering	[ ] 0802
Drug theft	[ ] 0803
Secure area key loss/missing	[ ] 0804
Major theft (over $250)	[ ] 0805
Amount:_____	
Minor theft	[ ] 0806
Amount:_____	
Personal property damage/loss	[ ] 0807
Amount:_____	
Hospital property damage	[ ] 0809
Amount:_____	
Other_____	[ ] 0810

SECTION 9
SAFETY INCIDENTS (patients and visitors only)

Body fluid exposure	[ ] 0901
Chemical exposure	[ ] 0902
Chemotherapy spill	[ ] 0903
Drug exposure	[ ] 0904
Hazardous material spill	[ ] 0905
Needlestick	[ ] 0906
Other_____	[ ] 0907

SECTION 10
EQUIPMENT INCIDENT

Disconnected	[ ] 1001
Electrical problem	[ ] 1002
Improper use	[ ] 1003
Malfunction/defect	[ ] 1004
Mechanical problem	[ ] 1005
Not available	[ ] 1006
Electrical shock	[ ] 1007
Electrical spark	[ ] 1008
Struck by	[ ] 1009
Wrong equipment	[ ] 1010
Tampered with	
By patient	[ ] 1011
Non-patient	[ ] 1012
Other_____	[ ] 1013

SECTION 11
FIRE INCIDENT

Equipment caused	[ ] 1101
Cigarette caused	[ ] 1102
Laser caused	[ ] 1103
Other_____	[ ] 1104

CONFIDENTIAL: This material is prepared pursuant to Code Annotated, §26-25-1, et seq., and 58-12-43(7, 8, and 9), for the purpose of evaluating health care rendered by hospitals or physicians and is NOT PART of the medical record.

Figure 5.11.   (Continued)

DO NOT COPY

SECTION 12   **EMPLOYEES DO NOT COMPLETE BELOW,**
FOR NURSE MANAGER/SUPERVISOR USE ONLY.

Recommendations and/or corrective actions based on review of report and discussion with employee:

NURSE MANAGER/SUPERVISOR Follow-Up [Check appropriate box(es)]/Corrective action]

Policy/Procedure:

Evaluate	[ ] 1201	**Discussed with:**
Recommend change . . . . [ ] 1202		Physician [ ] 1209
Changed	[ ] 1203	Staff. . . . . [ ] 1210
No action taken . . . . [ ] 1204		Patient [ ] 1211
Non-compliance	[ ] 1205	Other . . . . [ ] 1212
Inadequate . . . . [ ] 1206		
Needs enforcement	[ ] 1207	Date: _____
Review with involved individual(s). . . . [ ] 1208		Time: _____

Describe specific follow-up actions taken (if applicable include names of depts) _____

_____

_____

SIGN AND DATE: (Indicates review of report)

1. Quality Management/Risk Management _____   _____/____/____

2. Nurse Manager/Supervisor (as applicable) _____   _____/____/____

3. Department Head/DON (As applicable) _____   _____/____/____

4. QM Coordinator (As applicable)_____   _____/____/____

5. Other: Title_____   Name _____   _____/____/____

SECTION 13   BIOENGINEERING USE ONLY

Manufacturer contacted	[ ] 1301
Manufacturer instructions followed	[ ] 1302
Needs enforcement of policy/procedure	[ ] 1303
Include instructions in staff education and training	[ ] 1304
Preventative maintenance or biomedical evaluation of equipment ordered	[ ] 1305
Recommend repair or replacement	[ ] 1306
Removed from service	[ ] 1307
Other _____	[ ] 1308

SECTION 14   RISK MANAGEMENT USE ONLY
IMMEDIATE EFFECT OF THE INCIDENT

Alteration in skin integrity	[ ] 1401	Patient discomfort/inconvenience	[ ] 1411
Birth related injury . . . . [ ] 1402		Psycho/social trauma. . . . . [ ] 1412	
Breach of confidentiality	[ ] 1403	Reproductive injury or loss	[ ] 1413
Death . . . . [ ] 1404		Sensory impairment. . . . . [ ] 1414	
Disability	[ ] 1405	Severe internal injuries	[ ] 1415
Disfigurement. . . . . [ ] 1406		Substantial disability . . . . [ ] 1416	
Drug/blood reaction	[ ] 1407	Unanticipated neuro deficit	[ ] 1417
Fluid imbalance . . . . [ ] 1408		Unanticipated systemic deficit. . . . . . . [ ] 1418	
Neuro deficit	[ ] 1409	Indeterminate	[ ] 1419
Orthopedic injury . . . . [ ] 1410		None. . . . . [ ] 1420	
		Other_____	[ ] 1421

Description _____

_____

CONFIDENTIAL: This material is prepared pursuant to Code Annotated, §26-25-1, et seq., and 58-12-43(7, 8, and 9), for the purpose of evaluating health care rendered by hospitals or physicians and is NOT PART of the medical record.

Source: Shaw and others 2003.

Figure 5.12.   Example of a Progress Note Describing the Same Unanticipated Incident

PROGRESS NOTES	Med Rec # 00-05-45 Jackson, Julia DOB: 06/22/1923

DATE & TIME	NOTES MUST BE DATED AND TIMED
5/29/03	Patient developed a macular rash over entire trunk and
1650	extremities after 10 mg of Compazine given for nausea.
	Dr. Cook and house staff notified.
	Gwen Nelson, RN
5/29/03	Called to pt. for rash on trunk & extremities.
1700	Pt. examined, adverse reaction to Compazine
	most likely. Patient to receive 20 mg of
	Benadryl IM now. If nausea continues,
	Dramamine 50 mg IV prn.
	J. Lander, MD
5/29/03	Dr. Lander examined patient and ordered Benadryl
1700	20 mg IM. Patient injected IM 20 mg of Benadryl.
	Gwen Nelson, RN
5/29/03	Rash is subsiding and nausea less.
1810	Gwen Nelson, RN

PROGRESS NOTES

Source: Shaw and others 2003.

Health Informatics Standards

In an increasingly complex healthcare environment, hospitals and other healthcare organizations collect more data and need more information today than they did just a decade ago. Private organizations and government agencies gather data reported to them by healthcare organizations in huge state and national databases. These databases are used by reimbursement organizations, quality improvement organizations, clinical researchers, government policy makers, and others to plan and manage medical services and healthcare delivery systems. The universal implementation of electronic health record systems promises to make data collection, sharing, and analysis more efficient, but it also presents its own unique challenges.

One of the biggest obstacles to the widespread implementation of EHR systems has been the high cost of new and evolving communications technology. Hospitals have been reluctant to invest large amounts of capital in clinical information technology for two main reasons: the absence of clear financial incentives and the lack of a shared vision of what an EHR should include and how it should perform. However, this picture is changing, and the development and implementation of the HIPAA standards has increased policy and law makers' awareness of the need to modernize healthcare information management systems.

In the January 2004 State of the Union address, President George W. Bush called for the implementation of electronic health record (EHR) systems. Subsequently, in May 2004, the president announced the creation of a new federal post dedicated to the nationwide implementation of EHR systems within the next ten years. The Office of the National Coordinator of Health Information Technology has been established within the U.S. Department of Health and Human Services. The charge of the office is to guide the nationwide implementation of information technology in healthcare applications. Specifically, its long-term goals are to inform clinical practice, to connect clinicians, to personalize patient care, and to improve the health of the U.S. population.

Also in May 2004, Senator Edward Kennedy introduced the Health Care Modernization, Cost Reduction, and Quality Improvement Act in the U.S. Senate. The goal of the legislation is to improve the American healthcare system by implementing new information technology, basing payment on patient outcomes, and investing in disease prevention. In the area of health records, the bill calls for the full implementation of a broad-based system of electronic health records. One provision of the bill would be to increase reimbursement levels for providers that have implemented EHR systems and decrease payments for providers that have not.

Another substantial hurdle to the implementation of electronic health record systems has been the lack of standardization in the areas of clinical documentation and information technology. Here, too, recent efforts to address standardization issues are gaining momentum.

Health Data Standards

Efforts to standardize healthcare data began in the 1960s, when healthcare facilities first began using computers to process large amounts of clinical data. When regulators and researchers attempted to compare the data from multiple healthcare organizations, it was evident that organizations were not always collecting the same information or labeling the same information the same way. If meaningful data comparisons were to be made possible, facilities needed to start collecting the same data and using the same data definitions.

The first data standardization efforts focused on hospital discharge data. The need to compare discharge data from one hospital to the next led to the development of uniform data sets, lists of recommended or required data elements with uniform definitions. The data sets used most commonly in hospitals today include the Uniform Hospital Discharge Data Set (UHDDS), the

Data Elements for Emergency Department Systems (DEEDS), the Essential Medical Data Set (EMEDS), the Health Plan Employer Data and Information Set (HEDIS), and the Uniform Ambulatory Care Data Set (UACDS). (Healthcare data sets were discussed in more detail in chapter 3.)

The collection of uniform discharge data sets and the development of clinical databases made up of aggregate discharge data are still vital to healthcare operations and research today. In combination with diagnostic and procedural coded data, discharge data are used in accreditation, reimbursement, clinical research, delivery planning, and quality improvement as well as many other internal and external processes and programs.

The standardized data sets developed in the 1960s and still in use today were designed for paper-based systems and pre-Medicare healthcare delivery systems. The National Committee on Vital and Health Statistics (NCVHS) led the development of the first uniform data sets, and it is now leading efforts to develop data standards for modern healthcare delivery and computer-based health information systems in the United States. Collectively, these new standards are referred to as health informatics standards. **Health informatics standards** are standards that describe uniform methods for collecting, maintaining, and/or transferring healthcare data among computer information systems.

Health Informatics Standards

A number of national and international organizations develop voluntary standards for a variety of industries. The private and governmental organizations that actually publish standards are often referred to as standards development organizations. **Standards development organizations** (SDOs) design scientifically based models against which structures, processes, and outcomes can be measured. The American National Standards Institute (ANSI) coordinates the development of standards in the United States. The United Nations International Standards Organization (ISO) coordinates international standards development efforts.

Health informatics standards can be classified into five categories. Each of the categories has a specific purpose (Amatayakul 2004, pp. 122–24):

- **Vocabulary standards:** To establish uniform definitions for clinical terms

- **Structure and content standards:** To establish clear descriptions of the data elements to be collected

- **Transaction and messaging standards**: To facilitate **electronic data interchange** (EDI) among independent computer information systems

- **Security standards:** To ensure the integrity of patient-identifiable health information and to protect it from unauthorized disclosure, alteration, and destruction

- **Identifier standards:** To establish methods for assigning unique identifiers to individual patients, healthcare professionals, healthcare provider organizations, and healthcare vendors and suppliers

Many organizations are currently working on the development of health informatics standards. (See the list of SDOs in table 5.6.) For example, **Health Level Seven** (HL7) recently developed a draft functional model of the electronic health record. This effort is being supported by the **EHR Collaborative,** a group of representatives from healthcare-related professional and trade associations dedicated to the development and implementation of uniform EHR systems. (Participants include the American Health Information Management Association, the American Hospital Association, and the Health Information Management Systems Society.) The draft

Table 5.6.   Health Informatics Standards Development Organizations

Organization	Types of Standards	Description
Accredited Standards Committee X12 Data Interchange Standards Association (DISA) 333 John Carlyle Street, Suite 600 Alexandria, VA 22314 Telephone: (703) 548-7005 www.disa.org	Electronic data interchange for billing transactions The committee's particular area of focus has been computer-to-computer communications between healthcare providers and third-party payers	Chartered in 1979 by ANSI, the X12N subcommittee develops and maintains X12 standards, interpretations, and guidelines. X12N is one of the standards for EDI that is specified in the regulations of the Health Insurance Portability and Accountability Act of 1996. Subgroups of X12N include: *WEDI: Workgroup on Electronic Data Exchange* WEDI has been the prime mover in the development of insurance industry standards. In 1995, WEDI became a private standards advocacy group. *HIBCC: Health Industry Business Communications Council*
American College of Radiology—National Electrical Manufacturers Association (ACR-NEMA) American College of Radiology 1891 Preston White Drive Reston, VA 20191 Telephone: (703) 648-8900 www.acr.org National Electrical Manufacturers Association 1300 N. Seventeenth Street, Suite 1847 Rosslyn, VA 22209 Telephone: (703) 841-3200 www.nema.org	Exchange of digitized images	ACR is a professional association, and NEMA is a trade association. They have worked collaboratively to develop the Digital Imaging and Communications in Medicine (DICOM) standard, which promotes a digital image communications format and facilitates development by the American College of Radiology of picture archive and communications systems. DICOM may be used for electronic exchange of X rays, computed tomography (CT), magnetic resonance imaging (MRI), ultrasound, nuclear medicine, and other radiology images. Work is under way to support other diagnostic images.
American Society for Testing and Materials (ASTM) 100 Barr Harbor Drive West Conshohocken, PA 19428 Telephone: (610) 832-9585 www.astm.org	Multiple health informatics standards, including clinical content of patient records, exchange of messages about clinical observations, data security and integrity, healthcare identifiers, data modeling, clinical laboratory systems, Arden syntax (a coding system), and system functionality	Organized in 1898, the ASTM is one of the largest SDOs in the world. It provides a forum for vendors, users, consumers, and others to develop standards for a wide range of materials, products, systems, and services. It is composed of more than 140 subcommittees or working groups identified as E31 and E32. Since 1990, Committee E31 on Healthcare Informatics has developed standards for health information and health information systems. Standard E1384, discussed earlier, is a product of the E31 subcommittee of ASTM.
Health Level Seven (HL7) 3300 Washtenaw Avenue, Suite 227 Ann Arbor, MI 48104 Telephone: (734) 677-7777 www.hl7.org	Electronic interchange of clinical, financial, and administrative information among disparate health information systems	HL7 is an ANSI-accredited SDO. Level 7 refers to the highest level of the Open System Interconnection (OSI) model of the International Standards Organization. The HL7 standard addresses issues that occur within the seventh, or application, layer.
Institute of Electrical and Electronics Engineers (IEEE) 445 Hoes Lane P.O. Box 1331 Piscataway, NJ 08855-1331 Telephone: (732) 981-0060 www.ieee.org	Medical device information and general informatics format	The IEEE's Medical Data Interchange Standard (MEDIX) is a standard set of hospital system interface transactions based on the ISO standards for all seven layers of the OSI model. Another IEEE standard for a medical information bus (MIB) links bedside instruments in critical care with health information systems.
National Council on Prescription Drug Programs (NCPDP) 4201 N. Twenty-fourth Street, Suite 365 Phoenix, AZ 85016 Telephone: (602) 957-9105 www.ncpdp.org	Data interchange and processing standards for pharmacy transactions	The NCPDP has defined standards for transmitting prescription information from pharmacies to payers for prescription management services and for receiving approval and payment information back in near-real time. Other standards address adverse drug reactions and utilization review.

model has gone through the initial phase of review, and the result is a draft standard for trial use. The draft standard will undergo a two-year feasibility study to be conducted by healthcare organizations, starting in mid-2004. The goal for publication of the final EHR standard is 2006. The HL7 standard is an example of a content and structure standard.

The **American Society for Testing and Materials** (ASTM) has also developed a standard on the content and structure of computer-based health records. Standard E1384 describes the basic information categories in EHRs and segments the categories into specific data elements.

The **Systematized Nomenclature of Medicine Clinical Terms®** (SNOMED CT®) is an example of a vocabulary standard. It was developed jointly by the College of American Pathologists and the National Library of Medicine. SNOMED CT established a common language for capturing, sharing, and aggregating health data across specialties and care settings. The SNOMED core terminology includes over 357,000 healthcare concepts, each with a unique definition. Currently, it is available in English- and Spanish-language versions. Experts expect SNOMED CT to be adopted as a universal vocabulary standard for EHRs. SNOMED CT is available free for downloading as a part of the National Library of Medicine's Unified Medical Language System Metathesaurus (National Library of Medicine 2004).

The National Library of Medicine has also developed a clinical drug nomenclature in consultation with the Food and Drug Administration, the Department of Veterans Affairs, and HL7. (The FDA regulates the safety of food, drugs, medical devices, and cosmetics. The VA provides benefits to military veterans.) **RxNorm** provides standard names for clinical drugs and administered dose forms. Like SNOMED CT, the most recent update of RxNorm is available through the National Library of Medicine's Unified Medical Language System Metathesaurus (National Library of Medicine 2004).

The work being done to develop and establish health informatics standards will ensure the successful implementation of electronic health record systems in the near future. Compliance with such industry standards will probably continue to be voluntary. Generally, however, most hospitals and other healthcare organizations will find it beneficial to adopt health informatics standards because efficient information sharing is critical to so many areas of patient care and healthcare operations.

Internal Hospital Policies and Procedures

Every hospital must develop, implement, and enforce policies and procedures to ensure the quality of clinical care and the safety of patients, visitors, and staff. **Policies** are general written guidelines that dictate behavior or direct and constrain decision making within the organization. **Procedures** are written instructions that detail how functions and processes are to be carried out. Procedures should be designed specifically to fulfill the stipulations of general policies.

Hospitals generally model their internal policies and procedures after applicable state and federal regulations, legal guidelines, accreditation standards, clinical practice standards, and voluntary industry standards. However, internal policies must also reflect the facility's own service goals and standards of care.

Policies should use clear language and follow a consistent format. In addition, every policy, procedure, and revision should be dated to ensure effective version control.

Policies and procedures should be reviewed on a regular basis and communicated to employees and the medical staff during initial employee and provider orientation. Employees and caregivers may also be required to review and sign particularly important policies at regular intervals. Examples might include patient confidentiality and health record access and security policies. Many healthcare organizations post policies and procedures on their internal information networks to make them easy for staff to access.

Policies and procedures may apply across the hospital's departments or pertain specifically to one group of employees or one functional department. Hospital policies and procedures can be grouped into the following general categories:

- Administration, including health information management
- Medical Staff
- Nursing Services
- Human Resources
- Safety
- Environment of Care

Health Information Management Policies and Procedures

The director of health information management works with representatives of the hospital's clinical departments to develop health record policies and procedures. Like other hospital policies, health record policies must comply with applicable state and federal regulations, accreditation standards, and clinical standards. They must also fulfill the specific legal requirements that apply to the facility. (Figure 5.13 provides an example of an HIM policy. Figure 5.14 lists the policies and procedures commonly maintained by hospital HIM departments.)

Figure 5.13.   Example of an HIM Policy

Policy on Computer Terminal Controls

Purpose: To prevent unauthorized access to University Hospital data by providing terminal controls

Scope: University Hospital's terminals

Standard: Proper physical and software control mechanisms shall be in place to control access to and use of devices connected to University Hospital's computer systems

Guidelines:

1. Hardware Terminal Locking: In areas that are not physically secured, terminals should be equipped with locking devices to prevent their use during unattended periods. The locks should be installed in addition to programmed restrictions, such as automatic disconnect after a given period of inactivity.

2. Operating System Identification of Terminal: All terminal activity should be controlled by the operating system, which should be able to identify terminals, whether they are hardwired or connected through communications lines. The operating system should inspect log-on requests to determine which application the terminal user desires. The user should identify an existing application and supply a valid user ID and password combination. If the log-on request is valid, the operating system should make a logical connection between the user and the application.

3. Limitation of Log-On Attempts: Limit system log-on attempts from remote terminal devices. More than three unsuccessful attempts should result in termination of the session, generation of a real-time security violation message to the operator and/or the ISO (and log of said message in an audit file), and purging of the input queue of messages from the terminal.

4. Time-Out Feature: Ensure that the operating system provides the timing services required to support a secure operational environment. Inactive processes or terminals (in an interactive environment) should be terminated after a predetermined period.

5. Dial-Up Control: The communications software should ensure a clean end of connection in all cases, especially in the event of abnormal disconnection.

Source: Johns 2002c.

Figure 5.14. List of Common HIM Department Policies and Procedures

The following list provides an example of the types of policies and procedures that may be included in a manual for health information services. The titles and content of the policies and procedures may vary by facility or corporation. Some of the policies and procedures are listed more than once for cross-referencing purposes.

Abbreviations
Access to Automated/Computerized Records
Access to Records (Release of Information) by
    Resident and by Staff
Admission/Discharge Register
Admission Procedures
    Facility Procedures–Establishing/Closing the
        Record
    Preparing the Medical Record
    Preparing the Master Patient Index Card
    Readmission–Continued Use of Previous
        Record
    Readmission–New Record
Amendment of Clinical Records
Audit Schedule
Audit and Monitoring System
    Admission/Readmission Audit
    Audit/Monitoring Schedule
    Change in Condition
    Concurrent Audit
    Discharge Audit
    MDS
    Nursing Assistant Flow Sheet
    Pressure Sore
    Psychotropic Drug Documentation
    Restrictive Device/Restraint
    Specialized Audits (examples)
    Therapy
Certification, Medicare
Chart Removal and Chart Locator Log
Clinical Records, Definition of Records,
    and Record Service
Closing the Record
Coding and Indexing, Disease Index
Committee Minutes Guidelines
Computerization and Security of Automated
    Data/Records
Confidentiality (See Release of Information)
Consulting Services for Clinical Records and Plan
    of Service

Content, Record *(the list provided is not all-inclusive
    and should be tailored to the
    facility/corporation)*
    Advanced Directives
    Discharge against Medical Advice
    Discharge Summary
    General
    Interdisciplinary Progress Notes
    Medicare Certification/Recertification
    Physician Consultant Reports
    Physician History and Physical Exam
    Physician Orders/Telephone Orders
    Physician Services Guidelines and Progress Notes
    Transfer Form/Discharge Plan of Care
Copying/Release of Records—General
Correcting Clinical Records
Data Collection/Monitoring
Definition of Clinical Records/Health Information
    Service
Delinquent Physician Visit
Denial Letters, Medicare
Destruction of Records, Log
Disaster Planning for Health Information
Discharge Procedures
    Assembly of Discharge Record
    Chart Order on Discharge
    Closure of Incomplete Clinical Record
    Completing and Filing Master Patient Index Card
    Discharge Chart Audit
    Incomplete Record File
    Notification of Deficiencies
Emergency Disaster Evacuation
Establishing/Closing Record
Falsification of Records, Willful
Fax/Facsimile, Faxing
Filing Order, Discharge (Chart Order)
Filing Order, In-house (Chart Order)
Filing System
Filing System, Unit Record

Figure 5.14.   (Continued)

Forms, Release of Information

Forms, Subpoena

Forms Management

General Policies

   Access to Records

   Automation of Records (See also
      Computerization)

   Availability

   Change in Ownership

   Completion and Correction of Records

   Confidentiality

   Indexes

   Ownership of Records

   Permanent and Capable of Being
      Photocopied

   Retention

   Storage of Records

   Subpoena

   Unit Record

   Willful Falsification/Willful Omission

Guide to Location of Items in the Health
    Information Department

Guidelines, Committee Minutes

Incomplete Record File

Indexes

   Disease Index and Forms for Indexing

   Master Patient Index

   Release of Information Index/Log

In-service Training Minutes/Record

Job Descriptions

   Health Information Coordinator

   Health Unit Coordinator

   Other Health Information Staff (if applicable)

Late Entries

Lost Record—Reconstruction

Master Patient Index

Medicare Documentation

   Certification and Recertification

   Medicare Denial Procedure and Letter

   Medicare Log

Numbering System

Ombudsman, Review/Access to Records

Omission, Willful

Order of Filing, Discharge

Order of Filing, In-house

Organizational Chart for Health Information
    Department

Orientation/Training of Health Information
    Department

Outguides

Physician Visit Schedule, Letters, and Monitoring

Physician Visits, Delinquent Visit Follow-up

Quality Assurance

   Health Information Participation

   QA Studies and Reporting

Readmission—Continued Use of Previous Record

Readmission—New Record

Recertification or Certification (Medicare)

Reconstruction of Lost Record

Refusal of Treatment

Release of Information

   Confidentiality

   Confidentiality Statement by Staff

   Copying/Release of Records—General

   Faxing Medical Information

   Procedure for Release—Sample Letters
      and Authorizations

   Redisclosure of Clinical Information

   Resident Access to Records

   Retrieval of Records (sign-out system)

   Subpoena

   Witnessing Legal Documents

Requesting Information

   From Hospitals and Other Healthcare Providers

   Request for Information Form

Retention of Records and Destruction after Retention
    Period

   Example Statement for Destruction

   Retention Guidelines

Retrieval of Records

Security of Automated Data/Electronic Medical
    Records

   Back-up Procedures

   General Procedures

   Passwords

Sign-out Logs

Storage of Records

Telephone Orders

Thinning

   In-house Records

   Maintaining Overflow Record

Unit Record System

Source: Johns 2002c.

Medical Staff Bylaws, Rules, and Regulations

As noted earlier in this chapter, **medical staff bylaws, rules, and regulations** govern the conduct of the independent healthcare professionals who provide patient care services in acute care facilities. (Bylaws are similar to policies in that they describe general guidelines. Rules and regulations, like procedures, describe the specific activities to be performed to carry out the bylaws.) The bylaws describe the structure of the medical staff and its membership qualifications, rights, and responsibilities.

Rules and regulations are generally easier to amend and therefore should be used to communicate elements that are likely to change frequently. Medical staff rules and regulations establish the medical staff's specific responsibilities for patient care and health record documentation.

Summary

Acute care hospitals are regulated through a complex and constantly changing system of mandatory and voluntary standards promulgated by government agencies, accreditation organizations, professional organizations, and standards development organizations. In order for the health record to be considered a legal document, it must fulfill specific form and content requirements. Issues of release and disclosure as well as privacy and security have come to the fore with the advent of electronic health records and HIPAA implementation in 2003. Regulations vary at the federal, state, and local levels of government, and Medicare and Medicaid have their own *Conditions of Participation* based on the healthcare setting. Although several accreditation programs are available for contemporary hospitals, the Joint Commission on Accreditation of Healthcare Organizations brings together these disparate regulations and provides a launching point for most healthcare facilities. Recent efforts at developing standards for electronic health record systems hold promise for the adoption of fully modern documentation practices in the near future.

References

Amatayakul, Margret. 2002. Computer-based patient records. In *Health Information Management: Concepts, Principles, and Practice,* edited by Kathleen LaTour and Shirley Eichenwald. Chicago: American Health Information Management Association.

Amatayakul, Margret. 2004. *Electronic Health Records: A Practical Guide for Professionals and Organizations,* second edition. Chicago: American Health Information Management Association.

Amatayakul, Margret, and others. 2002. Practice Brief: Implementing the minimum necessary standard. *Journal of the American Health Information Management Association* 73(10). Available at www.ahima.org.

American Osteopathic Association. 2004a. About the Healthcare Facilities Accreditation Program. Available at http://do-online.osteotech.org.

American Osteopathic Association. 2004b. *Accreditation Requirements for Healthcare Facilities, 2004–2005.* Chicago: AOA:

Carpenter, Jennifer. 1999. Practice Brief: Managing health information relating to infection with the human immunodeficiency virus. *Journal of the American Health Information Management Association* 70(5). Available at www.ahima.org.

Centers for Medicare and Medicaid Services. 2004. Medicare *Conditions of Participation for Hospitals.* Available at www.access.gpo.gov.

Commission on Accreditation of Rehabilitation Facilities. 2004a. About Accreditation. Available at www.carf.org.

Commission on Accreditation of Rehabilitation Facilities. 2004b. *2004 Behavioral Health Standards Manual.* Tucson: CARF.

Commission on Accreditation of Rehabilitation Facilities. 2004c. *2004 Medical Rehabilitation Standards Manual.* Tucson: CARF.

Hjort, Beth. 2001. Practice Brief: A HIPAA checklist. *Journal of the American Health Information Management Association* 72(6). Available at www.ahima.org.

Hjort, Beth. 2003. Practice Brief: HIPAA privacy and security training. *Journal of the American Health Information Management Association* 74(10). Available at www.ahima.org.

Hjort, Beth, and Hughes, Gwen. 2002. Practice Brief: Consent for uses and disclosures of information. *Journal of the American Health Information Management Association* 73(10). Available at www.ahima.org.

Hughes, Gwen. 2002a. Practice Brief: Destruction of patient health information. *Journal of the American Health Information Management Association* 73(10). Available at www.ahima.org.

Hughes, Gwen. 2002b. Practice Brief: Laws and regulations governing the disclosure of health information. *Journal of the American Health Information Management Association* 73(10). Available at www.ahima.org.

Hughes, Gwen. 2002c. Practice Brief: Notice of information practice. *Journal of the American Health Information Management Association* 73(10). Available at www.ahima.org.

Hughes, Gwen. 2002d. Practice Brief: Required content for authorizations to disclose. *Journal of the American Health Information Management Association* 73(10). Available at www.ahima.org.

Johns, Merida. 2002a. Legal issues in health information management. In *Health Information Management Technology: An Applied Approach.* Chicago: American Health Information Management Association.

Johns, Merida. 2002b. *Information Management for the Health Professions,* second edition. Albany, NY: Delmar Learning.

Johns, Merida. 2002c. Supervision of health information technology functions. In *Health Information Management Technology: An Applied Approach.* Chicago: American Health Information Management Association.

Joint Commission on Accreditation of Healthcare Organizations. 2004a. About the Hospital Survey Process. Available at www.jcaho.org.

Joint Commission on Accreditation of Healthcare Organizations. 2004b. *2004 Comprehensive Accreditation Manual for Hospitals: The Official Handbook.* Oakbrook Terrace, Il.: JCAHO.

Joint Commission on Accreditation of Healthcare Organizations. 2004c. 2005 National Patient Safety Goals. Available at www.jcaho.org/news+room.

Joint Commission on Accreditation of Healthcare Organizations. 2004d. Shared Visions—New Pathways Q & A: Periodic performance review. Available at www.jcaho.org/accredited+organizations.

Kiger, Linda. 2002. Preservation of health records. In *Health Information Management: Principles and Organization for Health Information Services,* fifth edition, edited by Margaret Skurka. San Francisco: Jossey-Bass.

McCain, Mary Cole. 2002. Paper-based health records. In *Health Information Management: Concepts, Principles, and Practice,* edited by Kathleen LaTour and Shirley Eichenwald. Chicago: American Health Information Management Association.

McWay, Dana. 2002. *Legal Aspects of Health Information Management,* second edition. Clifton Park, New York: Delmar Learning.

National Committee for Quality Assurance. 2004. www.ncqa.org.

National Library of Medicine. 2004. Unified Medical Language System Metathesaurus. Available at www.nlm.nih.gov/research/umls.

Pozgar, G. 1999. *Legal Aspects of Health Care Administration.* Gaithersburg, Md.: Aspen Publishers.

Quinsey, Carol Ann, and Brandt, Mary. 2003. Practice Brief: Information security—An overview. *Journal of the American Health Information Management Association* 74(10). Available at www.ahima.org.

Rhodes, Harry. 2001. Practice Brief: Patient anonymity. *Journal of the American Health Information Management Association* 72(5). Available at www.ahima.org.

Rhodes, Harry, and Brandt, Mary. 2003. Practice Brief: Protecting patient information after a facility closure. *Journal of the American Health Information Management Association* 74(10). Available at www.ahima.org.

Rhodes, Harry, and Burrington-Brown, Jill. 2002. Practice Brief: Recommended regulations and standards for specific healthcare settings. *Journal of the American Health Information Management Association* 73(10). Available at www.ahima.org.

Rhodes, Harry, and Fletcher, Donna. 2002. Practice Brief: Retention of health information. *Journal of the American Health Information Management Association* 73(6). Available at www.ahima.org.

Rhodes, Harry, and Hughes, Gwen. 2003. Practice Brief: Redisclosure of patient health information. *Journal of the American Health Information Management Association* 74(4). Available at www.ahima.org.

Russell, Lynda. 2002. Legal issues in health information management. In *Health Information Management: Concepts, Principles, and Practice,* edited by Kathleen LaTour and Shirley Eichenwald. Chicago: American Health Information Management Association.

Shaw, Patricia, and others. 2003. *Quality and Performance Improvement in Healthcare: A Tool for Programmed Learning,* second edition. Chicago: American Health Information Management Association.

Zeman, Vicki. 2002. Clinical quality management. In *Health Information Management: Concepts, Principles, and Practice,* edited by Kathleen LaTour and Shirley Eichenwald. Chicago: American Health Information Management Association.

Review Quiz

Directions: Choose the best answer for each of the following items.

1. ___ Which of the following is a direct command that requires an individual or a representative of an organization to appear in court or to present an object to the court?
   A. Judicial decision
   B. Subpoena
   C. Credentialing
   D. Regulation

2. ___ What is a piece of legislation written and approved by a state or federal legislature and then signed into law by the state's governor or the president?
   A. Municipal code
   B. Statute
   C. Regulation
   D. Judicial decision

3. ___ What is it called when a hospital is allowed to claim reimbursement for services provided to Medicare beneficiaries without having to provide evidence that it meets the Medicare *Conditions of Participation for Hospitals*?
   A. Deemed status
   B. Judicial decision
   C. Subpoena
   D. Credentialing

4. ___ Which of the following is a rule established by an administrative agency of government?
   A. Municipal code
   B. Statute
   C. Subpoena
   D. Regulation

5. ___ Which process requires the verification of the educational qualifications, licensure status, and other experience of healthcare professionals who have applied for the privilege of practicing within a healthcare facility?
   A. Deemed status
   B. Judicial decision
   C. Subpoena
   D. Credentialing

6. ___ What is a rule established by a local government called?
   A. Municipal code
   B. Statute
   C. Judicial decision
   D. Regulation

7. ___ Which of the following is a ruling handed down by a court to settle a legal dispute?
   A. Municipal code
   B. Statute
   C. Deemed status
   D. Judicial decision

8. ___ General written guidelines that dictate behavior and/or direct and constrain decision making within the organization are known as what?
   A. Procedures
   B. Policies
   C. Standards
   D. Rules

9. ___ Which of the following would be an acceptable medium for reporting an individual's positive HIV test results to a state department of health?
   A. Certified e-mail
   B. Certified courier
   C. Telephone
   D. Facsimile

10. ___ When a physician learns about his or her patient's HIV status while the patient is hospitalized, what is this information considered to be?
    A. A privileged communication
    B. A disclosure
    C. A redisclosure
    D. A privileged diagnosis

11. ___ Why did the AOA first initiate its Healthcare Facilities Accreditation Program?
    A. To increase the number of osteopaths in practice
    B. To improve the quality of medical schools
    C. To ensure the quality of residency programs for osteopathic physicians
    D. To increase the public's awareness of the benefits of osteopathic treatments

12. ___ Which of the following dictates the maximum period of time that may elapse between an event and any consequent legal action in a specific geopolitical area?
    A. Statute of limitations
    B. Court order
    C. Subpoena
    D. Jurisdiction

13. ___ Which two inpatient services does CARF offer accreditation programs for?
    A. Behavioral health and neurosurgery
    B. Medical rehabilitation and behavioral health
    C. Medical rehabilitation and cardiology
    D. Neurosurgery and medical rehabilitation

14. ___ Burning, shredding, pulping, and pulverizing are all acceptable methods in which process?
    A. Deidentification of electronic documents
    B. Destruction of paper-based health records
    C. Deidentification of records stored on microfilm
    D. Destruction of computer-based health records

15. ___ Which JCAHO survey methodology involves an evaluation that follows the hospital experiences of past or current patients?
    A. Priority focus review
    B. Periodic performance review
    C. Tracer process
    D. Performance improvement

16. ___ Which type of regulation addresses a hospital's operational procedures, staffing, and environmental safety?
    A. Licensure
    B. Accreditation
    C. Certification
    D. Insurance

17. ___ Which legal doctrine was established by the *Darling v. Charleston Community Hospital* case of 1965?
    A. Hospital–physician negligence
    B. Clinical negligence
    C. Physician–hospital negligence
    D. Corporate negligence

18. ___ According to the Medicare *Conditions of Participation for Hospitals,* when must the patient's history and physical examination be performed?
    A. No more than 7 days before admission or within 48 hours after admission
    B. No more than 7 days before admission or within 24 hours after admission
    C. No more than 10 days before admission or within 48 hours after admission
    D. No more than 10 days before admission or within 24 hours after admission

19. ___ Which national database collects information on medical malpractice settlements, clinical privilege actions, and medical society actions taken against licensed healthcare providers?
    A. Healthcare Integrity and Protection Data Bank
    B. Medicare Protection Database
    C. National Practitioner Data Bank
    D. Healthcare Protection Database

20. ___ Which standard rating categories does the CARF accreditation program use?
    A. Insufficient compliance, partial compliance, satisfactory compliance, not applicable
    B. Denial of accreditation, preliminary accreditation, conditional accreditation, accreditation
    C. Nonconformance, partial conformance, conformance, exemplary conformance
    D. Insufficient compliance, sufficient compliance, exemplary compliance, not applicable

21. ___ What type of security safeguards depend on the use of fire alarms, smoke detectors, and sprinklers?
    A. Media control systems
    B. Surveillance systems
    C. Environmental safety systems
    D. Technical security systems

22. ___ What type of data were the first to be subject to data standardization efforts?
    A. Health informatics
    B. Credentialing
    C. Privacy
    D. Hospital discharge

23. ___ Under federal regulations, when can records of substance abuse treatment be released without the consent of the patient?
   A. For research and audit activities
   B. In response to a subpoena for a criminal case
   C. In response to a subpoena for a civil lawsuit
   D. For continuing treatment at an outpatient clinic

24. ___ Who owns the health records of patients treated in acute care hospitals?
   A. The patient
   B. The physician
   C. The hospital
   D. The patient's family

25. ___ Which of the following is a voluntary, systematic quality review process that evaluates the healthcare facility's performance against preestablished, written criteria?
   A. Accreditation
   B. Licensure
   C. Certification
   D. Performance improvement

26. ___ The JCAHO began using a new set of standard performance ratings in 2004. What are they?
   A. Insufficient compliance, partial compliance, satisfactory compliance, not applicable
   B. Denial of accreditation, preliminary accreditation, conditional accreditation, accreditation
   C. Nonconformance, partial conformance, conformance, exemplary conformance
   D. Insufficient compliance, sufficient compliance, exemplary compliance, not applicable

27. ___ Which of the following is a written description of a healthcare facility's procedures on the use and disclosure of protected health information?
   A. Minimum necessary standard
   B. Notice of privacy practices
   C. Notice of protected health information
   D. Minimum use requirement

28. __ Professional organizations that establish quality standards and conduct periodic assessments of the performance of individual healthcare organizations against those standards are called what?
   A. Standards development organizations
   B. Accreditation organizations
   C. State licensing organizations
   D. Public health organizations

29. ___ When does the JCAHO plan to move its accreditation process to completely unannounced surveys?
   A. 2005
   B. 2004
   C. 2008
   D. 2006

30. ___ Which type of standards describe the accepted methods for collecting, maintaining, and/or transferring healthcare data among computer systems?
   A. Privacy standards
   B. Performance standards
   C. Vocabulary standards
   D. Health informatics standards

31. ___ Which JCAHO accreditation activity converts presurvey data into information for planning survey activities, increasing consistency in the accreditation process, and customizing the accreditation process?
    A. Periodic performance review
    B. Presurvey review
    C. Tracer process
    D. Priority focus process

32. ___ What is hospital licensure?
    A. The voluntary process whereby independent organizations evaluate the performance of individual hospitals against established quality standards
    B. The mandatory process whereby state governments grant individual hospitals permission to operate within a specific geopolitical area
    C. The voluntary process whereby hospitals are granted permission to provide healthcare services to Medicare and Medicaid patients
    D. The mandatory process whereby the federal government grants hospitals permission to provide a specific range of healthcare services

33. ___ Which of the following accreditation categories would the JCAHO assign to a hospital that has not been accredited by the JCAHO in the past but has demonstrated compliance with selected standards in the first of two on-site surveys?
    A. Provisional accreditation
    B. Preliminary accreditation
    C. Accredited
    D. Conditional accreditation

34. ___ The process of releasing health record documentation originally created by a different provider is called what?
    A. Privileged communication
    B. Subpoena
    C. Jurisdiction
    D. Redisclosure

35. ___ According to the HFAP's accreditation standards, osteopathic physicians are required to perform what type of examination in addition to a traditional physical examination on or before a patient's admission to the hospital?
    A. Neurological
    B. Musculoskeletal
    C. Respiratory
    D. Cardiovascular

36. ___ What type of health record policy dictates how long individual health records must remain available for authorized use?
    A. Disclosure policies
    B. Legal policies
    C. Retention policies
    D. Redisclosure policies

37. ___ What does the JCAHO call unexpected occurrences that result in death or serious physical or psychological injury or the risk of death or serious injury?
    A. Priority focus areas
    B. Practice guidelines
    C. Sentinel events
    D. Medical errors

38. ____ What type of organization works under contract with the CMS to conduct Medicare/Medicaid certification surveys for hospitals that do not qualify for deemed status?
   A. Accreditation organizations
   B. Certification organizations
   C. State licensure agencies
   D. Conditions of participation agencies

39. ____ Written instructions that describe how functions and processes must be carried out are what kind of documents?
   A. Procedures
   B. Policies
   C. Standards
   D. Rules

40. ____ What should a hospital do when a state law requires more stringent privacy protection than the federal HIPAA privacy standard?
   A. Ignore the state law and follow the HIPAA standard
   B. Follow the state law and ignore the HIPAA standard
   C. Comply with both the state law and the HIPAA standard
   D. Ignore both the state law and the HIPAA standard and follow relevant accreditation standards

41. ____ Which national database was created to collect information on the legal actions (both civil and criminal) taken against licensed healthcare providers?
   A. Healthcare Integrity and Protection Data Bank
   B. Medicare Protection Database
   C. National Practitioner Data Bank
   D. Healthcare Safety Database

42. ____ What process involves overseeing the hospital's internal medical, legal, and administrative operations with the goal of minimizing the hospital's exposure to liability?
   A. Incident reporting
   B. Risk management
   C. Legal reporting
   D. Performance management

43. ____ Under the HIPAA privacy standard, which of the following types of protected health information must be specifically identified in an authorization?
   A. History and physical reports
   B. Operative reports
   C. Consultation reports
   D. Psychotherapy notes

44. ____ What does the JCAHO call its newly revised accreditation and survey process?
   A. Periodic Performance Review
   B. Shared Visions—New Pathways
   C. Patient Tracer Methodology
   D. Priority Focus Assessment

45. ____ What type of standard establishes uniform definitions for clinical terms?
   A. Identifier standard
   B. Vocabulary standard
   C. Transaction and messaging standard
   D. Structure and content standard

46. ___ What type of standard establishes clear descriptions of the data elements to be collected?
    A. Vocabulary standard
    B. Transaction and messaging standard
    C. Structure and content standard
    D. Security standard

47. ___ What type of standard facilitates electronic data interchange among independent computer information systems?
    A. Security standard
    B. Transaction and messaging standard
    C. Vocabulary standard
    D. Identifier standard

48. ___ What type of standard ensures the confidentiality of patient-identifiable health information and protects it from unauthorized disclosure, alternation, and destruction?
    A. Identifier standard
    B. Vocabulary standard
    C. Structure and content standard
    D. Security standard

49. ___ What type of standard establishes methods for creating unique designations for individual patients, healthcare professionals, healthcare provider organizations, and healthcare vendors and suppliers?
    A. Vocabulary standard
    B. Identifier standard
    C. Structure and content standard
    D. Security standard

50. ___ According to the JCAHO, how should the unanticipated death of a full-term infant be reported?
    A. As a sentinel event
    B. As a violation of a clinical practice guideline
    C. As an unfortunate accident
    D. As a medical complication

Appendix A
Bibliography

Abdelhak, Mervat and others, editors. 2001. *Health Information: Management of a Strategic Resource,* second edition. Philadelphia: W. B. Saunders.

Agency for Healthcare Research and Quality. 2002. *Health Care Costs.* Rockville, MD: U.S. Department of Health and Human Services.

AHIMA E-HIM Task Force. 2003. Practice Brief: E-mail as a provider–patient electronic communication medium and its impact on the electronic health record. *Journal of the American Health Information Management Association* 74(10). Available at www.ahima.org.

AHIMA E-HIM Task Force. 2003. Practice Brief: Implementing electronic signatures. *Journal of the American Health Information Management Association* 74(10). Available at www.ahima.org.

AHIMA E-HIM Task Force. 2003. Practice Brief: Speech recognition in the electronic health record. *Journal of the American Health Information Management Association* 74(10). Available at www.ahima.org.

Amatayakul, Margret, and others. 2001. Practice Brief: Definition of the health record for legal purposes. *Journal of the American Health Information Management Association* 72(10). Available at www.ahima.org.

Amatayakul, Margret, and others. 2002. Practice Brief: Implementing the minimum necessary standard. *Journal of the American Health Information Management Association* 73(10). Available at www.ahima.org.

American Osteopathic Association. 2004. About the Healthcare Facilities Accreditation Program. Available at www.do-online.osteotech.org.

American Osteopathic Association. 2004. *Accreditation Requirements for Healthcare Facilities.* Chicago: AOA.

American Society for Testing and Materials. 2004. Standard Guide for Content and Structure of the Electronic Health Record. Available at www.astm.org.

Burrington-Brown, Jill, and Hughes, Gwen. 2003. Practice Brief: Provider–patient e-mail security. *Journal of the American Health Information Management Association* 74(6). Available at www.ahima.org.

Carpenter, Jennifer. 1999. Practice Brief: Managing health information relating to infection with the human immunodeficiency virus. *Journal of the American Health Information Management Association* 70(5). Available at www.ahima.org.

Cassidy, Bonnie, and others. 1998. Practice Brief: Data quality management model. *Journal of the American Health Information Management Association* 69(6). Available at www.ahima.org.

Center for Studying Health System Change. 2003. Tracking health care costs. *Data Bulletin* 25:1–2.

Centers for Medicare and Medicaid Services. 2003. Medicare+Choice program in 2001 and 2002. Available at www.cms.hhs.gov.

Centers for Medicare and Medicaid Services. 2003. *Medicare Conditions of Participation for Hospitals.* Washington, D.C.: CMS.

Centers for Medicare and Medicaid Services. 2004. The facts about upcoming new benefits in Medicare. Available at www.cms.hhs.gov.

Commission on Accreditation of Rehabilitation Facilities. 2004. 2004 Behavioral Health Standards Manual. Tucson: CARF.

Commission on Accreditation of Rehabilitation Facilities. 2004. *2004 Medical Rehabilitation Standards Manual.* Tucson: CARF.

Commission on Accreditation of Rehabilitation Facilities. 2004. About Accreditation. Available at www.carf.org.

Detmer, Don, and others, editors. 1991. *The Computer-Based Patient Record: An Essential Technology for Health Care.* Washington, D.C.: National Academy Press.

Dick, Richard, and others, editors. 1997. *The Computer-Based Patient Record: An Essential Technology for Health Care,* revised edition. Washington, D.C.: National Academy Press.

Dougherty, Michelle. 2002. Practice Brief: Maintaining a legally sound health record. *Journal of the American Health Information Management Association* 73(9). Available at www.ahima.org.

Dougherty, Michelle. 2001. Practice Brief: Verbal/telephone order authentication and time frames. *Journal of the American Health Information Management Association* 72(2). Available at www.ahima.org.

Fletcher, Donna. 1999. Practice Brief: Best practices in medical record documentation and completion. *Journal of the American Health Information Management Association* 70(10). Available at www.ahima.org.

Fletcher, Donna. 1997. Practice Brief: Telemedical records. *Journal of the American Health Information Management Association* 68(4). Available at www.ahima.org.

Glondys, Barbara. 2003. Practice Brief: Ensuring the legibility of patient records. *Journal of the American Health Information Management Association* 74(5). Available at www.ahima.org.

Hjort, Beth. 2003. Practice Brief: HIPAA privacy and security training. *Journal of the American Health Information Management Association* 74(10). Available at www.ahima.org.

Hjort, Beth. 2001. Practice Brief: HIPAA privacy checklist. *Journal of the American Health Information Management Association* 72(6). Available at www.ahima.org.

Hjort, Beth, and others. 2001. Practice Brief: Patient photography, videotaping, and other imaging. *Journal of the American Health Information Management Association* 72(6). Available at www.ahima.org.

Hjort, Beth, and Hughes, Gwen. 2002. Practice Brief: Consent for uses and disclosures of information. *Journal of the American Health Information Management Association* 73(10). Available at www.ahima.org.

Hughes, Gwen. 2000. Practice Brief: Authentication of health record entries. *Journal of the American Health Information Management Association* 71(3). Available at www.ahima.org.

Hughes, Gwen. 2002. Practice Brief: Destruction of patient health information. *Journal of the American Health Information Management Association* 73(10). Available at www.ahima.org.

Hughes, Gwen. 2001. Practice Brief: Facsimile transmission of health information. *Journal of the American Health Information Management Association* 72(6). Available at www.ahima.org.

Hughes, Gwen. 2002. Practice Brief: Laws and regulations governing the disclosure of health information. *Journal of the American Health Information Management Association* 73(10). Available at www.ahima.org.

Hughes, Gwen. 2002. Practice Brief: Notice of information practice. *Journal of the American Health Information Management Association* 73(3). Available at www.ahima.org.

Hughes, Gwen. 2002. Practice Brief: Required content for authorizations to disclose. *Journal of the American Health Information Management Association* 73(10). Available at www.ahima.org.

Johns, Merida, editor. 2002. *Health Information Management Technology: An Applied Approach.* Chicago: American Health Information Management Association.

Joint Commission on Accreditation of Healthcare Organizations. 1995. *1995 Accreditation Manual for Hospitals.* Oakbrook Terrace, Il.: JCAHO.

Joint Commission on Accreditation of Healthcare Organizations. 2004. *2004 Comprehensive Accreditation Manual for Hospitals: The Official Handbook.* Oakbrook Terrace, Il.: JCAHO.

Joint Commission on Accreditation of Healthcare Organizations. 2004. About the Hospital Survey Process. Available at www.jcaho.org.

Kaiser Permanente. 2004. About Kaiser Permanente. Available at www.newsmedia.kaiserpermanente.org.

LaTour, Kathleen, and Eichenwald, Shirley, editors. 2002. *Health Information Management: Concepts, Principles, and Practice.* Chicago: American Health Information Management Association.

McWay, Dana. 2002. *Legal Aspects of Health Information Management,* second edition. Clifton Park, New York: Delmar Learning.

Pozgar, G. 1999. *Legal Aspects of Health Care Administration.* Gaithersburg, Md.: Aspen Publishers.

Prophet, Sue. 2002. *Health Information Management Compliance: A Model Program for Healthcare Organizations,* 2002 edition. Chicago: American Health Information Management Association.

Quinsey, Carol Ann, and Brandt, Mary. 2003. Practice Brief: Information security—An overview. *Journal of the American Health Information Management Association* 74(10). Available at www.ahima.org.

Rhodes, Harry. 1999. Practice Brief: The care and maintenance of charge masters. *Journal of the American Health Information Management Association* 70(7). Available at www.ahima.org.

Rhodes, Harry. 2001. Practice Brief: Patient anonymity. *Journal of the American Health Information Management Association* 72(5). Available at www.ahima.org.

Rhodes, Harry, and Brandt, Mary. 2003. Practice Brief: Protecting patient information after a facility closure. *Journal of the American Health Information Management Association* 74(10). Available at www.ahima.org.

Rhodes, Harry, and Burrington-Brown, Jill. 2002. Practice Brief: Recommended regulations and standards for specific healthcare settings. *Journal of the American Health Information Management Association* 73(10). Available at www.ahima.org.

Rhodes, Harry, and Fletcher, Donna. 2002. Practice Brief: Retention of health information. *Journal of the American Health Information Management Association* 73(6). Available at www.ahima.org.

Rhodes, Harry, and Hughes, Gwen. 2003. Practice Brief: Redisclosure of patient health information. *Journal of the American Health Information Management Association* 74(4). Available at www.ahima.org.

Schanz, S. J. 1999. *Developing and Implementing Clinical Practice Guidelines.* Chicago: American Medical Association.

Shaw, Patricia, and others. 2003. *Quality and Performance Improvement in Healthcare: A Tool for Programmed Learning,* second edition. Chicago: American Health Information Management Association.

Skurka, Margaret, editor. 2002. *Health Information Management: Principles and Organization for Health Information Services.* San Francisco: Jossey-Bass.

Smith, Cheryl. 2001. Practice Brief: Documentation requirements for the acute care inpatient record. *Journal of the American Health Information Management Association* 72(3). Available at www.ahima.org.

U.S. Census Bureau. 2003. *Health Insurance Coverage in the United States: 2002.* Washington, D.C.: U.S. Census Bureau.

Welch, Julie. 2000. Practice Brief: Authentication of health record entries. *Journal of the American Health Information Management Association* 71(3). Available at www.ahima.org.

Welch, Julie. 1999. Practice Brief: Correcting and amending entries in a computerized patient record. *Journal of the American Health Information Management Association* 70(8). Available at www.ahima.org.

Welch, Julie. 2000. Practice Brief: Storage media for health information. *Journal of the American Health Information Management Association* 71(6). Available at www.ahima.org.

Appendix B

Glossary

Accreditation: A voluntary process of institutional or organizational review in which a quasi independent body created for this purpose periodically evaluates the quality of the entity's work against preestablished written criteria; also, a determination by an accrediting body that an eligible organization, network, program, group, or individual complies with applicable standards

Accreditation Association for Ambulatory Health Care (AAAHC): A professional organization that offers accreditation programs for ambulatory and outpatient organizations such as single-specialty and multispecialty group practices, ambulatory surgery centers, college/university health services, and community health centers

Accreditation organization: A professional organization that establishes quality standards against which healthcare organizations are measured and conducts periodic assessments of the performance of individual healthcare organizations against the standards

Activities of daily living (ADL): The basic activities of self-care, including grooming, bathing, ambulating, toileting, and eating

Acute care: Medical care of a limited duration that is provided in a an inpatient hospital setting to diagnose and/or treat an injury or a short-term illness

Administrative information: Information used for administrative and healthcare operations purposes such as billing and quality oversight

Advance directive: A legal, written document that describes the patient's preferences regarding future healthcare or stipulates the person who is authorized to make medical decisions in the event the patient is incapable of communicating his or her preferences

Advanced decision support: Automated clinical practice guidelines that are built in to electronic health record systems and designed to support clinical decision making

Aggregate data: Data extracted from individual health records and combined to form de-identified information about groups of patients that can be compared and analyzed

Allied health professional: A credentialed healthcare worker who is not a physician, nurse, psychologist, or pharmacist (for example, a physical therapist, dietitian, social worker, or occupational therapist)

Alphabetic filing system: A system of health record identification and storage that uses the patient's last name as the first component of identification and his or her first name and middle name or initial for further definition

Alphanumeric filing system: A system of health record identification and storage that uses a combination of alphabetic letters (usually the first two letters of the patient's last name) and the health record number

Ambulatory care: Preventive or corrective healthcare services provided on a nonresident basis in a provider's office, clinic setting, or hospital outpatient setting

American Osteopathic Association (AOA): The professional association of osteopathic physicians, surgeons, and graduates of approved colleges of osteopathic medicine that inspects and accredits osteopathic colleges and hospitals

American Society for Testing and Materials (ASTM): A national organization whose purpose is to establish standards on materials, products, systems, and services

Ancillary services: Tests and procedures ordered by a physician to provide information for use in patient diagnosis or treatment

Authentication: The process of identifying the source of health record entries by attaching a handwritten signature, the author's initials, or an electronic signature; also, proof of authorship that ensures, as much as possible, that log-ins and messages from a user originate from an authorized source

Autopsy report: Written documentation of the findings from a postmortem pathological examination

Average record delinquency rate: The monthly average number of discharges divided by the monthly average number of delinquent records.

Biomedical research: The process of systematically investigating subjects related to the functioning of the human body

Board certified: A designation given to a physician or other health professional who has passed an exam from a medical specialty board and is thereby certified to provide care within that specialty

Capitation: A method of healthcare reimbursement in which an insurance carrier prepays a physician, hospital, or other healthcare provider a fixed amount for a given population regardless of the actual number or nature of healthcare services provided to the population

Care plan: The specific goals in the treatment of an individual patient, amended as the patient's condition requires, and the assessment of the outcomes of care

Case management: The ongoing, concurrent review performed by clinical professionals to ensure the necessity and effectiveness of the clinical services being provided to a patient; also, a term used to describe a process that integrates and coordinates patient care and needs across a continuum of care settings or the process of developing a specific care plan for a patient that serves as a communication tool to improve quality of care and reduce cost

Case mix: A description of a patient population based on any number of specific characteristics, including age, gender, type of insurance, diagnosis, risk factors, treatment received, and resources used

Centers for Disease Control and Prevention: A group of federal agencies that oversee health promotion and disease control and prevention activities in the United States.

Centers for Medicare and Medicaid Services (CMS): The division of the Department of Health and Human Services that is responsible for developing healthcare policy in the United States and for administering the Medicare program and the federal portion of the Medicaid program; called the Health Care Financing Administration (HCFA) prior to 2001

Certificate of destruction: A document that constitutes proof that a health record was destroyed and that includes the method of destruction, the signature of the person responsible for destruction, and inclusive dates for destruction

Certification: The process by which a duly authorized body evaluates and recognizes an individual, institution, or educational program as meeting predetermined requirements; also, an evaluation performed to establish the extent to which a particular computer system, network design, or application implementation meets a prespecified set of requirements

Chargemaster: A financial management form that contains information about the organization's charges for the healthcare services it provides to patients; also called the charge description master; also called charge description master (CDM)

Charting by exception: A system of health record documentation in which progress notes focus on abnormal events and describe any interventions that were ordered and the patient's response; also known as focus charting

Civilian Health and Medical Program—Veterans Administration (CHAMPVA):   The federal healthcare benefits program for dependents of veterans rated by the Veterans Administration as having a total and permanent disability, for survivors of veterans who died from VA-rated service-connected conditions or who were rated permanently and totally disabled at the time of death from a VA-rated service-connected condition, and for survivors of persons who died in the line of duty

Claims processing: The process of accumulating claims for services, submitting claims for reimbursement, and ensuring that claims are satisfied

Clinical data: Data captured during the process of diagnosis and treatment

Clinical data repository (CDR):   A central database that focuses on clinical information

Clinical decision support system (CDSS):   A special subcategory of clinical information systems that is designed to help healthcare providers make knowledge-based clinical decisions

Clinical information: Health record documentation that describes the patient's condition and course of treatment

Clinical pathway: A tool designed to coordinate multidisciplinary care planning for specific diagnoses and treatments; also called critical path or pathway or care map

Clinical practice guideline: A systematically developed statement designed to support clinical decision making for a specific medical condition that is issued by an authoritative organization such as a medical society or government agency

Clinical privileges: The authorization granted by a healthcare organization's governing board to a member of the medical staff that enables the physician to provide patient services in the organization within specific practice limits

Clinical protocol: Specific instructions for performing clinical procedures established by authoritative bodies, such as medical staff committees, and intended to be applied literally and universally

Code of Federal Regulations **(CFR):**   The official collection of legislative and regulatory guidelines that are mandated by final rules published in the *Federal Register*

Coding specialist: The healthcare worker responsible for assigning numeric or alphanumeric codes to diagnostic or procedural statements

Commission on Accreditation of Rehabilitation Facilities (CARF):   A private, not-for-profit organization that develops customer-focused standards for behavioral healthcare and medical rehabilitation programs and accredits such programs on the basis of its standards

Comorbidity: A medical condition that coexists with the primary cause for hospitalization and affects the patient's treatment and length of stay

Complication: A medical condition that arises during an inpatient hospitalization (for example, a postoperative wound infection)

Conditions of Participation: The administrative and operational guidelines and regulations under which facilities are allowed to take part in the Medicare and Medicaid programs; published by the Centers for Medicare and Medicaid Services, a federal agency under the Department of Health and Human Services

Confidentiality: A legal and ethical concept that establishes the healthcare provider's responsibility for protecting health records and other personal and private information from unauthorized use or disclosure

Consent to treatment: Legal permission given by a patient or a patient's legal representative to a healthcare provider that allows the provider to administer care and/or treatment or to perform surgery and/or other medical procedures

Consultation reports: Health record documentation that describes the findings and recommendations of consulting physicians

Continuous quality improvement (CQI): A management philosophy that emphasizes the importance of knowing and meeting customer expectations, reducing variation within processes, and relying on data to build knowledge for process improvement; also, a continuous cycle of planning, measuring, and monitoring performance and making knowledge-based improvements

Continuum of care: The range of healthcare services provided to patients, from routine ambulatory care to intensive acute care

Core measure/core measure set: Standardized performance measures developed to improve the safety and quality of healthcare (for example, core measures are used in the Joint Commission on Accreditation's ORYX initiative)

Corporate negligence: The failure of an organization to exercise the degree of care considered reasonable under the circumstances that resulted in an unintended injury to another party

Court order: An official direction issued by a court judge and requiring or forbidding specific parties to perform specific actions

Credentialing: The process of reviewing and validating the qualifications (degrees, licenses, and other credentials) of healthcare practitioners, granting medical staff membership, and awarding specific clinical privileges to licensed, independent practitioners

Data: The dates, numbers, images, symbols, letters, and words that represent basic facts and observations about people, processes, measurements, and conditions

Data Elements for Emergency Department Systems (DEEDS): A data set designed to support the uniform collection of information in hospital-based emergency departments

Data exchange standards: Protocols that help ensure that data transmitted from one system to another remain comparable

Data quality management: A managerial process that ensures the integrity (accuracy and completeness) of an organization's data during data collection, application, warehousing, and analysis

Database: An organized collection of data, text, references, or pictures in a standardized format, typically stored in a computer system for multiple applications

Database management system (DBMS): Computer software that enables the user to create, modify, delete, and view the data in a database

Deemed status: An official designation that a healthcare facility is in compliance with the Medicare *Conditions of Participation*; to qualify for deemed status, facilities must be accredited by the Joint Commission on Accreditation of Healthcare Organizations or the American Osteopathic Association

Deficiency systems: Paper- or computer-based processes designed to track and report elements of documentation missing from the health records of discharged patients

Demographic information: Information used to identify an individual, such as name, address, gender, age, and other information linked to a specific person

Destruction: The act of breaking down the components of a health record into pieces that can no longer be recognized as parts of the original record; for example, paper records can be destroyed by shredding, and electronic records can be destroyed by magnetic degaussing

Diagnostic codes: Numeric or alphanumeric characters used to classify and report diseases, conditions, and injuries

Digital signature: An electronic signature that binds a message to a particular individual and can be used by the receiver to authenticate the identity of the sender

Discharge summary: The final conclusions at the termination of a facility stay or treatment

Disclosure: The act of making information known; in the health information management context, the release of confidential health information about an identifiable person to another person or entity

Disease index: A list of diseases and conditions of patients sequenced according to the code numbers of the classification system in use

Do-not-resuscitate (DNR) order: An order written by the treating physician stating that in the event the patient suffers cardiac or pulmonary arrest, cardiopulmonary resuscitation should not be attempted

Dumping: The illegal practice of transferring uninsured and indigent patients who need emergency services from one hospital to another (usually public) hospital solely to avoid the cost of providing uncompensated services

EHR Collaborative: A group of healthcare professional and trade associations formed to support Health Level Seven, a healthcare standards development organization, in the development of a functional model for electronic health record sustems

Electronic data interchange (EDI): A standard transmission format using strings of data for business information communicated among the computer systems of independent organizations

Electronic document management system (EDM): A storage solution based on digital scanning technology in which source documents are scanned to create digital images of the documents that can be stored electronically on optical disks

Electronic health record (EHR): A computerized record of health information and associated processes; also called computer-based patient record

Electronic signature: Any representation of a signature in digital form, including an image of a handwritten signature; also, the authentication of a computer entry in a health record made by the individual making the entry

Essential Medical Data Set (EMEDS): A recommended data set designed to create a health history for an individual patient treated in an emergency service

Expressed consent: The spoken or written permission granted by a patient to a healthcare provider that allows the provider to perform medical or surgical services

Federal Register: The daily publication of the U.S. Government Printing Office that reports all changes in regulations and federally mandated standards, including HCPCS and ICD-9-CM codes

Fee-for-service (FFS) reimbursement: A method of reimbursement through which providers receive payment based on either billed charges for services provided or on annually updated fee schedules

Financial data: The data collected for the purpose of managing the assets of a business (for example, a healthcare organization, a product line); in healthcare, data derived from the charge generation documentation associated with the activities of care and then aggregated by specific customer grouping for financial analysis

Flow chart: A graphic tool that uses standard symbols to visually display detailed information, including time and distance, of the sequential flow of work of an individual or a product as it progresses through a process

Health informatics standards: A set of standards that describe accepted methods for collecting, maintaining, and/or transferring healthcare data among computer systems

Health Insurance Portability and Accountability Act of 1996 (HIPAA): The federal legislation enacted to provide continuity of health coverage, control fraud and abuse in healthcare, reduce healthcare costs, and guarantee the security and privacy of health information

Health Level Seven (HL7): A standards development organization accredited by the American National Standards Institute that addresses issues at the seventh, or application, level of healthcare systems interconnections

Health maintenance organization (HMO): A prepaid health plan that meets the requirements of the federal Health Maintenance Organization Act and provides healthcare services to a specified group in return for monthly premiums

Health record: A paper- or computer-based tool for collecting and storing information about the healthcare services provided to a patient in a single healthcare facility; also called a patient record, medical record, resident record, or client record, depending on the healthcare setting

Health record analysis: A concurrent or ongoing review of health record content performed by caregivers or HIM professionals while the patient is still receiving inpatient services to ensure the quality of the services being provided and the completeness of the documentation being maintained

Health record number: A unique numeric or alphanumeric identifier assigned to each patient's record upon admission to a healthcare facility

Healthcare Facilities Accreditation Program (HFAP): An accreditation program managed by the American Osteopathic Association that offers services to a number of healthcare facilities and services, including laboratories, ambulatory care clinics, ambulatory surgery centers, behavioral health and substance abuse treatment facilities, physical rehabilitation facilities, acute care hospitals, and critical access hospitals

Healthcare Integrity and Protection Data Bank (HIPDB): A national database that collects information on cases of healthcare fraud and abuse

History: The pertinent information about a patient, including chief complaint, past and present illnesses, family history, social history, and review of body systems

Home health care: The medical and/or personal care provided to individuals and families in their place of residence with the goal of promoting, maintaining, or restoring health or minimizing the effects of disabilities and illnesses, including terminal illnesses

Hospice care: The medical care provided to persons with life expectancies of six months or less who elect to forgo standard treatment of their illness and to receive only palliative care

Hospital inpatient: A patient who is provided with room, board, and continuous general nursing services in an area of an acute care facility where patients generally stay at least overnight

Hospitalist: Physicians employed by teaching hospitals to play the role that admitting physicians fulfill in hospitals that are not affiliated with medical training programs

Identifier standards: Recommended methods for assigning unique identifiers to individuals (patients and clinical providers), corporate providers, and healthcare vendors and suppliers

Implied consent: The type of permission that is inferred when a patient voluntarily submits to treatment

Incident: An occurrence in a medical facility that is inconsistent with accepted standards of care

Incident report: A quality/performance management tool used to collect data and information about potentially compensable events (events that may result in death or serious injury)

Indian Health Service (IHS): The federal agency within the Department of Health and Human Services that is responsible for providing federal healthcare services to American Indians and Alaska natives

Information: Factual data that have been collected, combined, analyzed, interpreted, and/or converted into a form that can be used for a specific purpose

Informed consent: An individual's voluntary agreement to participate in research or to undergo a diagnostic, therapeutic, or preventive medical procedure

Inpatient: *See* Hospital inpatient

Integrated health record: A system of health record organization in which all of the paper forms are arranged in strict chronological order and mixed with forms created by different departments

Integrated healthcare network: A group of healthcare organizations that collectively provides a full range of coordinated healthcare services ranging from simple preventive care to complex surgical care

Interval note: Health record documentation that describes the patient's course between two closely related hospitalizations directed toward the treatment of the same complaint

Intraoperative anesthesia record: Health record documentation that describes the entire surgical process from the time the operation began until the patient left the operating room

Joint Commission on Accreditation of Healthcare Organizations (JCAHO): A private, not-for-profit organization that evaluates and accredits hospitals and other healthcare organizations that provide acute care, home care, mental healthcare, ambulatory care, and long-term care services

Judicial decision: A ruling handed down by a court to settle a legal dispute

Jurisdiction: The power and authority of a court to hear and decide specific types of cases

Labor and delivery record: Health record documentation that takes the place of an operative report for patients who gave birth in the obstetrics department of an acute care hospital

Liability: A legal obligation or responsibility that may have financial repercussions if not fulfilled; also, an amount owed by an individual or organization to another individual or organization

Licensure: The legal authority or formal permission from authorities to carry on certain activities that by law or regulation require such permission (applicable to institutions as well as individuals)

Long-term care: Healthcare services provided in a nonacute care setting to chronically ill, aged, disabled, or mentally handicapped individuals

Longitudinal health record: A permanent, coordinated patient record of significant information listed in chronological order and maintained across time, ideally from birth to death

Managed care: A generic term for reimbursement and delivery systems that integrate the financing and provision of healthcare services by means of entering contractual agreements with selected providers to furnish comprehensive healthcare services and developing explicit criteria for the selection of healthcare providers, formal programs of ongoing quality improvement and utilization review, and significant financial incentives for members to use those providers associated with the plan

Managed fee-for-service reimbursement: A type of prepaid healthcare plan that uses traditional fee-for-service reimbursement methods and controls costs by controlling utilization of services (that is, by conducting prospective and retrospective reviews of medical necessity)

Master patient index (MPI): A list or database created and maintained by a healthcare facility to record the name and identification number of every patient who has ever been admitted or treated in the facility; also called a master population index or a master person index

Medicaid: An entitlement program that oversees medical assistance for individuals and families with low incomes and limited resources; jointly funded between state and federal governments

Medical necessity: The likelihood that a proposed healthcare service will have a reasonably beneficial effect on the patient's physical condition and quality of life at a specific point in his or her illness or lifetime

Medicare Provider Analysis and Review File (MEDPAR): A collection of data from reimbursement claims submitted to the Medicare program by acute care hospitals and skilled nursing facilities that is used to evaluate the quality and effectiveness of the care being provided

Medical specialties: A group of clinical specialties that concentrates on the provision of nonsurgical care by physicians who have received advanced training in internal medicine, pediatrics, cardiology, endocrinology, psychiatry, oncology, nephrology, neurology, pulmonology, gastroenterology, dermatology, radiology, or nuclear medicine

Medical staff bylaws: A collection of guidelines adopted by a hospital's medical staff to govern its business conduct and the rights and responsibilities of its members

Medicare: A federally funded health program established in 1965 to assist with the medical care costs of Americans sixty-five years of age and older as well as other individuals entitled to Social Security benefits owing to their disabilities

Medication record: Health record documentation that lists all of the medications administered to a patient while he or she is on a nursing unit

Messaging standards: *See* Transmission standards

Minimum necessary standard: A stipulation of the HIPAA privacy rule that requires healthcare facilities and other covered entities to make reasonable efforts to limit the patient-identifiable information they disclose to the least amount required to accomplish the intended purpose for which the information was requested

Municipal ordinance/code: A rule established by a local branch of government such as a town, city, or county

National Committee for Quality Assurance (NCQA): A private not-for-profit accreditation organization whose mission is to evaluate and report on the quality of managed care organizations in the United States

National Committee on Vital and Health Statistics (NCVHS): A public policy advisory board that recommends policy to the National Center for Health Statistics and other health-related federal programs.

National Practitioner Data Bank (NPDB): A data bank established by the federal government through the 1986 Health Care Quality Improvement Act that contains information on professional review actions taken against physicians and other licensed healthcare practitioners, which healthcare organizations are required to check as part of the credentialing process

National Vital Statistics System (NVSS): A federal agency responsible for the collection of vital statistics for the United States

Notice of Privacy Practices: A statement (mandated by the HIPAA privacy rule) issued by a healthcare organization that informs individuals of the uses and disclosures of patient-identifiable health information that may be made by the organization, as well as the individual's rights and the organization's legal duties with respect to that information

Notifiable disease: A disease that must be reported to a government agency so that regular, frequent, and timely information on individual cases can be used to prevent and control future cases of the disease

Numeric filing system: A system of health record identification and storage in which records are arranged consecutively in ascending numerical order according to the health record number

Nursing assessment: The assessment performed by a nurse to obtain clinical and personal information about a patient shortly after he or she has been admitted to a nursing unit

Nutritional assessment: The assessment performed by a registered dietitian to obtain information about a patient's diet history, weight and height, appetite and food preferences, and food sensitivities and allergies

Ongoing record review: A continuous health record quality review process performed by caregivers or HIM professionals to ensure that inpatient health records are complete and accurate and that the facility's clinical documentation practices meet relevant accreditation standards, state licensing laws, and federal regulatory requirements

Online analytical processing (OLAP): A data access architecture that allows the user to retrieve specific information from a large volume of data

Operation index: A list of the operations and surgical procedures performed in a healthcare facility that is sequenced according to the code numbers of the classification system in use

Operative report: A formal document that describes the events surrounding a surgical procedure or operation and identifies the principal participants in the surgery

Orders for restraint or seclusion: Physician's orders for physical or pharmaceutical restraint or seclusion to protect the patient or others from harm

Outguide: A device used in paper-based health record systems to track the location of records removed from the file storage area

Outpatient: A patient who receives ambulatory care services in a hospital-based clinic or department

Pathology report: A type of health record documentation that describes the results of a microscopic and macroscopic evaluation of a specimen removed or expelled during a surgical procedure

Patient assessment instrument (PAI): A standardized tool used to evaluate the patient's condition after admission to, and at discharge from, the healthcare facility

Patients' rights: The protections afforded to individuals who are undergoing medical procedures in hospitals or other healthcare facilities

Performance improvement (PI): The continuous study and adaptation of a healthcare organization's functions and processes to increase the likelihood of achieving desired outcomes

Periodic performance review (PPR): An organizational self-assessment conducted at the halfway point between triennial on-site accreditation surveys conducted by the Joint Commission on Accreditation of Healthcare Organizations

Personal health record (PHR): An electronic health record maintained and updated by an individual for himself or herself

Physician index: A list of patients and their physicians that is usually arranged according to the physician code numbers assigned by the healthcare facility

Physician's order: A physician's written or verbal instructions to the other caregivers involved in a patient's care

Policy: A statement that describes how a department or an organization is supposed to handle a specific situation

Population-based statistics: Statistics based on a defined population rather than on a sample drawn from the same population

Postoperative anesthesia record: Health record documentation that contains information on any unusual events or complications that occurred during surgery as well as information on the patient's condition at the conclusion of surgery and after recovery from anesthesia

Preferred provider organization (PPO): A managed care arrangement based on a contractual agreement between healthcare providers (professional and/or institutional) and employers, insurance carriers, or third-party administrators to provide healthcare services to a defined population of enrollees at established fees that may or may not be a discount from usual and customary or reasonable charges

Preoperative anesthesia evaluation: An assessment performed by an anesthesiologist to collect information on a patient's medical history and current physical and emotional condition that will become the basis of the anesthesia plan for the surgery to be performed

Primary care: The continuous and comprehensive care provided at first contact with the healthcare provider in an ambulatory care setting

Principal diagnosis: The disease or condition that was present on admission, was the principal reason for admission, and received treatment or evaluation during the hospital stay or visit; also called most significant diagnosis

Principal procedure: The procedure performed for the definitive treatment of a condition (as opposed to a procedure performed for diagnostic or exploratory purposes) or for care of a complication

Priority focus area (PFA): One of fourteen areas that the Joint Commission on Accreditation of Healthcare Organizations considers vital in the successful operation of a hospital; includes processes, systems, and structures that have a substantial effect on patient care services

Priority focus process: The part of the JCAHO's accreditation process that uses presurvey data to focus survey activities, increase consistency in the accreditation process, and customize the accreditation process to each specific hospital

Privacy and security standards: Standards that ensure the confidentiality and integrity of patient-identifiable information

Privileged communication: The protection afforded to the recipients of professional services that prohibits medical practitioners, lawyers, and other professionals from disclosing the confidential information that they learn in their capacity as professional service providers

Problem list: A list of illnesses, injuries, and other factors that affect the health of an individual patient, usually identifying the time of occurrence or identification and resolution; also called a summary list or a patient summary

Problem-oriented health record: A way of organizing information in a health record in which clinical problems are defined and documented individually

Procedural codes: The numeric or alphanumeric characters used to classify and report the medical procedures and services performed for patients

Procedure: A document that describes the steps involved in performing a specific function

Professional certification organizations: Private societies and membership organizations that establish professional qualification requirements and clinical practice standards for specific areas of medicine, nursing, and allied health professions

Progress note: The documentation of a patient's care, treatment, and therapeutic response that is entered into the health record by all of the clinical professionals involved in a patient's care, including nurses, physicians, therapists, and social workers

Prohibited abbreviations: Acronyms, abbreviations, and symbols that cannot be used in health records because they are prone to misinterpretation

Prospective payment system (PPS): A type of reimbursement system that is based on preset payment levels rather than actual charges billed after the service has been provided; specifically, one of several Medicare reimbursement systems based on predetermined payment rates or periods and linked to the anticipated intensity of services delivered as well as the beneficiary's condition

Prospective reimbursement: *See* Prospective payment system

Psychotherapy notes: Notes recorded in any medium by a mental health professional to document or analyze the contents of conversations between therapists and clients during private or group counseling sessions

Qualitative analysis: A review of the health record to ensure that standards are met and to determine the adequacy of entries documenting the quality of care

Quality improvement organization (QIO): An organization under contract with the Centers for Medicare and Medicaid Services to ensure that Medicare beneficiaries receive high-quality healthcare that is medically necessary and appropriate and meets professionally recognized standards of care; until 2002, called peer review organization

Quantitative analysis: A review of the health record to determine its completeness and accuracy

Recovery room record: A type of health record documentation used by nurses to document the patient's reaction to anesthesia and condition after surgery

Redisclosure: The process of releasing confidential health record information that was originally created and disclosed by another healthcare provider

Registry: A collection of case information related to a specific disease, condition, or procedure that makes health record information available for analysis and comparison

Regulation: A rule or order having the force of law issued by executive authority of the government

Rehabilitation care: The process of restoring a disabled insured to maximum physical, mental, and vocational independence and productivity (commensurate with their limitations) through the identification and development of residual capabilities, job modifications, or retraining

Reimbursement: Payment for services provided

Requisition: A request from an authorized health record user to gain access to a health record currently in storage in a hospital's HIM department

Release and disclosure: The processes that make health record information available to legitimate users

Retention: The process whereby inactive health records are stored and made available for future use in compliance with state and federal requirements

Retrospective payment system: A reimbursement system based on charges calculated after the delivery of healthcare services

Risk management (RM): A comprehensive program of activities designed to minimize the hospital's potential liability for wrongful injuries and deaths and to anticipate and respond to instances of liability when they do occur

RxNorm: A clinical drug nomenclature developed by the Food and Drug Administration, the Department of Veterans Affairs, and HL7 to provide standard names for clinical drugs and administered dose forms

Secondary care: A general term for healthcare services provided by a specialist at the request of the primary care physician

Security rule: The federal regulations created to implement the security requirements of the Health Insurance Portability and Accountability Act of 1996

Security standards: Statements that describe the processes and procedures meant to ensure that patient-identifiable health information remains confidential and protected from unauthorized disclosure, alteration, and destruction

Sentinel event: According to the JCAHO, an unexpected occurrence involving death or serious physical or psychological injury, or the risk thereof

Serial numbering system: A type of health record identification and filing system in which patients are assigned a different but unique numerical identifier for every admission

Serial–unit numbering system: A health record identification and filing system in which health record numbers are assigned in a numerical sequence but older records are brought forward and filed under the last number assigned

Shared Visions—New Pathways: The new accreditation process implemented by the Joint Commission on Accreditation of Healthcare Organizations in January 2004 and designed to focus on systems critical to the safety and quality of patient care, treatment, and services

Source-oriented health record: A system of health record organization in which information is arranged according to the patient care department that provided the care

Standard: A scientifically based statement of expected behavior against which structures, processes, and outcomes can be measured; also, a model or example established by authority, custom, or general consent or a rule established by an authority as a measure of quantity, weight, extent, value, or quality

Standards development organization (SDO): A private or governmental agency involved in the development of healthcare informatics standards at a national or international level

State Children's Health Insurance Program (SCHIP): The children's healthcare program implemented as part of the Balanced Budget Act of 1997; sometimes referred to as the Children's Health Insurance Program, or CHIP

Statute: A law enacted by the legislative body of a unit of government (for example, the U.S. Congress, state legislatures, and city councils)

Statute of limitations: A specific time frame allowed by statute or law for bringing litigation

Structure and content standards: Common data elements and definitions of the data elements to be included in an electronic patient record

Subacute care: A type of step-down care provided after a patient is released from an acute care hospital (including nursing homes and other facilities that provide medical care, but not surgical or emergency care)

Subpoena: A command to appear at a certain time and place to give testimony on a certain matter

Subpoena duces tecum: A written document directing individuals or organizations to furnish relevant documents and records

Surgical specialties: A group of clinical specialties that concentrates on the provision of surgical services by physicians who have received advanced training in obstetrics/gynecology, ophthalmology, orthopedics, cardiovascular surgery, otorhinolaryngology, trauma surgery, neurosurgery, thoracic surgery, urology, plastic and reconstructive surgery, anesthesiology, and pathology

Systematized Nomenclature of Medicine Clinical Terminology (SNOMED CT): A comprehensive, controlled clinical vocabulary developed by the College of American Pathologists

Telemedicine: A telecommunications system that links healthcare organizations and patients from diverse geographic locations and transmits text and images for (medical) consultation and treatment

Terminal-digit filing system: A system of health record identification and filing in which the last digit or group of digits (terminal digits) in the health record number determines file placement

Tertiary care: A type of highly specialized care provided by specialists (such as neurosurgeons, fertility specialists, or immunologists) who use sophisticated technology and support services

Third-party payer: An insurance company (for example, Blue Cross/Blue Shield) or healthcare program (for example, Medicare) that reimburses healthcare providers and/or patients for the delivery of medical services

Tracer methodology: An evaluation that follows (traces) the hospital experiences of specific patients to assess the quality of patient care; part of the new Joint Commission on Accreditation of Healthcare Organizations survey process

Transaction standards: *See* Transmission standards

Transcriptionist: A specially trained typist who understands medical terminology and translates physicians' verbal dictation into written reports

Transfusion record: Health record documentation that includes information on the type and amount of blood products a patient received and the patient's reaction to them

Transmission standards: Standards that support the uniform format and sequence of data during transmission from one healthcare entity to another; also referred to as communication, messaging, and transaction standards

TRICARE: The federal healthcare program that provides coverage for the dependents of armed forces personnel and for retirees receiving care outside military treatment facilities in which the federal government pays a percentage of the cost; formerly known as Civilian Health and Medical Program of the Uniformed Services

Uniform Ambulatory Care Data Set (UACDS): A data set developed by the National Committee on Vital and Health Statistics consisting of a minimum set of patient/client-specific data elements to be collected in ambulatory care settings

Uniform Hospital Discharge Data Set (UHDDS): A core set of data elements adopted by the U.S. Department of Health, Education, and Welfare in 1974, which are collected by hospitals on all discharges and all discharge abstract systems.

Unique identifier: A type of information that refers to only one individual or organization

Unit numbering system: A health record identification and filing system in which the patient receives a unique record number at the time of the first encounter that is used for all subsequent encounters

Utilization management (UM): The planned, systematic review of the patients in a healthcare facility against care criteria for admission, continued stay, and discharge; also, a collection of systems and processes to ensure that facilities and resources, both human and nonhuman, are used maximally and are consistent with patient care needs

Utilization review (UR): The process of determining whether the medical care provided to a specific patient is necessary according to preestablished objective screening criteria at time frames specified in the organization's utilization management plan

Vocabulary standard: A common definition for medical terms to encourage consistent descriptions of an individual's condition in the health record

Workers' compensation: The medical and income insurance coverage for certain federal employees in unusually hazardous jobs

Appendix C

Crosswalk between Acute Care Accreditation Standards and Medicare Conditions of Participation for Hospitals

Note: Empty cells indicate that the agency or accreditor does not have a standard or condition of participation (COP) for the domain.

Domain	2003 Medicare COPs for Hospitals	JCAHO 2004 Standards for Hospitals	AOA 2004 Standards for Hospitals
GENERAL			
A record is maintained for every individual evaluated or treated in the facility.	482.24 482.24(b)	IM.6.10	10.00.01 10.00.04
Health records are maintained for at least five years or longer as required by state or local laws and/or the facility's retention policy.	482.24(b)(1) 482.26(d)(2)(i) 482.26(d)(2)(ii)	IM.6.10, EP12	10.00.06 19.00.15
BASIC RECORD CONTENT			
Patient's name, gender, address, and date of birth as well as the name of the patient's authorized representative or legal guardian (when applicable)		IM.6.20, EP1	
Reason(s) for admission	482.24(c)(2)(ii)	IM.6.20, EP1	10.00.12
Documentation of informed consent	482.13(b)(2) 482.24(c)(2)(v) 482.51(b)(2)	RI.2.40, EP3 IM.6.20, EP1	10.00.19 18.00.15 28.00.26 28.00.27 30.00.17 30.03.04 31.00.09
Evidence of known advance directives (signed as necessary)	482.13(b)(3)	RI.2.80, EP4 IM.6.20, EP1	15.01.03 15.01.04 15.07.08
Evidence that the patient has been informed that access to care does not depend on having a signed advance directive	482.13(b)(3)	RI.2.80, EP3	15.01.03 15.17.08 31.00.09

Domain	2003 Medicare COPs for Hospitals	JCAHO 2004 Standards for Hospitals	AOA 2004 Standards for Hospitals
Legal status of patients admitted for behavioral health services	482.61(a)(1)	IM.6.20, EP1	27.01.02
Emergency care provided to the patient prior to arrival at the facility (when applicable)		IM.6.20, EP1	20.00.09
Patient assessment documentation and findings	482.23(b)(4) 482.43(c)(1)	IM.6.20, EP1	15.06.06 16.02.03 20.00.09
Diagnostic and therapeutic orders	482.24(c)(2)(vi) 482.57(b)(3)	IM.6.20, EP1	10.00.20 17.00.05
Reassessments and plan of care revisions (as indicated)	482.23(b)(4) 482.43(c)(4) 482.43(e)	IM.6.20, EP1	15.06.11 15.06.14 16.02.03 16.02.05 16.02.06 26.00.16 26.01.16 26.02.16 26.03.16 26.04.16
Patient's response to care	482.24(c) 482.24(c)(2)(iii)	IM.6.20, EP1	10.00.10 10.00.13
Medication(s) administered (every dose) and documentation of any adverse drug reactions	482.23(c)(1) 482.24(c)(2)(iv) 482.24(c)(2)(vi)	IM.6.20, EP1	10.00.20 10.00.18 16.02.04 25.01.06 25.01.23 25.01.26
Medication(s) dispensed or prescribed upon discharge		IM.6.20, EP1	15.06.08
Relevant diagnoses/conditions as established during the course of care	482.24(c) 482.24(c)(2)(iii)	IM.6.20, EP1	10.00.10 10.00.13
PATIENT ASSESSMENT AND REASSESSMENT			
Patient assessments cover the following areas: • Physical status • Psychological status • Social status • Nutritional/hydrational status • Functional status For patients receiving end-of-life care, assessments also include the following areas: • Spiritual status • Cultural status		PC.2.20, EP4	15.02.01 15.03.03 24.00.05

Domain	2003 Medicare COPs for Hospitals	JCAHO 2004 Standards for Hospitals	AOA 2004 Standards for Hospitals
Medical history and physical examination are performed within 48 hours after the patient's admission or no more than seven days before the patient's planned admission.	482.22(c)(5) 482.24(c)(2)(i) 482.51(b)(1)	PC.2.120, EP2	03.01.27 10.00.11 18.00.13 21.00.13 30.00.14 30.04.13
The initial nursing assessment is documented within 24 hours of inpatient admission.		PC.2.120, EP3	
The conclusions and impressions drawn from the medical history and physical examination are documented in the patient's record.		IM.6.20, EP1	
The patient's diagnoses, diagnostic impression, or conditions are documented in the record.	482.24(c)(2)(ii)	IM.6.20, EP1	10.00.12
The record includes sufficient information to support the stated diagnoses/conditions, to justify the care provided, and to promote the continuity of care.	482.24(c) 482.24(c)(2)(vi)	IM.6.10, EP6	10.00.10 10.00.20
The record documents the performance of a comprehensive pain assessment.		PC.8.10, EP1	16.02.03 16.02.05
Nutritional screening (when warranted) is documented within 24 hours of the patient's admission.		PC.2.120, EP4	24.00.05
Known allergies to foods and medications are documented in the patient's record.		IM.6.20, EP1	25.01.18
Functional status screening (when warranted) is documented within 24 hours of the patient's admission.		PC.2.120, EP5	15.02.01
Specialized assessments and reassessments as specified by the organization for various populations are conducted (when applicable).		PC.2.20, EP3	15.02.01
Evidence of the need for discharge or transfer planning is documented.	482.43(a) 482.43(b)(1) 482.43(b)(3) 482.43(b)(4) 482.43(b)(5) 482.43(b)(6) 482.43(c)(1) 482.43(c)(2) 482.43(d)	PC.15.20, EP2	15.06.01 15.06.02 15.06.03 15.06.05 15.06.06 15.06.07 15.06.09 15.06.12 15.06.13
Patient reassessment (as needed) is documented.	482.43(c)(4) 482.43(e)	PC.2.150, EP1	15.06.11 15.06.14
An integrated plan of care based on all assessments is documented.		PC.4.10, EP2	15.04.01 15.04.03
Evidence that care is appropriate to the patient's needs is documented.	482.21(a)(3)	PC.4.10, EP1	

Domain	2003 Medicare COPs for Hospitals	JCAHO 2004 Standards for Hospitals	AOA 2004 Standards for Hospitals
DOCUMENTATION OF PATIENT CARE			
Every health record entry is dated and authenticated by the person (as identified by name and discipline with written initials and/or signature, electronic signature, computer key, or rubber stamp) who is responsible for ordering, providing, or evaluating the service furnished, as dictated by the facility's policy and relevant laws and regulations.	482.23(c)(2) 482.24(b) 482.24(c)(1) 482.24(c)(1)(i) 482.24(c)(1)(ii) 482.26(d)(1) 482.51(b)(6) 482.53(d)(1) 482.53(d)(2)	IM.6.10, EP4	10.00.23 10.00.24 10.00.25 10.00.27 10.00.33 10.02.01 18.00.16 21.00.16 19.00.12 23.00.15 25.01.06 25.01.07 30.00.18 30.04.17
At a minimum, the following types of documentation are authenticated with a written signature, electronic signature, computer key, or rubber stamp: • History and physical examination reports • Consultation reports • Operative reports • Discharge summaries		IM.6.10, EP5	
Verbal orders are issued infrequently and include the following information: • The date of order • The originator of the order • The person who received the order • The person who implemented the order	482.23(c)(2)(i)	IM.6.50, EP2	10.01.01 15.00.05 25.01.07
As required by state and federal laws and regulations, verbal orders are authenticated by the physician as soon as possible or within the required time frame.	482.23(c)(2)(ii) 482.23(c)(2)(iii)	IM.6.50, EP3	10.01.01 15.00.05
Evidence of treatment/care plans (including specific goals) is documented in the patient's record.	482.23(b)(4) 482.56(b)	IM.6.20, EP1	15.04.03
The patient's progress is evaluated in comparison to the treatment/care plan goals.	482.23(b)(4)	PC.4.10, EP12	15.04.03
Relevant patient observations are documented in the health record.	482.24(c)(2)(iii)	IM.6.20, EP1	10.00.13 15.04.03
Progress notes by authorized clinicians are documented in the health record.		IM.6.20, EP1	15.03.04 15.07.09
All consultation reports are documented and authenticated.	482.24(c)(2)(iii)	IM.6.20, EP1	10.00.13
The effects of medication(s) on the patient, including the patient's own perceptions, as well as laboratory results, clinical responses, and medication profiles are documented in the health record.		IM.6.20, EP1	25.01.18 25.01.23 25.01.26

Domain	2003 Medicare COPs for Hospitals	JCAHO 2004 Standards for Hospitals	AOA 2004 Standards for Hospitals
Medication orders are documented in the health record.	482.24(c)(2)(vi)	IM.6.20, EP1	25.01.23 25.01.26
Orders for diagnostic and therapeutic procedures, tests, and results are documented in the health record.	482.24(c)(2)(vi) 482.53(d)(1)	IM.6.20, EP1	10.00.20 23.00.16
Records indicate the timely entry of information according to a schedule determined by the facility's policies.	482.24(c)(1)	IM.6.10, EP8	
Records are completed within 30 days of the patient's discharge from the facility.	482.24(c)(2)(viii)	IM.6.10, EP9	10.00.22
Medical record delinquency is monitored and reported no less frequently than once every three months.		IM.6.10, EP10	
EDUCATION			
Evidence of an assessment of the patient's learning needs and other educational considerations includes: • Cultural and religious beliefs • Emotional barriers • Desire and motivation to learn • Physical and/or cognitive limitations • Barriers to communication		PC.6.10, EP2	15.02.01
The record contains evidence that the educational process is coordinated among the disciplines providing care to the patient.		PC.6.30, EP2	15.04.03
The record contains evidence that the patient received education related to the plan for his or her care and treatment.	482.13(b)(1) 482.13(b)(2)	PC.6.10, EP3	15.02.02
The record contains evidence that the patient received education related to basic health and safety practices.		PC.6.10, EP3	15.04.03
The record contains evidence that the patient received education related to nutritional interventions, modified diets, and/or oral health.		PC.6.10, EP3	15.04.03
The record contains evidence that the patient received education related to the safe and effective use of medications.		PC.6.10, EP3	15.04.03

Domain	2003 Medicare COPs for Hospitals	JCAHO 2004 Standards for Hospitals	AOA 2004 Standards for Hospitals
The record contains evidence that the patient received education related to the safe and effective use of medical equipment or supplies (when provided by the facility).		PC.6.10, EP3	15.04.03
The record contains evidence that the patient received education related to the habilitation or rehabilitation techniques to be used in his or her care and treatment.		PC.6.10, EP3	15.04.03
The record contains evidence that the patient received education related to the pain management.		PC.6.10, EP3	15.04.03
The record contains evidence that services have been arranged to meet the patient's needs after discharge (when necessary and before discharge).	482.43(a)(5) 482.43(c)(3) 482.43(c)(5)	PC.15.20, EP8	15.06.08
The record contains evidence that the academic needs of children and adolescents have been addressed (when applicable).		PC.6.50	
DISCHARGE INFORMATION			
The patient's discharge summary includes concise information in the following areas: • Reason for hospitalization • Significant findings • Procedures and care provided • Patient's condition at discharge • Instructions to the patient and family (as appropriate)	482.24(c)(2)(vii)	IM.6.10, EP7	10.00.21
OPERATIVE AND OTHER INVASIVE PROCEDURES			
Provisional diagnoses are recorded in the patient's record by a qualified person before the operative procedure is performed.		IM.6.30, EP1	
The record contains evidence that a complete informed consent process was carried out.	482.51(b)(2)	RI.2.40, EP3	18.00.15 30.00.17
A presedation or preanesthesia assessment is conducted.	482.52(b)(1)	PC.13.20, EP10	30.01.06
The record contains evidence that a licensed independent practitioner with appropriate clinical privileges concurs with the planned anesthesia method before the patient undergoes sedation or anesthesia.		PC.13.20, EP11	

Domain	2003 Medicare COPs for Hospitals	JCAHO 2004 Standards for Hospitals	AOA 2004 Standards for Hospitals
The patient is reevaluated immediately before moderate or deep sedation and before anesthesia induction.		PC.13.20, EP12	
The record contains evidence that the patient's oxygenation, ventilation, and circulation were continually monitored during the procedure (intraoperative anesthesia record).	482.52(b)(2)	PC.13.30, EP1	30.01.08
Patients receive adequate postoperative care.	482.51(b)(4)		
Postoperative monitoring includes an assessment of the patient's physiological status.		PC.13.40, EP2	30.02.14
Postoperative monitoring includes an assessment of the patient's mental status.		PC.13.40, EP2	30.02.14
Postoperative monitoring includes an assessment of the patient's medications (including intravenous fluids).		IM.6.30, EP5	30.02.14
Postoperative monitoring includes an assessment of any blood and blood components administered (when applicable)		IM.6.30, EP5	30.02.14
Postoperative monitoring includes an assessment of the patient's vital signs and level of consciousness.		IM.6.30, EP5	30.02.14
Postoperative monitoring includes an assessment of the patient's pain level.		PC.13.40, EP2	30.02.14
Postoperative monitoring includes an assessment of any unusual events or complications and the management of those events or complications.		IM.6.30, EP5	30.01.09 30.04.18
An operative progress note is entered in the patient's record immediately after the procedure is complete.		IM.6.30, EP2	
For inpatients, a postanesthesia follow-up report is documented within 48 hours after surgery by a qualified individual.	482.52(b)(3)	PC.13.40, EP4 IM.6.30, EP6–EP8	30.02.13 30.02.14
For outpatients, a postanesthesia recovery evaluation is performed in accordance with approved discharge criteria.	482.52(b)(4)	PC.13.40, EP4 IM.6.30, EP6–EP8	30.02.13 30.02.14
Complete operative reports that describe surgical techniques, findings, specimens removed or altered, and other relevant information are prepared immediately after surgery and authenticated by the surgeon.	482.51(b)(6)	IM.6.30, EP3, EP4	30.00.18

Domain	2003 Medicare COPs for Hospitals	JCAHO 2004 Standards for Hospitals	AOA 2004 Standards for Hospitals
USE OF RESTRAINTS FOR ACUTE CARE AND SURGICAL CARE			
Health record documentation confirms that the use of restraints was initiated pursuant to either an individual order or an approved protocol (initiated by an individual order).	482.13(e)(3)(ii)	PC.11.40	15.05.01 15.05.04
Individual orders identify the rationale for any variation from policies and procedures for monitoring of the patient and for release from restraint before the order expires.		PC.11.50, EP2	
The patient's record contains evidence that an approved protocol for use of restraints was followed and that the protocol includes: • Guidelines for assessing the patient • Guidelines for applying restraint • Criteria for monitoring the patient and reassessing the need for restraint • Criteria for terminating restraint		PC.11.60, EP1	
The patient's record contains evidence that the restrained patient is continually assessed, monitored, and reevaluated.	482.13(e)(4)	PC.11.70, EP1, EP2	15.05.07
The patient's record includes documentation of the following: • Relevant orders for use • Results of patient monitoring • Results of patient reassessment • Significant changes in the patient's condition		PC.11.100, EP2	15.05.04 15.05.05 15.05.06 15.05.07
OUTPATIENT CARE			
For every outpatient receiving continuing ambulatory care, the patient's health record contains a list that summarizes all significant diagnoses, procedures, drug allergies, and medications.		IM.6.40, EP3	
A summary list is initiated for each patient by the third visit and maintained during subsequent visits.		IM.6.40, EP1 IM.6.40, EP3	15.04.02 15.04.03
The summary list is always stored in the same location for ease of access.		IM.6.40, EP2	
EMERGENCY CARE			
Records of emergency patients contain the following information: • Time and means of the patient's arrival • Documentation that the patient left against medical advice (when applicable) • Conclusions at termination of treatment, including final disposition, condition, and instructions for follow-up care, treatment, or services • Notation that a copy of the record is available to the practitioner or medical organization that will provide follow-up care		IM.6.10, EP14	20.00.09

Domain	2003 Medicare COPs for Hospitals	JCAHO 2004 Standards for Hospitals	AOA 2004 Standards for Hospitals
Appropriate information is communicated to any organization or provider to which the patient is transferred or discharged.	482.43(d)	PC.15.30, EP1	15.06.12
Information shared with another organization or provider includes (as appropriate): • Reason for transfer or discharge • Patient's physical and psychosocial status at transfer or discharge • Summary of care provided and progress toward goals • Community resources or referrals provided to the patient		PC.15.30, EP2	
RESEARCH, CLINICAL TRIALS, AND EXPERIMENTATION			
All research protocols are reviewed in relation to the facility's mission, values, and other guidelines and weighs the risks and benefits to the research subjects.		RI.2.180, EP1	
Facilities provide patients who are potential subjects with adequate information so that they can make informed decisions participation decisions.		RI.2.180, EP2	15.01.03 25.01.24
Patients are informed that refusing to participate or discontinuing participation will not compromise their access to care, treatment, or services.		RI.2.180, EP3	
Consent forms include the preceding information and: • Indicate the name of the person who provided the information to the patient and the date the form was signed • Address the participant's right to privacy, confidentiality, and safety		RI.2.180, EP4	
Subjects are told the extent to which their personally identifiable private information will be held in confidence.		RI.2.180, EP5	
All information given to subjects is documented in the health record or research file along with the consent forms.		RI.2.180, EP6	
When a research-related injury does occur, the principal investigator attempts to address any harmful consequences for the subject.		RI.2.180, EP7	

Domain	2003 Medicare COPs for Hospitals	JCAHO 2004 Standards for Hospitals	AOA 2004 Standards for Hospitals
SUBSTANCE ABUSE TREATMENT			
Patient assessments and reassessments include the following information: • History of substance use • Types of previous treatment and responses to that treatment • History of mental, emotional, and behavioral problems; their coincidence with substance abuse; and their treatment • History of associated biomedical complications and the patient's level of awareness regarding the relationship of the complications to the substance abuse • Psychosocial status		PC.3.120, EP1	
As appropriate, the following additional assessments are performed: • Vocational or educational • Legal • Other areas such as communication, self-care, and visual-motor coordination		PC.3.120, EP4	
CARE FOR EMOTIONAL OR BEHAVIORAL DISORDERS			
Assessments and reassessments of patients treated for emotional and behavioral disorders include at least the following information: • History of mental, emotional, behavioral, and substance abuse problems as well as their coincidence and treatment • Current mental, emotional, and behavioral functioning, including a mental status examination • Maladaptive or problem behaviors • Psychosocial status		PC.3.130, EP1	27.01.05
Vocational or educational assessments are conducted as appropriate.		PC.3.130, EP4	27.01.05
Assessments of the patient's legal status are conducted as appropriate.		PC.3.130, EP4	
The use of restraints and/or seclusion is documented in patient records as appropriate.	482.13(f)(3)(ii)	PC.12.70, EP1	27.04.03
Patient records contain evidence that episodes of restraint or seclusion were reported to the patients' families or legal representatives.		PC.12.80, EP1	
Patient records contain evidence of timely evaluation of patient by a physician or licensed independent practitioner after initiation of restraint or seclusion.	482.13(f)(3)(ii)(c)	PC.12.90, EP1	27.04.07
Patient records contain evidence that orders for restraint or seclusion are not written as standing orders or on an as-needed basis.	482.13(f)(3)(ii)(A)	PC.12.100, EP2	27.04.05
Patient records contain evidence that time limits and specific assessment criteria exist for orders and reorders for restraint and seclusion.	482.13(f)(3)(ii)(D)	PC.12.100, EP1	27.04.08

Domain	2003 Medicare COPs for Hospitals	JCAHO 2004 Standards for Hospitals	AOA 2004 Standards for Hospitals
Patient records contain evidence that the condition of the patient in restraint or seclusion is continually assessed, monitored, and reevaluated.	482.13(f)(5)	PC.12.110, EP5	27.04.08 27.04.11
Patient records contain evidence that patients in restraint or seclusion are monitored by competent and trained staff.	482.13(f)(4) 482.13(f)(5)	PC.12.140, EP1	27.04.12
Patient records contain evidence that the staff who have direct patient contact receive ongoing education about proper and safe restraint and seclusion techniques.	482.13(f)(6)	PC.12.30, EP4 PC.12.130, EP1	27.04.03 27.04.12 27.04.14
Patient records contain evidence that staff assist patients in meeting behavioral criteria that support the discontinuation of discontinuing restraints or seclusion.		PC.12.130, EP3	
LABORATORY SERVICES			
In cases where potentially HIV-infected blood was inadvertently administered to a patient, the facility notifies the patient's attending physician of the potential exposure within an eight-week timeframe that begins at the time the exposure was reported by the blood bank. The facility makes at least three attempts to notify the physician. If the physician is not available or fails to notify the patient of the exposure, the facility promptly makes at least three attempts to notify the patient or the patient's legal representative directly.	482.27(c)(4)		
In cases where potentially HIV-infected blood was administered and the facility is unable to notify the patient within the eight-week timeframe after making at least three attempts, the facility documents the extenuating circumstances in the patient's health record.	482.27(c)(5)(ii)		

Sources

The JCAHO hospital accreditation standards are used with permission from the *2004 Comprehensive Accreditation Manual for Hospitals.* Copyright ©2003 by the Joint Commission on Accreditation of Healthcare Organizations. All rights reserved.

The AOA hospital accreditation standards are used with permission from the *2004 Healthcare Facilities Accreditation Program Requirements for Healthcare Facilities.* Copyright ©2004 by the American Osteopathic Association. All rights reserved.

The 2003 *Medicare Conditions of Participation for Hospitals* were accessed April 15, 2004, on the Centers for Medicare and Medicaid Services Web site.

Appendix D

Principles of Form and Screen Design

Every acute care facility must institute a well-thought-out system for managing its patient care documentation tools. This requirement is the same whether the facility uses paper-based health records, computer-based health records, or a combination of preprinted health record forms, computer-generated reports, and data-entry software. As acute care facilities gradually move toward implementing paperless electronic health record (EHR) systems, the forms design process will evolve to a screen (or view) design process. Although the health record format will change, the principles of effective design and management will still apply.

Principles of Design: All Health Record Formats

- Every form or view should be designed with its end users in mind so that the form or view fulfills its purpose and is easy to complete.

- Every form or view should include completion instructions so that the data collected will be as consistent as possible.

- Every form or view should include a title that clearly represents the form/view's purpose.

- Every form or view should include adequate space provisions for dates, signatures, and other elements of authentication.

- Every form or view should be as simple as possible and still fulfill its purpose.

- Forms and views that include similar information and are utilized by the same users should be combined whenever feasible.

- The elements on each form or view should be arranged logically, and similar information should be grouped together.

- When possible, forms and views should use only standard medical symbols, acronyms, and abbreviations.

- When space limitations make it necessary to use unusual abbreviations and acronyms, a key should be added to the form, or a link to the definition should be made provided in an electronic system.

- Ambiguous abbreviations should never be used on health record forms or views.

Principles of Design: Paper-Based Health Records

- All of the paper-based health record forms used by a facility should follow a similar format. Typically:

  —Forms are 8.5 by 11 inches in size.

  —Forms are one-sided (that is, nothing is printed on the reverse side).

  —Form headings (top or bottom of the page) include the name of the facility and the name of the form, and headings are repeated on every page of multipage forms.

  —Pages of multipage forms are numbered in sequence.

  —A space is left blank at the same position on every page of every form to accommodate a patient identification label. Labels usually include at least the patient's full name, date of birth, and health record number. Some facilities also include the patient's Social Security number, the name of the patient's physician, the date of admission, or other identifying data. Most facilities now use bar codes in their identification systems to streamline access and filing processes.

  —Notations at the bottom of each form are used for version control and usually note the form's title and control number and indicate the date on which the form was last revised.

  —Margins are standardized to accommodate the style of chart holder used in the facility.

  —The same style of type (for example, all capital letters) and type size and font (for example, ten-point Helvetica) are used on every form. Type sizes below eight points are generally considered illegible.

  —Corner marks are placed in the form's top and bottom margins to make document scanning more efficient.

- The Joint Commission on Accreditation of Healthcare Organizations requires hospitals to prohibit the use of the following abbreviations in handwritten health record documentation:

  —U for unit

  —IU and iu

  —QD and qd

  —QOD and qod

  —Zero after the decimal point

  —No zero before the decimal point

  —MS, MSO4, and MgSO4

- Rules should be used to demarcate separate sections of a form or view.

- Care should be taken in using shading to highlight specific areas of a form because information in the shaded sections may become illegible in scanned documents.

- Adequate space should be provided to accommodate the information to be entered by the user (for example, three lines of space should be left blank to allow the user to fill in a mailing address).

- Space-saving devices such as checkoff boxes should be used whenever possible.

- The paper used for printing forms should be appropriate to the amount of use the record is likely to receive. Twenty-pound, white stock is generally adequate for use in printers, scanners, and photocopiers. Black ink reproduces more clearly than other colors.

Principles of Design: Electronic Health Records

- Menus and submenus should be provided to make navigation between views easy, and the menus and submenus should be sequenced in a logical order.

- Patient identifiers should be visible on every view to prevent errors in documentation.

- Printability should be considered in the use of color.

- Designs should be attractive but simple to allow maximum area for data content.

- Data fields should be large enough to accommodate the information to be collected.

- Default values such as the current date and automatic numbering should be used whenever possible to reduce the amount of keyboarding needed.

- Data editing functions should be protected by password to prevent unauthorized or unintentional alteration.

Principles of Management

- Acute care facilities should establish organizationwide guidelines for the creation and maintenance of the facility's information capture and health record documentation tools.

- Acute care facilities should institute an approval process to control the number of different health record forms and computer views in use.

- The roles and responsibilities of the facility's medical records committee in regard to health record content, format, and vocabulary should be spelled out in the facility's medical staff bylaws or health record policies.

- The roles and responsibilities of the facility's medical records committee in regard to the forms approval process should be spelled out in the facility's medical staff bylaws or health record policies.

- When new or revised paper forms are approved and implemented, the existing stock of out-of-date forms should be retrieved from patient care units and storage and then destroyed.

- Every paper form in use should be assigned a unique number, and a master list of forms that includes their titles, control numbers, and the approval date or the date when the form was last revised should be maintained.

- The collection of health record information should be streamlined to avoid unnecessary duplication of data and data collection efforts.

Sources

Kiger, Linda S. 2002. Information-capture design and principles. In *Health Information Management: Principles and Organization for Health Information Services,* fifth edition, edited by Margaret A. Skurka. San Francisco: Jossey-Bass.

McCain, Mary Cole. 2002. Paper-based health records. In *Health Information Management: Concepts, Principles, and Practice,* edited by Kathleen M. LaTour and Shirley Eichenwald. Chicago: American Health Information Management Association.

Appendix E

AHIMA Data Quality Management Model

The data quality management model developed by the American Health Information Management Association in 1998 is based on four domains:

- *Data applications:* The purposes for which data are collected

- *Data collection:* The processes by which data are collected

- *Data warehousing:* The processes and systems by which data are archived (saved for future use)

- *Data analysis:* The processes by which data are translated into information that can be used for designated application

The data quality management model applies the following basic characteristics to the four quality management domains:

- Accuracy

- Accessibility

- Comprehensiveness

- Consistency

- Currency

- Definition

- Granularity

- Precision

- Relevancy

- Timeliness

Data accuracy refers to the correctness of the data. The data should represent what was intended or defined by the original source of the data. For example, the patient's emergency contact information recorded in a paper record or a database should be the same as what the patient said it was. Results of laboratory testing for a particular patient should reflect the results generated by the laboratory equipment. Data related to the medication provided to a particular patient should reflect the actual date, time, and medication administered. The accuracy of the data placed in the health record depends on a number of factors, including:

- The patient's physical health and emotional state at the time the data were collected
- The provider's interviewing skills
- The provider's recording skills
- The availability of the patient's clinical history
- The dependability of the automated equipment
- The reliability of the electronic communications media

Data accessibility means that the data are easily obtainable. The following factors affect the accessibility of health record data and information:

- Whether previous health records are available when and where they are needed
- Whether dictation equipment is accessible and working properly
- Whether transcription of dictation is accurate, timely, and readily available to health-care providers
- Whether computer data-entry devices are working properly and are readily available to healthcare providers

Data comprehensiveness refers to the fact that all of the required data elements are included in the health record. In essence, comprehensiveness means that the record is complete. In both paper-based and computer-based systems, having a complete health record is critical to the organization's ability to provide excellent patient care and to meet all regulatory, legal, and reimbursement requirements. In general, the health record must include the following data elements:

- Patient identification
- Consents for treatment
- Problem list
- Diagnoses
- Clinical history
- Diagnostic test results
- Treatments and outcomes
- Conclusions and follow-up requirements

Data consistency refers to the reliability of the data. Reliable data do not change no matter how many times or in how many ways they are stored, processed, or displayed. Data values are consistent when the value of any given data element is the same across applications and systems. Related data items also should be reliable. For example, the clinical history for a male patient would never include a hysterectomy as a past surgical procedure.

Legitimate documentation inconsistencies do occur in health records. Any given health record may contain numerous references to the patient's diagnosis in terms of:

- The admitting diagnosis

- The diagnostic impression upon physical examination

- The postoperative diagnosis

- The pathology diagnosis

- The discharge diagnosis

Any inconsistencies among the various types of diagnosis would be legitimate. The different diagnoses incorporate the results of tests and findings not available at the time the previous documentation took place.

In other instances, however, data inconsistencies in the health record are not acceptable. For example, a nursing assessment might indicate that the patient is deaf when there is no documentation by the physician that the patient's hearing is compromised. Another unacceptable inconsistency occurs when different healthcare providers use different terminology. For example, different providers might use the words *cyst, lesion,* and *abscess* interchangeably in documenting a skin condition for the same patient. Such inconsistencies create difficulties for other caregivers and can be very confusing to external users of the health record.

Data currency and **data timeliness** refer to the requirement that healthcare data should be up-to-date and recorded at or near the time of the event or observation. Because care and treatment rely on accurate and current data, an essential characteristic of data quality is the timeliness of the documentation or data entry.

Data definition refers to the meaning of the data and information documented in the health record. For information to be meaningful, it must be pertinent. Further, users of the data must understand what the data mean and represent. Every data element should have a clear definition and a range of acceptable values.

Data granularity is another data quality characteristic that needs to be considered when establishing data definitions. It requires that the attributes and values of data be defined at the correct level of detail. For example, numerical values for laboratory results should be recorded to the appropriate decimal place as required for the meaningful interpretation of test results.

Data precision is the term used to describe expected data values. As part of data definition, the acceptable values or value ranges for each data element must be defined. For example, a precise data definition related to gender would include three values: male, female, and unknown. Precise data definition yields accurate data collection. In paper-based health records, much of the documentation and data is collected in narrative format and it is difficult to apply the concept of data precision to narrative text. The movement toward computer-based patient records provides the perfect opportunity to improve data precision in health records.

Data relevancy refers to the usefulness of the data in the health record. The reason for collecting the data element must be clear to ensure the relevancy of the data collected. In paper-based health records, the volume of detail provided sometimes limits the usefulness of the data and information. For example, nursing documentation is often lengthy, and physicians and other caregivers may not have sufficient time to review it.

Source

Cassidy, Bonnie, et al., 1998. Practice Brief: Data quality management model. *Journal of the American Health Information Management Association* 69(6).

Appendix F

Maintenance of the Master Patient Index

An accurate master patient, or person, index (MPI), whether in paper or electronic format, can be considered the healthcare organization's most important resource. The MPI tracks patient, person, or member activity within an organization (or enterprise) and across patient care settings.

The functions of the MPI include:

- Matching patients with their health records at the time of admission

- Minimizing the number of duplicate health records in the system

- Facilitating the merging of individual MPIs to create enterprise MPIs

- Facilitating links with clinical data repositories, pharmacies, and outside laboratories

- Facilitating access to longitudinal (lifetime) patient records

Some of the terms used in discussing MPIs include the following:

- *Master patient (person) index:* an index of patients, persons, members of healthcare plans, guarantors, physicians, healthcare practitioners, payers, employees, employers, and/or other individuals. The MPI may also be called an enterprise master patient index (EMPI), an enterprise patient index (EPI), a corporate person index (CPI), or another similar description. MPIs shared by two or more healthcare facilities may be considered enterprise, corporate, or multifacility MPIs.

- *Algorithm:* a mathematical formula using a combination of weighted MPI data elements to determine the probability of MPI duplicate, overlap, or overlay entries

- *Duplicate:* more than one entry or file for the same person in a facility-level MPI

- *Overlap:* more than one MPI entry or file for the same person in two or more facilities within an enterprise

- *Overlay:* one MPI entry or file for more than one person (that is, two people have been erroneously assigned the same identifier)

It should be noted that duplicate and overlay entries may represent information capture errors, but overlap entries do not.

Core Data Elements

The AHIMA recommends that facilities include the following core data elements in MPIs:

- Internal patient identification
- Patient's legal name
- Patient's date of birth
- Patient's gender
- Patient's race
- Patient's ethnicity
- Patient's address
- Patient's previous name or aliases
- Patient's Social Security number
- Patient's telephone number
- Facility or enterprise identification number

Healthcare facilities and enterprises may also choose to include the following optional data elements in their MPIs:

- Billing account number
- Date of admission or encounter
- Discharge date
- Encounter or service type
- Patient disposition
- Marital status
- Mother's maiden name
- Patient's place of birth
- Advance directive status
- Organ donor status
- Emergency contact information
- Patient's allergies
- Problem list

Maintenance of MPIs

The AHIMA recommends that the responsibility for MPI maintenance be centralized under the direction of health information management professionals. Employees responsible for MPI maintenance must be carefully trained and follow standardized processes to ensure consistent compliance with established guidelines. Specifically, the usefulness of MPI information depends on three factors: standardized data capture processes, well-established MPI content policies, and timely problem reporting:

1. Accurate data capture requires the standardization of the following processes:

    • Method for updating entries in the facility's MPI

    • Method for resolving overlap and overlay entries and data inconsistencies in the enterprise's MPI

    • Method for reporting facility MPI changes to the enterprise MPI

    • Method for resolving potential duplicate, overlap, and overlay entries and data inconsistencies in the enterprise's MPI

    • Method for reporting enterprise MPI changes to individual facilities

    • Method for monitoring progress on unresolved problems

2. Written maintenance policies ensure the consistency of MPI content in the following areas:

    • Search criteria to be used during patient registration

    • Use of suffixes, prefixes, aliases, nicknames, and punctuation

    • Resolution of duplicate entries within the facility

    • Resolution of overlap and overlay entries across the enterprise

    • Resolution of missing core data elements within the facility

    • Resolution of inconsistent core data elements for the same patient within the facility

    • Automatic (software-based) merging of entries (when applicable)

    • Physical merging of computer-merged entries (when applicable)

    • Resolution of urgent errors (those that affect patient care) and nonurgent errors

    • Monitoring of issues and resolution of errors

    • Reporting of MPI changes within the facility

    • Reporting of MPI changes across the enterprise

    • MPI access within the facility

    • MPI access across the enterprise

3. Detailed MPI reports ensure the timely resolution of problems in the following areas:

    • Potential duplicates within the same facility

    • Potential overlap and overlay entries across the enterprise

    • Missing core data elements within the same facility

    • Inconsistent core data elements for the same patient within the same facility

    • Inconsistent core data elements for the same person across the enterprise

    • Computer-merged entries (when applicable)

Sources

AHIMA MPI Task Force, 1997. Practice Brief: Maintenance of master patient index. *Journal of the American Health Information Management Association* 68(7).

AHIMA MPI Task Force, 1998. Practice Brief: Master patient index: Recommended core data elements. *Journal of the American Health Information Management Association* 69(6).

AHIMA MPI Task Force, 2004. Practice Brief: Building an enterprise master person index. *Journal of the American Health Information Management Association* 75(1).

Appendix G

Principles of Health Information Release and Disclosure

Protecting the confidentiality of patient health information has been an essential component of health information management (HIM) for decades. And until recently, medical professionals routinely asked for their patients' permission before sharing information related to their healthcare with other clinicians and health insurance representatives. Today, the professional practice standards of HIM professionals, medical professionals, and allied health professionals continue to dictate that disclosures of confidential, patient-identifiable information must be limited to the amount of information needed to fulfill a legitimate health-related purpose. However, recent federal legislation, along with older federal regulations with limited applicability as well as state privacy laws, have made protecting patient privacy a matter of law as well as professional practice.

Every healthcare organization and provider must develop and maintain health information release and disclosure policies that ensure compliance with the following federal regulations and state laws:

- The Medicare Conditions of Participation

- The federal Health Insurance Portability and Accountability Act of 1996, specifically the privacy and security standards developed to implement the act

- The federal Alcohol Abuse and Alcoholism Prevention, Treatment, and Rehabilitation Act of 1970

- The federal Drug Abuse Prevention, Treatment, and Rehabilitation Act of 1970

- The federal Privacy Act of 1974

- State healthcare facility licensure requirements

- State mental health regulations

- State public health surveillance and reporting requirements

- State privacy regulations

- State HIV testing and reporting requirements

In addition, health information release and disclosure policies must ensure compliance with any applicable voluntary accreditation standards. Most acute care facilities are accredited by either the Joint Commission on Accreditation of Healthcare Organizations or the American Osteopathic Association's Healthcare Facilities Accreditation Program. Specialty services and facilities may also be accredited by other accreditation organizations. For example, psychiatric departments within acute care hospitals and psychiatric hospitals may be accredited through the Commission on Accreditation of Rehabilitation Facilities.

To ensure compliance with federal regulations and state laws that govern the disclosure of confidential health information, the AHIMA recommends that HIM professionals should take the following steps:

- Study the privacy requirements of the HIPAA privacy standard, specifically, its stipulations regarding:

    —The release of information for the purposes of patient care, reimbursement, and healthcare operations

    —The minimum necessary limitation on the amount of confidential information to be disclosured

    —The patient's right to access and amend personal health-related information

    —The patient's right to control the disclosure of personal health-related information for purposes not related to patient care and healthcare operations

- Study the privacy requirements in the Medicare Conditions of Participation.

- Study the privacy requirements of any other federal regulations that apply to their organizations.

- Study the privacy requirements of applicable accreditation standards.

- Study the privacy requirements of applicable state laws.

- Understand when and how confidential health information may be requested.

- Recognize which categories of individuals and types of organizations have a legitimate need for patient information.

- Understand when and how confidential health information should be disclosed.

- Understand when and how requests for disclosure should be denied.

- Understand which requests for disclosure require the patient's written authorization and when and how such authorizations should be documented.

- Learn how to apply their organizations' information release and disclosure policies to ensure that the information disclosed is limited to the minimum necessary to fulfill the stated purpose.

- Learn how to apply regulatory and accreditation standards and their organization's release and disclosure policies when they request, use, or disclose confidential health information.

In addition, the AHIMA recommends that HIM professionals work within their organizations to ensure that internal release and disclosure policies and procedures are effectively designed and maintained. Specifically:

- Release and disclosure policies should be designed to fulfill the requirements of all applicable regulations, laws, and standards so that uniform release and disclosure procedures can be applied to all requests for patient information. In general, policies and procedures should reflect the most stringent requirements that apply. This approach assumes that less stringent requirements will then be fulfilled automatically.

- Release and disclosure policies and procedures should be designed to apply the minimum necessary standard as required by the HIPAA privacy regulations.

- Release and disclosure policies and procedures should specify how and when the organization will provide patients with a notice of the organization's privacy practices in order to comply with the HIPAA privacy standard.

- Release and disclosure policies and procedures should specify which types of health information disclosures do not require the patient's written authorization and which types of disclosures do require the patient's specific written authorization under the HIPAA privacy standard.

- Release and disclosure policies and procedures should specify the form and content for authorizations for disclosure of patient information as required under the HIPAA privacy standard.

- Release and disclosure policies and procedures should include provisions for patient access to their personal health records as required by the HIPAA privacy standard and applicable accreditation standards.

- Release and disclosure policies and procedures should include a process for maintaining detailed records of health record disclosures and providing patients with an accounting of past disclosures.

- Fee schedules for release of information services should comply with both state and federal regulations on the application of reasonable, cost-based charges for photocopying and postage.

- Release and disclosure policies should address the redisclosure of confidential information originally created by another healthcare provider.

- New or revised release and disclosure policies and procedures should be reviewed by the organization's legal counsel before they are implemented.

- The organization's release and disclosure policies and procedures should be included in the training and orientation programs provided to new staff members.

- Appropriate documentation of the organization's release and disclosure practices should be maintained to demonstrate compliance with all applicable regulations, laws, and standards.

- The organization should regularly monitor compliance with its policies on the release and disclosure of confidential patient information and immediately address instances of noncompliance.

- All contracts for services with business associates that use confidential patient information should be reviewed by legal counsel to ensure that the contract language is in compliance with the HIPAA privacy regulations.

Sources

Dougherty, Michelle. 2001. Practice Brief: Accounting and tracking disclosures of protected health information. *Journal of the American Health Information Management Association* 72(10).

Hjort, Beth. 2002. Practice Brief: Consent for uses and disclosures of information. *Journal of the American Health Information Management Association* 73(9).

Hjort, Beth, and Hughes, Gwen. 2003. Practice Brief: Understanding the minimum necessary standard. *Journal of the American Health Information Management Association* 74(3).

Hjort, Beth, and Rhodes, Harry B. 2004. Practice Brief: Release of information reimbursement laws and regulations. *Journal of the American Health Information Management Association* 75(4).

Hughes, Gwen. 2002. Practice Brief: Laws and regulations governing the disclosure of health information. *Journal of the American Health Information Management Association* 73(10).

Hughes, Gwen. 2002. Practice Brief: Required content for authorizations to disclose. *Journal of the American Health Information Management Association* 73(9).

Rhodes, Harry B., and Hughes, Gwen. 2003. Practice Brief: Redisclosure of patient health information. *Journal of the American Health Information Management Association* 74(4).

Appendix H

Principles of Health Record Retention and Destruction

Various regulations and standards dictate how long healthcare organizations must retain the health records of patients who have received services in their facilities. Federal agencies such as the Centers for Medicare and Medicaid Services and many state governments have established retention guidelines for health records. Specific information on these guidelines is available in an AHIMA Practice Brief published in 2002 and entitled "Retention of Health Information."

The destruction of confidential patient health information by healthcare organizations must be carried out in accordance with federal and state laws and as part of the organization's health record retention program. Some states require the creation of record abstracts or the notification of patients before the original records may be destroyed. A few states specify the method of destruction.

The AHIMA offers the following recommendations on health record retention and destruction that provide helpful guidance in the absence of state laws to the contrary.

AHIMA-Recommended Retention Guidelines

- Every healthcare organization should develop health record retention guidelines that ensure the availability of health record information to meet the needs of patients, physicians, researchers, and other legitimate users and comply with all applicable legal, regulatory, and accreditation requirements.

- Retention guidelines should specify what types of information should be stored, how long the information should be stored, and what storage medium (electronic, paper, microfilm, optical disk, magnetic tape, or other) should be used.

- Healthcare organizations should establish written policies that address the retention periods for all types of information, including clinical documentation, claims documentation, and regulatory compliance documentation.

- Most states have established specific retention requirements to be used as the basis for record retention policies. In general, however, healthcare organizations should keep health information for at least the period specified by the state's statutes of limitations or for a sufficient length of time to prove compliance with laws and regulations.

- Longer retention periods may be required for the records of infants, children, and adolescents. The records of minor patients should be retained until the patients reach the age of majority (as defined by state law) plus the period of the statute of limitations unless otherwise provided by state law.

- Unless longer retention periods are required by state or federal law, the AHIMA recommends that specific patient health information be retained for the following periods of time:

Diagnostic images	5 years
Disease indexes	10 years
Records of fetal heart monitoring	10 years after the infant reaches majority
Master patient indexes	Permanently
Operative indexes	10 years
Health records (adults)	10 years after the most recent encounter
Health records (minors)	Patient's age of majority plus the state statute of limitations
Physician indexes	10 years
Birth registers	Permanently
Death registers	Permanently
Surgery registers	Permanently

AHIMA-Recommended Destruction Guidelines

- The records should be destroyed in such a way that the information cannot be reconstructed.

- Appropriate methods for destroying paper records include burning, shredding, pulping, and pulverizing.

- Appropriate methods for destroying microfilm or microfiche include recycling and pulverizing.

- Because laser disks used in write once-read many document imaging applications cannot be recycled, pulverization is the only appropriate means of destruction.

- Approved methods for destroying electronic data include magnetic degaussing and overwriting. Proper degaussing ensures that there is insufficient magnetic remanence to reconstruct the data. Overwriting also destroys computerized data, but documents that have been overwritten as many as six times could be recovered. Total destruction of electronic data does not occur until the original data and all back-up information have been destroyed.

- Magnetic degaussing is the preferred method of destroying magnetic tapes. Although magnetic tapes can be overwritten, the process is time-consuming, and some areas on a tape may be unresponsive to overwriting.

- The destruction of patient records must be completely documented, and the documentation should be maintained permanently. Destruction records should include the following information:

  —Date of destruction

  —Method of destruction

  —Description of the records destroyed, including the dates of encounters included on the records

—Statement that the records were destroyed during the normal course of business

—Signatures of the individuals who supervised and witnessed the destruction

- When the healthcare organization contracts with an independent vendor for record destruction services, the contract must fulfill HIPAA requirements. In addition, the contract should indemnify the healthcare facility from loss due to unauthorized disclosure, require that the business associate maintain liability insurance, and require proof of destruction. The contract should also specify the method of destruction and the schedule for completion of the destruction process.

- Healthcare organizations should reassess the method of destruction annually and consider regulatory changes and the potential availability of new technologies and more cost-effective destruction services.

Sources

Fletcher, Donna M., and Rhodes, Harry B. 2002. Practice Brief: Retention of health information. *Journal of the American Health Information Management Association* 73(10).

Hughes, Gwen. 2002. Practice Brief: Destruction of patient health information. *Journal of the American Health Information Management Association* 73(6).

Appendix I

Documentation Regulations and Standards for Nonacute Care Settings

Standards/Regulations	Source
ALL PRACTICE SETTINGS	
State health information management association confidentiality, legal, or release of information manual (usually includes applicable state laws)	State health information management associations
State health information management associations	State departments of health
State laws relative to record retention and destruction	Individual state government Web sites
Health Insurance Portability and Accountability Act (HIPAA)	U.S. Department of Health and Human Services
Recording and Reporting Occupational Injuries and Illnesses (42 CFR 1904)	National Archives and Records Administration, Code of Federal Regulations
Patient Self-Determination Act (42 USC 1395-1396) (Advanced Directives)	The Office of the Law Revision Counsel
Medicare and Medicaid program manuals, memorandums, and transmittals	Centers for Medicare and Medicaid Services (CMS) Web site
Health utilization management standards	American Accreditation Healthcare Commission/URAC
Workers' compensation utilization management standards	American Accreditation Healthcare Commission/URAC
Health provider credentialing standards	American Accreditation Healthcare Commission/URAC
LONG-TERM CARE	
Conditions of Participation for Long Term Care (42 CFR 483)	National Archives and Records Administration, Code of Federal Regulations
Minimum Data Set 2.0	CMS Web site
Resident Assessment Instrument for Long-Term Care Facilities	CMS Web site

Standards/Regulations	Source
LONG-TERM CARE (Continued)	
Medicare skilled nursing facility prospective payment program manual	CMS Web site
Federal statutes, regulations, and policies governing the ICF/MR program	CMS Web site
Medicare interpretive guidelines for long-term care facilities	CMS Web site
Survey process for skilled nursing facilities and nursing facilities	CMS Web site
Office of Inspector General Compliance Plan for Nursing Facilities	Department of Health and Human Services Office of Inspector General
Comprehensive Accreditation Manual for Assisted Living	Joint Commission on Accreditation of Healthcare Organizations
Assisted Living Standards Manual	Commission on Accreditation of Rehabilitation Facilities
Comprehensive Accreditation Manual for Long-Term Care	Joint Commission on Accreditation of Healthcare Organizations
HOME HEALTH	
Conditions of Participation for Home Health (42 CFR 484)	CMS Web site
OASIS	CMS Web site
Medicare home health program manual	CMS Web site
Medicare home health prospective payment system	CMS Web site
Office of Inspector General Compliance Program Guidance	Department of Health and Human Services Office of Inspector General
Standards of Practice for Community Health	Community Health Accreditation Program
Comprehensive Accreditation Manual for Home Care	Joint Commission on Accreditation of Healthcare Organizations
HOSPICE CARE	
Conditions of Participation for Hospices (42 CFR 418)	National Archives and Records Administration, Code of Federal Regulations
Medicare payment policies for hospice care	CMS Web site
Survey procedures and interpretive guidelines for hospice organizations	CMS Web site
Medicare hospice program manual	CMS Web site
Office of Inspector General Compliance Program Guidance	Department of Health and Human Services Office of Inspector General
Comprehensive Accreditation Manual for Home Care	Joint Commission on Accreditation of Healthcare Organizations
Standards of Practice for Hospice	National Hospice and Palliative Care Organization
Community Health Accreditation Program Standards for Hospices	Community Health Accreditation Program

Standards/Regulations	Source
CLINICAL RESEARCH	
Protection of Human Subjects (45 CFR 46)	National Archives and Records Administration, Code of Federal Regulations
Animal Welfare (9 CFR, Ch. 1)	National Archives and Records Administration, Code of Federal Regulations
SUBSTANCE ABUSE TREATMENT	
Conditions of Participation for Drug, Alcohol and Substance Abuse (42 USC 290dd-3)	Office of the Law Revision Counsel
Code of Federal Regulations (42 CFR 2)	National Archives and Records Administration, Code of Federal Regulations
Comprehensive Accreditation Manual for Behavioral Health Care	Joint Commission on Accreditation of Healthcare Organizations
BEHAVIORAL HEALTH	
Conditions of Participation for Drug, Alcohol, and Substance Abuse (42 CFR 2)	National Archives and Records Administration, Code of Federal Regulations
Medicare interpretive guidelines and survey procedures for psychiatric hospitals	CMS Web site
Comprehensive Accreditation Manual for Behavioral Health Care	Joint Commission on Accreditation of Healthcare Organizations
Behavioral Health Standards Manual	Commission on Accreditation of Rehabilitation Facilities
Standards for the Accreditation of Managed Behavioral Healthcare Organizations	National Committee for Quality Assurance
PHYSICAL MEDICINE AND REHABILITATION	
Conditions of Participation for Specialized Providers (42 CFR 485)	National Archives and Records Administration, Code of Federal Regulations
Inpatient rehabilitation facility prospective payment system	CMS Web site
Medicare program manual for rehabilitation facilities	CMS Web site
Medicare survey forms for outpatient rehabilitation	CMS Web site
Conditions of Participation for Comprehensive Outpatient Rehabilitation Facilities	National Archives and Records Administration, Code of Federal Regulations
Interpretive guidelines for comprehensive outpatient rehabilitation facilities	CMS Web site
Medical Rehabilitation Standards Manual	Commission on Accreditation of Rehabilitation Facilities

Standards/Regulations	Source
RENAL DIALYSIS PROGRAMS	
Medicare Payment Systems Patient Profile Tables	CMS Web site
Conditions of Participation (42 CFR Part 405.2100, Subpart U)	National Archives and Records Administration, Code of Federal Regulations
Survey Procedures and Interpretive Guidelines	CMS Web site
Medicare Renal Dialysis Facility Manual	CMS Web site
AMBULATORY CARE SETTINGS	
Comprehensive Accreditation Manual for Ambulatory Care	Joint Commission on Accreditation of Healthcare Organizations
Medicare payment rules for ambulatory care	CMS Web site
Medicare documentation guidelines for evaluation and management services	CMS Web site
Interpretive guidelines for ambulatory surgical services	CMS Web site
Office of Inspector General Compliance Program for Physician Practices	Department of Health and Human Services Office of Inspector General
Medicare manual for rural health clinics	CMS Web site
Accreditation Handbook for Ambulatory Health Care	Accreditation Association for Ambulatory Health Care

Source

Burrington-Brown, Jill. 2002. Practice Brief: Recommended regulations and standards for specific healthcare settings. *Journal of the American Health Information Management Association* 73(10). Available at www.ahima.org.

Index

(continued on next page)

AHIMA Certification:
Your Valuable Career Asset

AHIMA offers a variety of credentials whether you're just starting out in the health information management (HIM) field, are an advanced coding professional, or play an important privacy or security role at your facility. Employers are looking for your commitment to the field and a certain competency level. AHIMA credentials help you stand out from the crowd of resumés.

✔ Registered Health Information Administrator (RHIA)/Registered Health Information Technician (RHIT)

✔ Certified Coding Associate (CCA), entry-level

✔ Certified Coding Specialist (CCS), advanced

✔ Certified Coding Specialist—Physician-based (CCS-P), advanced

✔ Certified in Healthcare Privacy (CHP)

✔ Certified in Healthcare Privacy and Security (CHPS), AHIMA in conjunction with HIMSS

In recent AHIMA-sponsored research groups, healthcare executives and recruiters cited three reasons for preferring credentialed personnel:

1. Assurance of current knowledge through continued education

2. Possession of field-tested experience

3. Verification of base level competency

AHIMA is a premier organization for HIM professionals, with more than 48,000 members nationwide. AHIMA certification carries a strong reputation for quality—the requirements for our certification are rigorous.

AHIMA exams are computer-based and available throughout the year.

Make the right move...pair your degree and experience with AHIMA certification to maximize your career possibilities.

For more information on AHIMA credentials and how to sit for the exams, you can either visit our Web site at www.ahima.org/certification, send an e-mail to **certdept@ahima.org,** or call **(800) 335-5535.**

Look for These Quality AHIMA Publications at Bookstores, Libraries and Online

Applying Inpatient Coding Skills under Prospective Payment

Basic CPT/HCPCS Coding

Basic ICD-9-CM Coding

The Best of In Confidence

Calculating and Reporting Healthcare Statistics

Clinical Coding Workout: Practice Exercises for Skill Development

Coding and Reimbursement for Outpatient Care

CPT/HCPCS Coding and Reimbursement for Physician Services

Documentation for Acute Care

Documentation for Ambulatory Care

Documentation and Reimbursement for Behavioral Healthcare Services

Documentation and Reimbursement for Long-term Care (book and CD)

Documentation and Reimbursement for Home Care and Hospice Programs

Effective Management of Coding Services

Electronic Health Record

Health Information Management

Health Information Management Technology

Health Information Management Compliance (book and CD)

HIPAA in Practice

ICD-9-CM Diagnostic Coding and Reimbursement for Physician Services

ICD-9-CM Diagnostic Coding for Long-Term Care and Home Care

ICD-10-CM and ICD-10-PCS Preview (book and CD)

Quality and Performance Improvement in Healthcare

Reimbursement Methodologies for Healthcare Services

More Information

Textbook details and easy ordering are available online at **ww.ahima.org/store.**
For textbook content questions, contact **publications@ahima.org,** and
for sales information contact **info@ahima.org** or **(800) 335-5535.**

AHIMA
American Health Information
Management Association®